DATA MODELING

MADE SIMPLE

WITH ERWIN DATA MODELER

by

JEFF HARRIS

STEVE HOBERMAN

Published by:

2 Lindsley Road

Basking Ridge, NJ 07920 USA

https://www.TechnicsPub.com

Cover design by Lorena Molinari

ISBN, printed 9781634628440

ISBN, PDF   9781634628471

ISBN, Kindle   9781634628457

ISBN, ePub   9781634628464

First Printing 2020

First Edition 2020

Printed in the United States of America

Library of Congress Control Number: 9781634628440

CONTENTS AT A GLANCE

TABLE OF CONTENTS

I would like to take this opportunity to thank some close and dear people that were instrumental in making this book possible.

My family is my world, and data modeling is my passion. Trying to fit my passion into my world is not easy, but with the family I am blessed with, they make it easy. They have been behind me every step I have taken, including the writing of this book. With that, I would like to thank my wife, Elsie, and my son, Jean-Michael, for putting up with all the "lost time" while I was writing and for being there when I needed the extra motivation to carry-on. For making sure that I kept my energy levels up with those meals in front of the computer and the regular questions of "can I bring you anything from downstairs?"

A special thanks to Gary for his wisdom and insight into writing a book. If it were not for his experience of writing, I most probably would not have had the courage to take on this challenge. He has been there in support every time that I felt I could not go any further, even if it were just by going out for an ice-cream. Not only is Gary a well credited fictional author, but he is also well versed in database architectures and an excellent sounding board for my ideas and thoughts for the book.

I would further like to thank Steve for inviting me to write this book with him. Steve, being a well-known author in the data arena, who knows the ups and downs of writing, has been an anchor through this whole process for me. He kept me honest and on track to deliver each step of the way up to the standard you would expect of a book like this.

To Mariann, Danny, Kathy, and all the rest of the people at erwin Inc., here is a thanks to you for providing the erwin Data Modeler product and being a devoted supporter of this book, without the support, this would not have been possible.

Numerous other people have crossed my path and have molded my career in some shape and form over time. Thanks to all those that have influenced the trajectory of my career, which led me to write this book.

And most importantly, I would like to give thanks to God for empowering me with the wisdom and knowledge to be successful in this endeavor. All things are possible through Him.

If you are like me, you usually skip book introductions and jump straight into Chapter 1. By calling this chapter 'Read me first!' instead of 'Introduction,' I am hoping you read this *first*. It helps you get the most out of this book by becoming familiar with the learning objectives and getting a glimpse of each lesson and chapter.

This book has ten key objectives:

1. Learn the fundamentals of data modeling and how to leverage erwin Data Modeler (erwin DM) to perform these tasks.
2. Read a data model of any size and complexity with the same confidence as reading a book.
3. Customize erwin DM's workspace, using the tools and functionality more efficiently.
4. Become empowered with the critical skills to build a data model of any size or complexity using erwin DM.
5. Apply erwin DM's Design Layer Modeling techniques to turn a conceptual data model into a logical data model, a logical data model into a physical data model, and a physical data model into a DDL (Data Definition Language) script.
6. Know the benefit of using erwin DM's templates, naming standards, data type standards, domains, themes, and other reusable functionalities.
7. Become confident in effectively and consistently communicating data model designs with varying data design consumer audiences.
8. Master erwin DM advanced functionality, such as Bulk Editor, Report Designer, Complete Compare, Reverse Engineering, and Forward Engineering.
9. Distinguish the traits of a good data model.
10. Learn about other data modeling tools to assist in delivering robust, accurate data architecture.

This book contains seven parts to laser focus on specific areas of data modeling:

- Part I provides a foundation in data modeling. Be able to explain data modeling concepts, use cases, and benefits.

- Part II provides a foundation in erwin DM. Build your first data models in erwin DM!

- Part III covers the design layer technique and its application using erwin DM. Know the difference between conceptual, logical, physical, and operational data models.

- Part IV provides you with an understanding of the critical, logical building block of data modeling, and how to implement them using erwin DM. Learn the various usages and requirements for entities, domains, attributes, key groups, validation rules, default rules, subject areas, and ER diagrams after this part.

- Part V provides you with an understanding of the physical data model and how to convert a logical data model to a physical data model in erwin DM. Become comfortable with tables, columns, indexes, and views.

- Part VI provides you with a deeper understanding of advanced functionalities within erwin DM. Master User Defined Properties, Naming Standards, the forward engineering engine, the reverse engineering engine, the Complete Compare tool, the report designer, and the bulk editor.

- Part VII takes a broader look beyond erwin DM. Become proficient with several data architecture tools, including erwin Data Catalog, its mapping manager, and more.

Each chapter starts with a Haiku, and contains exercises to keep it interactive and reinforce skills.

Let's get started!

Part I introduces data modeling and explains the purpose of a data model and its many variations. After completion of this part, you will be able to justify the need for a data model and know which type of data model is most useful for each situation. Also, be able to perform a very high-level assessment of a data model by identifying specific characteristics of the data model.

Chapter 1 introduces the concept of wayfinding and how it relates to data modeling. Furthermore, it presents the principle of data modeling and explains the benefits of developing a data model. This chapter also explains the power of a data model using a spreadsheet analogy, with its tabs, columns, and rows.

Chapter 2 explains the two core characteristics of a data model that make it so valuable: communication and precision. You will learn where communication occurs and about the three situations that can weaken data model precision. This chapter also explores the uses of a data model within the business and application areas.

Chapter 3 introduces the need for a data modeling tool. It provides an understanding of the benefits of a data modeling tool over a generic graphical tool. Furthermore, it lists some of the vital functions that a data modeling tool provides, such as documentation, automation reuse, and enforcement of database rules and requirements.

How do I get there?
Maps, blueprints, data models
Please show me the way

I gave the steering wheel a heavy tap with my hands as I realized that once again, I was utterly lost. It was about an hour before dawn, I was driving in France, and an important business meeting awaited me. I spotted a gas station up ahead that appeared to be open. I parked, went inside, and showed the attendant the address of my destination.

I don't speak French, and the attendant didn't speak English. The attendant did, however, recognize the name of the company I needed to visit. Wanting to help and unable to communicate verbally, the attendant took out a pencil and paper. He drew lines for streets, circles for roundabouts along with numbers for exit paths, and rectangles for his gas station and my destination, MFoods. The picture he drew resembled that which appears in Figure 1.

Figure 1. Simplification of Geographic Landscape

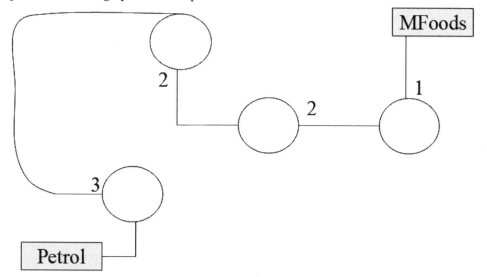

With this custom-made map, which contained only the information that was relevant to me, I arrived at my address without making a single wrong turn. This map was a model of the actual roads I needed to travel.

A map simplifies a complex *geographic* landscape in the same way that a data model simplifies a complex *information* landscape. This chapter explains the data model and its role as an invaluable wayfinding tool.

Wayfinding Explained

If the term 'data model' does not excite you or your business users, try the term 'wayfinding' instead. Wayfinding encompasses all the techniques and tools used by people and animals to find their way from one site to another. If travelers navigate by the stars, for example, the stars are their wayfinding tools. Maps and compasses are also wayfinding tools.

All models are wayfinding tools. A model is a set of symbols and text used to make a complicated concept easier to grasp. The world around us is full of obstacles that overwhelm our senses, making it very challenging to focus only on the relevant information needed to make intelligent decisions. A map helps a visitor navigate a city, like an organization chart, helps an employee understand reporting relationships, and a blueprint helps an architect communicate building plans. The map, organization chart, and blueprint are all types of models that represent a filtered, but simplified view of something complex. They all intend to improve a wayfinding experience by helping people understand part of the real world.

It would probably have taken me hours of trial and error to reach my destination in France. Whereas that simple map the gas station attendant drew provided me with an almost instantaneous broad understanding of how to reach my destination. A model makes use of standard symbols that allows you to grasp the content quickly. In the map he drew for me, the attendant used lines to symbolize streets and circles to symbolize roundabouts. His skillful use of those symbols helped me visualize the streets and roundabouts.

Data Model Explained

A data model is a wayfinding tool for both business and IT professionals. It uses a set of symbols and text to precisely explain a subset of real information that improves communication within the organization and thereby lead to a more flexible and stable application environment. A line represents a motorway on a map of France. A box with the word **Customer** within it represents the concept of a real **Customer**, such as Bob, IBM, or Walmart, in a data model.

In other words, a map simplifies a complex *geographic* landscape in the same way that a data model simplifies a complex *information* landscape. In many cases, the complexities in the actual data can make those roundabouts in France look ridiculously simple.

A data model is a set of symbols and text used for communicating a precise representation of an information landscape. There are many different forms available for describing the information landscape. Data models can look like box and line drawings, or they can take other forms, such as spreadsheets, or state transition diagrams. All these models are wayfinding tools designed with the single purpose of simplifying complex information in our real world.

Spreadsheets and Data Models

Have you ever opened a spreadsheet and did not know any context about the data in the spreadsheet? We usually create spreadsheets with metadata to explain the context of the data in the spreadsheet. Metadata is data or information that explains the contents of the data. The same applies to a database schema; we need a data model to explain what the database schema contains.

With a spreadsheet, we first give it a name to explain the general context of the spreadsheet. We give a spreadsheet a name to identify what it is we are trying to represent in the spreadsheet, for example, **Sales for Month**. In a data model, this would be the name of the data model, and most probably the name of the database schema that we are modeling. As in the spreadsheet example, we would give the data model a name like **Sales for Month**.

After opening the spreadsheet, we usually observe several tabs, each labeled according to their specific context. Typically, each containing some subset of information relevant to the overarching spreadsheet context. We usually don't keep information about a grocery shopping list in a spreadsheet intended for **Sales for Month**. Likewise, we do not keep several tabs, all having the same name and containing the same information. Unless there is a business reason for keeping duplicates of the same type of data, a typical business case for keeping duplicates of the same type of data may be for historical purposes, each separate month's sales on a separate tab. Which, in data modeling concepts, would typically be a data warehouse model. These tabs in our spreadsheet would equate to entities in a data model design, each entity designed for a specific set of data related to the overarching context of the data model.

Moreover, in the database schema, each tab would be a table containing the specific set of data related to the context of the database schema. We classify the name of the tab as the spreadsheet's metadata; likewise, we classify the name of the entity as the entity's metadata in the data model. Also, we classify the name of the table as the metadata of the table in the database schema. In addition to the name of the spreadsheet tab, the tab's color and whether it is hidden or not, would also be metadata.

As we look at each of the tabs, we observe a collection of data, listed in columns and rows. Usually, each column would have a column heading explaining what that column contains. If we didn't have column headings, we would not know what the data meant. Each of the columns in the spreadsheet would typically be an attribute in the data model or a column in the database schema. The column heading would, in turn, be an attribute name, once again being the metadata of the attribute and the database column. We might also observe other types of metadata in the spreadsheet, such as the type of data in the column and the format of the column.

In examining our spreadsheet, we further observe the rows of data; each row in our spreadsheet is unique. The same applies to our database schema—each row or record in our database schema is unique. Quite often, we have a specific column or collection of columns in our spreadsheet that makes the row unique. This unique column or columns, in a data model, is the primary key or primary key group. Although we do not represent the rows or records of data in a data model, we design the data model to manage the metadata of our database schema. Furthermore, in our comparison of a spreadsheet, the data model is only a reflection of the metadata in the spreadsheet, not the actual data.

Taking our spreadsheet comparison a bit further, we can also compare the spreadsheet's lookup formulas to the relationships in a data model. The data validation functionality in a spreadsheet is the same as a validation rule in a data model. There are several other similarities between the two, but it gives the basic concepts of how a spreadsheet compares to a data model.

Key Learnings

- Wayfinding encompasses all the techniques and tools used by people and animals to find their way from one site to another.

- A data model is a set of symbols and text used for communicating a precise representation of an information landscape.

- Data models come in many different forms. The most common and globally understood form is a spreadsheet.

Remove ambiguity

Introduce precision

Additional benefits

Data modeling is an essential part of building an application. Communication and precision are two core dynamics that make a data model so important. This chapter explains these two core dynamics, followed by a section that explains some other benefits gained by a data model. Learn where communication of a data model occurs, and about the three situations that can weaken data model precision.

Communication

People with different backgrounds and levels of experience across departments and functional areas need to speak with each other about business concerns and to make business decisions. Therefore, in conversation, there is a need to know how the other party views concepts such as **Customer** or **Sales**. A data model is an ideal tool for understanding, documenting, and eventually reconciling different perspectives.

Data models allow us to communicate the same information at different levels of detail. For example, I recently built a data model to capture consumer interactions within the snack food industry. If someone called up the company and complained about one of their products, the data model I built would store this complaint and related information. The business user and I built a very high-level data model showing the subjects that are relevant for the project.

The data model helped with the scoping of the project, understanding fundamental terms such as **Consumer**, **Product**, and **Interaction**, and building a relationship with the business. Several months later, I used a much more detailed data model of the same consumer interaction information, to communicate to the report developers the requirements of each report, with all the necessary selection criteria.

The communication we deliver from data modeling does not begin when the data modeling phase ends. That is, much knowledge gets communicated during the process of building the data model. The means are just as valuable as the end. Let's look at the communication benefits derived from both during and after the data modeling process in more detail.

Communicating During the Data Modeling Process

During the process of building data models, we are forced to analyze data and data relationships. We have no choice but to acquire a strong understanding of the content of what is being modeled. Knowledge is gained as the people involved in the data modeling process challenge each other about terminology, assumptions, rules, and concepts.

While data modeling a recipe management system for a large manufacturing company, I was amazed to witness team members with years of experience debate whether the concept of an **Ingredient** differed from the concept of **Raw Material**. After a 30-minute discussion on ingredients and raw materials, everyone who participated in this data modeling effort benefited from the debate and left the data modeling session with a better understanding of recipe management.

Communicating After the Data Modeling Process

The completed data model is the basis for discussing what to build in an application, or more fundamentally, how something works. The data model becomes a reusable map to which analysts, modelers, and developers can refer to understand how things work. In much the same way as the first mapmaker painfully learned and documented a geographic landscape for others to use for navigation. The data modeler goes through a similar exercise so that others can understand an information landscape.

Before I started working at a large manufacturing company, my soon-to-be manager gave me a large book containing a set of data models for the company. I read this book several times, becoming familiar with the key concepts in the business and their business rules. On my first day on the job, I already knew a lot about how the business worked. When my colleagues mentioned terms specific to the company, I already knew what they meant.

Precision

Precision means that there is a clear, unambiguous way of reading every symbol and term in the data model. One might argue with others about whether the rule is accurate, but that is a different argument. In other words, one can't view a symbol in a data model and say, 'I see A here' and for someone else to view the same symbol and respond, 'I see B here.'

Because the data model introduces precision, valuable time doesn't get wasted trying to interpret the data model. Instead, time gets spent debating, and then validating the concepts on the data model.

Three situations can degrade the precision of a data model:

1. **Weak definitions.** If the definitions behind the terms in a data model are inadequate or nonexistent, multiple interpretations of terms become a strong possibility. Imagine a business rule in our data model that states that an employee must have at least one benefit package. If the definition of **Employee** is something meaningless like '*An Employee is a carbon-based life form,*' we may conclude that **Employee** includes **Job Applicants**. Someone else may conclude that the **Employee** does not include **Job Applicants**, and one of us

would be wrong. Then stepping back to the business rule, one can imagine the implication that would have—we could end up providing a benefit package to a **Job Applicant**.

2. **Dummy data**. The second situation occurs when we introduce data that is outside the typical set of data values that one would expect in a data grouping. An old trick for getting around the rigor of a data model rule is to expand the set of values that a data grouping can contain. For example, if the data model states that 'a contact must have at least one phone number,' and a contact arrives in the application with no phone number, one can create a fake phone number such as 'Not Applicable,' '99,' or 'other,' so that the contact is enterable. In this case, adding the dummy data allows a contact to exist without a valid phone number, which violates and circumvents the original business rule.

3. **Vague or missing labels**. A data model is read in much the same way as a book is read, with proper sentence structure. An essential part of the sentence is the verbs. In a data model, when describing how concepts on the data model relate to each other, we capture these verbs. Concepts like **Customer** and **Order**, for example, may relate to each other through the verb 'place.' That is, 'A **Customer** may *place* one or many **Orders**.' Vague verbs such as 'associate' or 'have,' or missing verbs altogether, reduce the precision of the data model, as we cannot accurately read the sentences.

In a data model, precision is also the result of applying a standard set of symbols. The traffic circles that the gas station attendant drew for me were standard symbols that we both understood. There are also standard symbols used in data models, as demonstrated in the following chapters.

Additional Benefits of a Data Model

The data model is built during the analysis and design phases of a project for a new application and ensures that the requirements are fully understood and correctly captured before the actual creation of the database schema. Due to being precise, the data model has additional benefits:

- **To understand an existing application**. The data model provides a precise and straightforward picture of the concepts within an application. We can derive a data model from an existing application by examining the application's database schema and building a data model of its structures. The technical term for the process of building data models from existing applications is reverse engineering.

- To manage risk. A data model can capture the concepts and interactions that are impacted by a development project or program. What is the impact of adding or modifying structures for an application already in production? How many of an application's structures are for archival purpose requirements? Many organizations today purchase software and then customize it. One example of managing risk through impact analysis would be to use data modeling to determine what impact modifying its structures would have on the purchased software.

- To learn about the business. As a prerequisite to a significant development effort, it usually is necessary to understand how the business works before one can understand how the applications that support the business works. For example, before building an order entry system, one needs to understand the order entry business process. One of my favorite sentences in the classic 1978 book, Data and Reality, by William Kent occurs during a section discussing the steps required to build a database to store book information: 'So, once again, if we are going to have a database about books, before we can know what one representative stands for, we had better have a consensus among all users as to what 'one book' is.'

- To educate team members. When new team members need to come up to speed or developers need to understand requirements, a data model is an effective explanatory medium. Whenever a new person joined our department, I spent some time walking through a series of data models to educate the person on concepts as quickly as possible.

Key Learnings

- Two core dynamics of data modeling are communication and precision.

- Communication occurs both during the building of the data model and after its completion.

- Weak definitions, dummy data, and vague or missing labels can compromise a data model's precision.

- Communication and precision make a data model an excellent tool for building new applications.

- Other benefits of data models include understanding existing applications and business areas, performing an impact analysis, and educating team members.

Click of a button
Automatically apply
Reuse and comply

In the previous chapter, we identified that data modeling is an essential part of building an application. Also, communication and precision are two core dynamics that make a data model so important. So how does one build a data model that can form part of a communication strategy and provide the precision needed? We could always use the trusted old-fashioned way of a piece of paper and a pencil, but that would be time-consuming. It does not allow for reusability and could not ensure that the design is best for the DBMS. Besides the fact that a piece of paper can get lost, it only provides a single point in time view and does not age with the ongoing changes.

In this chapter, we cover where a data modeling tool like erwin Data Modeler (erwin DM) plays a beneficial part, and how it allows the user to represent complex data structures in an easily understood, graphical format. It can automate repetitive data modeling tasks, such as forward engineering of the data design into a database schema. It allows the user to make use of a library of data modeling objects that allow for reuse, bringing with it all the metadata associated with the object. It performs error checking to ensure that the data model adheres to standards that can improve the quality of the data design and database schema, reducing time and costs associated with the implementation and management of the data design and database structure.

Documenting the Data Design

In the fast-paced lives that we live today, documentation usually is one of the areas that is often overlooked or does not get the time that it deserves. I remember as a kid that I loved building kit model airplanes. It was through this experience that I learned to follow a set of instructions to get to the desired goal. When I did not follow the instructions, I inevitably found myself with leftover parts. Wondering where they needed to go, and what would happen if I did not put them in. It was when I attempted to fly the model airplane that I found out what those leftover parts should have gone, as the airplane came crashing down to the ground and broke into a million pieces.

The documentation of a data-design is no different from the model airplane's instructions. Without having the documentation, we can still use the database, but it won't be the best for the data. We may be inserting data into an incorrect place and won't be managing the data as intended. Like I did with the leftover parts of my model airplane—one ultimately wonders as to when it will all come to a crashing halt.

We find ourselves too focused on delivering to ever-growing business needs and tighter deadlines, instead of producing useful documentation to clarify why we did something and how that something should get used. By using a data modeling tool like erwin DM, the user has the benefit of producing both the design and the documentation in one integral process. Thus, allowing them to be able to deliver faster and communicate more consistently with enhanced precision and allowing a means of knowledge transfer for future understanding.

In erwin DM, when a user creates a data design using the intuitive graphical interface, the user is already working on the development of the documentation. Every time the user adds a new entity, attribute, or relationship to their data model, they are including these in the documentation for the data design. See Figure 2. The most convenient way of working in erwin DM is through the graphical interface, although the model is not stored as a graphic, but instead as a collection of data objects displayed as a graphic. This is one of the areas that differentiates a generic graphical tool from a real data modeling tool—a generic graphical tool only sees the data model as a collection of boxes and lines, where a real data modeling tool like erwin DM, sees the data model as a collection of data objects, like entities, attributes, and relationships. Because of these stored data objects, the user can quickly generate the data design documentation. The user can manipulate the data object metadata into whatever format the documentation is required, and interact with these objects for automation, as seen in the Automation of Tasks section below.

Figure 2. Data Model Represented Graphically

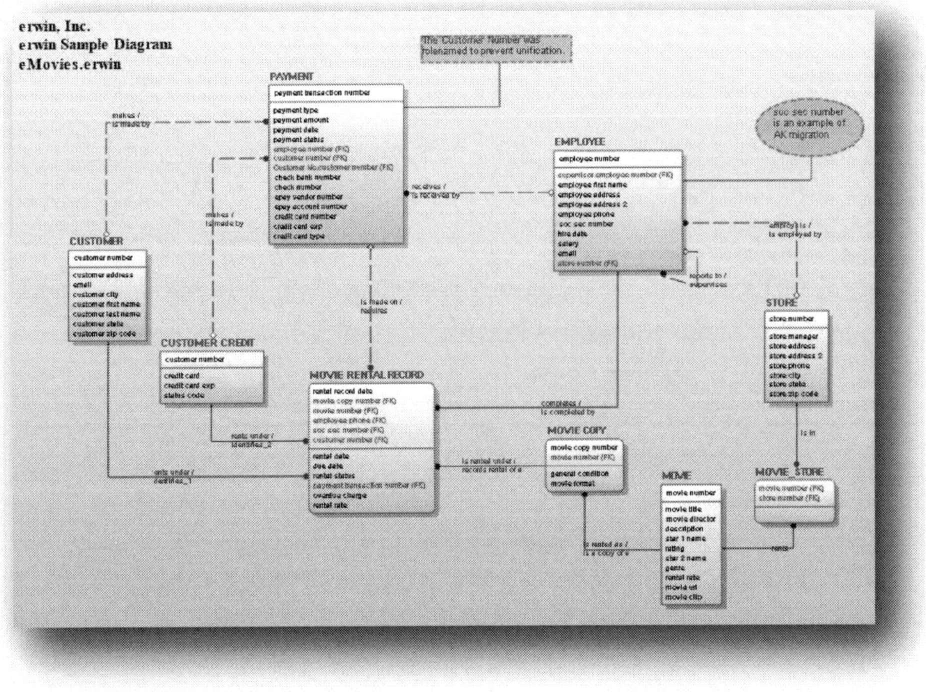

Automation of Tasks

When starting to use a data modeling tool like erwin DM, the user finds a critical need to automate some of the repetitive or time-consuming tasks. Automating tasks can make the modeling process go smoother or ensure that the data model is transformed into the database schema accurately. Data modeling tools provide a full spectrum of automation capabilities, some dealing with low-level automation of synchronizing the same definition across multiple attributes. Alternatively, high-level automation, like the forward engineering of a DDL (Data Definition Language) script, can generate a database schema.

Forward Engineering Engine

One of the significant benefits of using a real data modeling tool like erwin DM is the ability to generate the database schema directly from the tool. erwin DM gives the user the ability to forward engineer from within the tool. It gives the user the ability to generate a DDL (Data Definition Language) script file, should the user prefer not to apply changes blindly.

Figure 3. Forward Engineering Schema Generation Wizard Dialog

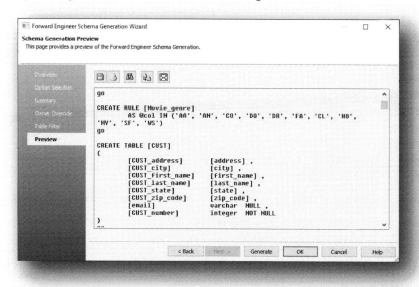

Reverse Engineering Engine

Reverse engineering is the reverse process of forward engineering. This feature allows the user to direct erwin DM towards a database schema, and 'suck in,' that is reverse engineer, the table and column structures into a data model. The benefit of this automation is that a user with an existing database schema that has no documentation can reverse engineer the database schema in a short space of time. It results in a workable data model reflective of the data structures within the database, although limited to the metadata of the database schema. The reverse engineering engine does provide some intelligence while reverse engineering to infer some of the relationships.

Figure 4. Reverse Engineering Dialog

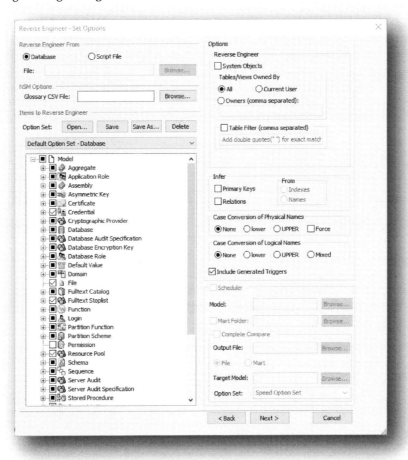

The Complete Compare Engine

The erwin DM Complete Compare automation tool allows a data modeler to compare two versions of a data model, a data model to a database schema, or even two database schemas. This engine provides the functionality to migrate new objects, change objects, and delete objects. If we had to call out one automation tool that has the most power in erwin DM, it would be the Complete Compare engine. See Figure 5.

The Bulk Editor

Another very intuitive tool in erwin DM is the Bulk Editor, as shown in Figure 6. As the name implies, it allows the user to edit data objects in bulk capacity, using a grid-style tool. The real power comes from the ability to export a list of objects in the Bulk Editor grid to a CSV file, and then to use the power of a spreadsheet tool to manipulate the data and import it back into their data model. An everyday use case for the Bulk Editor is to export all the entities and their definitions into a spreadsheet. Then to send the spreadsheet to the business owners to edit and update the definitions of the entities, and finally to import all those updated definitions back into the data model.

Figure 5. Complete Compare Resolve Differences Dialog

Transforms

Transforms are a collection of tools that can change a specific object in a data model from one state to another state, performing structural changes to the data model. The target data model structure transforms in a specific and predefined manner, dependent on the transform performed. There are automatic transforms such as the many-to-many relationship transform from the logical data model to the physical data model, and transforms which require user-intervention such as the roll-up denormalization transform. See Figure 7.

Reusability

Another area that improves the data modeling process in a data modeling tool, like erwin DM, is the ability to reuse objects. The key benefits of reusable objects are to standardize and reduce repetitive data modeling efforts. Reusable objects come in different forms, each with their specific purpose.

Figure 6. Bulk Editor Dialog

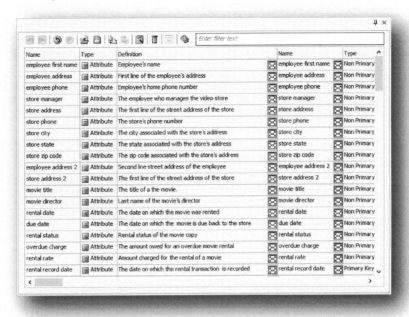

Figure 7. Table Denormalization Roll Up Transform Wizard Dialog

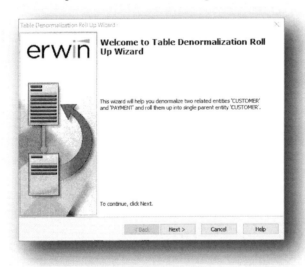

Domains

Domains provide an attribute or column level mini template. Let's assume, for example, that we are working for a retail organization. One of the commonly used attributes is **Store Number**. The **Store Number** domain would predefine the naming convention, data type, definition, and data rules associated with the **Store Number**. Every time there is a need to represent the **Store Number** in a data model, we would pull the **Store Number** domain into the relevant entity. With the **Store Number** domain comes all the predefined metadata automatically, thus removing the task of redefining it each time. Domains lead to standardization and consistency throughout all the data models within an organization. Now let's assume that due to the lack of foresight in the organization's original decision regarding the data type length of the **Store Number** field, we need to change the data length from 3 characters to 4 characters. If we had not managed the **Store Number** via a reusable domain, this would have been an enormous task locating all the **Store Number** attributes. By using the **Store Number** domain, one would change the **Store Number** domain's data type length, and allow the automatic rollout of the changed **Store Number** to all attributes related to **Store Number**.

Reusable Objects

Reusable Objects provide an entity or table level mini template, including all related relationships and data rules. Continuing from the previous example of the retail organization, assume that we have a standard design for **Customer**, and its associated **Address** and **Phone Number**. We could then create a mini template of **Customer**, and its associated **Address** and **Phone Number** in a Reusable Object data model, and pull them into a data model instead of recreating them anew each time. In erwin DM, one would store the Reusable Objects Model the same as any other data model, and then use the Complete Compare tool to pull this predefined mini template of **Customer** and its associated entities into the data model.

Template Models

Template Models provide a capability for reuse of the data model default values such as colors, themes, default settings, subject areas, ER Diagrams, User Defined Properties, and several other values. Templates not only provide the data model level objects, they also provide a means of managing organizational specific data modeling objects, such as domains. When thinking about Template Models in the context of erwin DM, these are data models in themselves. A template is stored like a data model and has all the same capabilities as a data model.

Enforcement of Database Rules and Requirements

As seen in the previous section on automation, erwin DM allows the user to perform forward engineering. However, for us to efficiently forward engineer a data model into a database schema, one needs to take into consideration the rules and requirements for the specific DBMS.

For example, there may be DBMS-specific issues with creating a unique index on the columns declared in a primary constraint. In this situation, a unique index is not allowed in SQL Server but is allowed in Oracle, provided the index statement precedes the constraint statement. Some DBMSs allow for materialized views, where others don't. SQL Server does not support the usage of the materialized view construct, yet Oracle does. SQL Server has a similar feature called an indexed view, which is a regular view with a clustered index. There is a minefield of DBMS-specific rules and requirements, and a data modeling tool needs to support all these nuances for the different Database Management Systems (DBMS). erwin DM 2020 R1 supports the following database natively:

- DB2 for i versions 5.x/6.x/7.x
- DB2 for LUW versions 9.7/10.x
- DB2 for z/OS version 8.1
- DB2 for z/OS version 12
- Informix versions 10.x/11.x/12.x
- Netezza version 7.2
- PostgreSQL version 9.6
- Redshift version 1.0
- SAP IQ (Intelligent Query), [originally known as Sybase IQ]
- SAS
- SQL Server version 2012
- SQL Server versions 2016/2017/2019
- Teradata versions 15.x/16.x

- DB2 for LUW version 9.5
- DB2 for LUW version 11.1
- DB2 for z/OS versions 9.1/10/11
- Hive version 2.1.x
- MySQL version 5.x
- Oracle versions 11g/12c
- Progress versions 9.x/10.x/11.x
- SAP ASE (Adaptive Server Enterprise) versions 15.x/16, [originally known as Sybase SQL Server]
- SQL Azure
- SQL Server version 2014
- Teradata version 14.10

For all other relational databases that support ANSI SQL, erwin DM supports them generically via ODBC (Open DataBase Connectivity).

 A database version listed on its own or at the beginning of a list, such as 2016 in 2016/2017/2019, implies a fully supported version of the database. A database version listed after a '/' in a list of versions, such as 2017 or 2019 in 2016/2017/2019, implies a partially supported version of the database. That means that all features in the first listed version remain fully supported in this version. However, any features introduced subsequently to the first version in the list do not have support. erwin DM drops support for a database version that is no longer supported by the database authors. This dropping of support occurs typically in the subsequent release of erwin DM.

Key Learnings

- Documenting the data design can easily be achieved by using a data modeling tool.

- A data modeling tool provides automation of repetitive and time-consuming tasks. Examples of automation are forward engineering, reverse engineering, complete comparing, bulk editing, and transforming of data model objects.

- The reuse of objects improves data modeling performance and standardization.

- Data modeling tools provide adherence to database rules and requirements.

erwin Data Modeler (erwin DM) is the industry-leading data modeling solution that enables organizations to discover, design, visualize, standardize, and deploy enterprise data through an intuitive, graphical interface. The solution combines business and technical views of data assets through integrated conceptual, logical, and physical data models to provide a detailed foundation for collaboration between data stakeholders across the enterprise. erwin DM enables organizations to:

- Master hybrid data architectures and infrastructure to accelerate data-centric innovations.

- Increase data quality and consistency to reduce analysis, development, and maintenance costs.

- Enable enterprise 'data fluency' to optimize stakeholder collaboration and accountability in the data management process.

- Centralize data model development for consistency and maximum reuse.

- Accelerate data source analysis and target schema design cycles in BI/analytics, master data management, and data warehouse/data lake initiatives.

- Reduce enterprise data silos because of interoperability with enterprise data modeling, data cataloging, and data literacy solutions.

Adapted from *https://erwin.com/*

Discover, design
Visual, deploy data
Intuitive, fun

In this chapter, we get started with erwin DM. Journey with us as we explore the various editions of erwin DM, and the different licensing options and functions for installing erwin DM.

erwin DM Editions

All editions of erwin DM use the same installation files—the only differentiator between the editions is the license that gets applied. erwin DM allows or disallows specific functionality based on the license. erwin DM is available in four editions:

- **erwin DM Standard Edition**. Helps organizations manage their hybrid data by providing a simple, graphical display to visualize a wide range of enterprise sources through a single interface, generating database designs directly from visual data models (forward engineering), generating data models from database designs (reverse engineering), increasing quality and efficiency with reusable standards, providing a point-and-click interface for creating PDF, HTML, and text-based reports, and including the Complete Compare feature for synchronizing data models, scripts, and databases.

- **erwin DM Workgroup Edition**. Includes the features from the Standard Edition plus the collaboration features of a centralized data model management repository. This powerful repository stores data models and templates, and enables managed access, collaboration and cross data model analysis, and governing data modeling practices and processes across the organization.

- **erwin DM Navigator Edition**. Helps organizations collaborate with read-only access for a wide range of roles within the organization. This edition allows the viewing of data models and definitions, and also provides point-and-click PDF, HTML, and text-based reporting for both diagrams and metadata.

- **erwin DM API Edition** (Special use licensing mode only). Allows access to specific functionality within erwin DM's COM Dynamic Link Libraries (DLL) via an Application Programming Interface (API). The API works in two different modes, standalone mode, and add-in mode. In standalone mode, the API is activated and controlled by a client application that hosts its process in the standalone mode. In this mode, erwin DM works in the background and does not allow for direct interactions, only via the API. In add-in mode, the API is activated and controlled within the erwin DM Add-In Manager as a COM DLL. The erwin DM executable owns a process, and all the client application DLLs run inside of that process. The application needs to be registered with the System Registry and with the erwin DM Add-In Manager so that it can be available for add-in mode activation.

erwin DM Licensing Models

erwin uses a cloud-based software licensing service to provide licenses for erwin DM, and the license code is a multi-use code, meaning users owning multi-editions of erwin DM only require one license code to manage all of their erwin DM editions and installations. In earlier releases of erwin DM, the user would need different license codes for each of the different editions owned. For each of the erwin DM editions, the following licensing models are available:

- **Node-locked licensing model**. This licensing model uses the computer ID to link the allocated license to the computer to grant access to erwin DM. These licenses cannot be shared between users on different computers unless a user returns the license first. However, there is a restriction on the number of times a node-locked license is returnable.

- **Concurrent licensing model**. This licensing model has a pool of licenses shared between several users in the organization. It provides simultaneous access to erwin DM and is available to as many users as the number of allowed users on a concurrent license. For example, if the user has a ten-user concurrent license, ten users can access erwin DM at a time using this license. If an 11th user tries to use erwin DM, erwin DM denies access.

Both the Node-Locked and Concurrent licensing models let the users activate licenses using either of the following mechanisms:

- **Online license activation**. This method connects to the cloud-based software licensing service over the Internet. The licensing service then validates and activates the license code that the user entered. Online license activation is the default and recommended method of activating the license. Please see the 'Activate erwin DM License Online' section below for more details.

- **Offline license activation**. Should the online license activation fail, then the user can perform an offline license activation. This method uses a multi-step activation process, in which the user needs to generate an activation certificate and send it to erwin Inc support. erwin Inc. support then generates a license certificate and sends it back to the user, who imports the license certificate to activate the license. Please see the 'Activate erwin DM License Offline' section below for more details.

Usage restriction based on network domain name or subnet IP can be implemented for each type of license if so desired by the organization. Please contact erwin Inc. for the availability and prerequisites of this licensing model.

Activate erwin DM License Online

The user needs to first obtain a license code from either erwin Inc. (https://support.erwin.com) or the organization's erwin license administrator. After obtaining the license code, the user needs to activate their erwin DM with the license code before the user can make use of erwin DM. After opening erwin DM for the first time, the erwin DM Licensing dialog box appears for activation of erwin DM with the license code, as shown in Figure 8.

Figure 8. erwin DM Licensing Dialog, Online Activation

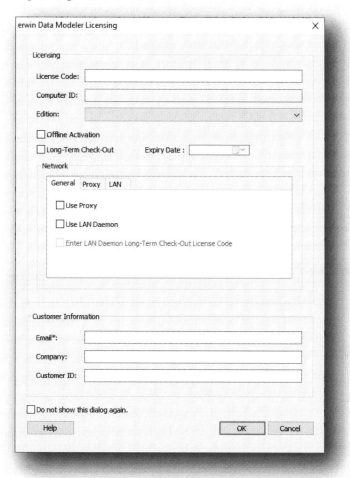

How to complete:

➢ **License Code.** Enter the license code received from erwin Inc. support or the organization's erwin license administrator. This field is greyed out and concealed if, during the install process, the license code was entered. This field is also greyed out and concealed if there was a silent install performed with the license code.

➢ **Computer ID**. This field is read-only, but is used to identify the computer for the license activation.

➢ **Edition**. Select the erwin DM edition, either Standard, Workgroup, Navigator, or API. To understand the difference between the different editions, please see the section on 'erwin DM Editions' above.

➢ **Offline Activation**. Leave this unselected. This checkbox identifies if the user wants to perform an offline activation.

➢ **Long-Term Check-Out and Expiry Date**. Select this checkbox if a Long-Term Check-Out of the license is required. If checked, an Expiry Date is required. A Long-Term Check-Out allows the user to hold the license for a specific period. After that period, the license is released for someone else's availability. A Long-Term Check-Out would be useful, for example, if a contractor needs to use a license just for the length of their assignment.

➢ **Use Proxy**. This checkbox defines whether the user needs to go through a proxy to access the internet. If checked, the Proxy tab requires completion with the relevant details about the proxy server. On the Proxy tab, set the proxy server's parameters, such as the server IP address or server web address, port number, and the credentials to access the internet. The organization's system administrator can usually provide these details. If a user needs to fill in their credentials to access an internet browser, this is a good indication that the user needs to use the proxy server settings.

➢ **Use LAN Daemon**. This checkbox defines whether the organization has set up a LAN Daemon for the license server. If checked, the LAN tab needs completion with the relevant details about the LAN Daemon license server. On the LAN tab, set the LAN Daemon's parameters, such as the server IP address, server name, port number, and credentials to access the LAN Daemon. The organization's system administrator can provide these details.

➢ **Email**. Enter the user's email address. The email address is the only required field under Customer Information.

➢ **Company**. Enter the company name, if a company or organization does not own the erwin DM license, leave it blank.

➢ **Company ID**. Enter the Company ID, if the company ID is not known, leave it blank.

➢ **Do not show this dialog again**. Click this box if you do not want this License Dialog window to appear whenever Data Modeler opens. Note that if you wish to revert this option at a later time, click the Help menu from the Ribbon, followed by the Licensing button, and then check or uncheck this box.

Activate the license by clicking the *OK* button. If all the details were correct from above, and a valid license is available for the Edition that was selected, the instance of erwin DM should open.

If erwin DM does not open, first check all the details above, confirming if there is a proxy in use. If all is correct, the user needs to use the offline activation option, as detailed next.

Activate erwin DM License Offline

The user needs to first obtain a license code from either erwin Inc. (https://erwin.com/) or the organization's erwin license administrator. After obtaining the license code, the user needs to activate their erwin DM with the license code before the user can make use of erwin DM. After opening erwin DM for the first time, the erwin DM Licensing dialog box appears as shown previously in Activate erwin DM License Online section. Follow the same instructions as for the online activation, except for clicking the Offline Activation checkbox. Click the *OK* button, and the Offline Activation dialog box appears, as shown in Figure 9.

Figure 9. Offline Activation Dialog

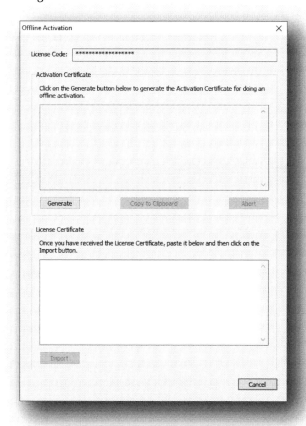

The License Code is greyed out and concealed, for the carrying forward of the license code from the previous dialog. Click the *Generate* button to generate and display an activation certificate. Click the *Copy to Clipboard* button and save the contents to a text file. Send this activation certificate file to erwin Inc. Support for a return of a License Certificate. Under the License Certificate, copy the received license certificate from erwin Inc. Support and paste it in this field. Click *Import*.

The offline License Certificate is only valid for 14 days for imports. After 14 days, a new License Certificate needs to be requested.

Setting the Expiry Reminders

1. In erwin DM, from the Ribbon, click the *Help* menu.

2. Then click the *Licensing* button, as shown in Figure 10.

   Figure 10. Open License Dialog from Ribbon toolbar to Set Expiry Reminders

   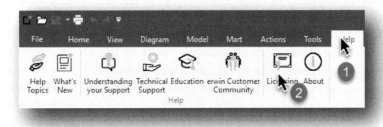

3. The Licensing dialog box appears, as shown in Figure 11.

4. The default reminder time for both, subscription expiry and maintenance end date, is 20 days. If the license is subscription-based or has maintenance, the user can set the reminder time.

5. Click the *Close* button.

6. Their reminders will now only appear on the new number of days before expiry.

Viewing and Returning an Online License

In erwin DM, when the user clicks *Help* > *Licensing*, the Licensing dialog box appears. It displays information about the license, such as:

➢ **License Code.** Masked and greyed out to reflect the license code provided during activation.

➢ **Edition.** Reflects the edition of erwin DM that is activated (Standard, Workgroup, Navigator, or API).

➢ **Computer ID.** Reflects a unique identifier for the computer used for license activation.

➢ **License Type**. Reflects whether the license is permanent or temporary and whether it is a node-locked or concurrent license.

➢ **Activation Type.** Reflects whether it was online or offline activation.

➢ **Total Activations.** Reflects the number of licenses available and the number of licenses used.

➢ **Subscription Expiry Date.** For subscription-based licenses, reflects the expiry of the license.

➤ **Maintenance End Date.** Reflects the expiry date of the license maintenance period.

➤ **Lease Expiry Date.** Reflects the expiry date of the license lease for lease-based licenses.

Figure 11. Change Expiration Reminder Time Frames

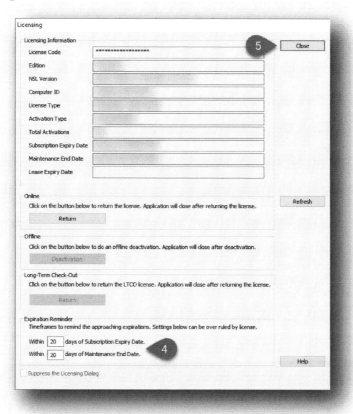

Based on the license activation model, this dialog box lets the user return or deactivate their license. The user might want to return a license in one of the following scenarios:

- Upgrading to a new PC
- Planning to reinstall the operating system
- Replacing a data modeling team member
- Returning or deactivating a license

To return an online or a long-term checked out license before it expires, follow the below process:

1. In erwin DM, from the Ribbon, click the *Help* menu.

2. Then click the *Licensing* button.

3. The Licensing dialog box appears, as shown in Figure 12, which displays all the information about their license. The availability of information, fields, and buttons depending on the license type.

Figure 12. Online License Return Dialog

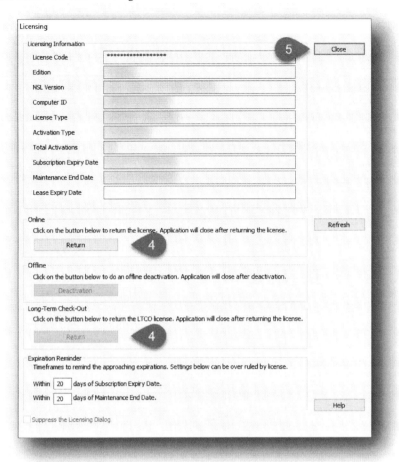

4. Click the *Return* button under the appropriate category. For online activated concurrent licenses, there is no need to follow the above process to return the license explicitly. Every time erwin DM closes, it returns the concurrent license.

5. Click the *Close* button.

6. The license is deactivated.

If there is any unsaved work in erwin DM, and the license expires or returned before expiry, erwin DM allows for the saving of work before closing. Once all work is saved, erwin DM closes.

Viewing and Returning an Offline License

In erwin DM, when the user clicks *Help > Licensing*, the Licensing dialog box appears. This dialog box lets the user return or deactivate their license. The user might want to return a license in one of the following scenarios:

- Upgrading to a new PC
- Planning to reinstall the operating system
- Replacing a data modeling team member

To return an online or a long-term checked out license before it expires, follow the below process:

1. In erwin DM, from the Ribbon, click the *Help* menu.

2. Then click the *Licensing* button.

3. The Licensing dialog box appears, which displays all the information about their license. The availability of information, fields, and buttons depending on their license type.

4. Click the *Deactivation* button under the appropriate category. For online activated concurrent licenses, there is no need to follow the above process to return the license explicitly. Every time erwin DM closes, it returns the concurrent license.

5. Click the *Generate* button on the Offline Deactivation dialog to generate the Deactivation Certificate.

6. Copy and send the generated Deactivation Certificate to erwin Inc. Support.

7. Click the *OK* button on the displayed dialog box.

8. Click the *Close* button.

9. The license is deactivated.

If there is any unsaved work in erwin DM, and the license expires or gets returned before expiry, erwin DM allows for the saving of work before closing. Once all work is saved, erwin DM closes.

Key Learnings

- erwin DM has several different editions available.

- erwin DM licensing can be either Node-Locked or Concurrent.

- The user can perform either an Online or Offline activation of their erwin DM.

- The License Dialog that displays whenever erwin DM opens is suppressible.

- There is a settable reminder for the expiry of the subscription and maintenance.

- The user can return their erwin DM license at any time for re-deployment.

Ribbons and toolbars
Optimize experience
Windows, panes, workspace

In this chapter, we cover the basics of the erwin DM toolbars, windows, panes, and associated options, to enable you to set up your workspace for optimal data modeling. See Figure 13.

Figure 13. The erwin DM Workspace

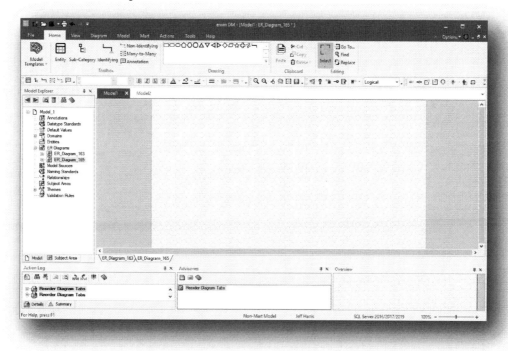

erwin DM Workspace Overview

The erwin workspace comprises of several work areas, namely:
- Title Bar and Quick Access Toolbar
- Ribbons
- Toolbars
- Diagram Window
- Model Explorer Pane
- Action Log Pane
- Advisory Pane
- Overview Pane
- Status Bar

Title Bar and Quick Access Toolbar

Figure 14. Title Bar and Quick Access Toolbar Location

The Title bar, as shown in Figure 14, consists of three sections. It displays the data model name, the subject area name, and the diagram name in the center. It also has the standard buttons to minimize, maximize, and close erwin DM on the right. On the left, it has the new Quick Access Toolbar, which contains a group of shortcut buttons for everyday tasks, such as creating, opening, saving, and printing a data model. It also houses the undo and redo action buttons. The Quick Access Toolbar is customizable via the customize button. For more information on the Quick Access Toolbar, please see the below section on the 'Quick Access Toolbar.'

Ribbons

Figure 15. Ribbon Location

The Ribbon, see Figure 15, is a collection of all the functions and actions of erwin DM. These functions and actions are grouped into tabs and categories and represented graphically using buttons. For more information on the Ribbons, please see the below section on 'Ribbons.'

Toolbars

The Toolbar, see Figure 16, is a set of individual customizable Toolbars that provide quick access to required tools and functionalities within erwin DM. The benefit of the Toolbars over the Ribbon is that Toolbars can always be visible, where a Ribbon menu button requires first the selection of the Ribbon category to be visible. Furthermore, they are small and can be floated and moved to a more accessible place for usage. For more information on the Toolbars, please see the below section on 'Toolbars.'

Figure 16. Toolbars Location

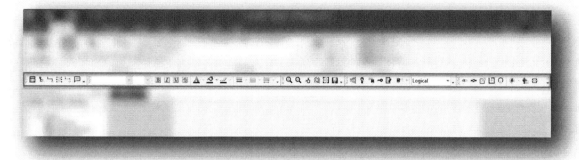

Diagram Window

Figure 17. Diagram Window Location

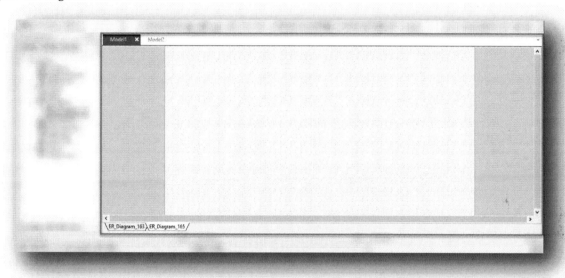

The Diagram Window, see Figure 17, is the area of erwin DM that the user performs the majority of their data modeling tasks. If the data models are in a maximized state, the Diagram Window lists all the data models that are open in a tabbed configuration across the top. The active data model is the highlighted tab, and the tabs can be re-arranged by dragging and dropping them in any order for ease of access. To close a data model, the user can make usage of the appropriate close button on the relevant tab, and any subsequent save dialogs display as usual. The Diagram Window also lists all the data model diagrams for the active subject area in a tabbed configuration across the bottom. The active diagram is the white highlighted tab, and the tabs can be rearranged by dragging and dropping them in any order for ease of access.

Model Explorer Pane

The Model Explorer pane, see Figure 18, is an expandable hierarchical list of all the data model objects. Depending on the bottom tab of the Model Explorer pane, this pane defines the scope of the objects in the list. When the Model tab is select, the default when opening erwin DM, all the data model objects are listed. When the Subject Area tab is selected, all the subject area's data model objects are listed. Depending on the model type of diagram in focus in the Diagram Window, either logical or physical, determines the context of each of the lists. A logical diagram lists only the logical data model objects, and the physical diagram lists only the physical data model objects.

Figure 18. Model Explorer Pane Location

By right-clicking on any of the categories in the Model Explorer pane, the *New* button appears, allowing the user to create a new instance of that object. By clicking on the expand icon (⊞), the hierarchy expands, displaying all the next level objects in the hierarchy. Likewise, by clicking on the collapse icon (⊟), the hierarchy collapses. Right-clicking on any of the objects allows the user to either select an option to delete the object or enter the context-sensitive properties dialog to edit the object. The one exception to this is the Domains category. The user has a further option of sorting the objects.

Action Log Pane

Figure 19. Action Log Pane Location

The Action Log pane, see Figure 19, displays a history of all the actions performed on the data model. The Action Log Pane, with the Advisory Pane, is the most commonly overlooked pane in erwin DM. They provide handy information when something does not perform as expected. Through this Action Log Pane, the user can undo and redo actions to a point in the log, or reverse an individual action.

Advisory Pane

Figure 20. Advisory Pane Location

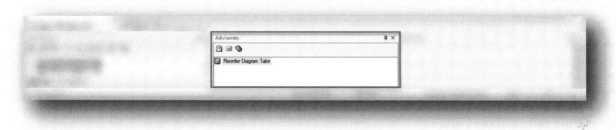

The Advisory pane, see Figure 20, displays a notification of the success or failure of the most recent actions performed on the data model. Through the Advisory Pane, the user can identify what the cause for something not happening, or what was the ripple effect of the action.

Overview Pane

Figure 21. Overview Pane Location

The Overview pane, see Figure 21, is what I refer to as the helicopter view of the data model, allowing the user to navigate around the data model, and zoom in and out of the data model. Further chapters demonstrate this functionality in deeper depth as we expand on erwin DM.

Status Bar

The Status Bar, Figure 22, provides critical information about the data model and erwin DM, such as the location of the data model, the user logged into the erwin Mart Server, and the target database of a physical or logical/physical data model. When in a physical diagram, the user can click on the target database area to change the target database type or version. This bar also provides a zoom function to zoom in or out of the data model quickly. The Status Bar can be hidden using the appropriate checkbox in the Panes category in the View Ribbon. For further information on this, please see the section on the View Ribbon Buttons.

Figure 22. Status Bar Location

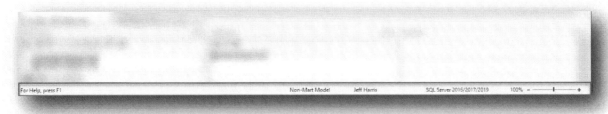

Bulk Editor Pane

Figure 23. Bulk Editor Pane Location

The Bulk Editor pane, Figure 23, is an advanced function within erwin DM. As the name implies, it allows the user to edit multiple data objects at once. The Bulk Editor is a grid-style tool that can list and edit objects and properties in a grid. The real power comes from the ability to export a list of objects in the Bulk Editor grid to a CSV file, and then to use the full power of a spreadsheet tool to manipulate the data and import it back into the data model.

An everyday use case for the Bulk Editor is to export all the entities and their definitions into a spreadsheet, have the business owners edit and update the entity definitions, and then re-import all those updated definitions back into the data model. For further information on the Bulk Editor functionality, please see Chapter 30.

Quick Access Toolbar

Figure 24. Quick Access Toolbar

The Quick Access Toolbar, Figure 24, contains a group of shortcut buttons for everyday tasks, such as creating, opening, saving, and printing a data model. It also houses the undo and redo action buttons. The Quick Access Toolbar is customizable via the customize button. The **default** shortcut buttons are:

Although this is on the Quick Access Toolbar, it is the icon for the erwin DM application. It behaves the same as a typical application icon—a single-click opens a drop-down menu to Restore, Move, Size, Minimize, Maximize, and Close, and a double-click closes the erwin DM application.

Opens the New Model dialog to start creating a new erwin Data Model.

Opens the Open Model dialog to allow for the selection of an existing data model to open.

Saves the active data model. If the active data model is a new data model that has not been saved yet, it opens the Save As dialog. It also provides a drop-down option to perform a Save As, which opens the Save As dialog.

Opens the Print dialog to allow the user to print the graphic of the active data model's active diagram.

Performs an undo function.

Performs a redo function.

Opens a drop-down menu for the customization of the erwin DM workspace. For more information, please the section on 'Customizing .'

Ribbons

erwin DM has adopted a modern graphical user interface to enable and empower the user to efficiently and effectively perform their data modeling tasks. One of the critical areas that they have adopted is the new Microsoft Office ribbon style menus instead of the older drop-down menu style. For users that are familiar with the older versions of erwin DM, the new Ribbon system provides the same functionality that they were familiar with in the older drop-down menus. The Ribbon is a collection of all functions and actions of the erwin DM. These functions and actions are grouped into tabs and categories and are represented graphically using buttons.

File Ribbon

Figure 25. File Ribbon

The File ribbon, Figure 25, provides all the functionality to interact with the data model files, including creating a new data model, opening an existing data model, closing a data model, saving a data model, and printing a data model. The user must not mistake this functionality with those for the erwin Mart Server data models.

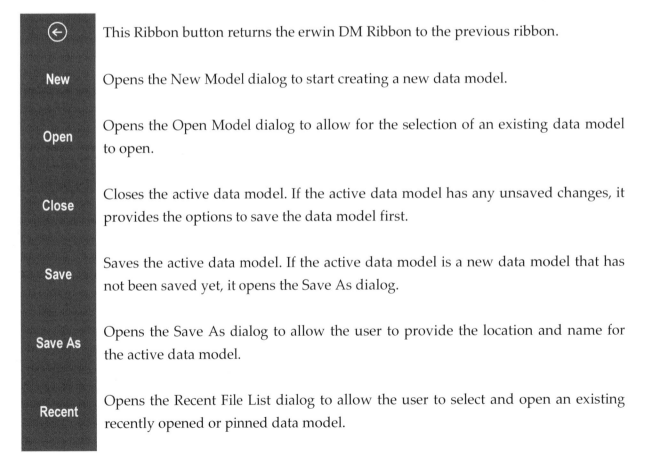

This Ribbon button returns the erwin DM Ribbon to the previous ribbon.

New — Opens the New Model dialog to start creating a new data model.

Open — Opens the Open Model dialog to allow for the selection of an existing data model to open.

Close — Closes the active data model. If the active data model has any unsaved changes, it provides the options to save the data model first.

Save — Saves the active data model. If the active data model is a new data model that has not been saved yet, it opens the Save As dialog.

Save As — Opens the Save As dialog to allow the user to provide the location and name for the active data model.

Recent — Opens the Recent File List dialog to allow the user to select and open an existing recently opened or pinned data model.

Print	Opens the Print dialog to allow the user to print the graphic of the active data model's active diagram.
Page Setup	Opens the Page Setup 'Default Page Setup' Editor dialog to allow the user to define the default print page for the data model.
Exit	Closes erwin DM and all open data models. If any of the data models have any unsaved changes, it provides the options to save the data model first.

Home Ribbon–Logical Model

Figure 26. Home Ribbon. Logical Model

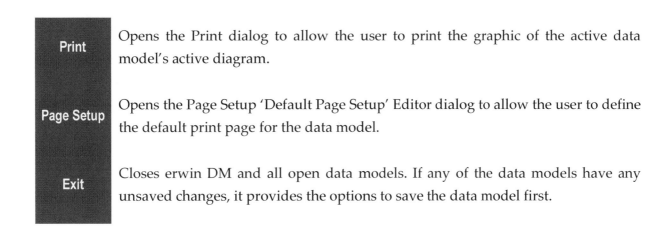

The Home ribbon, Figure 26, provides all the standard data modeling tools and functions for the logical data model, such as creating entities, relationships, and annotations.

Home Ribbon Buttons–Logical Model

 Opens the Template sub-menu to view the template information, bind a template, refresh a template, unbind a template, define filters for the bound template, or set the synchronization on load option.

Toolbox Category

Allows the user to create an Entity in the active Diagram Window.

Allows the user to create a Sub-Category in the active Diagram Window.

Allows the user to create an Identifying Relationship in the active Diagram Window.

Allows the user to create a Non-Identifying Relationship in the active Diagram Window.

Allows the user to create a Many-to-Many Relationship in the active Diagram Window.

Allows the user to create an Annotation in the active Diagram Window.

Drawing Category

Allows the user to draw a Rectangle in the active Diagram Window.

Allows the user to draw a Rounded Rectangle in the active Diagram Window.

Allows the user to draws an Ellipse in the active Diagram Window.

Allows the user to draw a Pentagon in the active Diagram Window.

Allows the user to draw a Hexagon in the active Diagram Window.

Allows the user to draw an Octagon in the active Diagram Window.

Allows the user to draw an Up Triangle in the active Diagram Window.

Allows the user to draw a Down Triangle in the active Diagram Window.

Allows the user to draw a Left Triangle in the active Diagram Window.

Allows the user to draw a Right Triangle in the active Diagram Window.

Allows the user to draw a Diamond in the active Diagram Window.

Allows the user to draw a Parallelogram in the active Diagram Window.

Allows the user to draw a Star in the active Diagram Window.

Allows the user to draw a Cross in the active Diagram Window.

Allows the user to draw a Graphical Line in the active Diagram Window. Not to be confused with relationship and connector lines.

Allows the user to draw a Connector in the active Diagram Window. (A connector is a line from an existing data modeling object to another, but is not a relationship)

Clipboard Category

 Allows the user to paste the contents of the clipboard.

 Allows the user to cut the select data modeling object/s into the clipboard.

 Allows the user to copy the select data modeling object/s into the clipboard.

 Allows the user to delete the selected data modeling object/s from the active diagram, the active subject area or, the active data model.

Editing Category

 Allows the user to change the selected data model object. They can either select the selected item in the active Diagram Window, select all in the active Diagram Window, erase the selection, invert the selection or select all objects in the neighborhood (all objects associated within one level from the object).

 Opens the Go To dialog for the user to go to a specific data model object.

 Opens the Find dialog for the user to find a specific data model object's property.

 Opens the Replace dialog for the user to replace a specific data model object's property.

Home Ribbon–Physical Model

This ribbon, see Figure 27, provides all the standard data modeling tools and functions for the physical data model, such as creating tables, views, relationships, and annotations. Note that buttons described in the previous section will not be described again here.

Figure 27. Home Ribbon. Physical Model

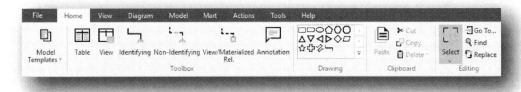

Home Ribbon Buttons–Physical Model

Toolbox Category

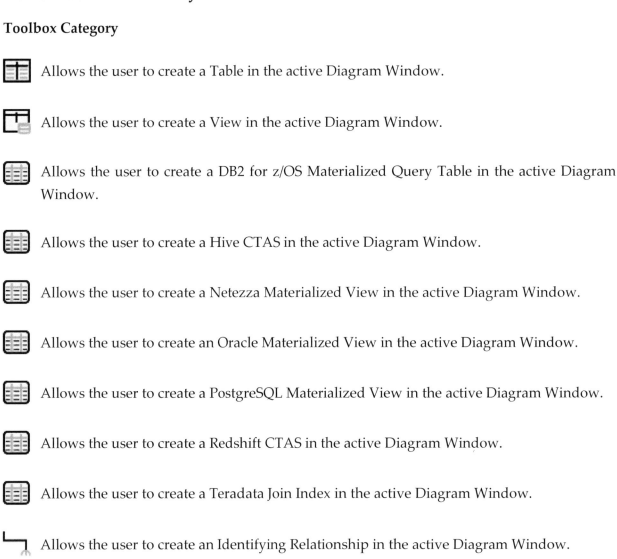

Allows the user to create a Table in the active Diagram Window.

Allows the user to create a View in the active Diagram Window.

Allows the user to create a DB2 for z/OS Materialized Query Table in the active Diagram Window.

Allows the user to create a Hive CTAS in the active Diagram Window.

Allows the user to create a Netezza Materialized View in the active Diagram Window.

Allows the user to create an Oracle Materialized View in the active Diagram Window.

Allows the user to create a PostgreSQL Materialized View in the active Diagram Window.

Allows the user to create a Redshift CTAS in the active Diagram Window.

Allows the user to create a Teradata Join Index in the active Diagram Window.

Allows the user to create an Identifying Relationship in the active Diagram Window.

Allows the user to create a Non-Identifying Relationship in the active Diagram Window.

Allows the user to create a View Materialized Relationship in the active Diagram Window.

Allows the user to create an Annotation in the active Diagram Window.

View Ribbon–Logical Model

Figure 28. View Ribbon. Logical Model

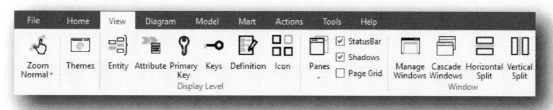

This ribbon, see Figure 28, provides all the tools and functionality in defining the view of the logical data model, such as zooming in and out of the data model, changing themes, changing display levels, managing the panes and windows.

View Ribbon Buttons–Logical Model

Changes the Zoom of the active Diagram Window. They can either Zoom In, Zoom Out, Zoom to Model, Zoom to Selection, or zoom using the interactive Zoom Tool.

Opens the Themes dialog for the user to modify the themes of the data model.

Display Level Category

Changes the display level to Entity Display Level. Entity Display Level shows only the entity name in the active Diagram Window. If one or more objects were selected when this button was pressed, only those objects would be impacted. This is true with all buttons in this category.

Changes the display level to Attribute Display Level. Attribute Display Level shows the entity name and all attributes in the active Diagram Window.

Changes the display level to Primary Key Display Level. Primary Key Display Level shows only the entity name and the primary key attributes in the active Diagram Window.

Changes the display level to Keys Display Level. Keys Display Level shows only the entity name and all the key attributes (primary key attributes and any other key attributes) in the active Diagram Window.

Changes the display level to Definition Display Level. Definition Display Level shows only the entity name and the definition of the entity in the active Diagram Window.

Changes the display level to Icon Display Level. Icon Display Level shows only the entity name and the icon associated with the entity in the active Diagram Window.

Panes Category

Allows the user to switch the display status of the panes in the erwin DM workspace. The Model Explorer pane, Action Log pane, Advisory pane, Overview pane, and Bulk Editor pane can have their display status switch on or off.

□ **Status Bar**   Switches on and off the status bar at the bottom of the erwin DM workspace.

□ **Shadows**   Switches on and off the shadow of all the data model objects in the Diagram Window of the active diagram.

□ **Page Grid**   Switches on and off the print page grid in the Diagram Window of the active diagram.

Window Category

Opens the Manage Windows dialog for the user to be able to manage which data models are open. It also allows the user to close any open data models.

Displays all the open maximized data models in a cascaded view.

Displays all the open maximized data models in a horizontal split view. Note that if there are more than three data models open, erwin tiles the open data models instead.

Displays all the open maximized data models in a vertical split view. Note that if there are more than three data models open, erwin tiles the open data models instead.

View Ribbon–Physical Model

Figure 29. View Ribbon. Physical Model

This ribbon, see Figure 29, provides all the tools and functionality in defining the view of the logical data model, such as zooming in and out of the data model, changing themes, changing display levels, managing the panes and windows. Note that buttons described in the previous section will not be described again here.

View Ribbon Buttons–Physical Model

Display Level Category

Changes the display level to Table Display Level, which shows only the table name in the active Diagram Window. If one or more objects were selected when this button was pressed, only those objects would be impacted. This is true with all buttons in this category.

Changes the display level to Column Display Level. Column Display Level shows the table name and all columns in the active Diagram Window in the column order.

Changes the display level to the Primary Key Display Level. Primary Key Display Level shows only the table name and the primary key columns in the active Diagram Window.

Changes the display level to Keys Display Level. Keys Display Level shows only the table name and all the key columns (primary key columns and any other key columns) in the active Diagram Window.

Changes the display level to Comment Display Level, which shows only the table name and the column of the table in the active Diagram Window. Depending on whether there was a selection in place when used, it determines the scope of tables whose display level changes.

Changes the display level to Icon Display Level. Icon Display Level shows only the table name and the icon associated with the table in the active Diagram Window.

Changes the display level to Physical Order Display Level. Physical Order Display Level shows the table name and all columns in the active Diagram Window in the physical order.

Diagram Ribbon

Figure 30. Diagram Ribbon

This ribbon, see Figure 30, provides all the tools and functionality of the diagrams, including the tools and functionality to layout the objects in the diagrams, such as creating and managing diagrams, aligning objects, grouping objects, and auto-layout options.

Diagram Ribbon Buttons

Diagram Category

 Allows the user to create a Diagram in the active Subject Area and make the new diagram the active diagram in the Diagram Window.

 Allows the user to delete the active Diagram and make the previous diagram the active diagram in the Diagram Window.

 Opens the Diagram Editor dialog for the user to be able to manage the diagram settings.

Alignment Category

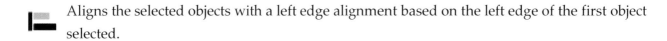 Aligns the selected objects with a left edge alignment based on the left edge of the first object selected.

Aligns the selected objects with a horizontal center alignment based on the horizontal center of the first object selected.

Aligns the selected objects with a right edge alignment based on the right edge of the first object selected.

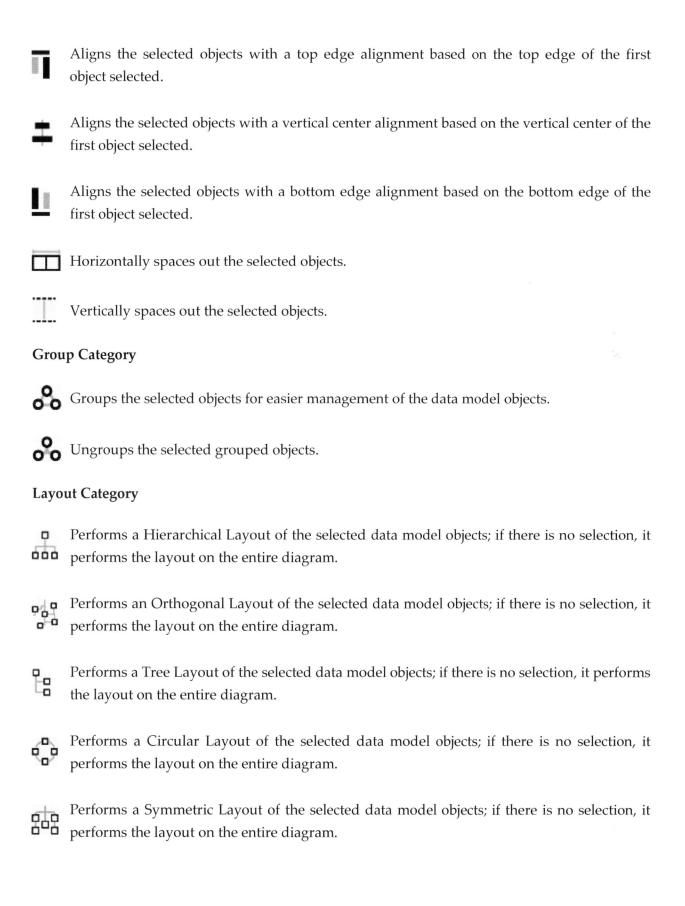

Aligns the selected objects with a top edge alignment based on the top edge of the first object selected.

Aligns the selected objects with a vertical center alignment based on the vertical center of the first object selected.

Aligns the selected objects with a bottom edge alignment based on the bottom edge of the first object selected.

Horizontally spaces out the selected objects.

Vertically spaces out the selected objects.

Group Category

Groups the selected objects for easier management of the data model objects.

Ungroups the selected grouped objects.

Layout Category

Performs a Hierarchical Layout of the selected data model objects; if there is no selection, it performs the layout on the entire diagram.

Performs an Orthogonal Layout of the selected data model objects; if there is no selection, it performs the layout on the entire diagram.

Performs a Tree Layout of the selected data model objects; if there is no selection, it performs the layout on the entire diagram.

Performs a Circular Layout of the selected data model objects; if there is no selection, it performs the layout on the entire diagram.

Performs a Symmetric Layout of the selected data model objects; if there is no selection, it performs the layout on the entire diagram.

Resets the size of the selected object/s to their default size and switches on the automatic resizing option.

 Resets the relationship lines to the default path.

☐ **Layout** Specifies whether to perform the layout option in the existing place, or to layout in a
In Place new area in the diagram page.

Model Ribbon–Logical Model

Figure 31. Model Ribbon. Logical Model

This ribbon, see Figure 31, provides all the tools and functionality to manage the logical data model, such as defining default values, creating and managing domains, managing entities, creating and managing subject areas, and managing data model properties.

Model Ribbon Buttons–Logical Model

Model Category

Opens the Default Value Editor dialog for the user to modify the default values in the data model at the logical level.

Opens the Domain Dictionary dialog for the user to modify the domains in the data model at the logical level.

Opens the Entity Editor dialog for the user to modify the entities in the data model at the logical level.

Opens the Relationship Editor dialog for the user to modify the relationships in the data model at the logical level.

Opens the Validation Rule Editor dialog for the user to modify the validation rules in the data model at the logical level.

 Opens the Model Source Properties dialog for the user to modify the model sources in the data model.

 Opens the Subject Area Editor dialog for the user to modify the subject areas in the data model.

 Opens the User Defined Properties dialog for the user to modify the user defined properties in the data model.

 Opens the Model Editor dialog for the user to modify the data model properties in the data model.

Model Ribbon–Physical Model

This ribbon, see Figure 32, provides all the tools and functionality to manage the physical data model, such as defining default values, creating and managing domains, managing tables, creating and managing subject areas, and managing data model properties.

Figure 32. Model Ribbon. Physical Model

Model Ribbon Buttons–Physical Model

Model Category

 Opens the database-specific Default Value Editor dialog for the user to modify the default values in the data model at the physical level.

 Opens the database-specific Domain Dictionary dialog for the user to modify the domains in the data model at the physical level.

Opens the database-specific Table Editor dialog for the user to modify the tables in the data model at the physical level.

Opens the database-specific Function Editor dialog for the user to modify the functions in the data model at the physical level.

Opens the database-specific Relationship Editor dialog for the user to modify the relationships in the data model at the physical level.

Opens the database-specific Script Template Editor dialog for the user to modify the script templates in the data model at the physical level.

Opens the database-specific Stored Procedure Editor dialog for the user to modify the stored procedures in the data model at the physical level.

Opens the database-specific Trigger Template Editor dialog for the user to modify the referential integrity trigger templates in the data model at the physical level.

Opens the database-specific Trigger Editor dialog for the user to modify the triggers in the data model at the physical level.

Opens the database-specific Validation Rule Editor dialog for the user to modify the validation rules in the data model at the physical level.

Opens the database-specific Materialized View Editor dialog for the user to modify the materialized views in the data model at the physical level.

Opens the database-specific View Editor dialog for the user to modify the views in the data model at the physical level.

Opens the database-specific options to modify other objects in the model at the physical level. For SQL Server, Aggregates, Assemblies, Database Audit Specifications, Databases, Files, Fulltext Catalogs, Fulltext Stoplists, Principals, Partitions, Permissions, Resource Pools, Schemas, Security, Sequences, Servers, Synonyms, Workload Groups, and XML Schema Collections appear. For Oracle, Clusters, Database, Database Links, Directories, Disk Groups, Libraries, Packages, Rollback Segments, Sequences, and Tablespaces appear.

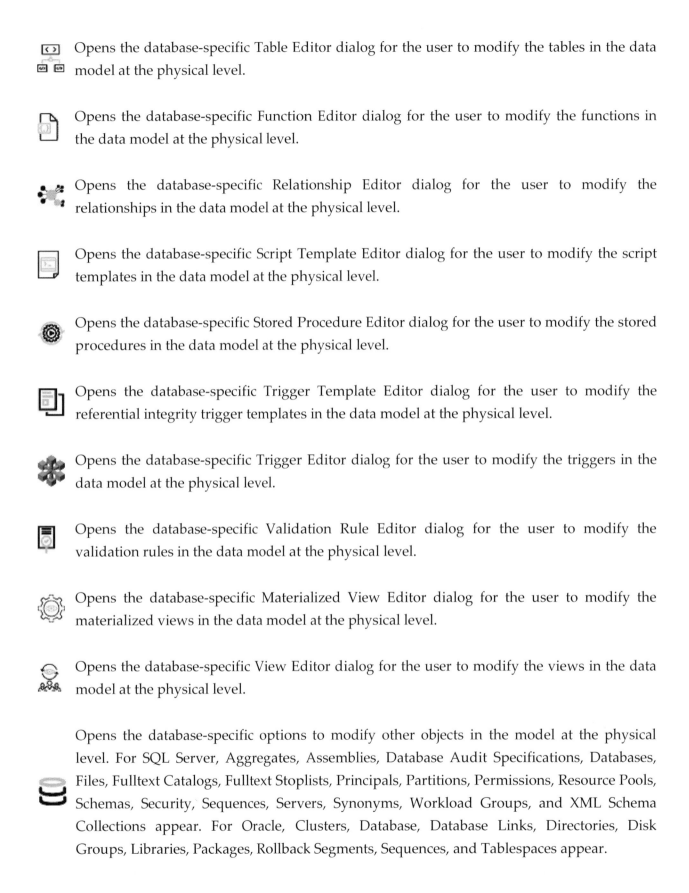

Opens the Model Source Properties dialog for the user to modify the model sources in the data model.

Opens the Subject Area Editor dialog for the user to modify the subject areas in the data model.

Opens the User Defined Properties dialog for the user to modify the user defined properties in the data model.

Opens the Model Editor dialog for the user to modify the data model properties in the data model.

Mart Ribbon

This ribbon, see Figure 33, provides all tools and functionality regarding management and interacting with the erwin Mart Server. The use of the erwin Mart Server repository is for storing the data models when working with the erwin DM Workgroup Edition.

Figure 33. Mart Ribbon

Mart Ribbon Buttons

Opens the Connect to Mart dialog for the user to input the erwin Mart Server details and login credentials.

Disconnects the user from the erwin Mart Server.

Opens the Open dialog for the erwin Mart Server for the user to be able to navigate and open a data model from the repository.

Forces erwin DM to save the active data model to the erwin Mart Server repository. The Save As dialog opens if the model is a new unsaved data model.

 Opens the Save As dialog for the user to save the active data model to the erwin Mart Server repository.

Opens the Lock sub-menu for the user to apply a lock on the active data model. It also displays the status of the lock applied.

  No Lock–A data model opened with 'No Lock' has no restrictions.

 Existence Lock–Stops other users from deleting the data model, but still allows for it to be moved and edited.

 Shared Lock–Data model becomes read-only to other users. They can still open the data model but can only save updates after the Shared lock is released.

 Update Lock–Restricts updates to the applying user. Other users cannot open the data model with an update lock in place.

 Exclusive Lock–Restricts updates to the applying user. Stops any other locks from being applied.

 Opens the Catalog Manager dialog to manage the data models on the erwin Mart Server.

 Opens the Merge dialog for the user to be able to merge the active data model with another data model from the erwin Mart Server. The dialog displayed is a specific version of the Complete Compare dialog.

 Opens the Review Difference to identify what has changed in their active data model. The dialog displayed is another particular version of the Complete Compare dialog, comparing the active data model to the version of the data model that was checked out.

 Opens the Refresh dialog for the user to refresh the data model from the erwin Mart Server repository. This functionality is useful when other users are working on the same data model. The dialog displayed is a specific version of the Complete Compare dialog, comparing the active data model to the version of the data model as it stands at the time.

Opens the Session Manager dialog for the user to be able to view and manage their sessions. Furthermore, it allows the user to manage any locks that they have applied to any of the data models that they have opened.

 Opens the Change Password dialog for the user to change their password to access the erwin Mart Server.

Actions Ribbon

Figure 34. Actions Ribbon

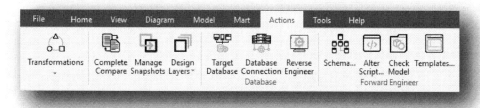

This ribbon, see Figure 34, provides all the action functionality regarding the advanced functionality of the erwin DM, such as transformations, complete compare, forward engineering, reverse engineering, and templates.

Actions Ribbon Buttons

 Opens a sub-menu with all the Transformation options. Depending on the object/s selected in the Diagram Windows, different options are available. The available transformation options are, Resolve All Transformations, Horizontal Partition transformation, Vertical Partition transformation, Supertype-Subtype Rollup transformation, Supertype-Subtype Rolldown transformation, Resolve to Supertype-Subtype Identity transformation, Two Table Rolldown transformation, Two Table Rollup transformation and Resolve Many-to-Many Relationship transformation.

 Opens the Complete Compare Wizard. More on complete compare in Chapter 31.

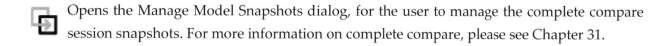 Opens the Manage Model Snapshots dialog, for the user to manage the complete compare session snapshots. For more information on complete compare, please see Chapter 31.

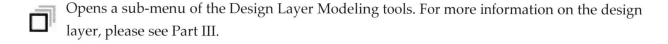 Opens a sub-menu of the Design Layer Modeling tools. For more information on the design layer, please see Part III.

Database Category

 Opens the Target Server dialog for the user to be able to change the target database for the data model. It is important to note that changing the target database triggers a significant change to the data model's metadata structure. Therefore, extreme caution needs to be taken when performing any of these changes.

 Opens the database-specific Connection dialog for the user to enter the connection details for the database. This connection is used to perform Forward Engineering of the physical level of the data model into the database.

 Opens the Reverse Engineering dialog for the user to be able to reverse engineer a database into a data model. It is important to note that erwin DM does not reverse engineer into an existing data model but creates a new data model. For more information on the reverse engineering process, please see Chapter 28 dedicated to this topic.

Forward Engineering Category

 Opens the Forward Engineering Schema Generation Wizard for the user to be able to forward engineer the physical data model into a physical database, or to generate a DDL script. More on forward engineering in Chapter 27.

 Opens the Forward Engineering Alter Script Schema Generation Wizard for the user to be able to forward engineer the deltas of the data model into a physical database, or to generate the DDL script. More on the alter script process in Chapter 27.

 Opens the Model Validation Report built-in to erwin DM that generates a report of found issues in the data model.

 Opens the Forward Engineering Template Editor for the user to be able to customize the used database-specific forward engineering template. The reason a user would customize the forward engineering temple would be to comply with the DDL generation standards that the organization has adopted.

Tools Ribbon

Figure 35. Tools Ribbon

This ribbon, see Figure 35, provides all the tools regarding the advanced tools of the erwin DM, such as naming standards, data type standards, volumetrics, reporting, and queries.

Tools Ribbon Buttons

Naming Category

Opens the Naming Standards dialog for the user to be able to manage the naming standards applied to the data model, including the options to manage the abbreviations.

Opens the Check Naming Standards Compliance dialog for the user to perform a check against the active data model's naming standards for compliance to the standard.

Opens the Name Hardening Wizard for the user to apply or remove name hardening.

Opens the Model Naming Options dialog for the user to set and manage the data model naming options.

Data Type Category

Opens the Data Type Standards dialog for the user to be able to manage the data type standards applied to the data model, including the options to manage data type conversions between different database types.

Volumetrics Category

Opens the Volumetrics dialog for the user to manage the physical database space requirements.

Add-In Category

 Opens the Add-Ins sub-menu for the user to make usage of the add-ins, including the option to open the Add-In Manage dialog for the user to manage the add-ins.

Diagram Picture Category

 Generates a picture report of the active diagram. The output of the generated picture is in the format of an enhanced metafile (*.EMF).

 Opens the Select Subject Area and Diagram dialog to generates a collection of picture reports of the selection. The output of the generated pictures is in the format of an enhanced metafiles (*.EMF).

Reporting Category

 Opens the erwin Report Designer dialog for the user to be able to execute a pre-built or build a new report.

 Opens the Query Tool dialog for the user to perform either database queries or queries against the active data model.

 Opens the erwin DM Scheduler for the user to schedule automated reverse engineering or complete compares.

Settings Category

 Opens the erwin DM Options dialog for the user to set the options of their erwin DM program. These options are not for the data model, but the erwin DM program.

 Opens the sub-menu of the Spelling Checker for the user to be able to customize the spelling checker options and dictionaries.

Bridges Category

 Opens the Import Bridge to convert and import the metadata of a data model from a format recognizable by another application to a format recognizable by erwin DM.

Opens the Export Bridge to convert and export the metadata of a data model from a format recognizable by erwin DM to a format recognizable by another application.

DM NoSQL Category

 Opens the Connect to erwin DM NoSQL dialog for the user to be able to establish a connection to the erwin DM NoSQL environment.

 Disconnects the user from the erwin DM NoSQL environment.

Uploads the active data model into the erwin DM NoSQL environment so the user can interact with the data model in erwin DM NoSQL.

Opens a session of the erwin DM NoSQL for the user to interact with the erwin DM NoSQL environment.

Help Ribbon

Figure 36. Help Ribbon

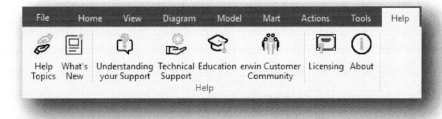

This ribbon, see Figure 36, provides all the links to the help facilities in erwin DM. It also provides access to the licensing dialog.

Help Ribbon Buttons

 Opens the Help Topics web page. Depending on the settings in the Options dialog, it will either open the page from the web or a local copy.

 Opens the What's New web page. Depending on the settings in the Options dialog, it will either open the page from the web or a local copy.

Opens the Understanding Support web page. Depending on the settings in the Options dialog, it will either open the page from the web or a local copy.

 Opens the Technical Support web page. Depending on the settings in the Options dialog, it will either open the page from the web or a local copy.

 Opens the Education web page. Depending on the settings in the Options dialog, it will either open the page from the web or a local copy.

 Opens the erwin Customer Community web page. Depending on the settings in the Options dialog, it will either open the page from the web or a local copy.

 Opens the Licensing dialog for the administration of the erwin DM license.

 Opens the About erwin DM dialog to provide information about the version of erwin DM installed.

Toolbars

The Toolbar is a set of customizable Toolbars that provide quick access to the required tools and functionality within erwin DM. The benefit of the Toolbars over the Ribbon is that Toolbars can always be visible, where a Ribbon button requires first the selection of the Ribbon tab to be visible. Furthermore, they are small and can be floated and moved to a more accessible place for usage, as demonstrated in the section 'Moving and Floating of Toolbars.'

Toolbox Toolbar–Logical Model

Figure 37. Toolbox Toolbar. Logical Model

This toolbar, see Figure 37, provides all the standard data modeling tools and functions for the logical data model, such as creating entities, relationships, and annotations.

Toolbox Toolbar Buttons–Logical Model

 Allows the user to create an Entity in the active Diagram Window.

Allows the user to create a Sub-Category in the active Diagram Window.

Allows the user to create an Identifying Relationship in the active Diagram Window.

Allows the user to create a Non-Identifying Relationship in the active Diagram Window.

Allows the user to create a Many-to-Many Relationship in the active Diagram Window.

Allows the user to create an Annotation in the active Diagram Window.

Opens a drop-down menu for the user to add or remove buttons on the toolbar.

X Reflects a floated toolbar, with the close button to close the toolbar.

Reflects a docked toolbar, with the grip to move and float the toolbar.

Toolbox Toolbar–Physical Model

Figure 38. Toolbox Toolbar. Physical Model

This toolbar, see Figure 38, provides all the standard data modeling tools and functions for the physical data model, such as creating tables, views, relationships, and annotations.

Toolbox Toolbar Buttons–Physical Model

 Allows the user to create a Table in the active Diagram Window.

Allows the user to creates a View in the active Diagram Window.

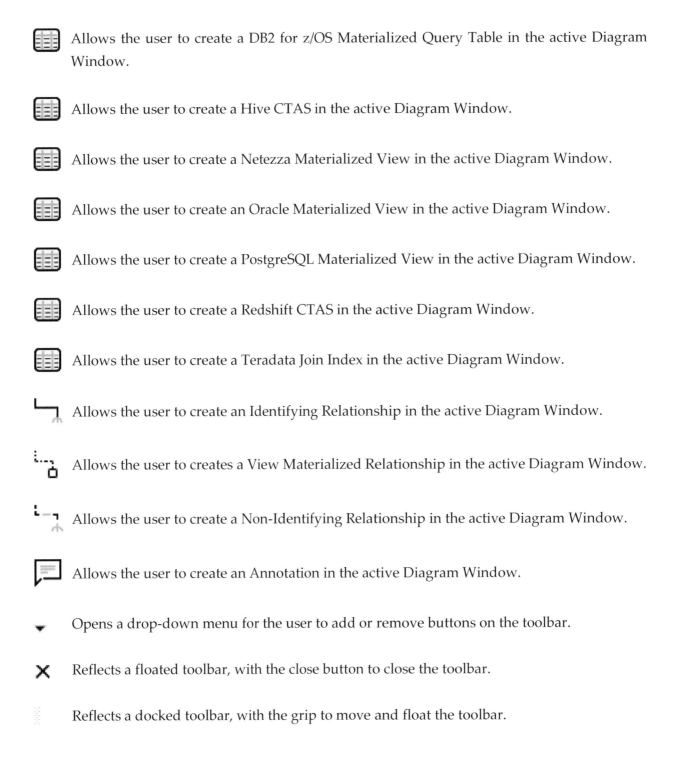

Allows the user to create a DB2 for z/OS Materialized Query Table in the active Diagram Window.

Allows the user to create a Hive CTAS in the active Diagram Window.

Allows the user to create a Netezza Materialized View in the active Diagram Window.

Allows the user to create an Oracle Materialized View in the active Diagram Window.

Allows the user to create a PostgreSQL Materialized View in the active Diagram Window.

Allows the user to create a Redshift CTAS in the active Diagram Window.

Allows the user to create a Teradata Join Index in the active Diagram Window.

Allows the user to create an Identifying Relationship in the active Diagram Window.

Allows the user to creates a View Materialized Relationship in the active Diagram Window.

Allows the user to create a Non-Identifying Relationship in the active Diagram Window.

Allows the user to create an Annotation in the active Diagram Window.

Opens a drop-down menu for the user to add or remove buttons on the toolbar.

Reflects a floated toolbar, with the close button to close the toolbar.

Reflects a docked toolbar, with the grip to move and float the toolbar.

Formatting Toolbar

This toolbar, see Figure 39, provides all the functionality to change the formatting of objects in the Diagram Window, such as changing the font, colors, and line styles.

Figure 39. Formatting Toolbar

Formatting Toolbar Buttons

Allows the user to change the font style of the selected object in the Diagram Window. The toolbar button applies to entity names, attribute names, table names, view names, column names, relationship names, relationship verb phrases, drawing shapes, and annotation text.

Allows the user to change the font size of the selected object in the Diagram Window. The toolbar button applies to entity names, attribute names, table names, view names, column names, relationship names, relationship verb phrases, drawing shapes, and annotation text.

Allows the user to change the font boldness of the selected object in the Diagram Window. The toolbar button applies to entity names, attribute names, table names, view names, column names, relationship names, relationship verb phrases, drawing shapes, and annotation text.

Allows the user to change the font italicization of the selected object in the Diagram Window. The toolbar button applies to entity names, attribute names, table names, view names, column names, relationship names, relationship verb phrases, drawing shapes, and annotation text.

Allows the user to change the font underlining of the selected object in the Diagram Window. The toolbar button applies to entity names, attribute names, table names, view names, column names, relationship names, relationship verb phrases, drawing shapes, and annotation text.

Allows the user to change the font strikethrough of the selected object in the Diagram Window. The toolbar button applies to entity names, attribute names, table names, view names, column names, relationship names, relationship verb phrases, drawing shapes, and annotation text.

Allows the user to change the font color of the selected object in the Diagram Window. The toolbar button applies to entity names, attribute names, table names, view names, column names, relationship names, relationship verb phrases, drawing shapes, and annotation text.

Allows the user to change the background color of the selected object in the Diagram Window. The toolbar button applies to entities, views, drawing shapes, annotations, and diagram backgrounds.

Allows the user to change the line or outline color of the selected object in the Diagram Window. The toolbar button applies to entities, views, relationships, drawing shapes, and annotations.

Allows the user to change the line or outline thickness of the selected object in the Diagram Window. The toolbar button applies to entities, views, relationships, drawing shapes, and annotations.

Allows the user to change the line or outline pattern of the selected object in the Diagram Window—applies to entities, views, relationships, drawing shapes, and annotations.

Allows the user to change the line end caps of the selected object in the Diagram Window. The toolbar button applies to line and connector drawing shapes only.

Opens a drop-down menu for the user to add or remove buttons on the toolbar.

Reflects a floated toolbar, with the close button to close the toolbar.

Reflects a docked toolbar, with the grip to move and float the toolbar.

Zoom Toolbar

Figure 40. Zoom Toolbar

This toolbar, see Figure 40, provides all of the zooming functionality.

Zoom Toolbar Buttons

Allows the user to zoom in on the active Diagram Window.

Allows the user to zoom out on the active Diagram Window.

Allows the user to set the zoom level to normal (100%).

Allows the user to zoom to fit all objects in the active Diagram Window.

Allows the user to zoom to selected objects on the active Diagram Window.

Allows the user to zoom in or out on the active Diagram Window using the interactive Zoom Tool.

Opens a drop-down menu for the user to add or remove buttons on the toolbar.

Reflects a floated toolbar, with the close button to close the toolbar.

Reflects a docked toolbar, with the grip to move and float the toolbar.

Display Toolbar–Logical Model

Figure 41. Display Toolbar. Logical Model

This toolbar provides all functionality for changing the display levels of the logical data model.

Display Toolbar Buttons–Logical Model

Changes the display level to Entity Display Level. Entity Display Level shows only the entity name in the active Diagram Window.

Changes the display level to Primary Key Display Level. Primary Key Display Level shows only the entity name and the primary key attributes in the active Diagram Window.

Changes the display level to Attribute Display Level. Attribute Display Level shows the entity name and all attributes in the active Diagram Window.

Changes the display level to Keys Display Level. Keys Display Level shows only the entity name and all the key attributes in the active Diagram Window.

Changes the display level to Definition Display Level. Definition Display Level shows only the entity name and the definition of the entity in the active Diagram Window.

Allows the user to open the Subject Area editor dialog for the user to apply changes to the subject areas.

Reflects whether the active diagram is logical or physical, and allows the user to change the active diagram between logical and physical.

Opens a drop-down menu for the user to add or remove buttons on the toolbar.

Reflects a floated toolbar, with the close button to close the toolbar.

Reflects a docked toolbar, with the grip to move and float the toolbar.

Display Toolbar–Physical Model

Figure 42. Display Toolbar. Physical Model

This toolbar provides all functionality for changing the display levels of the logical data model.

Toolbox Toolbar Buttons–Physical Model

Changes the display level to Table Display Level. Table Display Level shows only the table name in the active Diagram Window.

Changes the display level to Column Display Level. Column Display Level shows the table name and all columns in the active Diagram Window.

Changes the display level to Primary Key Display Level. Primary Key Display Level shows only the table name and the primary key columns in the active Diagram Window.

Changes the display level to Keys Display Level, showing only the table name and all key attributes in the active Diagram Window.

Changes the display level to Definition Display Level. Definition Display Level shows only the table name and the definition of the table in the active Diagram Window.

Allows the user to open the Subject Area editor dialog for the user to apply changes to the subject areas.

Reflects whether the active diagram is logical or physical, and allows the user to change the active diagram between logical and physical.

Opens a drop-down menu for the user to add or remove buttons on the toolbar.

Reflects a floated toolbar, with the close button to close the toolbar.

Reflects a docked toolbar, with the grip to move and float the toolbar.

Mart Toolbar

Figure 43. Mart Toolbar

This toolbar, see Figure 43, provides all tools and functionality regarding management and interacting with the erwin Mart Server. The use of the erwin Mart Server repository is for storing all the data models when working with the erwin DM Workgroup Edition.

Mart Toolbar Buttons

Opens the Connect to Mart dialog for the user to input the erwin Mart Server details and their login credentials.

Disconnects the user from the erwin Mart Server.

Opens the Open dialog for the erwin Mart Server for the user to be able to navigate and open a data model from the repository.

Forces erwin DM to save the active data model to the erwin Mart Server repository. If the data model is a new unsaved data model, the Save As dialog opens.

Opens the Save As dialog for the user to save the active data model to the erwin Mart Server repository.

Opens the Lock sub-menu for the user to apply a lock on the active data model.

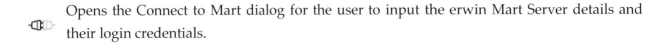

No lock–A data model opened with 'No Lock' has no restrictions.

Existence Lock–Stops other users from deleting the data model, but still allows for it to be moved and edited.

Shared Lock–Data model becomes read-only to other users. They can still open the data model but can only save updates after the Shared lock is released.

Update Lock–Restricts updates to the applying user. Other users cannot open the data model with an update lock in place.

Exclusive Lock–Restricts updates to the applying user. Stops any other locks from being applied.

Opens the Catalog Manager dialog for the user to manage the data models on the erwin Mart Server.

Opens the Merge dialog for the user to be able to merge the active data model with another data model from the erwin Mart Server.

Opens the Review Difference dialog for the user to identify what has changed in their active data model. The dialog displayed is another particular version of the Complete Compare dialog, comparing the active data model to the version that was checked out.

 Opens the Refresh dialog for the user to refresh the data model from the erwin Mart Server repository. This functionality is particularly useful when other users are working on the same data model. The dialog displayed is also a specific version of the Complete Compare dialog, comparing the active data model to the version as it stands at the time.

 This toolbar button the Session Manager dialog for the user to be able to view and manage their sessions. Furthermore, it allows the user to manage any locks that they have applied to any of the data models that they have opened.

 Opens the Change Password dialog for the user to change their password to access the erwin Mart Server.

Opens a drop-down menu for the user to add or remove buttons on the toolbar.

Reflects a floated toolbar, with the close button to close the toolbar.

Reflects a docked toolbar, with the grip to move and float the toolbar.

Key Learnings

- The Title bar consists of three sections: Quick Access Toolbar, data model name, and standard Windows buttons. The Quick Access Toolbar contains shortcut buttons for everyday tasks, such as creating, opening, saving, and printing a data model. The Status Bar provides critical information about the data model and erwin DM.

- The Ribbon is a collection of buttons grouped into tabs and categories and represented graphically, and the Toolbar provides quick access to the tools and functionalities.

- The Action Log pane displays a history of all the actions performed on the data model, the Advisory pane displays a notification of the success or failure of the most recent actions, the Overview pane allows the user to zoom in and out of the data model, and the Model Explorer pane is an expandable hierarchical list of all the data model objects.

- The Bulk Editor pane allows the user to edit data objects in a bulk manner.

Let's play with erwin
Open, close data models
Use panes and toolbars

In this chapter, we cover the foundational interactions with erwin DM, such as the opening of data models, interacting with the layout, and relocating panes and toolbars. Also covered in this chapter is the layout of data models in the Diagram Window.

Up to now, we have covered erwin DM from an informative perspective. From now on, use this book as a tutorial and replicate what we do, step by step. Replicating the steps not only gives you an understanding of each of the steps, but it also gives you valuable practice. To fully embrace the rest of this book, have an installed copy of erwin DM. This can include the trial version at: *https://erwin.com/products/erwin-data-modeler/*.

Opening an Existing erwin Data Model

As the saying goes, 'there's more than one way to verb a noun,' the same applies to most of the interaction with erwin DM. There is more than one way to open a data model. The user could double-click on the data model file in file explorer, and rely on the file type association in Windows to open erwin DM with the file. Alternatively, the user could open erwin DM, and then use the Quick Access Toolbar, the Ribbon, or the Toolbars to open a data model.

However, what I demonstrate is what I believe to be the best usage of erwin DM and the optimal route to achieving a result. Every extra click is time wasted. The user is more than welcome to use an alternative way to achieve the same result, whatever makes them comfortable in working with erwin DM. So, without further ado, open erwin DM and follow my lead:

1. Using the Quick Access Toolbar, click on the *Open* button. See Figure 44.

    Figure 44. Click the Open Button

2. Navigate to the **My Models** folder in the **Documents** folder, then select the '*eMovies.erwin*' data model.

If you do not find the 'eMovies.erwin' and 'PublicationSystemSample.erwin' data model files in the 'My Models' folder in the 'Documents' folder, there is a copy of these files in the '<Installation Directory>\erwin\Data Modeler r9\BackupFiles\Samples\ Standard' folder. Copy these files to the 'My Models' folder.

3. Click on the *Open* button.

4. eMovies data model opens, as shown in Figure 45.

Figure 45. eMovies Data Model Open

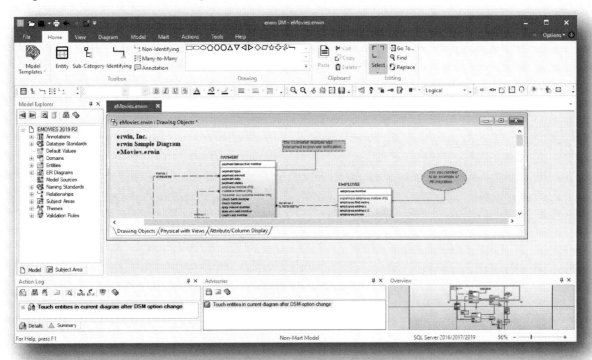

5. Using the Quick Access Toolbar, click on the *Open* button again.

6. This time, select the '*PublicationSystemSample.erwin*' data model.

7. Click on the *Open* button.

8. Both the *eMovies* and *PublicationSystemSample* data models are open.

Floating and Docking of Panes

For the next section of the tutorial, change the erwin DM's window state to 'normal,' not 'maximized.' See Figure 46.

Figure 46. erwin DM's Normal Window State

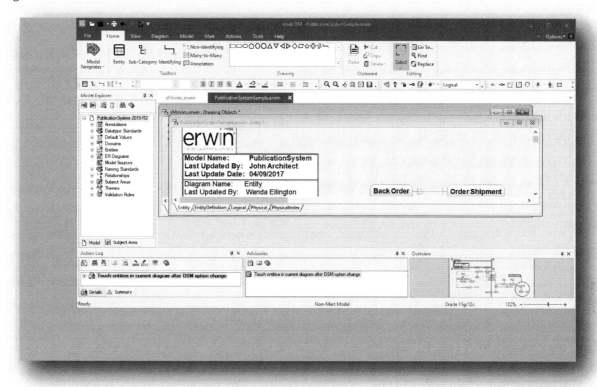

 To set an application to its 'normal' state, without using the Windows buttons, drag it away from the edges of the screen by its title bar or double-click the title bar. You can also use the Windows Key (⊞) and the Down Arrow (↓) shortcut to step down from 'maximized' to 'normal,' or from 'normal' to 'minimized.' The same combination, substituting the Up Arrow (↑) instead, reverses the steps.

1. Click and hold on the Model Explorer title bar.

2. Drag the Model Explorer pane to the left, clear of the erwin DM window, and release the mouse button. See Figure 47.

 These steps have effectively floated the Model Explorer pane, but the same is doable with any of the erwin DM panes. The Diagram Window, Ribbon, Status Bar, and Title Bar are the only ones that cannot float.

The next set of steps of this tutorial covers the first possible method to re-dock a floating pane.

3. Double click on the Model Explorer title bar. See Figure 48.

Figure 47. Floating the Model Explorer Pane

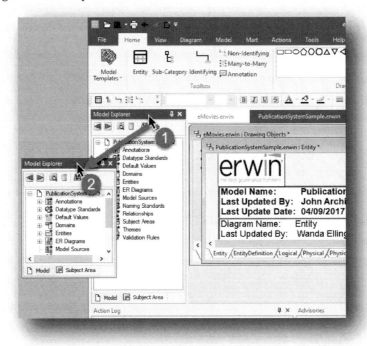

Figure 48. Double Click Model Explorer Title Bar to Re-Dock

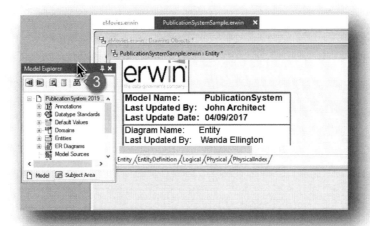

4. Observe that the Model Explorer pane re-docked in the pace it was before floating.

 This process works, irrespective of the number of moves the pane goes through, as long as you don't dock it anywhere else first. erwin DM remembers the last docked location of the pane and returns it to that location, even if the last docked location was not the default location. In the above tutorial, we used the original default location, so it returned to the default location.

The next set of steps covers another possible alternative method to re-dock a floating pane. However, before re-docking the pane, we need to float it again.

5. Click and hold on the Model Explorer title bar.

6. Drag the Model Explorer pane to the left, clear of the erwin DM window again, and release the left mouse button.

However, before re-docking, we explore the ability to change the size of the floated pane.

7. Drag the bottom edge of the Model Explorer pane down. See Figure 49.

Figure 49. Drag Edge of Model Explorer Pane

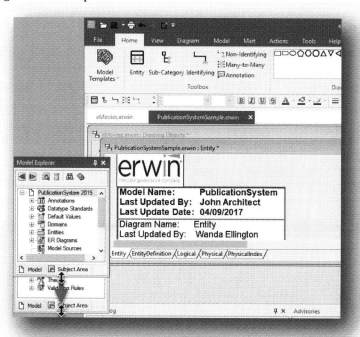

 The same action is performable on the left, top, and right edge of a floated pane. This functionality allows for the resizing of the panes to suit working requirements.

 When one has multiple monitors, it might be more efficient to have the primary monitor dedicated to core data modeling tasks. The secondary monitor to display all the auxiliary panes for ease of reach, but not cluttering the main work area.

8. Click and hold on the Model Explorer title bar.

9. Drag the Model Explorer pane to the right to over the erwin DM's Diagram Window again. See Figure 50.

Figure 50. Drag Model Explorer Pane Back

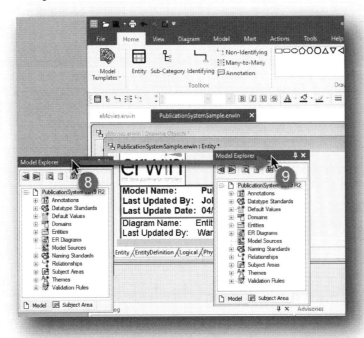

10. Observe the appearance of the Pane Docking Hotspots, to aid in the re-docking of the pane.

The Pane Docking Hotspots have two different types.

- **Workspace Hotspots.** These hotspots place the pane inside the erwin DM Workspace, but on the inside edges, either the top, bottom, left, or right edges.

- **Pane Hotspots.** These hotspots place the re-docked pane relative to the pane hovered over by the mouse pointer. This type of hotspot has two different types. The Diagram Window version of the pane hotspot allows the user to drop the re-docked pane to the top, bottom, left, or right of the Diagram Window. The supplementary pane's hotspot provides the same functionality as the Diagram Window's hotspot, plus allows the user to drop it in the center cluster to have the two panes in a tabbed configuration. See Figure 51.

11. Now hover over each of the docking hotspots and observe the blue shadow indicating the pane's docking location for that specific hotspot.

12. Once done, dock the Model Explorer pane back where it came from, that is to the left of the Diagram Window. See Figure 52.

Figure 51. Location of Pane Docking Hotspots

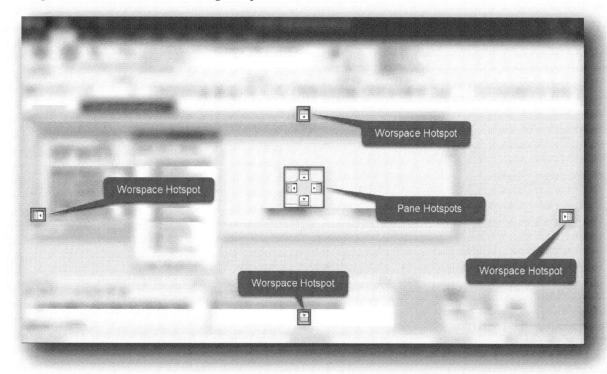

Figure 52. Re-Dock Pane Where It Came From

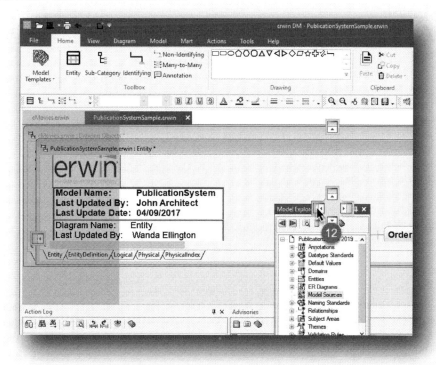

13. Click and hold on the Action Log title bar.

14. Drag the Action Log pane to the right over the Advisory pane, noting that the Advisory pane and the Overview pane automatically resize.

15. Release the Action Log pane over the center of the Pane Docking Hotspots, the tabbed icon. See Figure 53.

Figure 53. Dock Action Log Pane as a Tab on the Advisory Pane

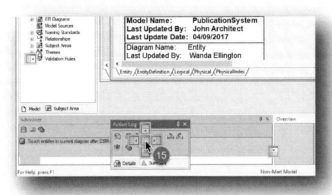

16. Observe the docking action resulted in the panes being joined together with two tabs, one for the Action Log pane and one for the Advisory pane.

 All interactions with the joined panes via the title bar behaves as one pane.

17. Click and hold on the Action Log tab.

18. Drag the Action Log pane to over the Advisory pane's Pane Docking Hotspots, noting that the Advisory pane and the Overview pane once again automatically resized.

19. Release the Action Log pane over the left of the Pane Docking Hotspots. See Figure 54.

Figure 54. Re-Docking the Action Log Pane

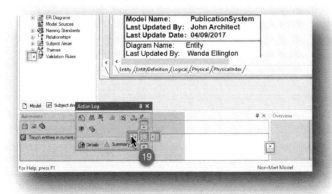

20. Observe that the Action Log pane has returned to its original location.

Auto-Hiding of Panes

For the next section of the tutorial, change the erwin DM's window state back to 'maximized.'

 To set an application to its 'maximized' state, without using the Windows buttons, drag it to the top edges of the screen by its title bar or double-click the title bar. You can also use the Windows Key (⊞) and the Up Arrow (↑) shortcut to step up from 'normal' to 'maximized,' or from 'minimized' to 'normal.'

1. Click on the pin icon (📌) in the Model Explorer title bar. See Figure 55.

    Figure 55. Click Pin Icon in Model Explorer Title Bar

    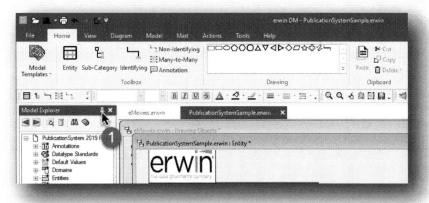

2. Observe how the Model Explorer pane slides to the side; the Model Explore pane is now an Auto-Hidden pane.

3. Hover over the Model Explorer flyout title bar and observe how the Model Explorer pane flies out from the side edge. See Figure 56.

 The size of the pane stretches the full height of the erwin DM Workspace in the Auto-Hidden state and is not limited to the height of the original location.

4. While the Model Explorer pane is still exposed, click once more on the *Pin* icon (📌).

5. Observe that the Model Explorer pane returns to a regularly docked pane.

 Note the change in orientation of the pin; vertical pin implies a pinned pane, horizontal implies an auto-hidden pane.

Figure 56. Hover Over Model Explorer Title

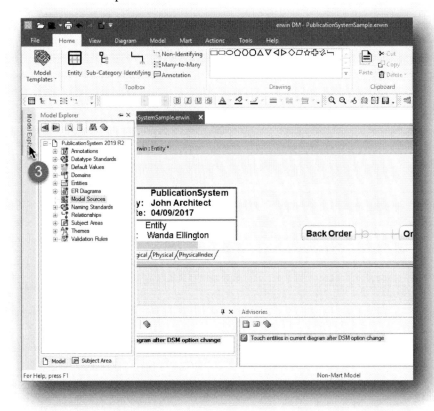

Closing and Re-Opening of Panes

1. Click on the *Close* icon (✖) in the Model Explorer title bar. See Figure 57.

    Figure 57. Close the Model Explorer Pane

    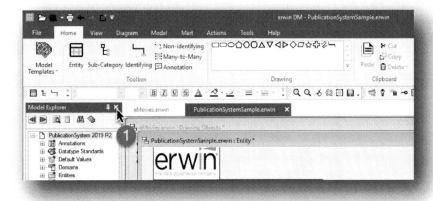

2. Observe how the Model Explorer pane closes completely.

When a pane closes, it does not mean that the data in the pane is lost—it is just not visible anymore. The Action Log pane, Advisory pane, and the Bulk Editor pane all maintain their data. After re-opening a closed pane, it returns the data to its state as before closing.

3. Click on the *View* tab in the Ribbon.

4. Then click on the *Panes* button.

5. Finally, click on the *Model Explorer* pane option.

6. Observe how the Model Explorer pane re-opens in its last location.

 Take note of the shortcut keys available to re-open closed panes:

Model Explorer pane	Ctrl + E
Action Log pane	Ctrl + L
Advisory pane	Ctrl + D
Bulk Editor pane	Ctrl + B

Moving and Floating of Toolbars

The ability to float and dock the erwin DM toolbars is similar to that of the panes. In this section of the tutorial, we are going to demonstrate this capability.

1. Click and hold on the *Grip* button ( ) on the Toolbox toolbar. The grip button is only visible on a docked toolbar. See Figure 58.

Figure 58. Click and Hold the Grip Button for the Toolbox Toolbar

2. Drag the Toolbox toolbar to the left of the Model Explorer pane. Notice that as the Toolbox toolbar moves down, it opens a new line for the toolbars below the exiting one. For our tutorial, don't dock it in this new toolbar line, but dock it on the left edge of the erwin DM Workspace.

3. Once the toolbar reflects on the left side of the Model Explorer, release the mouse button to dock the toolbar in this location. Observe that the toolbar is dockable anywhere in the new side toolbar column on the left of the Model Explorer.

 Toolbars are dockable at the top, left, right, and bottom of the erwin DM Workspace.

4. Once again, click and hold on the *grip* button ( ) on the Toolbox toolbar — this time dragging and releasing it inside the erwin DM Workspace. See Figure 59.

Figure 59. Float the Toolbox Toolbar

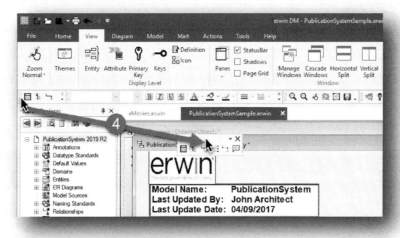

5. Observe that the grip button disappears, replaced with the close button.

6. Although the location chosen for the toolbar may be unsuitable for data modeling, it reflects the ability to float a toolbar over any other window or pane. The same floating that we experienced with the panes applies to the toolbars and thus is floatable onto a second monitor.

7. Now click on the close button on the Toolbox toolbar to close it.

8. Observe that the Toolbox toolbar has closed. Through this method, one can close all the toolbars that are not needed or used.

9. Click on the Customization button on the Quick Access Toolbar to display the drop-down menu. See Figure 60.

Figure 60. Customization Button Drop-Down Menu

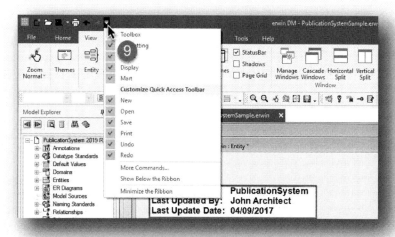

10. Observe the absence of the tick for the Toolbox toolbar, indicating a closed toolbar. Select the Toolbox toolbar menu option to open the Toolbox toolbar again.

11. Observe that the Toolbox toolbar has reappeared.

12. Click and hold on the *grip* button (   ) on the Toolbox toolbar — this time dragging and releasing it in its original location. See Figure 61.

Figure 61. Re-Dock the Toolbox Toolbar in its Original Location

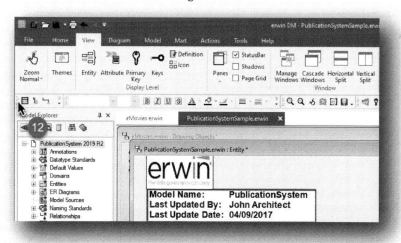

13. Observe how the other toolbars move to make space for the Toolbox toolbar again.

Customizing Toolbars

As was observed with the previous section, the Customization button on the Quick Access Toolbar provides the ability to close and open the toolbars. It also provides the ability to customize which buttons get displayed on the toolbars, including the Quick Access Toolbar itself. The customization drop-down menu is broken down into four areas (see Figure 62):

a. Toolbars close and open options

b. Quick Access Toolbar buttons hide and display options

c. Open the Customization dialog

d. Ribbon display options

Figure 62. Customization Button Drop-Down Menu Option

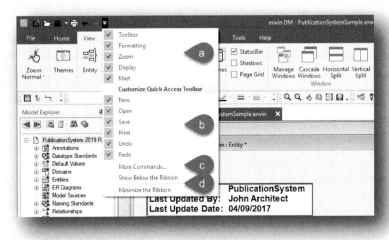

1. Click on the *Customization* button on the Quick Access Toolbar to display the drop-down menu.

2. Click on the *Save* menu option under the Customize Quick Access Toolbar. See Figure 63.

Figure 63. Close Save Button on Quick Access Toolbar

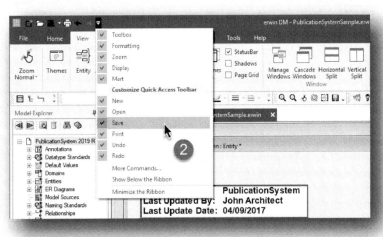

3. Observe that the *Save* button on the Quick Access Toolbar disappeared.

4. Once again, click on the *Customization* button on the Quick Access Toolbar to display the drop-down menu.

5. Click on the *Save* menu option under the Customize Quick Access Toolbar again. See Figure 64.

Figure 64. Enable Displaying Save Button on Quick Access Toolbar

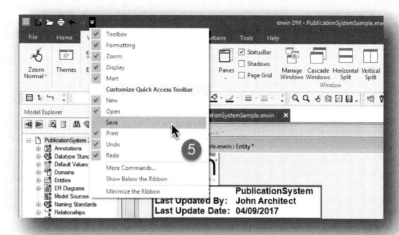

6. Observe that the Save button on the Quick Access Toolbar reappeared but in the wrong order.

7. Once again, click on the *Customization* button on the Quick Access Toolbar to display the drop-down menu.

8. This time click on the *More Commands* option. See Figure 65.

Figure 65. Open Customize Dialog

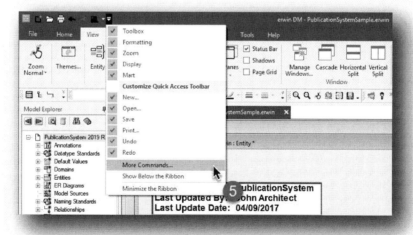

 In erwin DM, whenever you see a menu option with an ellipses after it (…), this implies that there is a dialog behind the menu option.

9. The Customize dialog appears, as displayed in Figure 66.

Figure 66. The Customize Dialog

10. Observe that the Customize dialog opens on the *Quick Access* tab. On the right-hand side of the tab, it allows for the customization of the order of the buttons. Also, the **Save** button option is at the bottom of the list. Select the Save button option.

11. Click the up arrow button three times to move it up to its original location. Its original location was between Open and Print.

12. Observe that on the left-hand side of the tab, it provides all the available buttons that are addable to the Quick Access Toolbar. From the *Choose Commands From* drop-down menu, select the **View** option. This option provides all the typical view related buttons.

13. Select the **Logical Model** button option.

14. Click the **Add** button to add it to the Quick Access Toolbar. See Figure 67.

15. Repeat the same steps for the **Physical Model** button option.

16. Observe that the list on the right-hand side of the tab includes the *Logical Model* and *Physical Model* buttons.

17. Explore the rest of the button options under the other *Choose Commands From* drop-down menu. When finished, click the **Close** button to close the Customize dialog.

 When working with data models from the erwin Mart Server, I usually hide the **Open** and **Save** buttons on the Quick Access Toolbar, and then replace them with the **Open** and **Save** buttons from the Mart drop-down list. These buttons make it easier to open and save the active data models to the erwin Mart Server.

18. Reopen the Customize dialog by clicking on the **Customization** button on the Quick Access Toolbar to display the drop-down menu.

Figure 67. Add Quick Access Toolbar Button

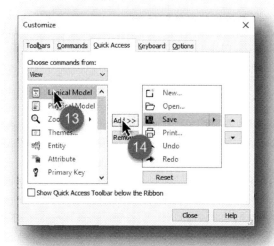

19. Click on the **More Commands** option once again.

20. On the Customize dialog, click on the **Toolbar** tab.

21. The Toolbars tab allows for the opening and closing of the various toolbars; only the *Ribbon* is not closable. The Toolbar tab also allows for the creation of new custom toolbars.

22. Click on the **New** button.

23. In the New Toolbar dialog, give the new toolbar a name of '**My Tools.**'

24. Then click the **OK** button.

25. Observe that a new toolbar has appeared in the toolbar row. See Figure 68.

Figure 68. New Toolbar Added

26. Click on the *Commands* tab. Observe the Commands that are available for inclusion in the toolbars.

27. Drag the Print toolbar option from the Command side of the Customize dialog to the new toolbar. See Figure 69.

Figure 69. Add New Button To New Toolbar

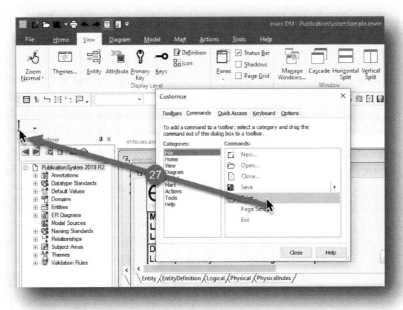

28. Observe the new *Print* button on the new toolbar. This functionality can be used to build a collection of regularly used buttons for easy access.

29. Return to the Toolbars tab on the Customize dialog. Observe the ability to rename the **My Tools** toolbar.

30. Seeing that we are not going to be needing the My Tools toolbar, ensure that the **My Tools** toolbar is selected, click the *Delete* button.

 erwin DM prevents a user from accidentally deleting the built-in toolbars by greying out the Delete button when a built-in toolbar is in focus.

31. Confirm the deletion by clicking the *OK* button.

32. Observe that there is a button to reset the built-in toolbars to their default configuration.

33. Click on the *Keyboard* tab in the Customize dialog.

34. On this tab, the user can change and assign the shortcut keys.

35. Click on the *Options* tab in the Customize dialog.

36. On this tab, the user can personalize the behavior of the menus and toolbars.

37. When finished exploring all the options, click the *Close* button.

Diagram Windows Management

erwin DM allows the user to have multiple data models open at the same time. This ability can be quite an advantage when there is a need to jump between different data models. erwin DM provides a couple of diagram management tools to assist the user.

1. With the two data models open from the earlier section, and ensuring that you are on the View Ribbon tab, click on the *Horizontal Split* button. See Figure 70.

   Figure 70. Click on the Horizontal Split Button

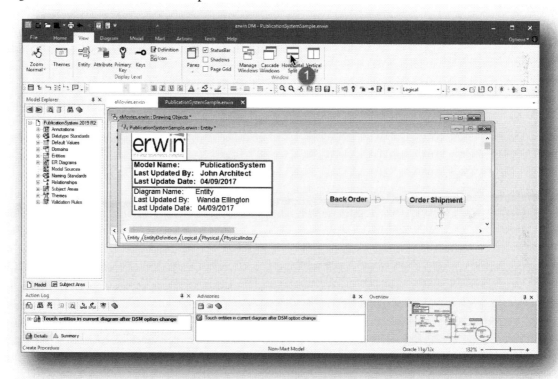

2. Observe that erwin DM lays out the two data models horizontally.

3. Click on the *Vertical Split* button.

4. Observe that erwin DM lays out the two data models vertically.

 erwin DM provides the ability to split the diagram window vertically or horizontally with up to three non-minimized data models. The split operation excludes all minimized data models. Should the number of non-minimized data models exceed three, erwin DM tiles the data models instead.

5. Click on the *Cascade Windows* button.

6. Observe that erwin DM lays out the two data models in a cascaded style.

7. The cascaded style is the typical style when opening data models.

8. Note that the standard Windows button operates in the Diagram Window, as they would for a typical Windows application.

9. Click on the *Manage Windows* button to open the Manage Windows dialog.

10. The Manage Windows dialog provides a dialog for all the open data models to be managed. The columns displayed in the Manage Windows dialog are:

➡	Indicate if the data model marked for activation as the active data model.
✖	Indicate if the data model marked for closing.
🖫	Indicate if the data model marked for saving.
Model Name	The internal name of the data model displayed.
File Name	The filename of the data model displayed.
Model Path	The location of the data model.

The actions that are performable from the Manage Windows dialog:

🖒	Either selects or unselects the highlighted row for activation as the active data model.
✖	Either selects or unselects the highlighted row's data model for closing.
🖫	Either selects or unselects the highlighted row's data model for saving.
🔄	Inverts the current selection.
🗁	Opens the file browser for a Save As action of the selected data model.
🗄	Opens the Mart browser for a Save As action of the selected data model.
📖	Opens the help web page.

 As much as erwin DM provides action buttons to mark the highlighted row for either closing or saving, it is a lot faster to use the included checkboxes to mark.

11. Select the checkbox to *close* the **Publication System Rx** data model.

12. Click the *OK* button.

13. Observe that the *PublicationSystemSample.erwin* data model closed.

14. Click the maximize button to maximize the data model in the Diagram Window. See Figure 71.

Figure 71. Maximize Data Model in the Diagram Window

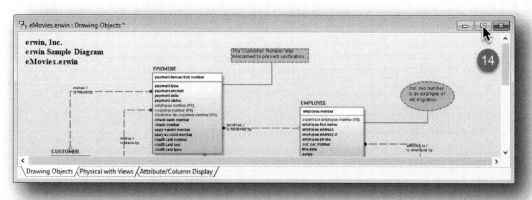

Navigating the Data Model with the Overview Pane

One of the most commonly overlooked features is the Overview Pane. I regularly refer to it as the helicopter view. It provides a way to move around and navigate large diagrams easily.

1. Identify the location of the Overview Pane. Observe that in the Overview Pane there is a reflection of the entire data model diagram. Furthermore, there is a blue rectangle in the Overview Pane, with four corner grips. The grips are the small blue squares outside of the corners of the rectangle. See Figure 72.

Figure 72. Overview Pane

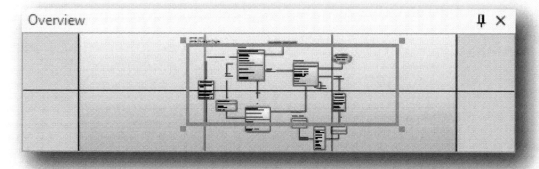

2. Use the scroll bars in the Diagram Window to move around the diagram, observe that with each move of the scroll bars, the Overview Pane's blue rectangle moves synchronously.

3. Place your cursor in the middle of the blue rectangle in the Overview Pane, observer the cursor changes to a hand icon.

4. Click and drag the rectangle around the Overview Pane. See Figure 73.

Figure 73. Drag Rectangle Around Overview Pane

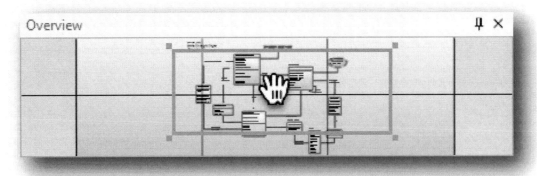

5. Observe how the main Diagram Window moves synchronously.

6. Click the *Zoom Normal* button on the View Ribbon. Remember from the previous chapter, this allows for zooming to Normal scale, i.e., 100%. Observe that the Diagram Window zoomed in on the data model diagram, and likewise on the Overview Pane.

7. Hover the cursor over the bottom right grip. Observe the change in the cursor to a double-sided arrow.

8. Click and drag the double-sided arrow cursor out and in, observing the change of the zoom in the Diagram Window synchronously.

9. While still dragging the double-sided arrow cursor, drag it over to the top left-hand side. Observe it switches to another zoom of the data model, furthermore, the proportion of the blue rectangle matches the proportion of the Diagram Window. Release the mouse button.

10. Move the cursor outside of the blue rectangle. Observe the change of the cursor to a magnifying glass.

11. Click and drag the magnifying glass cursor up to the left-hand side. Observe that the dragging creates a new zoom window in the Overview Pane.

Closing an erwin Data Model

There are several methods of closing a data model, one which we covered with the Manage Windows dialog in the previous section. In this section, we observe the other option for closing a data model.

1. In the erwin Diagram Window, observe the close button on the model tab. See Figure 74.

2. In the erwin DM window, observe the data model close button up below the application close button. See Figure 75.

3. On the File Ribbon, observe the close button. See Figure 76.

Figure 74. Close Data Model Option A

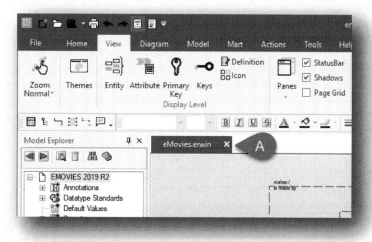

Figure 75. Close Data Model Option B

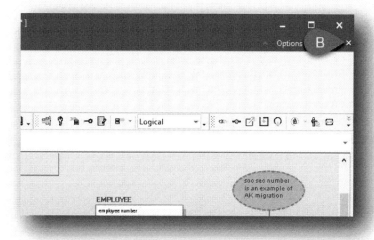

Figure 76. Close Data Model Option C

4. The final option is to close erwin DM completely, thus forcing all open data models to close. See Figure 77.

Figure 77. Close Data Model Option D

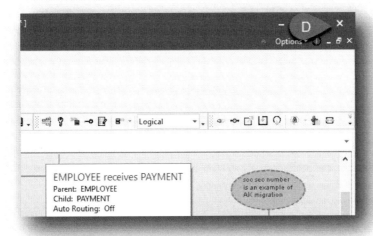

1. For the tutorial, use option A, click the *Close* button on the model tab in the Diagram Window.

2. Observe the pop-up Save Model dialog to allow for the saving of the data model. Even though we did not knowingly make any changes to the data model in the tutorial, by changing the zoom of the diagram, there were changes made, thus providing the Save Model dialog. See Figure 78.

Figure 78. Save Model Dialog

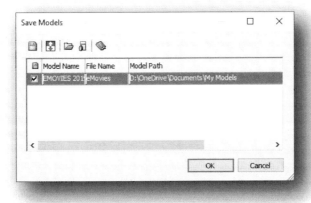

3. Seeing the changes were insignificant, *unselect* the save checkbox.

4. Click the *OK* button.

5. Observe that the data model closed without saving.

6. Close erwin DM.

The 'Cancel' button reverts to the previous data modeling session, and it does not save the data model, nor close it.

 erwin DM uses the same Save Model dialog for all methods of closing a data model, allowing for applying decisions to multiple data models in one process, if the closing process allows for multiple data models.

The Save Model dialog provides an interface for closing an open data model. See Figure 79.

Figure 79. Save Model Dialog Explained

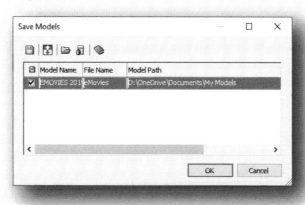

The columns displayed in the Save Model dialog are:

🖫	Indicate if the data model marked for saving.
Model Name	The internal name of the data model displayed.
File Name	The filename of the data model displayed.
Model Path	The location of the data model.

The actions buttons on the Save Model dialog:

🖫 Either selects or unselects the highlighted row's data model for saving.

📑 Inverts the current selection.

📂 Opens the file browser for a save-as action of the selected data model.

🗄 Opens the Mart browser for a save-as action of the selected data model.

🔖 Opens the help web page.

Key Learnings

- The panes in erwin DM are floatable, for locating on the second monitor in a dual monitor environment.

- The panes are also auto hideable, thus freeing up space for the Diagram Window in a single monitor environment.

- The toolbars have a similar characteristic to the panes.

- The Diagram Window has the functionality to split horizontally or vertically, or cascade the open data models.

- The overview pane provides easy navigation around a large diagram.

- Several methods can be used to close a data model.

Create a model
Check the spelling of the text
Lots of save options

In this chapter, we are going to start the building of a data model from the ground up, understanding all the requirements, settings, options, and properties of a new data model. We use this new data model in future chapters, so it is essential to follow all the steps to ensure consistency with the future chapters' tutorials.

Tutorial: Background to MyMovie

We have been approached by a movie rental company, MyMovie, to build a solution for the management of their movies and rentals. Furthermore, it needs to track the employees, and at which stores they work. As the data architect for the team, you have been tasked to develop a data model that encompasses the business requirements that can be rolled out to a SQL Server 2019 database. To set the stage before the initial requirements session, you decided to start the data model proactively.

Tutorial: Creating a Data Model

Before we can start a data model, we need to understand the context and usage of the data model. In our MyMovie tutorial, we know that it is for an operational system–this means that it is a relational data model. Secondly, it needs to encompass the business requirements–this means that it has to have a logical design. Thirdly, it needs to roll out to a database–this means it has to have a physical design. Fourthly, it needs to roll out to a SQL Server 2019 database–this means that the database is SQL Server 2019.

erwin DM provides the capability to design using different types of data models: a logical data model, a physical data model, and a combined logical\physical data model. The type of data model is chosen based on its specific purpose and its specific consumers.

A logical data model would reflect the business data requirements and should be independent of any implementation aspects that may be introduced by specific DBMS or organizational database design standards. Logical data models for different purposes can contain different levels of detail. Logical data models used for project scoping are often referred to as conceptual data models, and would contain less detail than data models looking at the details of a specific system.

Enterprise data models are logical data models covering the whole enterprise. These data models are at a level that only includes enterprise-wide significant objects. Different names may be used to refer to different categories of data models, including 'conceptual,' 'subject area,' or 'fully attributed' data models, but they are all built using the same foundation of a logical data model.

Physical data models in erwin DM are always database-specific, including the generic ODBC data model, which only provides for the ANSI core physical data objects. Dimensional data models are physical data models using the dimensional relationship notation and which may have additional data warehousing support options enabled. Those additional data warehousing support options are not dependent on using the dimensional notation.

Combined logical/physical data models are two data models combined into one. Combined logical/physical data models have two sides, one logical and one physical, with singular data modeling objects reflecting on both sides. There are setting, per data modeling objects, that can set them to be only logical or only physical.

The different types of data models and the integration between them are explored more in Part III. However, for our tutorial, we need a combined logical/physical data model.

1. Open erwin DM.

2. Using the Quick Access Toolbar, click on the *New* button. See Figure 80.

    Figure 80. Click the New Button

    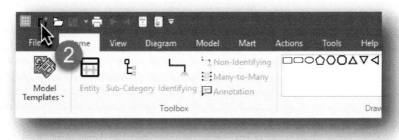

3. The New Model dialog appears. See Figure 81. The New Model dialog is broken down into three distinct sections:

    Type–This is where the user selects the type of data model they want to create.

    - Logical–This is a logical only data model
    - Physical–This is a physical only data model.
    - Logical/Physical–This is a combined logical and physical data model.
    - Match Template–This is used to match the type of data model from a pre-existing template model.

    Target Server–This is where the user defines the target database type and is only available for data models that have a physical side to it.

- Match Template Target Server–This is used to match the database type from a pre-existing template model.
- Database–This is used to select the database for the data model.
- Version–This is used to select the database version for the data model.

Template–This is where the user selects the template model, noticing that they can either be file-based or Mart-based.

Figure 81. The New Model Dialog

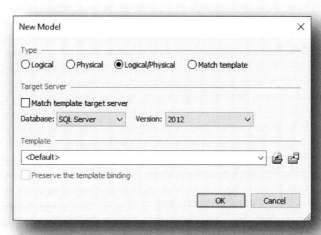

4. Select the 'Logical/Physical' option for the data model type.

5. Select 'SQL Server' for the database.

6. Select '2016/2017/2019' for the version of the database.

7. Leave all the rest of the settings as they are, then click the *OK* button.

8. Observe the created new data model.

 Although we have not used a template for our data model, erwin DM has three built-in templates. One for a logical only data model, one for the physical only data model, and one for the logical/physical data model. Each of these introduces the default objects in a data model; without these, we would not be able to start data modeling.

Tutorial: Defining the Data Model Properties

After creating a new data model, it is always a good practice to set all the properties for the data model.

1. Click on the **Model** ribbon tab to display the Model ribbon buttons.

2. Click on the *Model Properties* button. See Figure 82.

Figure 82. Open Model Properties Dialog

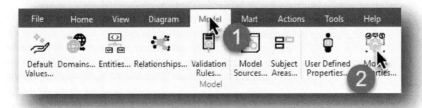

3. On the Model Editor dialog, click on the *General* tab. See Figure 83. The General tab lets the user enter the name and author of the data model, and review the target server and version. Furthermore, it allows the changing of the notation used in the diagrams and the data modeling features, such as the dimensional data model option and the data movement option.

Figure 83. Model Editor General Tab

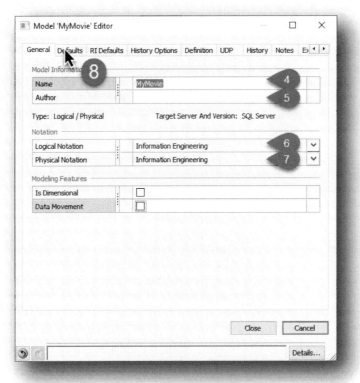

Model Information

Name   Allows the user to specify the name of the data model.

Author   Allows the user to specify the person responsible for the creation of the data model.

Type	This field reflects the type of data model.
Target Server and Version	This field reflects the target database and version of a physical or logical/physical data model.

Notation

Logical Notation	Allows the user to select the notation of the logical data model, either IDEF1x or Information Engineering notations.
Physical Notation	Allows the user to select the notation of the logical data model, either IDEF1x, Information Engineering, or Data Warehousing notations.

Notation

Is Dimensional	Allows the user to activate the dimensional data modeling functionality in the data model.
Data Movement	Allows the user to activate the data movement rules and sources. The user can then import and create data sources, data source tables, and columns, and assign data source columns to data model columns.

4. Change the name of the data model to 'MyMovie.'

 While every data model is given a default name in the form of 'Model_n,' where 'n' is a numeral, it is best practice to use meaningful names. The numeral 'n' is reset to 1 for every erwin DM session, resulting in many data models having the name 'Model_1.' It is challenging to identify data models when listed by name if these default names are not changed.

5. Fill in your name as the author of the data model.

6. Select 'Information Engineering' for logical notation.

7. Select 'Information Engineering' for physical notation.

 erwin DM provides for both the IDEF1x and the Information Engineering (variance of Crows Foot) notations for both logical and physical data models. The Data Warehousing (Dimensional) notation is also available for the physical data models.

8. When finished, click on the *Defaults* tab. See Figure 84. The Defaults tab in the Model Editor dialog allows the user to choose default values for null options, data types, themes, and object ownership.

Figure 84. Model Editor Defaults Tab

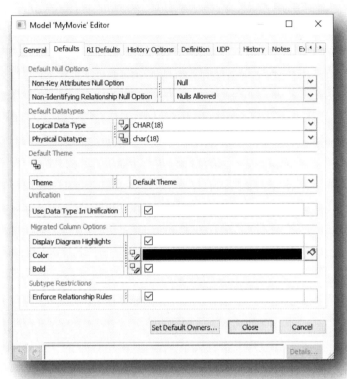

Default Null Options

Non-Key Attributes Null Option

Allows the user to specify whether they can have null as a value for a non-key attribute or column.

Non-Identifying Relationship Null Option

Allows the user to specify whether they can have null as a value for an attribute or a column that has a non-identifying relationship.

Default Data Types

Logical Data Type

Allows the user to specify the default data type for all attributes. They can change the data type for a specific attribute in the Attributes Editor dialog. They can also select whether the data type is inherited (⊞) or overridden (⊞).

Physical Data Type

Allows the user to specify the default data type for all columns. They can change the data type for a specific column in the Columns Editor. They can also select whether the data type is inherited (⊞) or overridden (⊞).

Default Theme

Theme	Allows specifying the default theme for the data model, including all the font, color, and formatting options for data model objects.

Unification

Use Data Type in Unification	Allows specifying whether they want to use the data type when you unify three or more entities. We cover unifications in Chapter 18.

Migrate Column Options

Display Diagram Highlights	Allows specifying the default settings for highlighting the primary and foreign keys on hovering over a relationship line.
Color	Allows the user to assigns a color for the highlighted relationship line and associated attributes or columns.
Bold	Allows specifying the bolding of the associated attributes or columns when clicking on the relationship line.

Subtype Restrictions

Enforce Relationship Rules	Allows specifying whether a supertype-subtype relationship between two different subtype entities belonging to the same or different supertype groups should be allowed. We cover subtypes in Chapter 18.
Set Default Owners Button	Opens the Set Default Owner dialog where the user can set a global default for all objects or individual objects. The user enters an owner name, and can optionally reset the ownership for all objects when you click Set Owner For All Objects. **Important:** although you can quickly reset the ownership for all objects using this feature, it cannot be undone.

9. When finished, click on the *RI Defaults* tab. See Figure 85. The RI Defaults tab lets the user set the default referential integrity rules for relationships in the data model.

Action Buttons and Options

	Allows the user to rebind all Referential Integrity settings on all relationships. This button applies the new default settings to any existing relationship in the data model. If the user changes the default settings in an existing data model, they can use this button to implement the new settings in the data model for all existing relationships. If the new settings are saved, but not rebound, the defaults affect the new relationships only.

Allows the user to reset all the Referential Integrity default settings to their system default settings.

☐ **Automatically Create RI Triggers**

Allows the user to specify whether they want to create database triggers for the Referential Integrity defaults automatically.

Grid Columns

Action

This column lists a SQL action in each row. For each SQL action, the user selects a default Referential Integrity action for each of the relationship type columns.

Identifying

Allows the user to specify the Referential Integrity setting for each of the SQL actions in the Action column. This setting applies to all identifying relationships in the data model.

Non-Identifying, Nulls Allowed

Allows the user to specify the Referential Integrity setting for each of the SQL actions in the Action column. This setting applies to all non-identifying relationships in the data model for which nulls are allowed.

Non-Identifying, No Nulls

Allows the user to specify the Referential Integrity setting for each SQL action in the Action column. The setting applies to all non-identifying relationships in the data model for which nulls are not allowed.

Subtype

Allows the user to specify the Referential Integrity setting for each of the SQL actions in the Action column. This setting applies to all subtype relationships in the data model.

Some databases, such as Oracle, use different terminology for Referential Integrity trigger actions. Use the Referential Integrity setting appropriate for the chosen database.

10. When finished, click on the *History Options* tab. See Figure 86. The History Options allows the user to configure the objects and events for which they want the history tracked for the data model. History Objects allow the user to select from a list of the standard data model objects which they want the history saved. History Events enable the user to select from a list of the standard data model events that they want the history saved.

Note that the History Options tab on the logical side of the data model, list the logical data model objects only. However, the History Options tab on the physical side of the data model lists the logical data model objects, plus the physical only additions.

Figure 85. Model Editor RI Defaults Tab

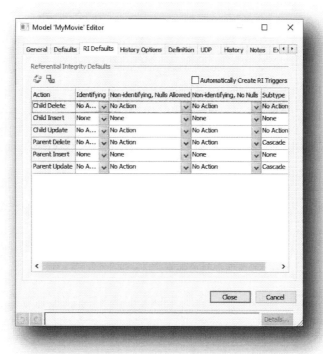

Figure 86. Model Editor History Options Tab

The History record does not provide versioning data but merely that the event occurred at a specific time and the user that actioned the event. A user can add a comment to the event record.

11. When finished, click on the *Definition* tab. See Figure 87. The Definition is useful to record the purpose of the data model. The definition can be added to over time to record significant changes to the data model's purpose, content, or scope.

Figure 87. Model Editor Definition Tab

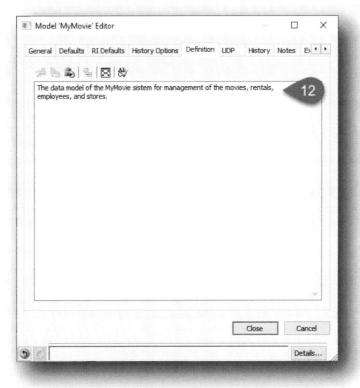

Action Buttons

Allows the user to cut the selected text into the clipboard.

Allows the user to copy the selected text into the clipboard.

Allows the user to paste the contents of the clipboard.

Allows the user to reset the definition to restore the inheritance.

Note: This option is available only for content that is inherited. Also, this option becomes available only when you change the definition value.

Allows the user to open the context-sensitive dialog to edit the definition.

Allows the user to open the Check Spelling dialog to check the spelling of the definition text.

12. Enter the definition for the MyMovie data model of 'The data model of the MyMovie sistem for management of the movies, rentals, employees, and stores.'

Note: The spelling of the word 'sistem' and not 'system' is intentional.

13. When finished, click on the **UDP** tab. See Figure 88. The User Defined Properties (UDP) are custom properties that can be defined by the user for any object. After the user has created User Defined Properties for the data model, they can specify the values in the UDP tab. We explain more about UDPs in Chapter 25.

Action Buttons

Allows the user to open the User Defined Properties Editor to add a UDP or edit an existing one.

Allows the user to reset the selected UDP to restore the inheritance.

Note: This option is available only for UDPs that are inherited. Also, this option becomes available only when you change the UDP value.

Figure 88. Model Editor UDP Tab

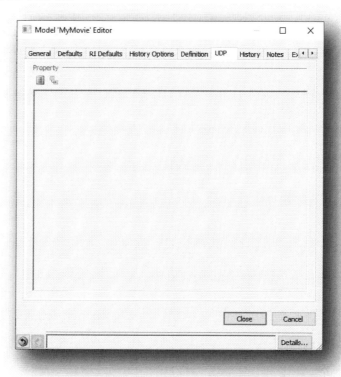

14. When finished, click on the **History** tab. See Figure 89. The History tab allows the user to review the tracked history for the data model. The list of History records is dependent on the settings in the History Options tab.

Figure 89. Model Editor History Tab

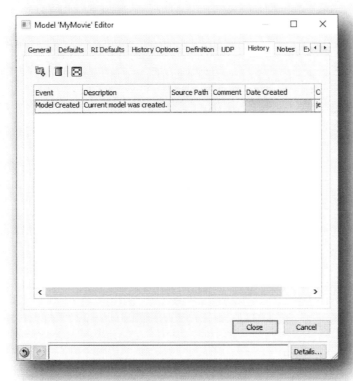

Action Buttons

 This interactive button allows the user to sort the History records according to the creation date ascending or descending. This button reflects the current state of the sort order.

       Ascending order

       Descending order

Allows the user to delete the selected History record.

Allows the user to edit the comment on the History record. Necessary to recognize the difference between the Comment and the Description of the historical record.

Grid Columns

Event   This column lists the event that caused the creation of the History record.

Description   This column lists the description of the History record.

Source Path   This column lists the source path of the History record. The source path column is empty for the create event. Source path is formatted as follows:

<ModelPath>\<ModelName>\<EntityName>\<AttributeName>

Where <ModelPath> is the path for the data model in the local computer or the path for a Mart data model in the Mart Server.

Comment   This column lists the editable comment of the History record.

Date Created   This column lists the creation date of the History record.

Created By   This column lists the user name of the person that actioned the event that created the History record.

 When the user configured the data model to track the history of data model objects, they can view the recorded history for those objects. They can view the history for a specific object in the History tab of the relevant object type editor. Click the History tab in any of the following editor dialogs to view the recorded events for that object: Entities, Attributes, Table, Columns, Views, and Cached Views.

15. When finished, click on the **Notes** tab. See When finished, click on the **Extended Notes** tab. See Figure 91. The Extended Notes tab allows the user to add, edit, view, or delete extended notes. The user can add Extended Notes apart from adding definitions in the Definition or Comment tab and adding comments in the History tab. The user can transfer a note from the Extended Notes tab to the Notes tab. They can also transfer a note from the Notes tab to the Extended Notes tab. Extended Notes are data model objects, and therefore the following tasks may be performed on them:

- Search for Extended Notes using the Find and Replace dialog.
- Compare the properties of Extended Notes added to data model objects using Complete Compare.
- Edit multiple Extended Notes at once using Bulk Editor.
- Create Extended Notes through the API.

16. Figure 90. The Notes tab allows the user to add, edit, view, or delete notes. The user can add notes apart from adding the definition in the Definition or Comment tabs and adding comments in the History tab. The user can transfer a note from the Notes tab to the Extended Notes tab. They can also transfer a note from the Extended Notes tab to the Notes tab.

Action Buttons

This interactive button allows the user to sort the Notes records according to the creation or modified date ascending or descending, or note order.

Creation date ascending order

Creation date descending order

Modification date ascending order

Modification date descending order

Note order

Allows the user to create a new Note record.

Allows the user to delete the selected Notes record.

Allows the user to reset the selected Notes to restore the inheritance.

Allows the user to transfer the selected Notes to the Extended Notes tab.

When using the Note Order option, this button allows the user to move the selected Notes to the top of the list.

When using the Note Order option, this button allows the user to move the selected Notes up one level of the list.

When using the Note Order option, this button allows the user to move the selected Notes down one level of the list.

When using the Note Order option, this button allows the user to move the selected Notes to the bottom of the list.

Allows the user to edit the comment on the Note record.

Grid Columns

Transfer	This checkbox allows the user to select or unselect the Note record for transfer to the Extended Notes tab or to change the order.
Event	This column lists the event that caused the creation of the Note record, typically 'User Note.'
Comment	This column lists the editable comment of the Note record.
Date Created	This column lists the creation date of the Note record.
Created By	This column lists the user name of the person that created the Note record.

Date Modified   This column lists the modified date of the Note record.

Modified By   This column lists the user name of the person that modified the Note record.

17. When finished, click on the ***Extended Notes*** tab. See Figure 91. The Extended Notes tab allows the user to add, edit, view, or delete extended notes. The user can add Extended Notes apart from adding definitions in the Definition or Comment tab and adding comments in the History tab. The user can transfer a note from the Extended Notes tab to the Notes tab. They can also transfer a note from the Notes tab to the Extended Notes tab. Extended Notes are data model objects, and therefore the following tasks may be performed on them:

- Search for Extended Notes using the Find and Replace dialog.
- Compare the properties of Extended Notes added to data model objects using Complete Compare.
- Edit multiple Extended Notes at once using Bulk Editor.
- Create Extended Notes through the API.

Figure 90. Model Editor Notes Tab

When the user transfers a Note from the Extended Notes tab to the Notes tab, the following implication occurs:

- The Name, Importance, and Status information gets deleted.

- The value in the Author field gets replaced with the current user and is displayed in the Created By field.

- The value in the Event field gets replaced with 'User Note.'

Action Buttons

This interactive button allows the user to sort the Extended Notes records according to the creation date ascending or descending, the modified date ascending or descending, or an extended note order. The button reflects the current state of the sort order.

        Creation date ascending order

        Creation date descending order

        Modification date ascending order

        Modification date descending order

        Extended Note order

Allows the user to create a new Extended Note record.

Allows the user to delete the selected Extended Notes record.

Allows the user to reset the selected Extended Notes to restore the inheritance.

Allows the user to transfer the selected Extended Notes to the Notes tab. Please see the writeup above about the implications thereof.

When using the Extended Note Order option, this button allows the user to move the selected Extended Notes to the top of the list.

When using the Extended Note Order option, this button allows the user to move the selected Extended Notes up one level of the list.

When using the Extended Note Order option, this button allows the user to move the selected Extended Notes down one level of the list.

When using the Extended Note Order option, this button allows the user to move the selected Extended Notes to the bottom of the list.

Allows the user to edit the comment on the Extended Note record.

Grid Columns

Transfer   This checkbox allows the user to select or unselect the Extended Note record for transfer to the Notes tab or to change the order.

Name   This column lists the editable name of the Extended Note record.

Event   This column lists the editable event that caused the creation of the Extended Note record.

Comment   This column lists the editable comment of the Extended Note record.

Author   This column lists the editable user name of the person that created the Extended Note record.

Important   This dropdown allows the user to specify the importance of the Extend Note. Valid options are:

<Blank>
Not Rated
1 Star
2 Star
3 Star
4 Star
5 Star

Note Status   This dropdown allows the user to specify the status of the Extend Note. Valid options are:

<Blank>
Candidate
Approved
Rejected

Time Created   This column lists the creation date of the Extended Note record.

Figure 91. Model Editor Extended Notes Tab

18. When finished, click on the *Close* button to close the Model Editor dialog.

Tutorial: Saving a Data Model

In Chapter 6, we covered the closing of a data model without saving. In this section, we save a data model and close a data model while saving.

1. Using the Quick Access Toolbar, click on the *Save* button. See Figure 92.

2. Observe that the Save As dialog appears because the data model has not been saved, as of yet.

3. Give the data model a file name of **MyMovie_Ver1** and ensure that the data model location is in the **My Models** folder in the **Documents** folder.

    Figure 92. Click on the Save Button

    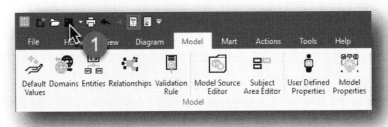

4. Click the *Save* button.

5. Re-open the Model Properties dialog. Click the *Model* tab in the Ribbon and the *Model Properties* button, as before.

6. Click on the *Definition* tab in the Model Editor dialog.

7. While taking note of the misspelled word of 'sistem,' click on the *Spell Check* button.

8. Observe that the Check Spelling dialog opens with the *'Not in Dictionary'* reflecting the 'MyMovie' word.

 Installations of erwin DM performed without using the 'Run As Administrator' option, can find that the spelling checker does not locate its dictionary. The same might occur with automated rolled-outs that have not taken into consideration the appropriate right to the dictionary folders. The best method of repairing this issue is to re-install erwin DM, taking into consideration the correct installation method, as documented by erwin Inc.

9. Seeing that the 'MyMovie' is not an actual English word, click the *Ignore* button to move to the next word.

10. Observe that this time it has found the incorrect spelling of the 'sistem' word. Furthermore, observe the list of suggested words below, with the correct spelling of the word being the second one down.

11. Click on the correct spelling of 'system.'

12. Then click on the *Change* button.

13. Observe that the spelling of the word was corrected and that the Check Spelling dialog dismissed.

14. The erwin DM's Spell Checker goes through all the words in the appropriate textbox. Once finished checking all the words, the Check Spelling dialog closes.

15. Click the *Close* button on the Model Editor dialog.

16. Using the Quick Access Toolbar, click on the *Save* button again.

17. Observe that this time the Save As dialog did not appear and that erwin DM saved the model with no further interaction.

18. There are several other methods of saving a model, and we have covered the quickest and easiest method. You are welcome to explore those alternatives, as detailed in the Ribbons and Toolbars sections in Chapter 5.

Key Learnings

- The internal name of the data model is vital for working with the data models, and should always be changed when creating a new data model.

- Several properties need defining in a new data model.

- The spelling checker tool in erwin DM can assist weeding out wrong spellings.

- When saving a new data model, the Save As dialog appears, allowing the user to provide a file name.

Part III explores the different types of data models: enterprise, conceptual, logical, physical, and operational. An Enterprise Data Model (EDM) represents the high-level business objects of the entire organization. Whereas, a Conceptual Data Model (CDM) represents the high-level business needs with a defined scope of either an application or business process. A Logical Data Model (LDM) is an attributed view of the conceptual data model detailing the application or business process needs down to low-level business data objects. Whereas, a Physical Data Model (PDM) is a detailed technical design of the logical data model, incorporating all the physical database aspects. An Operational Data Model (ODM) is a technical data model reflective of all data objects as implemented in a database. Over the next couple of chapters, we look into each of these types of data models.

Also, when it comes to the conceptual and logical data models, there are two different modeling mindsets: relational and dimensional. A relational data model captures how the business works; it achieves this by precisely representing the business rules. While a dimensional data model captures the monitoring of the business; it achieves this by precisely representing navigation.

The following table summarizes these levels of data models in combination with the two modeling mindsets, leading to the seven different types of models:

Table 1. Levels of Data Models with Modeling Mindsets

		Mindset	
		Relational	**Dimensional**
Types of data models	EDM	Organization-wide business objects at a fundamental level, including basic business rules, unbiased of any application, or technology, such as *'Customers place Orders.'*	
	CDM	Key concepts and their business rules, such as *'Each Customer may place one or many Orders.'*	Key concepts focused around one or more measures, such as *'I want to see Gross Sales Amount by Customer.'*
	LDM	All attributes required for a given application or business process. Neatly organized into entities according to strict business rules and independent of technology such as *'Each Customer ID value must return at most one Customer Last Name.'*	All attributes required for a given reporting application. Focused on measures and independent of technology such as *'I want to see Gross Sales Amount by Customer and view the customer's first and last name.'*
	PDM	The LDM modified for a specific technology such as a database or access software. For example, 'To improve retrieval speed, we need a non-unique index on Customer Last Name.' Alternatively, 'To improve retrieval speed, we need to embed this MongoDB collection within that MongoDB collection.'	
	ODM	The reverse-engineered data model of the database or access software. For example, 'I need to verify the implementation of the physical data model to ensure that no changes have occurred.'	

A detailed explanation of each of these models awaits in the following chapters:

- **Chapter 8** provides an overview of the design layers (types of data models) and how each of the layers inter-relate with one another.
- **Chapter 9** introduces the enterprise data model, discussing the benefits of it, and how to build this type of model.
- **Chapter 10** goes into detail on the conceptual data model, discussing the variations along with how to build this type of model.
- **Chapter 11** focuses on the relational and dimensional logical data model.
- **Chapter 12** focuses on the physical data model, going through the different techniques for building a practical design, such as denormalization and partitioning.
- **Chapter 13** discusses the importance and usage of the operational data model and why it is critical to maintaining an updated data architecture.

Blueprints and models
Which model type do I use?
Why all these layers?

From the introduction to Part III, we learn that there are five different types of data models. We also learned about the two different mindsets, resulting in seven different variations of a data model. See Table 2.

Table 2. Data Model Scope Perspectives

Model	Perspective	Scope
EDM	Executive	The scope of the enterprise data model is to provide a 'One-pager' on organization-wide business objects and rules. A business object is an idea that is both *fundamental* and *critical* to the organization. A business rule is a definition of how business objects relate to each other. An enterprise data model correlates to an executive summary for an overview of the data landscape of the organization.
CDM	Business Management	The scope of the conceptual data model is also to provide a 'One-pager' on business objects and rules relevant to a solution. The business object is a more detailed level and is relevant for the solution they are representing. A conceptual data model correlates to a synopsis for an overview of the data landscape of a solution.
LDM	Architect	The scope of the logical data model is to provide a business-readable model of what businesspeople require to understand the data landscape for a project and to generate the schema of the database. The logical data model uses a standard set of symbols to reflect the business objects as entities and the business rules as relationships.
PDM	Engineer	The scope of the physical data model is to provide a technical view of the logical data model for technicians to be able to understand the requirements for a project. The physical data model also makes use of a standard set of symbols to reflect the logical entities as tables and relationships as deployable indexes and constraints.
ODM	Technician	The scope of the operational data model is to provide a detailed technical representation of the implemented database. It conforms to all the physical data model notations and symbols. It differs from the physical data model by the fact that it represents the as-is database, whereas the physical data model is reflective of the to-be database.

As demonstrated in this table, each of the five types of data models serves a different purpose and has a different scope. These different types of data models are what we refer to as layers. Take a look at Figure 93 for an example of how each of the data models interacts with the different layers, highlighting the various perspectives and scopes. Also, observe how an enterprise data model can have multiple conceptual models, each for their solution. And that a conceptual model may have multiple logical data models representing the individual projects that make up the solution. Multiple physical data models can result out of a singular logical data model, each encapsulating the separate database requirements. Typically, there would an operational data model linked to a physical data model, but this is not always necessary or possible.

Figure 93. Design Layer Modeling

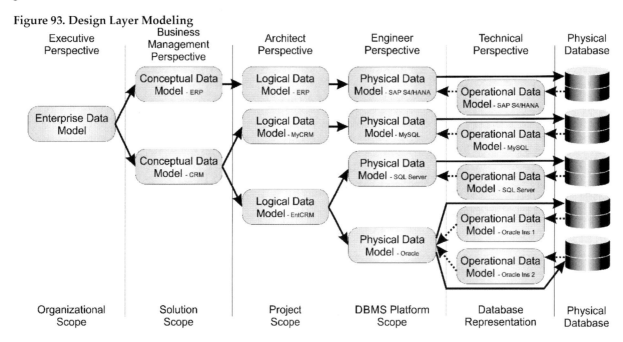

Blueprints and Data Models

A blueprint, characterized by white lines on a blue background, introduced by Sir John Herschel in 1842, is a negative of the original of a technical drawing using a contact print process on light-sensitive sheets. The process itself is now obsolete due to more modern technologies, but the term still survives to refer to any architectural plans or drawings.

So what does building a house and building a data model have in common, besides the fact that I have done both? Jokes asides, let's take a look at a set of architectural blueprints. There are different types of architectural blueprints, and each type has a different scope. Sound familiar? The same concepts that apply to the data model layers apply to architectural blueprints. An architectural blueprint is a drawing showing the technical details of an architectural subject, and often uses symbols rather than detailed drawings to represent lower-level details. Let's compare the similarities of these to data models and why there are different types.

Urban Planning Blueprint

The urban planning blueprint, an example shown in Figure 94, is the tool the municipalities use to set broad goals and objectives for city planning, guiding land usage, growth, and development. The urban planning blueprint is an opportunity to express the town or city's vision and values. It also provides a tangible representation of what a town or city looks like, and what they want it to look like in the future. The significant elements of an urban planning blueprint are:

- Statement of objectives and policies,

- Land usage plan,

- Transportation plan,

- Utilities and facilities plan,

- Recommended implementation program,

- Statement of how urban planning relates to neighborhood planning.

Figure 94. Example of an Urban Planning Blueprint

In comparing the elements of an urban planning blueprint to an enterprise data model, one can easily see the similarities. The enterprise data model states the objective and policies of the organization in a graphical format. It further states the data usage plan, what types of data does the organization consume, and what it looks like—similar to the land usage plan of the urban planning blueprint. Transportation, utilities, and facilities plans are similar to the relationships or business rules of the enterprise data model. It further provides a recommended implementation of the data assets of the organization, and finally provides the conduit down to the conceptual models or neighborhood blueprints in the urban planning blueprint comparison.

Neighborhood Blueprint

Whenever a developer starts laying out a new piece of land for development into housing or businesses, they need to draft a neighborhood blueprint, an example shown in Figure 95. They start by surveying the land to set the scope of the development, using the urban panning blueprint to guide then as to where the existing roads, utilities, and facilities are. They also consult the recommended implementation plan and the land usage plan to see what they are allowed to do on the land. Once they have this information, they can now set the goals of the new neighborhood, such as how many houses, and so on. Finally, they plan the layout of the roads, utilities, and lots of lands. This is an iterative process as new challenges and obstacles are constantly getting discovered.

Figure 95. Example of a Neighborhood Blueprint

Now, let's compare the steps taken by the developer of a neighborhood to those taken on the conceptual data model. Similar to the developer surveying the land, the data modeler scopes the solution requiring the data model. The data modeler also needs to consult the enterprise data model to understand where the existing data is stored and what interfaces are available, similar to the developer needing to know the placement of the existing roads and utilities. It is only then that the data modeler can start laying out the business objects that are needed, reiterating through the design process as they discover the challenges and obstacles. In the end, the data modeler delivers a conceptual data model for the solution, the same as a developer delivers a neighborhood blueprint.

House Perspective Blueprint

Once you have purchased land and decide to build a house, you need to sit down with an architect. The first thing the architect is going to ask you is to provide an idea of what your house needs to look like. Guiding them is the neighborhood blueprint as the boundaries and basic requirements for the house blueprint. As the architect draws out your ideas and puts them into a visual that a layperson would be able to interpret, see Figure 96, the design of your new house emerges. Seeing that this blueprint has a lot of changes and variations happening iteratively, the architect holds off on the more technical drawings. Eventually, we hopefully reach the point where you are satisfied with the representation of your new house.

Figure 96. Example of a House Perspective Blueprint

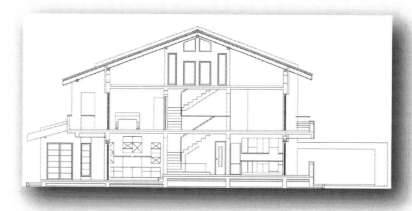

Comparing this process to the design of a logical data model, first, we can notice that the architect needs to leverage the neighborhood blueprint to define the boundaries and requirements. The same would be for the data modeler, and they would need to know the scope of the project and the basics of the requirements. Business objects don't define the entities completely and need the inclusion of all the attributes. The data modeler adds entities and attributes, similar to the architect laying out rooms and doors. The architect goes through many iterations, similar to the data modeler, hence why we hold off on the physical design.

Furthermore, the people that the data modeler is talking to is the business, and they would not necessarily want to see all the details. The business people are the laypersons in the data modeling world and do not need to deal with the technical constraints of a table.

House Technical Blueprint

Once you have a set of house blueprints that meet your requirements, the architect can get down to the details of the blueprint. See Figure 97. They take the approved house blueprint and start adding all the technical details, such as the plumbing, cabling, and air-conditioning ducts. The architect may need to consult with structural engineers and others to ensure the effectiveness of the technical house blueprint. The result is a technical house blueprint that would guide the builder to build your house physically to your requirements.

Figure 97. Example of a House Technical Blueprint

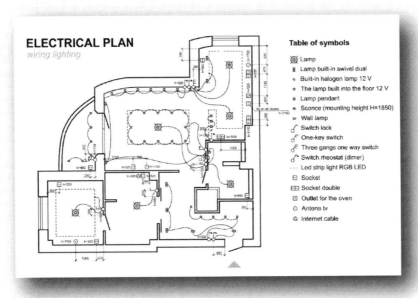

The data modeler would take the business-agreed logical data model and start the process of converting it to a physical data model, similar to the technical house blueprint. Adding physical objects where necessary and making technical changes to the existing objects. Just like the architect having to consult with structural engineers, the data modeler may need to consult with database specialists to ensure an effective implementation. The resulting physical data model would be a data model that the database administrator could implement in the database environment. The database administrator is the equivalent of the builder of your house.

As-Built Blueprint

A challenge with building a house is that what the architect plans is not always physically possible. For example, the architect might have planned running a plumbing pipe down a particular section of the wall. But when the builder builds the house, they discover that it might be better to run the plumbing pipe down another section of the wall. Alternatively, the builder might see that a particular passageway might be a bit cramped to walk down. They notice that there are six inches of unused space on the other side of the internal wall. Therefore the builder moves the internal wall by six inches into the unused space, thus making the passageway six inches wider. Technically there is no difference between the two, and making decisions during the building phase is a regular practice.

The database administrator, while implementing the database, might identify that by tweaking a unique clustered index parameter, it reduces the time it takes whenever the front-end does a customer lookup. Or by including another column to a non-unique index, data load performance improves, thus freeing up valuable time for the batch processes. These are the same sort of changes that the builder did to our house.

Irrespective of whether they were tweaks to the database or tweaks to the house, the product is slightly different from the original design. In the house building process, these tweaks and changes need to be introduced into the house blueprints to reflect the current state of the house. These blueprints are the as-built blueprints, but in the modern, fast-paced environments we live, and due to the cost and time involved, these as-built blueprints get overlooked typically. The same applies to our modeling practices, and we are too busy pushing to get into the next project or phase, that we overlook the operational data model.

Even worse, imagine that in three years we decide to break open a wall to put a doorway in it. But unfortunately, the section of the wall was the section that the builder ran the plumbing pipe. Because the blueprints reflected a different location for this pipe, we demo the wall based on the blueprint, and now there is water spraying all over the place. The same consequences could happen if we built an addition to a database, but are not using a model that reflects the current operational schema. When it comes to operational data models, erwin DM has an excellent capability of managing this with little effort and ease.

How does erwin DM Support Design Layers?

erwin DM provides five distinct actions to support Design Layer modeling. Each of these actions performs within the scope of design layers, but each is used for different purposes with different outcomes. erwin DM's design layer modeling actions are links between any two models. These links are very similar to a relationship in a data model in that:

- There is a parent (source model),
- There is a child (target model),
- The reference information is held in the child (target model),
- The parent (source model) can partake in a relationship (link) with many children (target models),
- The child (target model) can partake in a relationship (link) with many parents (source models),
- A model can be a child in one relationship (link) and can be a parent in another relationship (link).

Further to that, there are some other fundamentals about the links between these models, and they are:

- Initializing of synchronization is performed between two linked models and is always from the target model,

- A link between two models comprises:

    o   the identity of the source model,

    o   the location of the source model,

    o   the name mapping options (naming standards),

    o   the last time they were synchronized and

    o   a collection of object mappings.

- An object mapping links two objects in the two models, based on their internal identifiers,

- There is one limitation that needs consideration, and that is a child's objects need their parent objects to be linked first for them to be linked. For example, to link two attributes, their parent entities need to be linked first.

The five erwin Design Layer actions are:

- Add Model Source
- Link Model Source
- Derive New Model
- Split Model
- Sync with Model Source

Add Model Source

You use the Add Model Source action to link two independent models and specify that one model is a source for the other. The current model is the target model into which a model source that you select contributes a set of objects. The Add Model Source copies and links a selection of objects from the source model, as shown in Figure 98.

Figure 98. Add Model Source.

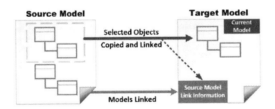

The Add Model Source wizard includes sections that let you do the following:

- In the Target Model tab, select the model for the target of the Add Model Source wizard. By default, the current model is selected, as shown in Figure 99.

- In the Source Model tab, select the model for the source of the Add Model Source wizard. If there are two or more open models, the next model in the list will be selected. See Figure 100.

Figure 99. Add Model Source. Target Tab

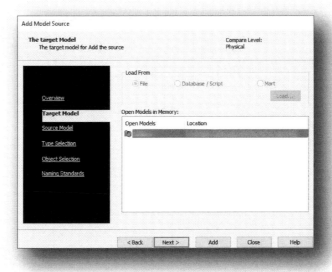

Figure 100. Add Model Source. Source Tab

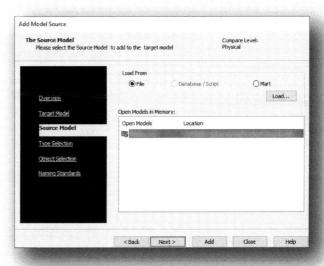

- In the Type Selection tab, see Figure 101, apply filters to control the type of added objects. You can filter by logical, physical, or database level objects, and use a customized option set of filter options.

- In the Object Selection tab, see Figure 102, select the model objects to add from the source to the target model.

- In the Naming Standards tab, see Figure 103, define the model object naming rules, and designate a naming standards file to use when enforcing standards in the target model. It only applies when linking a logical data model as the source.

Figure 101. Add Model Source. Type Selection Tab

Figure 102. Add Model Source. Object Selection Tab

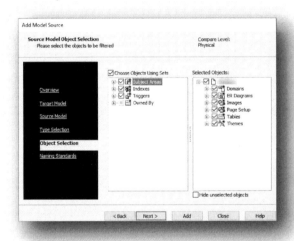

Figure 103. Add Model Source. Naming Standards Tab

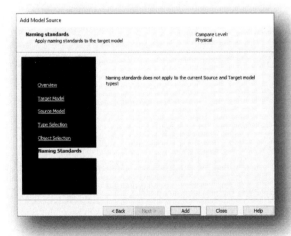

Link Model Source

You use the Link Model Source action to link two independent models and specify that one model is a source for the other. The current model is the target model to which a model source is linked, via the Link Model Source wizard. Then a second dialog, the Complete Compare dialog, provides the means to link and copy at the object level.

Figure 104. Link Model Source – Step 1

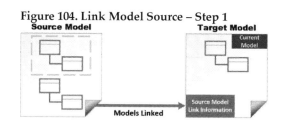

Figure 105. Link Model Source – Step 2

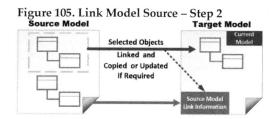

The Link Model Source wizard includes sections that let you do the following:

- In the Target Model tab, select the model for the target of the Link Model Source wizard. By default, the current model is selected.

- In the Source Model tab, select the model for the source of the Link Model Source wizard. If there are two or more open models, the next model in the list will be selected.

- In the Type Selection tab, apply filters to control the type of linked objects. You can filter by logical, physical, or database level objects, and use a customized option set of filter options.

- In the Object Selection tab, select the model objects to link from the source to the target model.

- The Naming Standards tab does not allow for the applying of naming standards, as the target model already manages these.

- After completing the Link Model Source wizard, the Complete Compare dialog displays, as shown in Figure 106. This dialog allows for the granular level linking and copying of objects. Note that objects can be copied in either direction.

For more information on the Complete Compare dialog, please refer to Chapter 31, dedicated to the topic.

Derive New Model

You use the Derive New Model action to create a new model linked to the current model. The current model is the source model from which you select a set of objects needed in the new model. The new model is the target model. The Derive New Model wizard includes sections that let you do the following:

- In the Source Model tab, select the model for the source of the Derive New Model wizard. By default, the current model is selected.

Figure 106. Link Model Source. Complete Compare

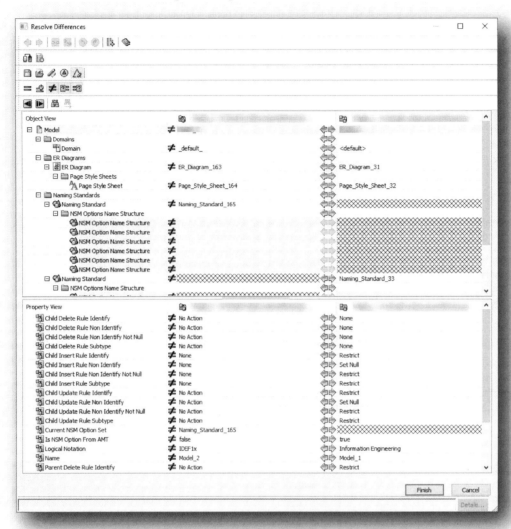

- In the Target Model tab, select the new model type, and all relevant model details. Chapter 7 contains information on creating a new model.

- In the Type Selection tab, apply filters to control the type of added objects. You can filter by logical, physical, or database level objects, and use a customized option set of filter options.

- In the Object Selection tab, select the model objects to add from the source to the new target model.

- In the Naming Standards tab, define the model object naming rules, and designate a naming standards file to use when enforcing standards in the target model. It only applies when linking a logical data model as the source of a new physical data model as the target.

- For more information on Naming Standards, please refer to Chapter 26, dedicated to the topic.

Split Model

You can split a logical/physical data model into an independent physical data model and a logical data model, as graphically demonstrated in Figure 107. The new physical data model includes the physical data model objects, such as columns, tables, indexes, views, triggers, and stored procedures, from the original logical/physical data model. The new logical data model includes the logical data model objects, such as entities, attributes, and key groups from the original logical/physical data model. The new logical data model serves as the model source for the new physical data model, allowing one to synchronize the two models in the future. There is no link to the original combined logical/physical data model.

Figure 107. Split Model

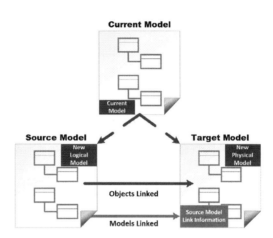

- When you choose Design Layers, Split Model from the Actions menu, you are prompted to save the new data models. erwin DM pre-empts the name of the data models by suffixing it with -LOGICAL and -PHYSICAL, respectively.

- All the data models remain open in the workspace, and the original combined logical/physical data model remains unchanged.

- The new physical data model includes the physical data model objects, such as columns, tables, indexes, views, triggers, and stored procedures, from the original combined logical/physical data model. The new logical data model includes the logical data model objects, such as entities, attributes, and key groups from the original combined logical/physical data model.

- The new logical data model serves as the model source for the new physical data model, allowing you to synchronize the two data models in the future. There is no link to the original combined logical/physical data model.

Sync with Model Source

At any time, you can synchronize a data model with its model source. When using the Sync with Model Source, by default, the left data model is the source model, and the right data model is the target model. When you export changes in the Resolve Differences dialog, export changes from right to left using the left arrows. To verify which model is the source and which is the target, one can expand the windows in the Resolve Differences dialog to view the entire path of the model.

• With the target model open, click Design Layers, Sync with Model Source on the Actions menu. Remember that the target model stores the information about the target model; only this model is aware of the link. Therefore it is not possible to initialize the sync with model source from the source model.

• The Sync with Model Wizard opens, as shown in Figure 108.

Figure 108. Sync with Model Source Dialog

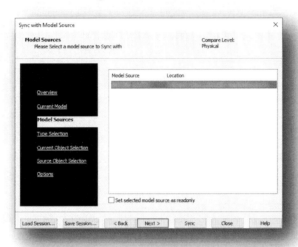

• In the Current Model tab, erwin DM populates the current model that was used to initialize the sync with model source. See Figure 109.

Figure 109. Sync with Model Source. Current Model Tab

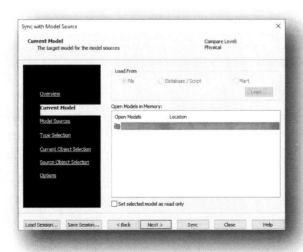

- In the Model Sources tab, erwin DM populates all the model sources for the current model. A model can have multiple sources; therefore, it allows for the selection of the source model that is needing synchronization. See Figure 110.

Figure 110. Sync with Model Source. Model Sources Tab

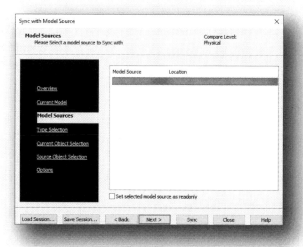

- In the Type Selection tab, apply filters to control the type of objects for synchronization, by default, erwin DM remembers the previous options selected. See Figure 111.

Figure 111. Sync with Model Source. Type Selection Tab

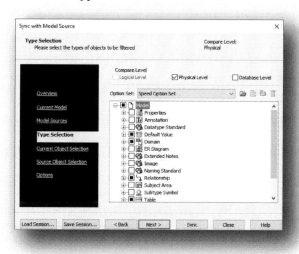

- In the Current Object Selection tab, one can change the current data model objects to synchronize between the source model and the target model. See Figure 112.

Figure 112. Sync with Model Source. Current Object Selection Tab

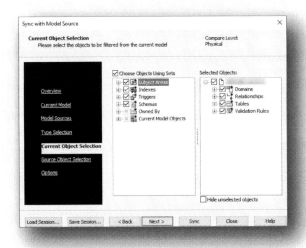

- In the Source Object Selection tab, one can change the source data model objects to synchronize between the source model and the target model. See Figure 113.

Figure 113. Sync with Model Source. Source Object Selection Tab

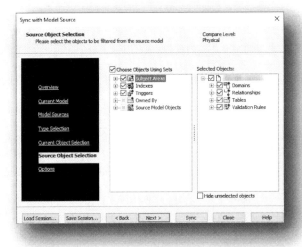

- In the Options tab, one can change the options of the Complete Compare dialog. For more information on these options, please refer to Chapter 31 on Complete Compare.

- After clicking the Sync button, the Complete Compare dialog displays. This dialog allows for the granular level of synchronizing of data model objects. Note that objects can be copied in either direction. For more information on the Complete Compare dialog, please refer to Chapter 31, dedicated to the topic.

Key Learnings

- Design layers are like architectural blueprints. Each architectural blueprint has a scope, purpose, and perspective.

- There are five different and distinct design layers, each having a different and distinct type of data model.

- Data models in the design layer modeling approach are progressive, one building on the foundation of the previous.

- erwin DM provides a rich set of functionality to support design layer modeling.

- Add model source functionality links, and adds data objects from a source model to a target model.

- Link model source functionality only links the data models from a source model to a target model. It then provides the Complete Compare dialog to synchronize data objects selectively.

- Derive new model functionality creates a new data model and links them together.

- Split model functionality splits a combined logical/physical data model into two separate linked data models, one logical and one physical data model.

- Sync with model source functionality provides the ability to synchronize data objects between two linked data models.

Reason in business?
Must understand the business
Build an EDM!

The highlighted row in Table 3 shows the focus of this chapter: the Enterprise Data Model (EDM).

Table 3. The Enterprise Data Model is the Focus of this Chapter

	Relational	Dimensional
Enterprise Data Model (EDM)	'One-pager' on organization-wide business objects and rules	
Conceptual Data Model (CDM)	'One-pager' on business rules	'One-pager' on navigation
Logical Data Model (LDM)	Detailed business solution on business rules	Detailed business solution on navigation
Physical Data Model (PDM)	Detailed technical solution	
Operational Data Model (ODM)	Technical implementation	

An enterprise data model shows the organization-wide fundamental business objects, setting the context of the business rules, unbiased of any application or technology. It is independent of how the data is physically stored or processed. This chapter defines business objects, followed by an explanation of the importance of the enterprise data model and business object definitions. Then we provide a summary of the five-step approach to building an enterprise data model. Finally, we show how an enterprise data model can be built using erwin DM and the benefits of building it with erwin DM.

Business Objects Explained

A business object is an idea that is both *fundamental* and *critical* to your organization. Fundamental means this term is probably mentioned many times a day in conversations with the people in the organization. Critical means the organization would be very different or non-existent without this business object.

The majority of business objects are easy to identify and include ideas that are common across industries, such as **Customer** and **Employee**. An airline may call a **Customer** a **Passenger**, and a hospital may call a **Customer** a **Patient**, but in general, they are all people who receive goods or services. Each idea becomes more detailed, as we progress from conceptual, logical, to physical design phases.

However, many business objects can be more challenging to identify. They may be ideas to specific audiences, but not to others in the same department, organization, or industry. For example, an **Account** would most likely be a business object for a bank and a manufacturing company. However, the audience for the bank enterprise data model might also require **Checking Account** and **Savings Account** to be in their model. Whereas the audience for the manufacturing enterprise data model, instead, might need **General Ledger Account** and **Accounts Receivable Account** to be in their model.

In our tutorial for the MyMovie organization, a fundamental and critical business object can be **Customer**. But **Address** can also be a fundamental and critical business object in a general context. Should the enterprise data model contain an **Address** business object as well? To answer this question, we need to know whether, and to what degree, the **Address** is fundamental and critical to the MyMovie organization.

Enterprise Data Model Explained

Business objects, such as those in the preceding discussion, need representation in an enterprise data model. An enterprise data model is a one-page data model that captures the organizational scope, designed for a high-level overview. Limiting the enterprise data model to one page is important because it forces the modeler and participants to select only vital business objects to the organization. A good rule of thumb, therefore, is to ask yourself if the audience for this model would include this business object as one of the top business objects in their organization. By doing this, it rules out business objects that are at too low a level of detail; they can appear in the more detailed conceptual and logical data models. If you're having trouble limiting the number of business objects, think about whether or not there are other business objects into which they are groupable. Such as grouping **Order Line** into **Order** or **Customer Address** into **Customer**. These higher business objects are the ones you should include in the enterprise data model.

The enterprise data model includes business objects, their definitions, and the relationships that show how these business objects interact with each other. Unlike the logical and physical data models, as demonstrated later, enterprise data models may contain many-to-many relationships. A simplified example of an enterprise data model for an airline organization appears in Figure 114.

Business object definitions:

- **Booking**–A booking is a record of the intention of a customer to fly with the airline organization from point A to point B.

- **Employee**–An employee is a person employed by the airline organization for a specific role. Note the role-up of role into the employee business object.

Figure 114. Simplified Enterprise Data Model of Airline Organization

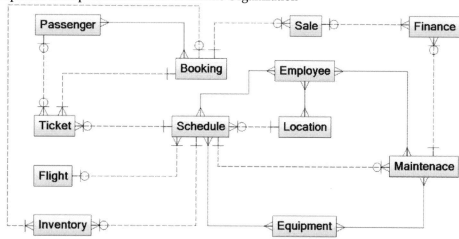

- **Equipment**–Equipment is the grouping of all physical business objects that the airline organization makes use of to perform their operations, including their aircraft.

- **Finance**–Finance is the grouped financial business objects that perform the financial requirements of the airline organization.

- **Flight**–A flight is an allocation from the FAA for a flying route.

- **Inventory**–Inventory is the grouping of seats of a scheduled flight with other inventory items, such as meals, drinks, and similar items that are associated with a flight. Not to be confused with equipment.

- **Location**–A location is a physical location, an employee, which is vital for a flight or a maintenance requirement.

- **Maintenance**–Maintenance is the physical implementation of a servicing or repair of a piece of equipment by an employee.

- **Passenger**–A passenger is any person that interacts with the airline organization to fly from point A to point B.

- **Sale**–A sale is a financial transaction for a booking.

- **Schedule**–A schedule is a date and time allocation of a flight or a piece of equipment is in for maintenance.

- **Ticket**–A ticket is issued to allow a passenger onto a scheduled flight of the airline organization.

Business Rules:

- Each **Passenger** may make several **Booking**s from the airline organization.

- For each **Booking** to exist, it needs at least one **Passenger**.

- If several **Passenger**s are flying together, they can make one **Booking** for all **Passenger**s

- Each **Passenger** is issued a separate **Ticket** for a **Booking**.

- Furthermore, for each **Booking** to exist, it further needs to have an available **Inventory** of a seat on a **Schedule**d **Flight**.

- Each **Flight** can have multiple **Schedule**s, but it needs at least one for it to exist.

- Each **Schedule** requires either a **Flight** or a **Maintenance** requirement to exist.

- And each **Schedule**d **Flight** can have zero, one, or more **Inventory** items and requires at least one piece of **Equipment** and at least one **Employee**.

- Also, for each **Booking** to exist, it further needs to have one or many **Ticket**s — one **Ticket** per **Schedule**d **Flight**.

- Note that each **Schedule**d **Flight** does not necessarily need to have any **Ticket**s issued for it, i.e., Flight to take an aircraft to a location for maintenance requirements.

- Each **Maintenance** requirement needs a **Schedule** for one or many pieces of **Equipment** and one or many **Employee**s at a specific **L**ocation.

- Each **Maintenance** requirement can have a **Financial** cost to perform the operations.

- Each **Sale** needs to have one Booking to exist, and also can produce one or many **Financial** transactions.

Notice in the model in Figure 114 that business objects such as **Passenger** and **Flight** are likely to be considered business objects throughout the airline industry. There are also slightly more specific business objects in this model, such as **Schedule** and **Location**, which are considered fundamental and critical for this airline organization. Therefore, they are business objects in the enterprise data model. Yet these more detailed business objects may not be considered *fundamental* and *critical* business objects within a different organization in the same industry or may be grouped into alternative business objects.

During the enterprise data modeling exercise, documenting clearly and thoroughly what each business object means is critical. All too often, we wait until it is too late in the process to get definitions. Waiting too long usually leads to not writing definitions at all or doing a rush job by writing quick definition phrases that have little or no usefulness. If the definitions behind the terms in a data model are nonexistent or weak, multiple interpretations of the concept become a strong possibility.

By agreeing on definitions at the enterprise level, the more detailed conceptual, logical, and physical analysis goes smoother and take less time. For example, definitions can address the question, 'Does Customer include potential customers or only existing customers?' When the enterprise data model is complete, which includes business object definitions, it is a powerful tool that can provide several significant business benefits:

- **To provide a broad understanding.** We can capture extremely complex and encompassing business processes, application requirements, and even entire industries on a single piece of paper, enabling people with different backgrounds and roles to understand and communicate with each other.

- **It defines scope and direction.** By visually showing business objects and their business rules, we can more easily identify a subset of the model for an application development effort. For example, we can model the entire enterprise and then scope out of this a subset for a particular application that we would like to build. The broad perspective of an enterprise data model can help us determine how the to-be and existing applications can coexist. It can provide direction and guidance on what new functionality the business needs next.

- **It offers proactive analysis.** By developing an enterprise understanding of the organization, there is a strong chance we can identify critical issues or concerns, saving substantial time and money later on. Examples include business object definition differences and different interpretations of the project scope.

- **It builds rapport between IT and the business.** A majority of organizations have some level of internal communication issues between the business and IT departments. Building an enterprise data model together is a great way to remove or reduce these communication barriers.

Designing an Enterprise Data Model

There are five steps to enterprise data modeling, as illustrated in Figure 115.

Figure 115. Five Steps to Enterprise Data Modeling

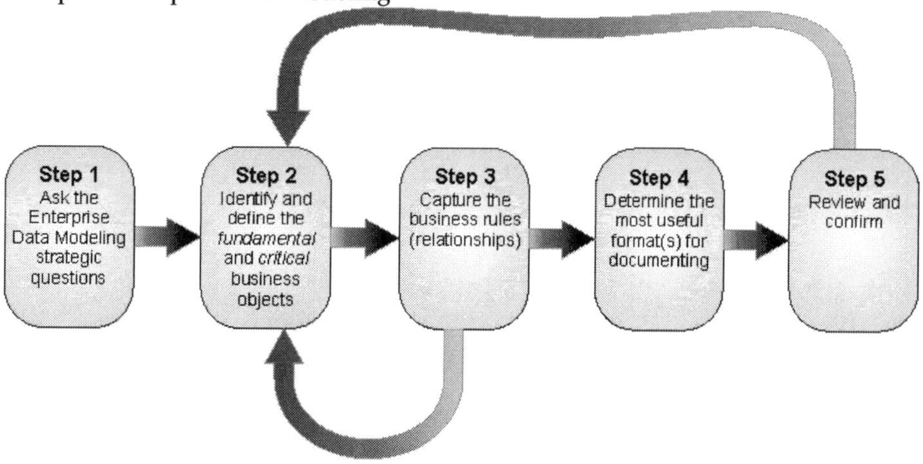

Before you begin an enterprise data model exercise, the enterprise data model strategic questions need answering (Step 1). These questions are a prerequisite to the success of any enterprise data modeling exercise. Next, identify all of the business objects within the scope of the organization (Step 2). Make sure each business object is clearly and completely defined. Then determine how these business objects are related to each other (Step 3). Often, you need to go back to Step 2 at this point because in capturing relationships, you often come up with new business objects, which results in new relationships between these new business objects. Next, decide the most useful form for your work (Step 4). Someone needs to review your work, so deciding on the most useful form is an important step. As a final step, review your work to get approval on the enterprise data model (Step 5).

Step 1: Ask the Enterprise Data Model Five Strategic Questions

Enterprise data model five strategic questions that need answering. Precisely and clearly document the answers to these questions in a few sentences each.

1. **What is the scope of the enterprise data model?** As much as we define the enterprise data model as having the entire organization in scope, this is still an important question because the definition of the entire organization in itself has ambiguities. For example, an organization might be the holding company of several other companies through acquisitions. The scope of an enterprise data model might be at the holding company level, encompassing all the sub-companies. Or it might be at one of the sub-company levels. The same could apply to an organization comprising of several independent divisions, and a specific division might frame the scope of the enterprise data model for themselves. Or it might be framed at the overarching organization. Knowing this answer sets the boundaries, or edges of the enterprise data model, but it also highlights where the overflow or overlaps would occur. Assuming our previous example of a division, the edges where there is overlap would occur is found in mutual business objects, like Customer. This insight leads to the building of the definition for the Customer.

2. **What is the context of the enterprise data model?** Traditionally we view an enterprise data model to be an as-is model, but it can be extended to define a future state, which is typically a to-be model. For example, an organization that is branching out into new business areas could require an enterprise data model that includes the new business area. It could require this to identify where the overlaps, similarities, or differences are in the existing and new business areas.

3. **Who is the consumer of the enterprise data model?** Like the previous questions, it is essential to know who are the users, or consumers of the enterprise data model. It is a good policy with anything you produce to determine early the validators and consumers of the model. This question ensures the correct choice of the display format for the enterprise data model. If the consumers vary considerably in expertise, the enterprise data model may need

more than one format. Step 4 discusses the various display formats, but before getting to step 4, one needs to understand in advance the requirements of the display format(s).

4. **Who is the validator of the enterprise data model?** As much as we have defined the users that consume the enterprise data model, we also need to ensure that what we are sharing is a real and accurate reflection of the scope and context of the enterprise data model. It is essential to assign validators accountability for checking the enterprise data model. The organization is relying on the enterprise data model to make vital decisions, hence why the accuracy of the model is of paramount importance.

5. **Who is the owner of the enterprise data model?** Bearing in mind that the typical as-is enterprise data model is not static, but a living model. As the organization changes, so does the enterprise data model, in all its display formats. So it is just as important to identify the owner of the enterprise data model so that they can take full responsibility for maintaining the model after completion.

Step 2: Identify and Define the Business Objects

Now that we have direction, we can work with the business experts to identify the business objects within the scope of the enterprise data model, and then come up with an agreed-upon definition for each business object. So, how does one come up with the *fundamental* and *critical* business objects? The business object needs to be a noun or a noun phrase that fits into one of six categories: who, what, when, where, why, or how. Table 4 contains a definition of each of these business object categories, along with examples.

Table 4. Definitions and Examples of Business Object Categories

Category	Definition	Examples
Who	Person or business of interest to the organization. That is, '*Who* is important to the organization?' Often a *Who* is associated with a role such as a Customer or a Vendor.	Employee, Patient, Player, Suspect, Customer, Vendor, Student, Passenger, Competitor, Author
What	Product or service of interest to the organization. It often refers to what the organization makes that keeps it in business. That is, '*What* is important to the organization?'	Product, Service, Raw Material, Finished Good, Course, Song, Photograph, Title
When	Calendar or time interval of interest to the organization. That is, '*When* is the organization in operation?'	Time, Date, Month, Quarter, Year, Semester, Fiscal Period, Minute

Category	Definition	Examples
Where	Location of interest to the organization. Location can refer to real places as well as electronic places. That is, '*Where* is business conducted?'	Mailing Address, Distribution Point, Website URL, IP Address
Why	Event or transaction of interest to the organization. These events keep the business afloat. That is, '*Why* is the organization in business?'	Order, Return, Complaint, Withdrawal, Deposit, Compliment, Inquiry, Trade, Claim
How	Documentation of the event of interest to the organization. Documents record the events such as a Purchase Order recording an Order event. That is, '*How* does the organization keep track of events?'	Invoice, Contract, Agreement, Purchase Order, Speeding Ticket, Packing Slip, Trade Confirmation

We can use these six categories to create a Business Object Template for capturing the business objects on our enterprise data model. See Table 5.

Table 5. Business Object Template

Who?	What?	When?	Where?	Why?	How?
1.	1.	1.	1.	1.	1.
2.	2.	2.	2.	2.	2.
3.	3.	3.	3.	3.	3.
4.	4.	4.	4.	4.	4.

Table 6 contains a completed Business Object Template for the airline organization example shown earlier. It is vital to note that in a real-world situation, the list of business objects would be a lot longer. And would require several iterations of refining down to a minimal list.

Table 6. Example of Completed Business Object Template for Airline Organization

Who?	What?	When?	Where?	Why?	How?
1. Passenger	1. Ticket	1. Schedule	1. Location	1. Sale	1. Equipment
2. Employee	2. Flight	2.	2.	2. Finance	2. Maintenance
3.	3. Inventory	3.	3.	3.	3.
4.	4. Booking	4.	4.	4.	4.

Here are some of the business object definitions:

Table 7. Example Business Object Definitions of Airline Organization

Business Object	Definition
Booking	A booking is a record of the intention of a customer to fly with the airline organization from point A to point B.
Employee	An employee is a person employed by the airline organization for a specific role. Note the role-up of role into the employee business object.
Equipment	Equipment is the grouping of all physical business objects that the airline organization makes use of to perform their operations, including their aircraft.
Finance	Finance is the grouped financial business objects that perform the financial requirements of the airline organization.
Flight	A flight is an allocation from the FAA for a flying route.
Inventory	Inventory is the grouping of seats of a scheduled flight with other inventory items, such as meals, drinks, and similar items that are associated with a flight. Not to be confused with equipment.
Location	A location is a physical location, an employee, which is vital for a flight or a maintenance requirement.
Maintenance	Maintenance is the physical implementation of a servicing or repair of a piece of equipment by an employee.
Passenger	A passenger is any person that interacts with the airline organization to fly from point A to point B.
Sale	A sale is a financial transaction for a booking.
Schedule	A schedule is a date and time allocation of a flight, or a piece of equipment is in for maintenance.
Ticket	A ticket is issued to allow a passenger onto a scheduled flight of the airline organization.

When sitting with a business team to build an enterprise data model, use a whiteboard with the Business Object Template drawn on it. Then break the team into small groups to write down on a set of sticky notes all the business object that they can imagine in their organization. Then start putting the business object sticky notes on the board as a combined team. Sticky notes give you the ability to stack them for grouping and allow for easy moving. Lastly, the team attempts to define a definition for each of the business objects. Business objects often get moved, and renamed during this phase as the team slowly gets to grips with what are the business objects.

Step 3: Capture the Business Rules (Relationships)

Our objective at the enterprise data model level is to determine which business objects relate to each other and then articulate the business rules that substantiate the relationship. For each relationship between business objects, we need to ask the following questions: two on participation and two on optionality. Try re-wording the question in your mind using examples of the business objects. See Table 8.

Table 8. Questions to Ask for Each Relationship

Question	Yes	No
Can a *Business Object A* be related to more than one *Business Object B*?		
Can a *Business Object B* be related to more than one *Business Object A*?		
Can a Business Object A exist without a Business Object B?		
Can a Business Object B exist without a Business Object A?		

The first two questions are on participation, and the answers to these questions determine the type of relationship between the two business objects. For example, if 'Yes' for Business Object A can be related to more than one Business Object B, then there is a many-symbol on the relationship line next to Business Object B.

The next two questions are on optionality, and the answers to these questions determine whether there is a zero-symbol on the relationship line next to either business object. For example, if 'Yes' for Business Object A can exist without Business Object B, then there is a zero-symbol on the relationship line next to Business Object B. Shading differentiates the questions for each relationship in the above table for ease of reading, but are not necessary for your practice. Take careful note of the relationship between *Passenger* and *Booking* (first group of questions and answers), review the enterprise data model in Figure 117, and notice the many-to-many relationship and then review the answers to the first two questions. The first two questions with both having an answer of 'Yes' implies that there is a many-symbol on both sides, which is a many-to-many relationship.

Table 9. Partial Set of Answers to the Questions for the Airline Organization Example

Question	Yes	No
Can a *Passenger* be related to more than one *Booking*?	✓	
Can a *Booking* be related to more than one *Passenger*?	✓	
Can a *Passenger* exist without a *Booking*?	✓	
Can a *Booking* exist without a *Passenger*?		✓
Can a *Ticket* be related to more than one *Booking*?		✓
Can a *Booking* be related to more than one *Ticket*?	✓	
Can a *Ticket* exist without a *Booking*?		✓
Can a *Booking* exist without a *Ticket*?		✓
Can a *Schedule* be related to more than one *Equipment*?	✓	
Can an *Equipment* be related to more than one *Schedule*?	✓	
Can a *Schedule* exist without an *Equipment*?		✓
Can an *Equipment* exist without a *Schedule*?	✓	

During this step, it is not uncommon to have to return to Step 2 to redefine the business objects. The questions and answers quite often uncover alternative thoughts on the business objects, their definitions, and business rules.

Step 4: Determine the Most Useful Format(s)

Some people need to validate the enterprise data model, and others need to make use of it, so deciding the most useful format is an important step. We know the validators for the model after answering enterprise data model Strategic Question #4 from Step 1: *Who is the validator of the enterprise data model?* And we know the users for the model after answering enterprise data model Strategic Question #3 from Step 1: *Who is the consumer of the enterprise data model?* If the validators and users are already familiar with data modeling notation, the decision is an easy one. Use the traditional data modeling notation they are comfortable with, such as this example in Figure 116 and the fully defined version in Figure 117.

However, the validator and users are not always familiar with the traditional data modeling notation or don't want to see it as a data model. In these situations, be creative with how you display the enterprise data model, coming up with a visual that the audience for the model would understand. For example, Figure 118 contains a business diagram that can be used instead of the traditional data modeling notation.

Figure 116. Traditional Data Modeling Notation

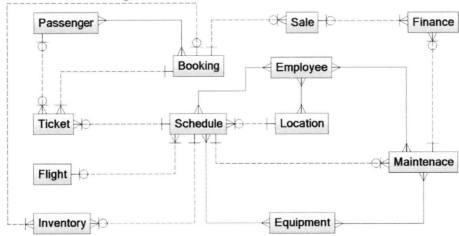

Figure 117. Traditional Data Modeling Notation with Definitions

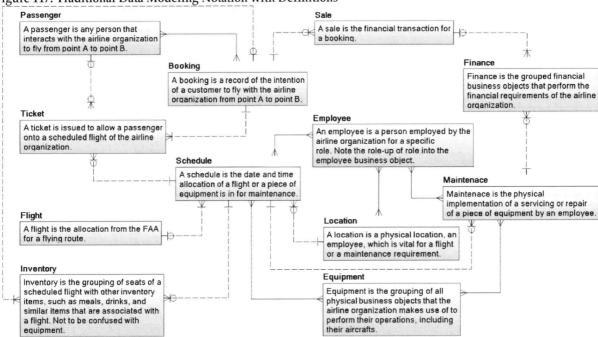

Note the usage of the arrowheads, representing the many-side of the relationship, and the double arrowheads for the many-to-many relationships.

Step 5: Review and Confirm

The validators need to review the enterprise data model, and frequently, during this step, some changes require returning to Step 2 and redefining the business objects. Most likely (and hopefully), the validators were involved during the process of building the enterprise data model, and therefore in many cases, this review step becomes a formality. But it is essential not to be overlooked, as the validators still need to take accountability for the accuracy of the enterprise data model. The organization is relying on the enterprise data model to make vital decisions, hence why the accuracy of the model is of paramount importance.

Figure 118. Business Diagram Instead of the Traditional Data Modeling Notation

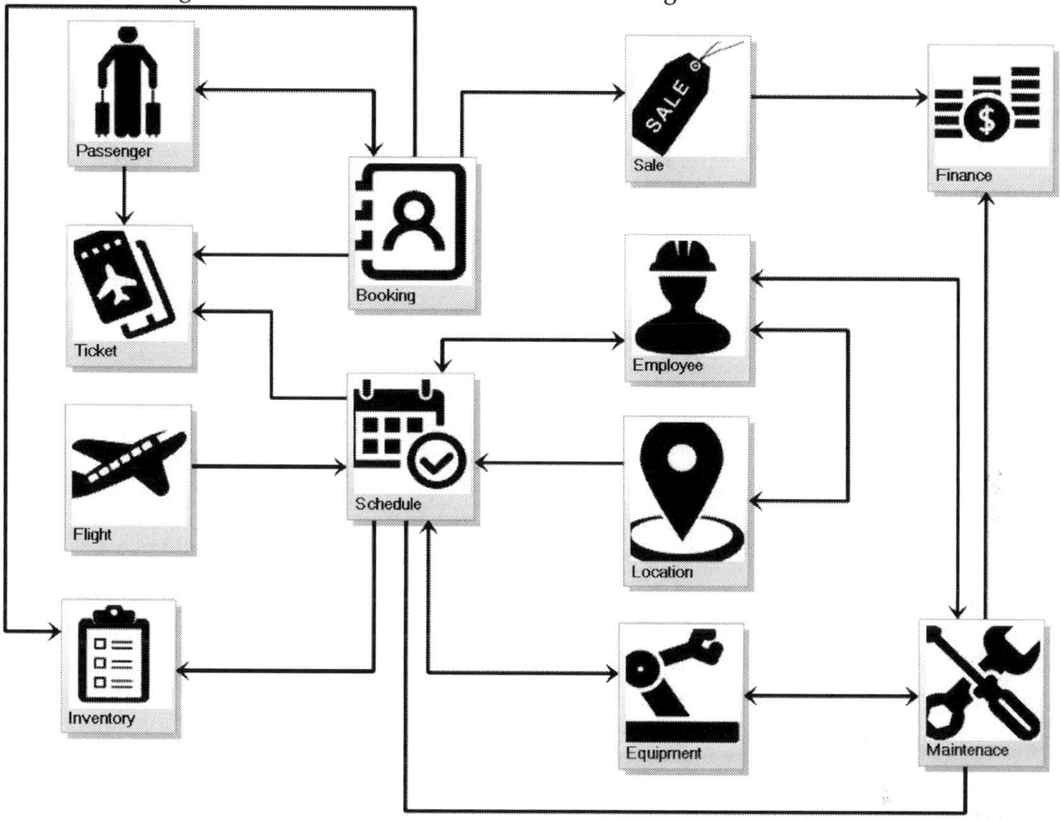

erwin DM Support for Enterprise Data Models

erwin DM provides several features to support enterprise data modeling. erwin DM supports several data modeling notations, including the Information Engineering (crows-foot) notation. erwin DM also provides several different display levels for the diagrams: Entity Display Level as shown in Figure 116, Definition Display Level as shown in Figure 117, and Icon Display Level as shown in Figure 118.

Another feature that erwin Data Modeling provides to support enterprise data modeling is the drawing feature. By using this option, one can draw connectors or lines between business objects, or use shapes to group business objects graphically, as demonstrated in Figure 119.

Finally, erwin DM provides the ability to make usage of color for business objects to identify their ownership, as demonstrated in Figure 120.

As demonstrated, erwin DM provides may features that can assist in enterprise data modeling, all of which are usable in whatever combination that suits your requirements.

Figure 119. Enterprise Data Model using Drawing Objects

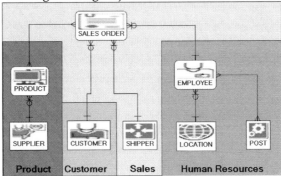

Figure 120. Enterprise Data Model using Colors

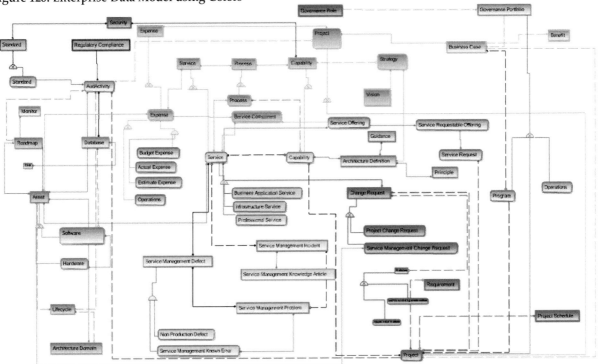

Key Learnings

- A business object is an idea that is both *fundamental* and *critical* to your audience.

- An enterprise data model is a set of symbols and text that represents organization-wide fundamental business objects and the rules binding them for a particular audience.

- An enterprise data model is unbiased of any application or technology. It is independent of how the data is physically stored or processed.

- erwin DM provides a selection of features that can assist in the documenting of the enterprise data model.

Need a one-pager?
Learn how this relates to that
Build a CDM!

The highlighted row in Table 10 shows the focus of this chapter: the Conceptual Data Model (CDM).

Table 10. The Conceptual Data Model is the Focus of this Chapter

	Relational	Dimensional
Enterprise Data Model (EDM)	'One-pager' on organization-wide business objects and rules	
Conceptual Data Model (CDM)	'One-pager' on business rules	'One-pager' on navigation
Logical Data Model (LDM)	Detailed business solution on business rules	Detailed business solution on navigation
Physical Data Model (PDM)	Detailed technical solution	
Operational Data Model (ODM)	Technical implementation	

A conceptual data model shows the critical business objects limited to a particular solution and how these business objects interact with each other relevant to that solution. This chapter defines the importance of the conceptual data model and the similarities and differences from the enterprise data model. Finally, we show how both a relational and dimensional conceptual data model can be built using erwin DM.

Conceptual Data Model Explained

Business objects, such as those introduced in Chapter 9, are also used in a conceptual data model. A conceptual data model is a one-page data model that captures the business solution needs, designed for a particular audience. As with the enterprise data model, limiting the conceptual data model to one page is important because it forces the modeler and participants to select only vital business objects for the solution. Once again, think about whether or not there are other business objects into which the ones you're discussing are groupable. These higher business objects are the ones you should include in the conceptual data model.

The conceptual data model includes business objects, their definitions, and the relationships that show how these business objects interact with each other. Unlike the logical and physical data models, both the enterprise data model and the conceptual data models may contain many-to-many relationships.

Recall from the introduction to this part, that relational data models capture how the business *works*; while dimensional data models capture the *monitoring* of the business.

Relational Conceptual Data Model Example

The relational conceptual data model includes business objects, their definitions, and the relationships that capture the business rules binding these business objects, framed by the scope of the solution. An example of a conceptual data model for an airline organization that we used in the previous chapter appears in Figure 121.

Figure 121. Airline Organization Relational Conceptual Data Model

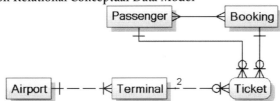

Business object Definitions:

• **Booking**–A booking is a record of the intention of a customer to fly with the airline organization from point A to point B.

• **Passenger**– A passenger is any person that interacts with the airline to fly from point A to B.

• **Ticket**–A ticket is issued to allow a passenger onto a scheduled flight of the airline organization.

• **Terminal**–A terminal is a gate that allows passengers to embark or disembark from an aircraft for a flight.

• **Airport**–An airport is the place where aircraft depart from and land at, and comprises of one or many terminals.

Business Rules:

  • Each **Passenger** may have one or many **Bookings**.
  • Each **Booking** can have one or many **Passengers**.
  • Each **Booking** may issue one or many **Tickets**.
  • Each **Ticket** must be issued by one **Booking**.
  • Each **Passenger** may have one or many **Tickets**.
  • Each **Ticket** must belong to one **Passenger**.
  • Each **Ticket** must have two **Terminals** (One for the departure and one for the destination).
  • Each **Terminal** can have one or many **Tickets**.

Notice how the relational conceptual data model looks like a subset of the enterprise data model. It is because it is the same business object, just the scope of the data model changed. The enterprise data model's scope is of the whole organization, where the conceptual data model is of the solution only. Another aspect that is not as predominant at this stage is that both the enterprise data model and the conceptual data model are a reflection of how the business *works*.

Dimensional Conceptual Data Model Example

To understand and document our reporting requirements, we can also build a dimensional conceptual data model to reflect the *monitoring* of the business, such as the example in Figure 122. In this case, we would like to see specific measures around **Ticket**s (**Ticket Price** as **Ticket Sales Amount**) at **Airport**, **Booking**, and **Day** level. And then navigate to higher levels (e.g., viewing **Ticket Sales Amount** at a **State** level). We take measures such as **Ticket Sales Amount** up and down hierarchies. A hierarchy is when an entity instance is a child of at most one other entity instance. Such as the day April 1st, 2020, belongs to only the month of April, which belongs only to the year 2020.

Figure 122. Airline Organization Dimensional Conceptual Data Model

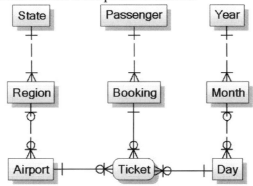

Business object definitions:
- **Booking**–A booking is a record of the intention of a customer to fly with the airline organization from point A to point B.

- **Passenger**–A passenger is any person that interacts with the airline to fly from point A to B.

- **Ticket**–A ticket is issued to allow a passenger onto a scheduled flight.

- **Airport**–An airport is a location that a flight may take off from or land.

- **State**–A state is one of the official states of the USA.

- **Region**–Region a geographical grouping of airports for air traffic control purposes.

- **Day**–A day is a time-based period, measured from midnight to midnight in GMT.

- **Month**–A month is one of the twelve named periods into which a year is divided.

- **Year**–A year is the time taken by the earth to make one revolution around the sun.

Designing a Conceptual Data Model

The process of designing a conceptual data model is similar to that of the enterprise data model. The enterprise data model can be a good source for the conceptual data modeling process, but there are distinct differences. The five steps to conceptual data modeling are shown in Figure 123.

Figure 123. Five Steps to Conceptual Data Modeling

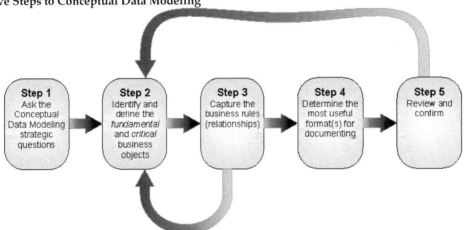

Before you begin a conceptual data model exercise, the conceptual data model strategic questions need answering (Step 1). These questions are a prerequisite to the success of any application effort. Next, identify all of the business objects within the scope of the application you are building (Step 2). Make sure each business object is clearly and completely defined. Then determine how these business objects are related to each other (Step 3). Often, you need to go back to Step 2 at this point because in capturing relationships, you often come up with new business objects, which results in new relationships between these new business objects. Next, decide the most useful form for making sure the practical usage of your work (Step 4). Someone needs to review your work, so deciding on the most useful form is an important step. As a final step, review your work to get approval on the conceptual data model (Step 5).

Step 1: Ask the Conceptual Data Model Five Strategic Questions

You need to answer five strategic questions:

1. **What is the solution going to do?** Precisely and clearly document the answer to this question in a few sentences. Make sure to include whether you are replacing an existing system, delivering new functionality, or integrating several existing solutions. Always begin with the end in mind so you know what you are going to deliver. This question helps determine the scope of the solution.

2. **'As-Is' or 'To-Be'?** You need to know if there is a requirement to understand and model the current business environment (that is, the 'as-is' view). Or to understand and model a proposed business environment (that is, the 'to-be' view).

3. **Is analytics a requirement?** Analytics, in informal terms, is the field of playing with numbers. That is, taking measurements such as **Ticket Sales Amount** or **Inventory Count** and viewing them at different levels of granularity such as by day or year. If there is a requirement for analytics, at least part of your solution needs to be dimensional. Relational modeling focuses on business rules, and dimensional modeling focuses on business questions.

4. **Who is the audience?** That is, who is the person or group who is the validator and can confirm your understanding of the conceptual data model, and who is the consumer of the conceptual data model? It is a good policy with anything you produce to determine early on who checks your work (the validators) and who uses your work. This question ensures you choose the ideal display format for your conceptual data model. Note that if the validators and users vary considerably in their technical skills, you may need more than one form for the conceptual data model.

5. **Flexibility or simplicity?** In terms of design, there is always a balancing act between flexibility and simplicity. If you are leaning more towards flexibility, you will most likely use some generic terms such as **Event** instead of **Order** or **Person** instead of **Employee**.

Step 2: Identify and Define the Business Objects

Now that we have direction, we can work with the business experts to identify the business objects within the scope of the solution. And then come up with an agreed-upon definition for each business object.

For Relational

We can use these six categories to create a Business Object Template for capturing the business objects on our conceptual data model. Table 11 contains a completed Business Object Template for the airline organization example shown earlier. It is vital to note that in a real-world situation, the list of business objects would be a lot longer. Table 12 contains the business object definitions.

Table 11. Example of Completed Business Object Template for Airline Organization

Who?	What?	When?	Where?	Why?	How?
1. Passenger	1. Ticket	1. Schedule	1. Location	1. Sale	1. Equipment
2. Employee	2. Flight	2.	2.	2. Finance	2. Maintenance
3.	3. Inventory	3.	3.	3.	3.
4.	4. Booking	4.	4.	4.	4.

Table 12. Example Business Object Definitions of Airline Organization

Business Object	Definition
Booking	A booking is a record of the intention of a customer to fly with the airline organization from point A to point B.
Employee	An employee is a person employed by the airline organization for a specific role. Note the role-up of role into the employee business object.
Equipment	Equipment is the grouping of all physical business objects that the airline organization makes use of to perform their operations, including their aircraft.
Finance	Finance is the grouped financial business objects that perform the financial requirements of the airline organization.
Flight	A flight is an allocation from the FAA for a flying route.
Inventory	Inventory is the grouping of seats of a scheduled flight with other inventory items, such as meals, drinks, and similar items that are associated with a flight. Not to be confused with equipment.
Location	A location is a physical location, an employee, which is vital for a flight or a maintenance requirement.
Maintenance	Maintenance is the physical implementation of a servicing or repair of a piece of equipment by an employee.
Passenger	A passenger is any person that interacts with the airline organization to fly from point A to point B.
Sale	A sale is a financial transaction for a booking.
Schedule	A schedule is a date and time allocation of a flight, or a piece of equipment is in for maintenance.
Ticket	A ticket is issued to allow a passenger onto a scheduled flight of the airline organization.

For Dimensional

We need to determine the specific business questions that need answering. For example, we work with the business analysts for airline organization and identify the following four questions:

1. Show me the number of bookings made by non-loyalty passengers over the last year that made more than one booking in the year. (From the Loyalty Department)

2. Show me the number of bookings for flights by departure airport that had only one flight (no connecting flights) for the last four months. (From the Strategy Department)

3. How many bookings that changed their seat after making the booking, by flight for the last month? (From the Budgeting Department)

4. How many bookings made for the last ten days? I want to compare loyalty to non-loyalty passengers and by different aircraft types. (From the Finance Department)

Step 3: Capture the Business Rules (Relationships)

For Relational

This step of relational conceptual modeling is all about capturing the business rules. Our objective at the relational conceptual level is to determine which business objects relate to each other and then articulate the rules. For each relationship line on our model, we find ourselves asking up to eight questions: two on participation, two on optionality, and up to four questions on subtyping. See Table 13.

Table 13. Questions to Ask for Each Relationship

Question	Yes	No
Can a *Business Object A* be related to more than one *Business Object B*?		
Can a *Business Object B* be related to more than one *Business Object A*?		
Can a Business Object A exist without a Business Object B?		
Can a Business Object B exist without a Business Object A?		
Are there examples of *Business Object A* that would be valuable to show?		
Are there examples of *Business Object B* that would be valuable to show?		
Does a *Business Object A* go through a lifecycle?		
Does a *Business Object B* go through a lifecycle?		

The first two questions are on participation, and the answers to these questions determine the type of relationship between the two business objects. For example, if 'Yes' for Business Object A can be related to more than one Business Object B, then there is a many-symbol on the relationship line next to Business Object B. The next two questions are on optionality, and the answers to these questions determine whether there is a zero-symbol on the relationship line next to either business object. For example, if 'Yes' for Business Object A can exist without Business Object B, then there is a zero-symbol on the relationship line next to Business Object B.

The answers to the next four questions determine where we introduce subtyping on the conceptual data model. When examples aid communication or if it is essential to explain the lifecycle of a concept, then subtyping needs to be added to the model. Table 14 shows a partial set of answers to the questions for the airline organization example.

Table 14. Partial Set of Answers to the Questions for the Airline Organization Example

Question	Yes	No
Can a *Passenger* be related to more than one *Booking*?	✓	
Can a *Booking* be related to more than one *Passenger*?	✓	
Can a *Passenger* exist without a *Booking*?	✓	
Can a *Booking* exist without a *Passenger*?		✓
Are there examples of *Passenger* that would be valuable to show?	✓	
Are there examples of *Booking* that would be valuable to show?		✓

Question	Yes	No
Does a *Passenger* go through a lifecycle?	✓	
Does a *Booking* go through a lifecycle?	✓	
Can a *Ticket* be related to more than one *Booking*?		✓
Can a *Booking* be related to more than one *Ticket*?	✓	
Can a *Ticket* exist without a *Booking*?		✓
Can a *Booking* exist without a *Ticket*?		✓
Are there examples of *Ticket* that would be valuable to show?	✓	
Are there examples of *Booking* that would be valuable to show?		✓
Does a *Ticket* go through a lifecycle?	✓	
Does a *Booking* go through a lifecycle?		✓
Can a *Schedule* be related to more than one *Equipment*?	✓	
Can an *Equipment* be related to more than one *Schedule*?	✓	
Can a *Schedule* exist without an *Equipment*?		✓
Can an *Equipment* exist without a *Schedule*?	✓	
Are there examples of *Schedule* that would be valuable to show?	✓	
Are there examples of *Equipment* that would be valuable to show?	✓	
Does a *Schedule* go through a lifecycle?	✓	
Does an *Equipment* go through a lifecycle?	✓	

During this step, it is not uncommon to have to return to Step 2 to redefine the business objects. The questions and answers quite often uncover alternative thoughts on the business objects, their definitions, and business rules.

For Dimensional

We need to take the business questions we identified in the previous step and create a Grain Matrix. A Grain Matrix is a spreadsheet where the measures from the business questions become columns, and the dimensional levels from the business questions become rows. The purpose of a Grain Matrix is to scope analytic applications efficiently. It is possible to elicit hundreds of business questions, and plot these questions on a Grain Matrix. We make the observation that questions from different departments can be very similar to each other. By consolidating questions, we can scope applications that address the needs of more than one department. Table 15 contains a completed Grain Matrix for our Airline Application.

In this Grain Matrix, we took each of the four questions from Step 2 and parsed them so that the measure from each question (**Booking Count**) became a column. The levels of detail in each question became rows. The numbers in the Grain Matrix refer back to the question numbers.

Table 15. Completed Grain Matrix for an Airline Application

	Booking Count
Passenger Loyalty	1, 4
Time (Year, Month & Day)	1, 2, 3, 4
Location (Departure Airport)	2
Ticket (Number of Flights)	2
Flight	3
Inventory (Seat Changed)	3
Equipment (Aircraft Type)	4

Step 4: Determine the Most Useful Format(s)

Someone needs to review your work and use your findings during development, so deciding the most useful form is an important step. We know the users for the model after getting an answer to Strategic Question #4 from Step 1: *Who is our audience?* What person or group is the validator and can confirm our understanding of the conceptual data model, and who the users of the conceptual data model?

For Relational

If the validators and users are already familiar with data modeling notation, the decision is an easy one. Use the traditional data modeling notation they are comfortable with, such in Figure 116, the fully defined version in Figure 117, or the business diagram in Figure 118.

For Dimensional

Figure 124 shows the dimensional conceptual data model with the traditional notation.
Figure 125 shows my favorite conceptual dimensional form, the Axis Technique. The Axis Technique is when you put the measured business object in the center (e.g., **Bookings**) with each axis representing a dimension. The notches on each axis represent the levels of detail that are required to see the measures in the meter. This form works very well when the audience has limited exposure to data modeling.

Step 5: Review and Confirm

The validators need to review the conceptual data model, and frequently, during this step, some changes require returning to Step 2 and redefining the business objects. Most likely (and hopefully), the validators were involved during the process of building the enterprise data model, and therefore in many cases, this review step becomes a formality. But it is essential not to be overlooked, as the validators still need to take accountability for the accuracy of the enterprise data model. The organization is relying on the enterprise data model to make vital decisions, hence why the accuracy of the model is of paramount importance.

Figure 124. Traditional Data Modeling Notation

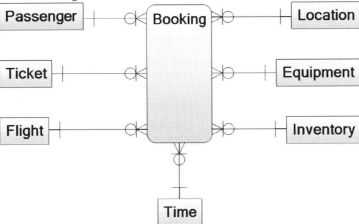

Figure 125. Axis Technique in erwin DM

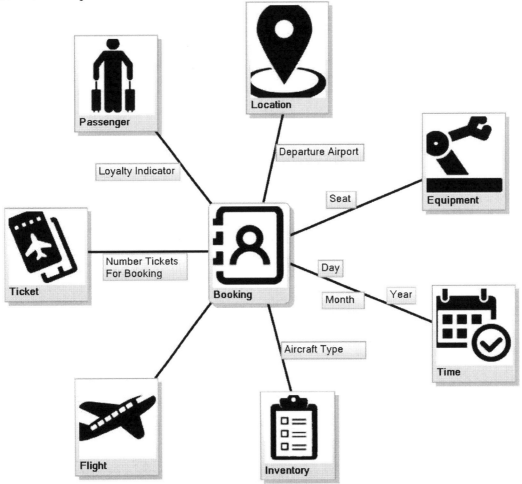

Tutorial: Initial Requirements Session with 'MyMovie'

As we dive deeper into data modeling, we are going to continue expanding our MyMovie tutorial. We spend a half-day with the MyMovie company to define the initial requirements of the solution. At the initial requirements session, you start working through the five steps to conceptual data modeling, as detailed in Designing a Conceptual Data Model section earlier in this chapter.

Step 1: Conceptual Data Model Five Strategic Questions

In Figure 126 is the answers to Step 1, ask the conceptual data model five strategic questions.

Figure 126. Answers to the Conceptual Data Model Strategic Questions for MyMovie

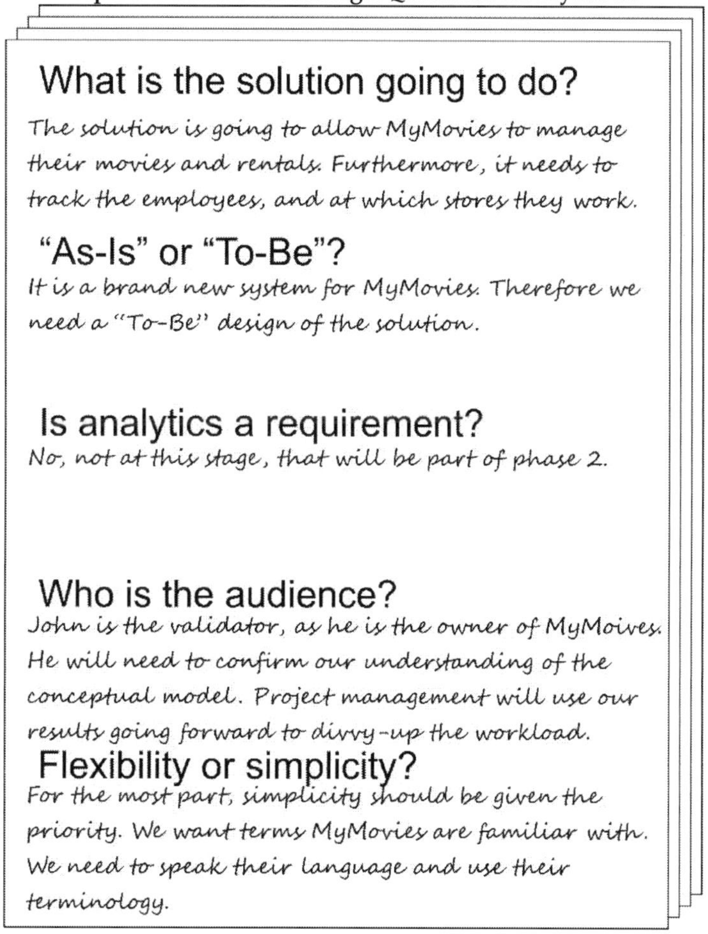

Step 2: Identify and Define the Business Objects

Next, we move onto Step 2, identify and define the Business Objects. After an hour of deliberation, and many sticky notes, we eventually agree on the Business Object Template, as detailed in Table 16.

Table 16. Business Object Template for MyMovie

Who?	What?	When?	Where?	Why?	How?
1. *Customer*	1. *Movie*	1.	1. *Store*	1. *Payment*	1. *Movie Rental*
2. *Employee*	2. *Movie Copy*	2.	2.	2.	2.

Movie Copy gave us some exciting challenges, which gave us a good insight into the business. MyMovie usually has multiple copies of the same movie. However, we still need to keep information about the contents of the **Movie** itself.

Here are the business object definitions:

Table 17. Business Object Definitions of MyMovie

Business Object	Definition
Customer	A CUSTOMER is a person or organization who has rented a movie within the past year.
Employee	EMPLOYEE is a person that works at the MyMovie STORE.
Movie	A MOVIE is any video that can be rented.
Movie Copy	A MOVIE COPY is a single copy of a MOVIE.
Store	A STORE is the physical location of MyMovies stores.
Payment	A PAYMENT is received when a CUSTOMER rents a MOVIE COPY.
Movie Rental	A MOVIE RENTAL is a record that is kept on every MOVIE in the STORE on who and when a MOVIE is rented.

Step 3: Capture the Business Rules (Relationships)

Exciting session thus far, but our job is only getting started. Next is Step 3, capture the business rules (Relationships). For this, we identify the business rules that relate to different business objects. We identify the following business rules:

- a customer rents movie rentals
- a movie rental is rented by a customer
- a customer makes payments
- a payment is made by a customer
- a payment is made for movie rentals
- a movie rental requires a payment
- an employee receives payment s
- a payment is received by an employee

- an employee completes movie rentals
- a movie rental is completed by an employee
- a movie copy is rented under movie rentals
- a movie rental records rental of a movie copy
- a movie is rented as movie copies
- a movie copy is a copy of a movie
- a store employs employees
- an employee is employed by a store
- movies are in stores
- stores rents movies

We then use the eight questions for each business rule. For space purposes, we show the answers to only the first three relationships in Table 18 through Table 20, with a summary of how the questions translate into the Zero, One and Many options in Table 21.

- *CUSTOMER* to *MOVIE RENTAL*, we identify that we need to maintain a relationship between these two because the business rule states, 'a customer rents movie rentals' and 'a movie rental is rented by a customer.'

Table 18. Relationship 8 Questions for MyMovie. Customer to Movie Rental

Question	Yes	No
Can a *CUSTOMER* be related to more than one *MOVIE RENTAL*?	✓	
Can a *MOVIE RENTAL* be related to more than one *CUSTOMER*?		✓
Can a *CUSTOMER* exist without a *MOVIE RENTAL*?	✓	
Can a *MOVIE RENTAL* exist without a *CUSTOMER*?		✓
Are there examples of *CUSTOMER* that would be valuable to show?	✓	
Are there examples of *MOVIE RENTAL* that would be valuable to show?		✓
Does a *CUSTOMER* go through a lifecycle?	✓	
Does a *MOVIE RENTAL* go through a lifecycle?		✓

- *CUSTOMER* to *PAYMENT*, we identify that we need to maintain a relationship between these two because the business rule states, 'a customer makes payments' and 'a payment is made by a customer.'

Table 19. Relationship 8 Questions for MyMovie. Customer to Payment

Question	Yes	No
Can a *CUSTOMER* be related to more than one *PAYMENT*?	✓	
Can a *PAYMENT* be related to more than one *CUSTOMER*?		✓
Can a *CUSTOMER* exist without a *PAYMENT*?	✓	
Can a *PAYMENT* exist without a *CUSTOMER*?		✓

Question	Yes	No
Are there examples of *CUSTOMER* that would be valuable to show?	✓	
Are there examples of *PAYMENT* that would be valuable to show?	✓	
Does a *CUSTOMER* go through a lifecycle?	✓	
Does a *PAYMENT* go through a lifecycle?		✓

 Notice the highlighted repetition of the 'example' and 'lifecycle' questions for 'Customer.' Since these questions were answered previously, one does not need to do extra work by re-answering them.

 Also, notice that we have discovered that 'Customer' does go through a lifecycle, and from earlier in this chapter, we need to identify if we need to reflect subtyping of the 'Customer' business object. In this case, we decide not to represent the subtyping on our conceptual data model; we deal with this later in the logical data model.

- *PAYMENT* to *MOVIE RENTAL*, we identify that we need to maintain a relationship between these two because the business rule states, 'a payment is made for movie rentals' and 'a movie rental requires a payment.'

Table 20. Relationship 8 Questions for MyMovie. Payment to Movie Rental

Question	Yes	No
Can a *PAYMENT* be related to more than one *MOVIE RENTAL*?	✓	
Can a *MOVIE RENTAL* be related to more than one *PAYMENT*?		✓
Can a *PAYMENT* exist without a *MOVIE RENTAL*?		✓
Can a *MOVIE RENTAL* exist without a *PAYMENT*?		✓
Are there examples of *PAYMENT* that would be valuable to show?		
Are there examples of *MOVIE RENTAL* that would be valuable to show?		
Does a *PAYMENT* go through a lifecycle?		
Does a *MOVIE RENTAL* go through a lifecycle?		

Table 21. Business Rules Summarized

From Business Object	To Business Object	Type of Business Rule
Customer	Movie Rental	One to Zero, One or Many
Customer	Payment	One to Zero, One or Many

From Business Object	To Business Object	Type of Business Rule		
Payment	Movie Rental	One	to	One or Many
Employee	Payment	One	to	Zero, One or Many
Employee	Movie Rental	One	to	Zero, One or Many
Movie Copy	Movie Rental	One	to	Zero, One or Many
Movie	Movie Copy	One	to	One or Many
Store	Employee	One	to	One or Many
Movie	Store	Many	to	Many

Step 4: Determine the Most Useful Format(s)

In speaking with John, the owner of the MyMovie company, we showed him all the options for the conceptual data model, and he stated that he is comfortable with the standard data modeling notation. It is now our job to encapsulate all we received from the initial interview into a conceptual data model based on the standard data modeling notation.

Tutorial: Creating a Conceptual Data Model in erwin DM

1. Open erwin DM.

2. Using the Quick Access Toolbar, click on the **Open** button.

3. Select the **MyMovie_Ver1** data model, from the previous portion of the tutorial, in the **Open** dialog.

4. Click on the **Open** button.

5. The MyMovie model opens in erwin DM. Before starting with the conceptual data model, lets first go through the different display levels that are available in erwin DM. In a logical data model, there are six different Display Levels, as described in Table 22.

Table 22. Logical Data Model Display Levels

Display Level	Description	Example
Attribute	This display level displays an entity, with all its attributes inside the entity box. Note that the entity box has two sections, the top is for the primary key attributes. And the bottom half is for all the non-primary key attributes. The attribute display level is the default display level in erwin DM and is the standard format used in the data modeling industry for a logical data model. Most commonly used in logical data models.	CUSTOMER customer number customer address email customer city customer first name customer last name customer state customer zip code

Display Level	Description	Example
Definition	This display level displays the entity name and the entity definition inside the entity box. Most commonly used in enterprise data models and conceptual data models.	CUSTOMER A CUSTOMER is a person or organization who has rented a movie within the past year.
Entity	This display level displays the entity name inside the entity box. Most commonly used in enterprise data models and conceptual data models, although they also are used in the logical data model.	CUSTOMER
Icon	This display level displays an icon that is representative of the entity with the name of the entity inside the entity box. Most commonly used in enterprise data models and conceptual data models.	 CUSTOMER
Keys	This display level displays the entity name and all the attributes that are part of a key group inside the box. Note that the entity box has two sections, the top is for the primary key group attributes, and the bottom half is for all the other key group attributes. Most commonly used in logical data models.	CUSTOMER customer number customer address customer last name
Primary Key	This display level displays the entity name and the primary key group attributes inside the entity box. Most commonly used in logical data models, although they also are used in the enterprise data models and conceptual data models.	CUSTOMER customer number

For a better understanding of when to use and how to use these display levels, please see Part IV, which covers the logical data model in more detail.

In a physical data model, there are seven different Display Levels, as described in Table 23.

Table 23. Physical Data Model Display Levels

Display Level	Description	Example
Column	This display level displays a table, with all its columns inside the table box. Note that the table box has two sections, the top is for the primary key columns. And the bottom half is for all the non-primary key columns. The column display level is the default display level in erwin DM and is the standard format used in the data modeling industry for a physical data model. Most commonly used in physical data models.	CUSTOMER customer_number customer_address customer_city customer_first_name customer_last_name customer_state customer_zip_code email
Comment	This display level displays the table name and the table comment (the physical version of a definition) inside the table box. Not very commonly used, but found in unique physical data models.	CUSTOMER A CUSTOMER is a person or organization who has rented a movie within the past year.
Icon	This display level displays an icon that is representative of the table with the name of the table inside the table box. Not very commonly used, but found in unique physical data models.	CUSTOMER
Keys	This display level displays the table name and all the columns that are part of an index or constraint (key) inside the table box. Note that the table box has two sections, the top is for the primary index columns, and the bottom half is for all the other index and constraints columns. Most commonly used in physical data models.	CUSTOMER customer_number customer_address customer_last_name

Display Level	Description	Example
Order	Most commonly used in physical data models. This display level displays a table, with all its columns inside the table box. Note that the table box does not separate the primary key index columns from the non-primary key index columns. Most commonly used in physical data models.	CUSTOMER customer_address customer_city customer_first_name customer_last_name customer_number customer_state customer_zip_code email
Primary Key	This display level displays the table name and the primary key index columns inside the table box. Most commonly used in physical data models.	CUSTOMER customer_number
Table	This display level displays the table name inside the table box. Most commonly used in physical data models.	CUSTOMER

For a better understanding of when to use and how to use these display levels, please see Part V, which covers the physical data model in more detail.

6. In the Model Explorer pane, click on the expand icon (⊞) next to the *ER Diagrams* node, to display all the ER Diagrams in the data model. See Figure 127.

Figure 127. Maximize the ER Diagram Node

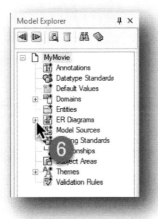

7. Right-click on the **ER_Diagarm_163** diagram.

8. Select the *Properties* option. See Figure 128.

Figure 128. Select the Properties Option

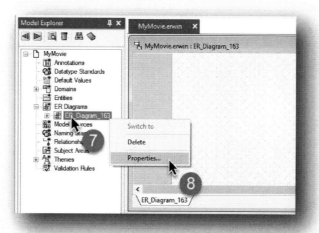

9. Note that the ER Diagram Editor dialog opens, and that there is only one diagram. Whenever an erwin Data Model is created, by default, it creates one ER Diagram. In Chapter 20, we discuss Subject Areas and Diagrams in more detail. See Figure 129.

Figure 129. ER Diagram Editor Dialog

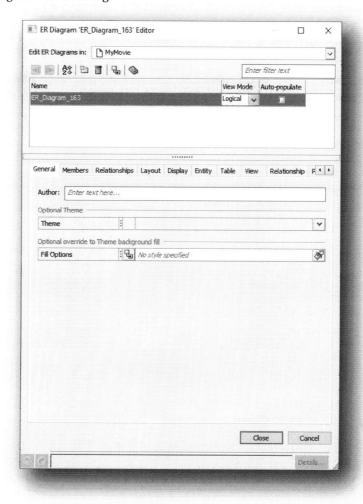

ER stands for Entity Relation. The ER Diagram is an Entity Relational Diagram, and in the earlier days, erwin was spelled ERwin, which stood for Entity Relation for Windows.

10. Click once on the name of the diagram to enter the edit state of the name. Then change it to **Conceptual Model**. See Figure 130.

Figure 130. Rename the Diagram to Conceptual Model

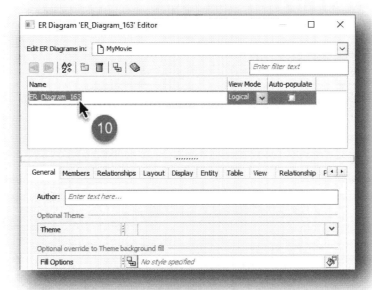

11. Click on the *Entity* tab to change the display level to definition.

12. On the Entity tab, note the section to change the *display level*, click on the drop-down to expose all the display levels, and select the *Definition* display level. See Figure 131.

13. While we are here, let us take a quick tour of how the erwin DM dialogs operate. Notice in Figure 132 the five sections of the dialog pane.

The top section is the parent object section, which is where one can change the parent object level. Once the parent object has changed, the focus of objects changes to the possible objects of the new parent. The next section is the object section, which is where one can change the object in focus. The properties section is where one can interact with the object in focus, changing all the available properties. In our tutorial, we changed the display level, and this is a property of the diagram. The action section allows one to apply the changes or to cancel all the changes performed from when the dialog opened. The advisory section provides a close view of the advisory pane, with the undo and redo buttons. When something does not work as expected, this provides insight as to why it did not perform as expected.

Figure 131. Change the Display Level to Definition

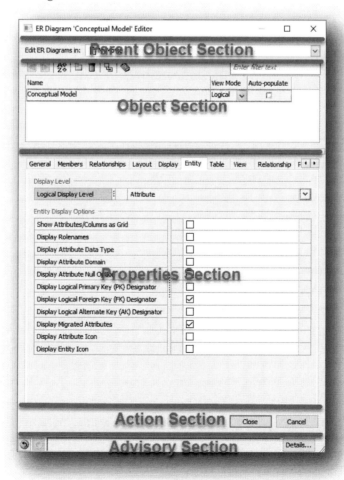

Figure 132. erwin DM Dialog Sections

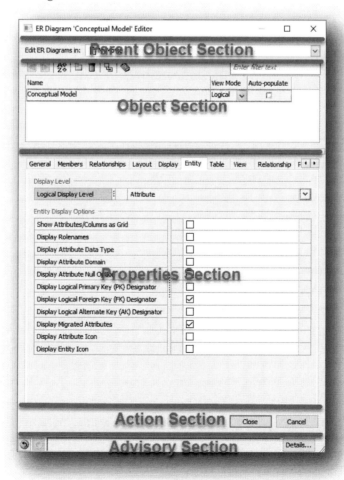

As we explore more of erwin DM over the following chapters, you will notice a common trend in how the dialogs are structured. Whenever the dialog has an object that has a parent, the parent object section is available, and there usually is always an object section. One exception to this is the model properties dialog, which does not have this section. Almost all dialogs have a properties and action section. And those dialogs that have a direct impact on the data model have the advisory section. You might also have picked up on our terminology earlier about applying changes or canceling changes. It is always essential to understand that whatever one does in the dialogs gets applied immediately to the model. In other words, as you change the display level earlier, if there were entities in the data model, they would change as you changed the property in the dialog. Also, notice that instead of an apply button on the dialog, there is a close button. This is because the changes get applied immediately to the model. Furthermore, the cancel button behaves like an undo command for all changes that occurred since the dialog opened.

 If an accidental action cannot be easily unchecked or reversed, and if you do not want to cancel all the changes performed in the dialog screen session by using the Cancel button, then the Undo button in the advisory section can perform an undo of the action and take into consideration all the ripple effects that the action caused.

14. When finished, click the *Close* button to dismiss the ER Diagram dialog.

15. Click on the Maximize button to maximize the model in the diagram pane. See Figure 133.

Figure 133. Maximize Data Model in Diagram Pane

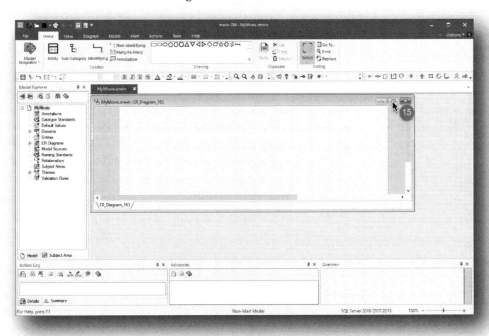

Now that we have finished setting up the display format, we need to create the business objects in the conceptual data model from the initial requirements session step 2.

16. Click on the *Entity* button on the ribbon to add our first business object. See Figure 134.

Figure 134. Click on the Entity Button

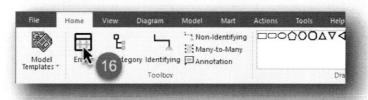

17. Now click in the data model diagram to create our first business object.

18. While the business object name is highlighted, rename it to **Customer**. See Figure 135.

Figure 135. Rename Business Object to Customer.

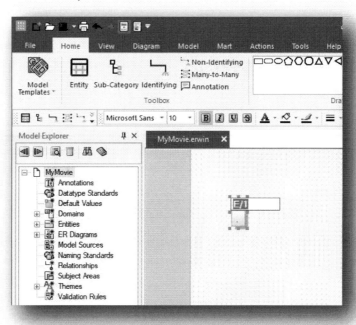

19. Click outside of the business object to apply the name change, taking note of the display level applied to the business object, the Definition Display Level.

20. We are going to repeat the same steps, but this time hold the Ctrl key in during the placement of the new business objects. Do this for six more business objects, releasing the Ctrl key after placing the sixth one.

21. Next, we need to rename the business object and capture their definitions.

In erwin DM, holding in the Ctrl key allows for the placement of multiple objects in succession. But note that it does not give the ability to name the objects immediately.

22. Click twice on the name of the **E/2** business object. Do not double-click, but instead pause between clicks. If the Entity dialog opens, close it and re-attempt the two clicks, making sure to pause in between and that you are clicking on the name and not the business object.

23. Observe that the name of the business object is highlighted for renaming. Rename it to **Employee**. Click outside of the business object to apply the name change.

24. This time double click on the **E/3** business object. Notice that the Entity editor dialog appears. The Entity Editor dialog is the dialog that is used to manage all interactions with the entity objects. Even though we refer to them as business objects at the enterprise and conceptual data model levels, in erwin DM, they refer to them as entities.

25. Note that the Entity Editor dialog does not have a Parent Object Section, as observed in the Diagram Editor dialog. All entity parents are the data model itself, and therefore there is only one parent object and no need to have this displayed in the dialog.

26. If the Definition tab is not displayed, click on the *Definition* tab. See Figure 136.

Figure 136. Click on the Definition Tab

27. Click once on the **E/3** business object name to enter the rename mode. Rename it to **Movie**.

28. Click in the *Definition* field to add the definition of the **Movie** business object.

29. Enter the following definition 'A MOVIE is any video that can be rented.'

30. Click on the **E/4** business object and repeat the process of capturing the name and definition of all the business objects, as per Table 24. Don't forget to do the definition of **Customer** and **Employee**.

Table 24. Business Object Definitions of MyMovie

Business Object	Definition
Customer	A CUSTOMER is a person or organization who has rented a movie within the past year.
Employee	EMPLOYEE is a person that works at the MyMovie STORE.
Movie	A MOVIE is any video that can be rented.
Movie Copy	A MOVIE COPY is a single copy of a MOVIE.
Movie Rental	A MOVIE RENTAL is a record that is kept on every MOVIE in the STORE on who and when a MOVIE is rented.
Payment	A PAYMENT is received when a CUSTOMER rents a MOVIE COPY.
Store	A STORE is the physical location of MyMovies stores.

31. When finished, press the *Close* button to dismiss the Entity Editor dialog. Observe the Conceptual Data model with all the business objects and their definitions displayed.

32. Click outside of the business objects to release any selected objects.

33. Click on the *Diagram* ribbon to display the layout options. See Figure 137.

Figure 137. Click the Diagram Ribbon

34. Click on the *Hierarchical* layout option to lay out all the business objects neatly. See Figure 138.

Figure 138. Click on the Hierarchical Layout Options

35. Observe how the conceptual data model lays this out neatly.

36. Next, we need to capture the business rules from the initial requirements session's step 3. In Table 25, we have repeated the summarized output of step 3 for ease of reading.

Table 25. Business Rules Summarized

From Business Object	To Business Object	Type of Business Rule
Customer	Movie Rental	One to Zero, One or Many
Customer	Payment	One to Zero, One or Many
Payment	Movie Rental	One to One or Many
Employee	Payment	One to Zero, One or Many
Employee	Movie Rental	One to Zero, One or Many
Movie Copy	Movie Rental	One to Zero, One or Many
Movie	Movie Copy	One to One or Many
Store	Employee	One to Zero, One or Many
Movie	Store	Many to Many

37. Click the **Identifying** relationship button on the Toolbox Toolbar. See Figure 139.

Figure 139. Click the Identifying Relationship Button

38. Click on the **Customer** business object to select the from business object in the business rule.

39. Then click on the **Movie Rental** business object to select the to business object to capture the business rule between these two objects.

40. While holding down the Ctrl key, capture the remaining business rules that are *One-To-...*, as listed in Table 25.

41. You might notice that all the relationships are defined as *One-to-Zero, One or Many*. Still, according to our table, the relationships between **Payment** to **Movie Rental** and **Movie** to **Movie Copy** are meant to be *One-to-One or Many*. To correct these, double click on the business rule from **Payment** to **Movie Rental** to open the Relationship Editor dialog. See Figure 140.

Figure 140. Double Click on Business Rule Between 'Payment' to 'Movie Rental'

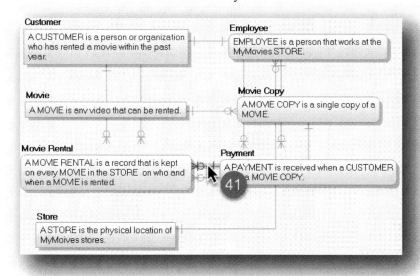

42. In the Relationship Editor dialog, click on the *General* tab.

43. Under Cardinality, change it to *One or More* to reflect the business rule. See Figure 141.

Figure 141. Change the Cardinality to One or More

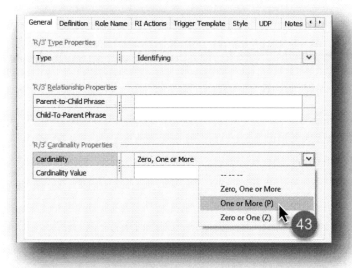

44. In the object section of the dialog, change to the **Movie** to **Movie Copy** business rule, and change the cardinality to *One or More*.

45. Notice how difficult it was to identify the business rule as all the business rules are labeled 'R/n,' where 'n' is the numeric value of the business rule. We return to this in step 51.

46. There is still one business rule that is not captured yet, the business rule between **Movie** and **Store**, that is the *Many-to-Many* relationship.

47. Click the *Close* button to close the Relationship Editor dialog.

48. Click the *Many-to-Many* relationship button on the Toolbox Toolbar. See Figure 142.

Figure 142. Click on the Many-to-Many Relationship Button

49. Click on the **Movie** business object, then click on the **Store** business object to capture the last remaining business rule.

50. Now let's rename the business rules to something more meaningful. Double click on the business rule you just created between **Movie** and **Store** to open the Relationship Editor dialog again.

51. Observe in the Relationship Editor dialog that there are three descriptive verbs that we are interested in capturing to reflect the business rule, as shown in Figure 143:

- Business Rule Name,
- Parent-to-Child Phrase (this explains the business rule from the parent's perspective),
- Child-to-Parent Phrase (this explains the business rule from the child's perspective).

52. Click on the **Movie** to **Store** business rule name, it should be called 'R/9' at this point, and rename it to '**MOVIEs is in STOREs.**'

53. Change the Parent-to-Child Phrase to 'is in.' Notice that one would read the business rule as 'MOVIEs is in STOREs,' also notice how it reflects the name of the business rule.

54. Change the Child-to-Parent Phrase to 'rents.' This reads as 'STOREs rents MOVIEs.'

55. Capture the rest of the business rule descriptive verbs.

56. When finished, click the *Close* button to close the Relationship Editor dialog.

57. We have finished capturing all the conceptual data model objects, but it still does not look elegant.

58. Next, we are going to explore the functionality in erwin DM to layout the model neatly.

Before we do this, click outside of the business objects to release any selected objects. We need to do this as erwin DM allows for laying out a selection within the data model. Seeing that we want to lay out the entire data model, we need to release any selected objects first.

Figure 143. The Three Descriptive Verb of a Business Rule

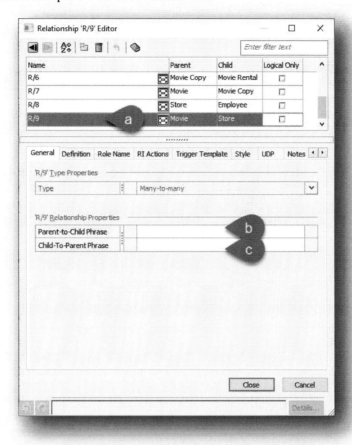

 erwin DM has a switch 'Layout in Place' that allows the layout of objects in the location that they were. If this switch is off, erwin DM will layout the objects in a new area in the diagram.

59. Explore and test all the layout options to see how they can automate the layout of the data model, including selecting a subset and using the 'Layout in Place' switch.

60. Finally, ensure no objects are selected and click on the *Hierarchical* layout option to lay out all the business objects neatly. See Figure 144.

Figure 144. Click on the Orthogonal Layout Options

61. Observe how the conceptual data model lays out neatly.

62. Save and close your MyMovie data model.

Key Learnings

- A conceptual data model is a set of symbols and text that represents business objects and the rules binding them for a specific application scope and a particular audience.

- The conceptual data model differs from the enterprise data model due to its scope.

- The relational conceptual data model includes business objects, their definitions, and the relationships that capture the rules binding these business objects.

- The dimensional conceptual data model includes business objects, their definitions, and the navigation paths required to analyze measures at different levels of detail.

- Follow a five-step approach to building a conceptual data model.

- erwin DM provides a rich set of features to support conceptual data modeling, including display levels, notations, and layout options.

Requirements now

Forget the technology

Enter logical

The highlighted row in Table 26 shows the focus of this chapter, which is the Logical Data Model (LDM).

Table 26. The Logical Data Model is the Focus of this Chapter

	Relational	Dimensional
Enterprise Data Model (EDM)	'One-pager' on organization-wide business objects and rules	
Conceptual Data Model (CDM)	'One-pager' on business rules	'One-pager' on navigation
Logical Data Model (LDM)	Detailed business solution on business rules	Detailed business solution on navigation
Physical Data Model (PDM)	Detailed technical solution	
Operational Data Model (ODM)	Technical implementation	

A logical data model takes the business needs that were defined in the conceptual data model down to the next level of a business solution. Once you understand at a broad level the scope of a project, the next step is to come up with a resolution in the form of a logical data model. This chapter explains the logical data model, along with a comparison of relational and dimensional mindsets. Then, for relational models, normalization is discussed.

Logical Data Model Explained

A logical data model is a business solution to a business problem. It is how the modeler captures the business requirements without complicating the model with implementation database-specific concerns.

In the conceptual data model, we might learn, for example, what the terms, business rules, and scope, would be for a new order entry system. After understanding the requirements for the order entry system, we create a logical data model containing all of the attributes and business rules needed to deliver the application. For example, the conceptual data model shows that a **Customer** may place one or many **Orders**. The logical data model captures all of the details behind **Customer** and **Order,** such as the customer's name, their address, the order number, and what is ordered.

Relational and Dimensional Logical Data Models

Recall from the introduction earlier, that relational data modeling is the process of capturing how the business *works* by precisely representing business rules, while dimensional data modeling is the process of capturing how the business is *monitored* by precisely representing navigation. There are both relational and dimensional logical data models. You have seen examples of both relational and dimensional conceptual data models (recall Figure 121 and Figure 122 from Chapter 10 on conceptual data modeling); Figure 145 and Figure 146 show these two examples at a logical level. Let's go through how to build each of these, starting with relational.

Relational Logical Data Model Example

The relational logical data model includes entities along with their definitions, relationships, and attributes. For example, Figure 145 contains a subset of the airline organization's relational logical data model.

Business Rules:

- Each **Passenger** may have one or many **Bookings**.
- Each **Booking** can have one or many **Passengers**. (Notice the translation of the Many-to-Many relationship in the data model)

Alternatively, one could interpret these differently if there was a business value of the intermediate entity, such as:

- Each **Passenger** may have one or many **Passenger Booking**s.
- Each **Passenger Booking** must be made by one **Passenger**.
- Each Passenger Booking must have one Booking.
- Each **Booking** must have one or many **Passenger Booking**s.

As demonstrated, the term **Passenger Booking** is not a typical term used in the airline organization; hence it has no business value. So when interpreting the business relationship, we shortcut these to a many-to-many relationship when explaining the relationship.

- Each **Booking** may issue one or many **Tickets**.
- Each **Ticket** must be issued by one **Booking**.
- Each **Passenger** may have one or many **Tickets**.
- Each **Ticket** must belong to one **Passenger**.
- Each Ticket must have one Departure Terminal.
- Each **Departure Terminal** can have one or many **Tickets**.
- Each Ticket must have one Destination Terminal.
- Each **Destination Terminal** can have one or many **Tickets**.

Figure 145. Airline Organization Relational Logical Data Model

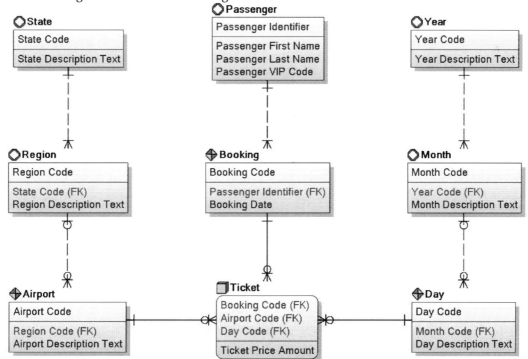

 A quick way to identify if the intermediate entity has any business value is to see if any attributes could be classified under the intermediate entity, besides the two foreign keys. Next is to identify if there is a business name for this object. If both are 'No,' then it is an intermediate entity in a many-to-many relationship.

Dimensional Logical Data Model Example

Figure 146. Airline Organization Dimensional Logical Data Model

We take measures such as **Ticket Price Amount** up and down hierarchies. In this case, we would like to see **Ticket Price Amount** at an **Airport**, **Booking**, and **Day** level, then navigate to higher levels such as viewing **Ticket Price Amount** at a **Region** or **State** level instead of the more granular **Airport** level.

The **Airport** is an exciting hierarchy level to discuss. Often when building a dimensional data model, we trace back the measures and ways of looking at these measures to a relational data model that eventually becomes the source for the dimensional data. On our relational data model in Figure 145, we have an **Airport Departure Terminal** and an **Airport Destination Terminal** in the **Ticket** entity. On the corresponding dimensional data model, however, there is no need to know what the **Airport Destination Terminal** is, only the **Airport Departure Terminal**. Therefore we only need to trace one of the relationships to the **Terminal** entity. Furthermore, there is no need to know the **Terminal**, only the higher level of **Airport**. Therefore, each **Airport** has to be derived from the corresponding **Airport Code** because, in this case, **Airport** was requested as a more manageable level to navigate than **Terminal**.

Creating a Relational Logical Data Model

Normalization is the main technique to create the relational logical data model. Normalization is the process of applying a set of rules to organize attributes, and these rules can be summarized in one sentence:

> *Make sure every attribute is* <u>*single-valued*</u> *and* <u>*provides a fact*</u> <u>*entirely*</u> *and* <u>*only*</u> *about its primary key.*

The underlined terms require more of an explanation.

<u>Single-valued</u> means an attribute must contain only one piece of information. If **Consumer Name** contains both the consumer's first and last name, for example, we must split **Consumer Name** into two attributes: **Consumer First Name** and **Consumer Last Name**.

<u>Provides a fact</u> means that a given primary key value always returns no more than one of every attribute that is identified by this key. If a **Customer Identifier** value of *'123'*, for example, returns three customer last names (*'Smith,' 'Jones,' and 'Roberts'*), it violates this part of the normalization definition.

<u>Entirely</u> means that the minimal set of attributes that uniquely identify an instance of the entity is present in the primary key. For example, if there are two attributes in an entity's primary key, but only one is needed for uniqueness, the additional attribute should be removed from the key.

<u>Only</u> means that each attribute must provide a fact about the primary key and nothing else. That is, there can be no hidden dependencies. For example, assume an **Order Number** identifies an **Order**. Within **Order**, there are many attributes, including **Order Scheduled Delivery Date**, **Order Actual Delivery Date**, and **Order On Time Indicator**. **Order On Time Indicator** contains either a *'Yes'* or a *'No,'* providing a fact about whether the **Order Actual Delivery Date** is less than or equal to the **Order Scheduled Delivery Date**. **Order On Time Indicator**, therefore, provides a fact about **Order Actual Delivery Date** and **Order Scheduled Delivery Date**, not

directly about **Order Number**. **Order On Time Indicator** is an example of a derived attribute, meaning it is calculated. Derived attributes are removed from a normalized model.

We apply normalization in a series of rules in small steps, where each step (or level of normalization) checks something that moves us towards our goal. Most data professionals would agree that the full set of normalization levels is the following:

- first normal form (1NF)
- second normal form (2NF)
- third normal form (3NF)
- Boyce/Codd normal form (BCNF or 3.5NF)
- fourth normal form (4NF)
- fifth normal form (5NF)
- sixth normal form (6NF)

Each level of normalization includes the lower levels of rules that precede it. If a model is in 5NF, it is also in 4NF, BCNF, and so on. Even though there are higher levels of normalization than 3NF, many interpret the term *normalized* to mean 3NF.

Because the higher levels of normalization (BCNF, 4NF, 5NF, and 6NF) cover specific situations that occur less frequently than the first three levels, this chapter details only the first three normal forms. See Figure 147, which contains a bunch of employee attributes.

Figure 147. Chaotic Pre-normalized State

Often definitions are of poor quality or missing entirely, and let's assume that this is the case with this **Employee** entity. We are told, however, that **Employee Vested Indicator** captures whether an **Employee** is eligible for retirement benefits (a value of 'Y' for 'yes' means the employee is eligible, and a value of 'N' for 'no' means the employee is not eligible). And this indicator is derived from the employee's start date. For example, if an employee has worked for the company for at least five years, then this indicator contains the value 'Y.'

What is lacking at this point, and is solved through normalization, is putting these attributes into the right entities.

It is beneficial to have some sample values for each of these attributes, so let's assume the spreadsheet in Table 27 is a representative set of employee values.

Table 27. Sample Employees

Emp Id	Dept Cd	Phone 1	Phone 2	Phone 3	Emp Name	Dept Name	Emp Start Date	Emp Vested Ind
123	A	973-555-1212	678-333-3333	343-222-1111	Henry Winkler	Data Admin	4/1/2012	N
789	A	732-555-3333	678-333-3333	343-222-1111	Steve Martin	Data Admin	3/5/2007	Y
565	B	333-444-1111	516-555-1212	343-222-1111	Mary Smith	Data Warehouse	2/25/2006	Y
744	A	232-222-2222	678-333-3333	343-222-1111	Bob Jones	Data Admin	5/5/2011	N

First Normal Form (1NF)

Recall that the series of rules can be summarized as: *Every attribute is single-valued and provides a fact entirely and only about its primary key.* First Normal Form (1NF) is the 'single-valued' part. It means that for a given primary-key value, we can find, at most, one of every attribute that depends on that primary key. Ensuring each attribute provides a fact about its primary key, includes correcting the more glaring issue shown in Table 27. As well as addressing repeating groups and multi-valued attributes. Specifically, the modeler needs to:

- **Move repeating attributes to a new entity**. When there are two or more of the same attribute in the same entity, they are called repeating attributes. The reason repeating attributes violate 1NF is that for a given primary key value, we are getting more than one value back for the same attribute. Repeating attributes often take a sequence number as part of their name, such as phone numbers in this employee example.

- **Separate multi-valued attributes**. *Multi-valued* means that within the same attribute, we are storing at least two distinct values. In other words, at least two different business objects are hiding in one attribute. For example, **Employee Name** may contain both a first name and last name. **Employee First Name** and **Employee Last Name** can be considered distinct attributes, and therefore, 'Henry Winkler' is multi-valued because it contains both 'Henry' and 'Winkler.' After talking with a business expert and answering these questions based on the sample data from Table 27, we update the model, which appears in Figure 148.

We learned that although **Phone Number 1**, **Phone Number 2**, and **Phone Number 3** appear as repeating attributes. They are three different pieces of information based upon the sample values given. **Phone Number 3** contained the same value for all four employees, and we learned after validating with the business expert that this is the organization's phone number. **Phone Number**

2 varied by department, so we renamed this attribute to **Department Phone Number**. **Phone Number 3** is different for each employee, and we learned that this is the **Employee Phone Number**. We also were told that **Employee Name** does contain more than one piece of information and, therefore, should be split into **Employee First Name** and **Employee Last Name**.

Figure 148. From Chaos to 1NF

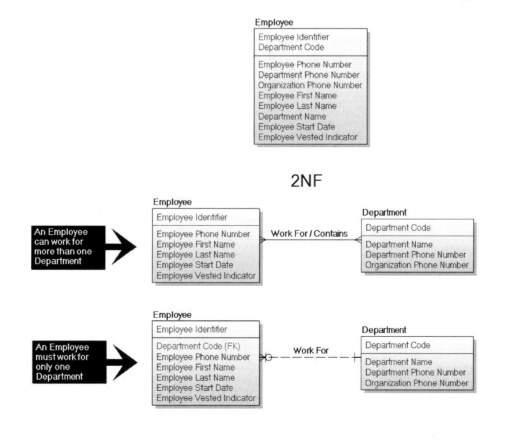

Second Normal Form (2NF)

Recall that the series of rules can be summarized as: *Every attribute is single-valued and provides a fact entirely and only about its primary key.* First Normal Form (1NF) is the 'single-valued' part. Second Normal Form (2NF) is the 'entirely' part. Meaning that each entity must have a minimal set of attributes that uniquely identify each entity instance.

Figure 149. Employee Example in 2NF

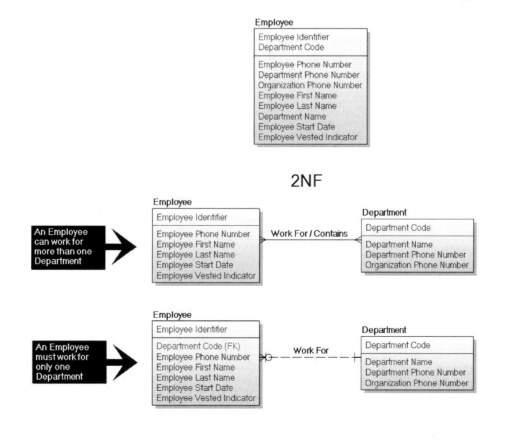

Third Normal Form (3NF)

Recall that the series of rules can be summarized as: *Every attribute is single-valued and provides a fact entirely and only about its primary key*. First Normal Form (1NF) is the 'single-valued' part. Second Normal Form (2NF) is the 'completely' part. Third Normal Form (3NF) is the 'only' part.

3NF requires the removal of hidden dependencies. Each attribute must be directly dependent on the primary key and not directly dependent on any other attributes within the same entity.

The data model is a communication tool. The relational logical data model communicates which attributes are facts about the primary key and only the primary key. Hidden dependencies complicate the model and make it difficult to determine how to retrieve values for each attribute.

To resolve a hidden dependency, you either need to remove the attribute that is a fact about the non-primary key attribute(s) from the model. Or you need to create a new entity with a different primary key for the attribute that is dependent on the non-primary key attribute(s).

Note that **Employee Vested Indicator** may be a fact about **Employee Start Date** as **Employee Vested Indicator** is a calculated 'Y' or 'N' based upon the employee's start date. Figure 150 shows the model now in 3NF after removing the derived attribute, **Employee Vested Indicator.**

Figure 150. Employee Example in 3NF

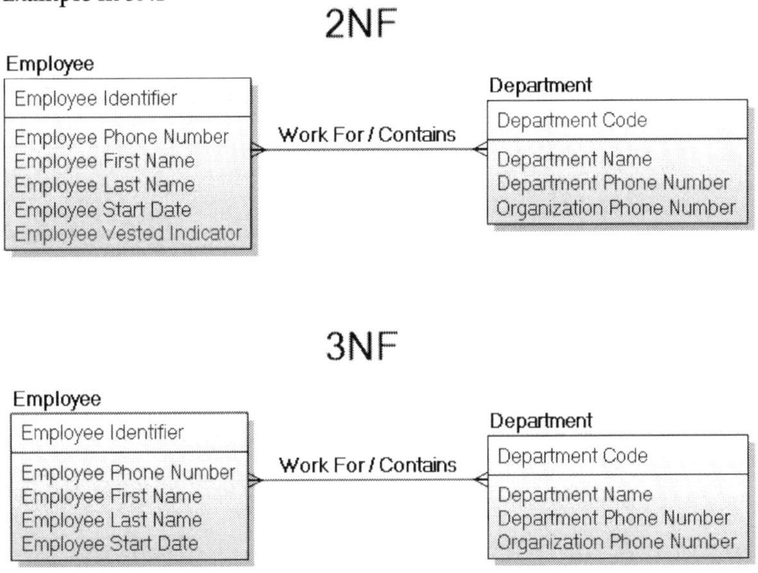

2NF

```
Employee                                    Department
┌─────────────────────────┐                 ┌─────────────────────────────┐
│ Employee Identifier      │                 │ Department Code              │
├─────────────────────────┤ Work For / Contains ├─────────────────────────────┤
│ Employee Phone Number    │─────────────────┤ Department Name              │
│ Employee First Name      │                 │ Department Phone Number      │
│ Employee Last Name       │                 │ Organization Phone Number    │
│ Employee Start Date      │                 └─────────────────────────────┘
│ Employee Vested Indicator│
└─────────────────────────┘
```

3NF

```
Employee                                    Department
┌─────────────────────────┐                 ┌─────────────────────────────┐
│ Employee Identifier      │                 │ Department Code              │
├─────────────────────────┤ Work For / Contains ├─────────────────────────────┤
│ Employee Phone Number    │─────────────────┤ Department Name              │
│ Employee First Name      │                 │ Department Phone Number      │
│ Employee Last Name       │                 │ Organization Phone Number    │
│ Employee Start Date      │                 └─────────────────────────────┘
└─────────────────────────┘
```

Creating a Dimensional Logical Data Model

Recall the dimensional data model from earlier in this chapter, repeated here in Figure 151.

Ticket is an example of a meter, which is an entity containing a related set of measures, distinguished by the meter icon (▢). A meter is not a person, place, event, or thing, as we find on the relational model. Instead, it is a bucket of standard measures; in this case, just the measure

Ticket Price Amount. As a group, standard measures address a business process such as **Profitability**, **Employee Satisfaction**, or **Sales**.

The meter icon is represented by a square, the meter, and several layers extending back from the square signifying many meters.

The dimension icon is represented by a multi-dimensional image, signifying the different dimensions.

The snowflakes icon is represented by an image that is surrounding the outside of the dimension image, signifying that it is not a dimension, but is closely connected to it.

Figure 151. Airline Organization Dimensional Logical Data Model

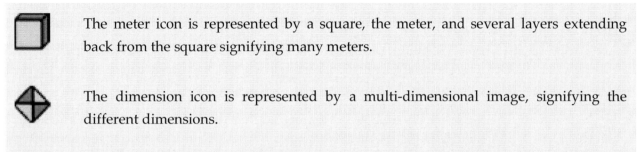

A meter is further classified into one of four types:

- **Aggregate**. Also known as summarization, an aggregate contains stored information at a higher level of granularity than translation level details. Aggregates provide quick access to data and can be very user-friendly structures for users and reporting tools. **Ticket Price** is an aggregate.

- **Atomic**. It contains the lowest level of detail available in the business, often the same level of detail that exists in operational systems. An example of an atomic meter in the airline ticketing system could be that **Ticket Price** is the sum of the base airfare, federal excise taxes, flight segment taxes, passenger facility charges, and security fees.

- **Cumulative**. Also known as accumulating, cumulative captures how long it takes to complete a business process. For example, tracking how long it takes from application through completion of a home mortgage application would be represented in a cumulative meter.

- **Snapshot**. It contains time-related information that details specific steps in the life of the entity. For example, snapshot information about a sale could contain information such as when the order was created, confirmed, shipped, delivered, and paid.

Airport, **Booking**, and **Day** are examples of dimensions, distinguished by the dimensions icon (⬦). A dimension is a subject whose purpose is to add meaning to the measures. All of the different ways of filtering, sorting, and summing measures make use of dimensions. Dimensions have their own attributes.

A dimension is further classified into one of six types:

- **Fixed Dimension**. Also known as a Type 0 Slowly Changing Dimension (SCD for short), a fixed dimension contains values that do not change over time. For example, Gender is a fixed dimension containing the values 'Male' and 'Female.'

- **Degenerate**. A dimension whose attribute(s) are moved to the meter. A degenerate dimension is most common when the original dimension contained only a single data attribute, such as a transaction identifier like an **Order Number**.

- **Multi-Valued**. A multi-valued dimension can help you model a situation where there are multiple values for an attribute or column. For example, a health care bill can have a line item of **Diagnosis** for which there could be multiple values. Best practice modeling dictates that there should be a single value for each line item. To model this multi-valued situation, you could create a multi-valued structure that captures the diagnosis information and weighs each diagnosis so that the total adds up to one.

- **Ragged**. In a ragged dimension, the parent of at least one member is missing from the level immediately above the member. Ragged dimensions allow for hierarchies of indeterminate depth, such as organizational charts and parts explosions.

- **Shrunken**. A shrunken table is a version of the meter often containing attributes that are not measures. Often it is used when there are large text strings that are at the same level of detail as the meter and stored in a separate structure for space or query efficiency reasons.

- **Slowly Changing Type 0 through 6**. Slowly Changing Dimension (SCD) Type 0 is equivalent to the fixed dimension concept, where values do not change over time. Slowly Changing Dimension Type 1 means we are only storing the current view and ignoring history. Slowly Changing Dimension Type 2 means we want all history (Type 2 is the Time Machine). Slowly Changing Dimension Type 3 means we want only some history, such as the most current state and the previous state or the most current state and the original state. Slowly Changing Dimension Type 6 is when we have a complex dimension with varying history needs; for example, if part of the dimension is a Type 1, part is a Type 2, and part is a Type 3 (1 + 2 + 3 = 6). Types 0, 1, 2, and 3 are the building blocks for more advanced history requirements such as the Type 6.

Region & **State**, **Month** & **Year,** and **Passenger** are examples of snowflakes, distinguished by the snowflakes icon (⬡). These are higher levels in a hierarchy. A hierarchy is when a higher level can contain many lower levels, but a lower level can belong to at most one higher level. These higher levels indicate that we can view the measures in the meter at these levels, as well. For example, we can view **Ticket Price Amount** at the **State**, **Year**, and **Passenger** levels. Snowflakes can also have their own attributes.

Key Learnings

- A logical data model represents a detailed business solution.

- A relational logical data model represents how the business works. A dimensional logical data model represents what the business is monitoring.

- Normalizing is a formal process of asking business questions. Normalization ensures that every attribute is a fact about the key (1NF), the whole key (2NF), and nothing but the key (3NF).

- There are several essential terms unique to dimensional modeling, including meters and dimensions.

- There are different types of meters, including aggregate, atomic, cumulative, and snapshot.

- There are different types of dimensions, including fixed dimension, degenerate, multi-valued, ragged, shrunken, and slow-changing.

Let's get Physical
Compromise the Logical
Efficiency rules

The highlighted row in Table 28 shows the focus of this chapter, which is the Physical Data Model (PDM).

Table 28. The Physical Data Model is the Focus of this Chapter

	Relational	Dimensional
Enterprise Data Model (EDM)	'One-pager' on organization-wide business objects and rules	
Conceptual Data Model (CDM)	'One-pager' on business rules	'One-pager' on navigation
Logical Data Model (LDM)	Detailed business solution on business rules	Detailed business solution on navigation
Physical Data Model (PDM)	Detailed technical solution	
Operational Data Model (ODM)	Technical implementation	

A physical data model takes the business solution defined in a logical data model to the next level of a technical solution. That is, once you solve the problem independent of software and hardware concerns, you can then make adjustments for software and hardware.

This chapter explains the most popular techniques for making adjustments to a business solution (logical data model) to create an efficient technical solution (physical data model). We explain the physical data model and then discuss the techniques of denormalization, views, indexing, and partitioning. Although these techniques apply to relational, dimensional, and NoSQL models, their names may differ depending on which type of model they apply.

Physical Data Model Explained

The physical data model is the logical data model compromised for specific software or hardware. On the enterprise data model, we learn about the terms and business rules. On the conceptual data model, we identify the scope and needs, leveraging the understandings from the enterprise data model. After understanding the need for a new solution, we create a logical data model representing the business solution. It contains all of the attributes and business rules needed to deliver the solution. For example, the enterprise data model shows **Customer** and **Order**, and that are related to each other. The conceptual data model shows that a **Customer** may place one or many **Orders**, in the context of the solution. The logical data model captures all of the details behind **Customer** and **Order,** such as the customer's **Name**, their **Address**, and the **Order Number**. After understanding the business solution, we move on to the technical solution and build the physical data model. We may make some modifications to **Customer** and **Order** structures, for example, for factors such as performance or storage.

Relational and Dimensional Physical Data Models

Recall from this section's introduction, that relational data modeling is the process of capturing how the business *works* by precisely representing business rules, while dimensional data modeling is the process of capturing how the business is *monitored* by precisely representing navigation. There are both relational and dimensional physical data models.

You have seen examples of both relational and dimensional conceptual and logical data models (recall Figure 121 and Figure 122 from the chapter on conceptual data modeling and Figure 145 and Figure 146 from the chapter on logical data modeling). Figure 152 and Figure 153 show these two examples at a physical level. Let's go through how to build each of these, starting with relational.

Relational Physical Data Model Example

The relational physical data model includes entities with their definitions, relationships, and columns along with their definitions. Note that in Database Management Systems (DBMS), the term *table* is used instead of the term *entity* and *column* instead of *attribute*. Figure 152 contains part of the airline organization's relational physical data model. Compromises such as combining **Terminal** and **Airport** into one structure are made to this model to improve data retrieval performance or to make it easier for developers to extract, transform, and load (ETL) data.

Figure 152. Airline Organization Relational Physical Data Model Subset

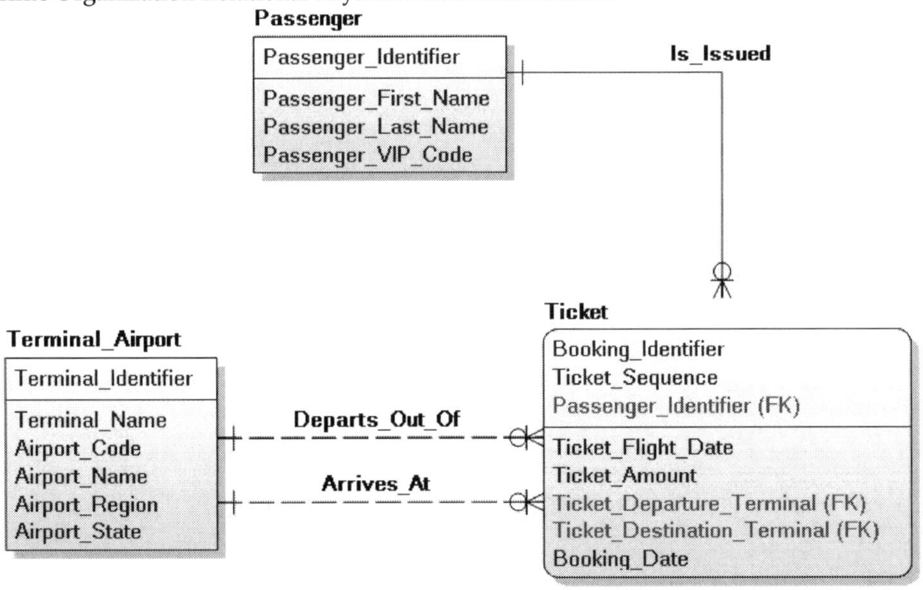

Dimensional Physical Data Model Example

To understand and document our reporting requirements, we can also build a dimensional physical data model, such as the example in Figure 153. This model, called a star schema, is similar to its logical counterpart, except that each dimension from the dimensional logical data model has been flattened on the model from Figure 146 into one structure, or the more recognized data warehousing notation in Figure 154.

Figure 153. Airline Organization Dimensional Physical Data Model

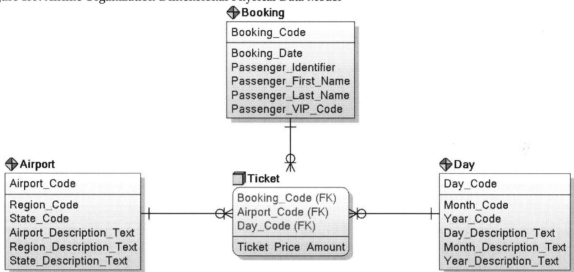

Figure 154. Previous Example Using Data Warehousing Notation

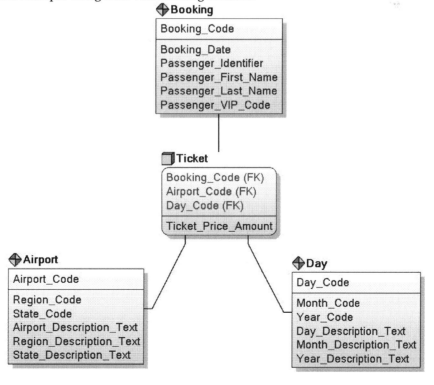

Denormalization

Denormalization is the process of selectively violating normalization rules and reintroducing redundancy into the data model and database. This extra redundancy can reduce data retrieval time, which is the primary reason for denormalizing. We can also denormalize to create a more user-friendly model. For example, we might decide to denormalize company information into an entity containing employee information because usually, when employee information is retrieved, company information is also retrieved.

There are several different ways to denormalize. In this section, we'll discuss the two most common, Rolldown and Rollup. Let's illustrate denormalization with an example of a company that sells ice cream toppings. An **Offering** is an ice cream topping such as 'chocolate sprinkles' or 'hot fudge.' A **Category** is a way of organizing these toppings, such as the 'Sprinkles' category containing the **Offerings** 'Chocolate Sprinkles' and 'Rainbow Sprinkles.' An **Offering** can belong to more than one **Category** as well, such as 'Chocolate Sprinkles' belonging to both the 'Sprinkles' and 'Chocolate' **Categories**.

We apply the rolldown and rollup techniques to **Offering**, **Category**, and **Assignment**. See Figure 155 for the normalized starting point, and Figure 156 and Figure 157 for their physical counterparts using each of these two techniques. Note that **Category Priority Number** is the popularity rating of a **Category**, and **Assignment Priority Number** is the popularity of an **Offering** within a **Category**.

Figure 155. Logical Data Model Example. Normalized Starting Point

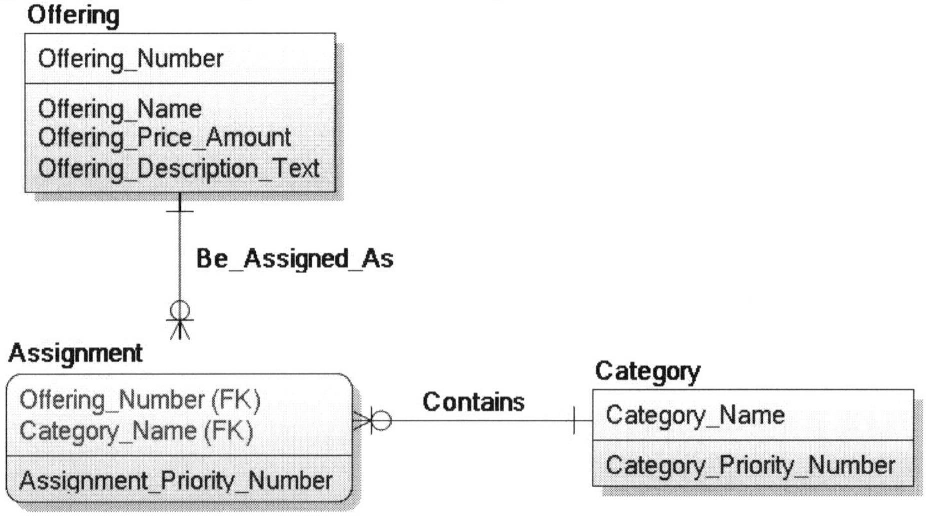

Rolldown Denormalization

Rolldown is the most common of the denormalization techniques. The parent entity in the relationship disappears, and all of the parent's columns and relationships move down to the child entity. You'll recall that the child entity is on the many side of the relationship and contains a foreign key back to the parent entity, which appears on the one side of the relationship.

Figure 156. Logical Data Model Example. Rolldown Denormalization

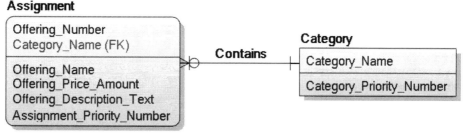

Figure 157. Logical Data Model Example. Rollup Denormalization

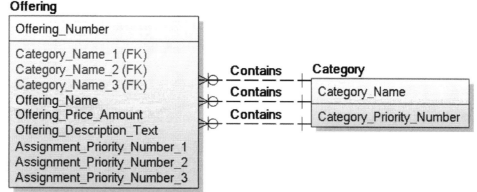

In addition to choosing denormalization because of the need for faster retrieval time or more user-friendly structures, often rolldown is chosen in the following situations:

- **When you need to maintain the flexibility of the normalized model.** Folding the columns and relationships together using rolldown still allows one-to-one and one-to-many relationships to be stored (but not enforced in the database). In Figure 156, for example, we did not lose the flexibility that an **Offering** can belong to many **Categories**.

- **When you want to reduce development time and complexity.** There is a direct relationship between the number of tables and relationships on a model and the amount of effort it takes to develop the application. A developer needs to write code that jumps from one table to another to collect specific columns, and this can take time and add complexity. Denormalizing into fewer tables using rolldown means the columns and relationships from different entities now exist in the same entity. In Figure 156, for example, if the developer needs to retrieve both offering information and the category name, they can easily do so from the same entity, **Assignment**.

Rollup Denormalization

In rollup, the same column or group of columns is repeated two or more times in the same entity. Also known as an *array*, rollup requires making the number of times something can occur static. Recall that in 1NF, we removed repeating groups; rollup means we are adding back in repeating groups. We had to decide in Figure 157, for example, that the maximum number of categories an offering can be assigned is three. In addition to choosing denormalization because of the need for faster retrieval time or more user-friendly structures, repeating groups are chosen in the following situations:

- **When it makes more sense to keep the parent entity instead of the child entity.** When the parent entity is going to be used more frequently than the child entity. Or when there are rules and columns to preserve in the parent entity format, it makes more sense to keep the parent entity.

- **When an entity instance never exceeds the fixed number of columns added.** In Figure 157, we are only allowing up to three categories for an offering. If we had a fourth category for an offering, for example, how would we handle this?

Star Schema

A star schema is the most common dimensional physical data model structure. The term *fact table* in the dimensional physical data model replaces the term *meter* in the dimensional logical data model, and the term *outrigger* in the dimensional physical data model replaces the term *snowflake* in the dimensional logical data model. A star schema results when each outrigger table is flattened into a single dimension table. The fact table is in the center of the model, and each of the dimensions relates to the fact table at the lowest level of detail. A star schema is relatively easy to create and implement, and it visually appears simplistic to both IT and the business. Recall the dimensional data model examples from Figure 151 and Figure 153. A star schema is when each hierarchy flattens into a single table. So on this star schema, **Passenger** flattens into **Booking**, **State** and **Region** flatten into **Airport**, and **Year** and **Month** flatten into **Day**.

Partitioning

Partitioning is the splitting up of a table into two or more tables. Vertical partitioning is the splitting up of columns as shown in Figure 158, and horizontal partitioning is the splitting up of rows as shown in Figure 159. It is common for both horizontal and vertical to be used together. That is, when splitting rows apart, we in many cases learn that certain columns only belong with one set of rows.

Both vertical and horizontal partitioning are common techniques when building analytics systems. A table might contain a large number of columns, and perhaps only a subset are volatile and change often. So this subset can be vertically partitioned into a separate table. Or we might have ten years of orders in a table. And to improve query performance, we horizontally partition by year so that queries run within a given year, perform much faster.

Partitioning can be used as a reactive technique, meaning that even after an application goes live, the designer might choose to add partitioning after monitoring performance and space and determine that an improvement is needed.

Figure 158. Vertical Partitioning Example

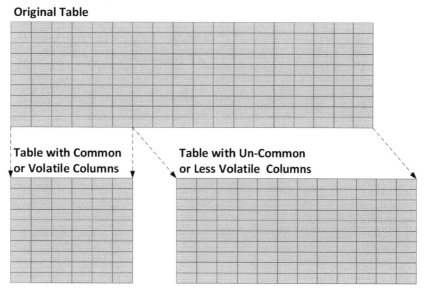

Figure 159. Horizontal Partitioning Example

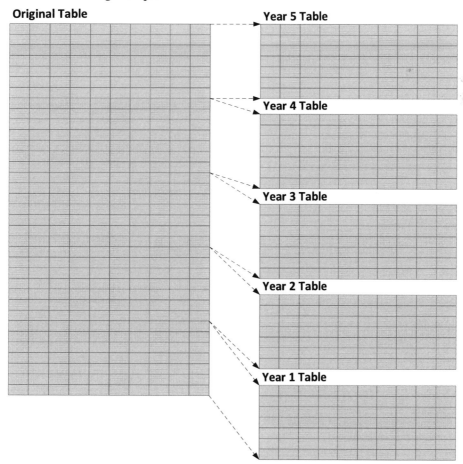

Key Learnings

- The physical data model builds upon the logical data model to produce a technical solution.

- Rolldown means the parent entity in the relationship disappears, and all of the parent's columns and relationships move down to the child entity.

- Rollup means the same column or group of columns is repeated two or more times in the same entity.

- A star schema results when each set of tables that make up a dimension, are flattened into a single table.

- Partitioning is the splitting up of a table into two or more tables. Vertical partitioning is the splitting up of columns, and horizontal partitioning is the splitting up of rows.

Beyond PDM

Model the DBMS

Need to know the start

The highlighted row in Table 29 shows the focus of this chapter, the Operational Data Model (ODM).

Table 29. The Operational Data Model is the Focus of this Chapter

	Relational	Dimensional
Enterprise Data Model (EDM)	'One-pager' on organization-wide business objects and rules	
Conceptual Data Model (CDM)	'One-pager' on business rules	'One-pager' on navigation
Logical Data Model (LDM)	Detailed business solution on business rules	Detailed business solution on navigation
Physical Data Model (PDM)	Detailed technical solution	
Operational Data Model (ODM)	Technical implementation	

An operational data model shows the technical implementation of a database. It is created by reverse-engineering the physical database and is used to compare against the physical data model to ensure that the physical data model is in sync with the database. It only holds physically implemented objects and properties of the database.

Operational Data Model Explained

If we go back to Chapter 8 and remember our comparison to the blueprints, the as-built blueprint was a reflection of the house as built. The same applies to the operational data model, and it has no more detail than what is physically in the database. The operational data model has only a loose connection to the physical data model through the comparison process, but it is a stand-alone data model. It provides a historical view of the state of the database at a point in time. This fact can be significant in the process of understanding how to implement new changes to the database. But unfortunately, this step gets neglected, and an operational data model does not get used, resulting in changes getting pushed into production that conflict with the physical database.

By using the operational data model, one can apply the production database schema to the physical data model. This process ensures that any future changes applied don't conflict with what is in production.

Creating an Operational Data Model in erwin DM

First, one needs to understand the purpose and scope of the operational data model. An operational data model is used to provide a true reflection of what is in the database at a current point in time.

From this, we can understand that the operational data model has close ties to the database and not the physical data model. Therefore, we do not use the traditional erwin DM design layer functionality of link, add, derive, and sync model source. For us to create a new operational data model, one needs to leverage different functionality, the reverse engineering functionality. We cover the reverse engineering functionality in Chapter 28 in-depth with a tutorial; this is just a high-level overview of the creation of an operational data model. Reverse engineering is the process of creating a data model from a database or a script. erwin DM creates a graphical representation of the selected data objects and the relationships between the data objects.

 In erwin DM, one can reverse engineer only into a new empty data model. One cannot reverse engineer into an existing data model.

During a reverse engineering process, the explicitly defined information of the database is reverse engineered in the physical database. However, reverse engineering also infers information from the database and incorporates it into the data model. For example, if the target database supports foreign key declarations, the reverse engineering process infers identifying and non-identifying relationships and default role names. This inferred information is essential to take note of in this process as we want the operational data model to be an accurate reflection of the physical database.

To reverse engineer an operational data model, one would follow the below steps:

1. Click on the *Actions* ribbon in the ribbon toolbar. See Figure 160.

    Figure 160. Click on the Actions Ribbon

2. Then click on the *Reverse Engineering* button. See Figure 161.

Figure 161. Click on the Reverse Engineering Button

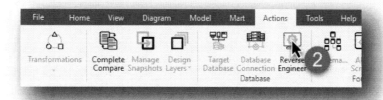

3. Observe that the New Model dialog opens. As pointed out earlier in the introduction to this section, the reverse engineering process can only reverse engineer into a new empty data model.

Because we are creating a new empty data model, we need to define all the properties of this new empty model. For more information on the properties of a data model, please see Chapter 7. In this example, we are using a SQL Server 2019 database to reverse engineer. Further to that, seeing that we are reverse engineering an operational data model, operational data models are physical data models. Therefore, we need to select the data model type of physical. And lastly, we do not want to apply any templates, as these can change the properties of the data objects. We want as clean and close to the database data objects as possible.

4. Click the *Next* button. A new data model gets created in erwin DM in the background. The Reverse Engineering dialog appears.

5. For Reverse Engineering, we are going to use the default options, taking careful note that we do not infer any primary key or relationships. Also, take note of the Scheduler section in the Reverse Engineering dialog, which assists us in automating the creation of an operational data model. We discuss this more in detail in Chapter 28.

6. Click the *Next* button and observe in Figure 162 that the database-specific Connection dialog appears. Database-specific means that each type of supported database has a tailored Connection dialog for the specific database type. Because we selected SQL Server 2019 as the database, the SQL Server 2019 Connection dialog is displayed. On the SQL Server Connection dialog, fill in all the connection details to connect to the database, then click the *Connect* button.

7. Observe the Reverse Engineer from Database progress screen.

8. Depending on the size of the database being reverse engineered, the time of processing may vary.

Figure 162. SQL Server Connection

9. Save the data model with an appropriate name. Operational data models typically do not require being laid out, having their diagrams renamed, or anything else. The objective of the operational data model is to ensure the accuracy of the physical data model only.

   Please refer to Chapter 7 for more on the Reverse Engineering process, and the new scheduling functionality.

Managing an Operational Data Model in erwin DM

As much as the reverse-engineered operational data model is a critical step in the design layer modeling concept, it still has no value until we use it in identifying the differences between the physical data model and what is in the database itself. To do this, we perform a comparison between the operational data model and the physical data model using erwin DM's Complete Compare functionality. To perform this, we need to follow the steps below.

1. With the operational data model open, open the physical data model.

2. Once both models are open, I always recommend displaying both models in view in the erwin DM's diagram pane. To do this, click on the *View* ribbon in the ribbon toolbar.

3. Then click on the *Vertical Split* button. See Figure 163.

4. Click on the tab of the operational data model, and we do this to ensure which data model is the left data model and which one is the right data model in erwin DM's Complete Compare process. See Figure 164. I prefer to work from left to right with the Complete Compare

process, and the objective is to move differences from the operation data model (left) to the physical data model (right).

Figure 163. Click on the Vertical Split Button

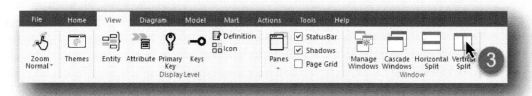

Figure 164. Click on the Operational Data Model Tab

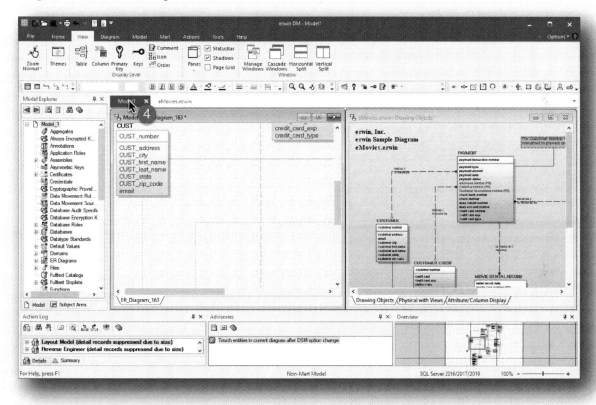

5. Click on the *Actions* ribbon in the ribbon toolbar. See Figure 165.

Figure 165. Click on the Actions Ribbon

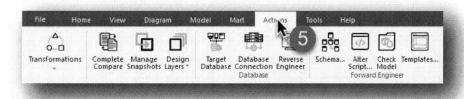

6. Then click on the ***Complete Compare*** button. Observe that the Complete Compare Wizard dialog opens, with the Complete Compare's Left Model, prepopulated with the left model in

the diagram pane, the operational data model. And the Complete Compare's Right Model, prepopulated with the right model in the diagram pane, the physical data model.

7. Click on the *Type Selection* tab in the Complete Compare Wizard dialog. See Figure 166.

Figure 166. Click on the Type Selection Tab

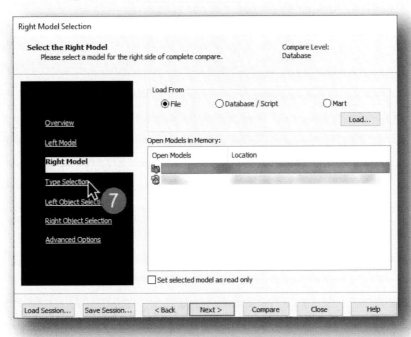

8. Ensure that the Compare Level is set to *Database Level*, and that the Option Set is set to *Speed Option Set*.

 The Speed Option Set is a new option set built into erwin DM to provide an efficient set of options for comparing a physical data model and a physical database.

9. In the Type Selection tab's Options, one can tweak the options for performing the Complete Compare. Depending on the known criteria that the database was generated, one can change the options to match. For example, if one did not implement the definitions in the database, one needs to exclude these from the options to be compared, as they may be flagged as different. Another good example is domains, and if these were not implemented as custom types in the database, one needs to exclude these from the complete compare session.

10. When finished tweaking the Type Selection tab's Options, click the *Compare* button.

11. Observe the Resolve Differences dialog appears. This dialog reflects all of the differences between the operational model on the left and the physical data model on the right.

12. In this example, one can identify that there are differences between the two models. One being a changed data type for the domain, and subsequent columns, for **zip_code**. It is also evident from the above resolve differences that there are indexes that were not applied in the physical database.

13. In a real-world scenario, one would want to capture the changed **zip_code** data type into the physical data model, and then roll it up into the logical data model too. This can be achieved by clicking on the move from the left to right arrow button (⇨) corresponding to the **zip_code** domain, as demonstrated below.

14. Observe the updated list of differences as shown in Figure 167, and how the **CUST_zip_code** was also updated and removed from the list of differences. This removal occurred because the **CUST_zip_code** column data type was dependent on the **zip_code** domain data type.

Figure 167. Click the Move from Left to Right Arrow Button

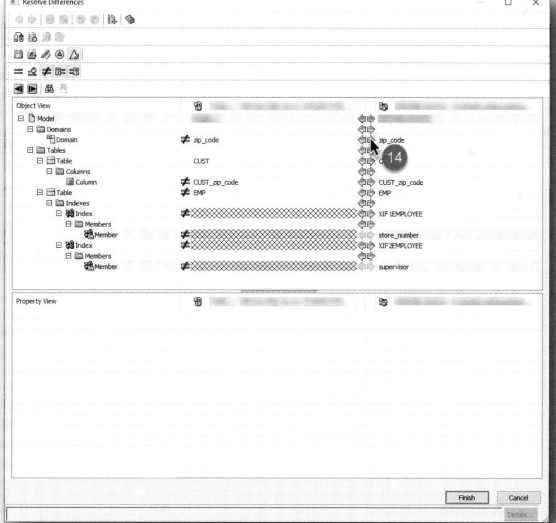

15. In the scenario with the missing indexes, this might have been caused due to a failure of the DBAs to execute the DLL correctly. For this, we would want to re-generate the appropriate DDL just for the indexes. Click on the move from the right to left arrow buttons (◀) corresponding to the indexes.

16. This should resolve all differences between the operational data model and the physical data model. Remember that we applied a change to the operational data model; this needs to be applied to the database.

17. Click on the *Left Alter Script/Schema Generation* button. Make sure that you don't use the Right Alter Script/Schema Generation button.

18. Observe the Forward Engineering Alter Script Schema Generation Wizard dialog opens.

19. Click on the *Preview* tab in the Forward Engineering Alter Script Schema Generation Wizard dialog.

20. Observe the DDL for forward engineering the changes of the indexes into the database are displayed.

This shows a highlight of the process of managing the operational data model and applying reverse changes back into the database—we cover the forward engineering process in Chapter 27. For more information on the reverse engineering functionality, please see Chapter 28 and for more information on the complete compare functionality, please see Chapter 31.

Key Learnings

- Operational Data Models are the 'true' reflection of the physical database.

- Operational Data Models maintain the as-is state of the database and are maintained for historical purposes.

- Typically, the Operational Data Model has no direct link to the physical data model, but it can be used to bring a physical data model in line with what is actually in the database.

Part IV explains all of the symbols and text in a data model. By the time you finish this section, you should be able to 'read' and navigate a data model of any size or complexity.

- **Chapter 14** defines an entity and discusses the different categories of entities. Entity instances are also defined. The different levels at which entities may exist, enterprise, conceptual, logical, physical, and operational, are also explained, as well as the concepts of weak and strong entities.
- **Chapter 15** defines the concept of a domain and discusses the value of domains in data modeling.
- **Chapter 16** defines an attribute and discusses the interrelationship of attributes and domains.
- **Chapter 17** defines keys and distinguishes the terms candidate, primary, alternate key. Surrogate keys and foreign keys are also defined, along with a discussion on their importance.
- **Chapter 18** defines rules and relationships. Data rules distinguish from action rules. Cardinality and labels explain so that we can read any data model as effectively as reading a book. Other types of relationships are also discussed, such as recursive relationships, and subtyping.
- **Chapter 19** defines validation rules and default values and identifies when to use validation rules and the options thereof. Furthermore, the chapter also defines what default values are and the usage of them.

- **Chapter 20** defines subject areas, highlighting what a subject area is, and why we would want to use subject areas in a data model.

Concepts of interest
Who, What, When, Where, Why, and How
Entities abound

This chapter defines the concept of an entity and discusses the different categories (Who, What, When, Where, Why, and How) of entities. Entity instances are also defined. The different levels of entities, enterprise, conceptual, logical, physical, and operational, are explained, as well as the concepts of a weak versus strong entity.

Entities Explained

An entity represents a collection of information about something that the business deems important and worthy of capture. Each entity is identified by a noun or noun phrase and fits into one of six categories: who, what, when, where, why, or how, as explained in Chapter 9.

Entity instances are the occurrences or values of a particular entity. Think of a spreadsheet as being an entity where the column headings represent the pieces of information that gets recorded for each entity. Each spreadsheet row containing the actual values represents an entity instance. The entity **Customer** may have multiple customer instances with the names 'Bob,' 'Joe,' 'Jane,' and so on. The entity **Account** can have instances of Bob's checking account, Bob's savings account, Joe's brokerage account, and so on.

Entity Types

The beauty of data modeling is that you can take the same information and show it at different levels of detail, depending on the audience. The previous Part introduced design layer modeling and the various levels of detail at each: enterprise, conceptual, logical, physical, and operational. Entities are components of all these levels.

The enterprise means the high-level business, as a whole. In contrast, the conceptual means the high-level business solution to a business process or application effort, frequently defining scope, and essential terminology. The logical means the detailed business solution to a business process or application effort. And the physical means the specific technical solution to an application effort — finally, the operational reflects the business in motion.

For an entity to be relevant at an enterprise level, it must be both *fundamental* and *critical* to the business. An entity at the conceptual level must be both *fundamental* and *critical* at the application or solution level. Therefore what is *fundamental* and *critical* at the conceptual level depends very much on the scope of the application or solution.

At a universal level, there are certain concepts familiar to most companies, such as **Customer**, **Product**, and **Employee**. Making the scope slightly narrower, a given industry may have certain unique concepts. **Campaign**, for example, will be a valid concept for the advertising industry but perhaps not for all other industries.

Entities described at a logical level represent the business in more detail than at the conceptual level. Frequently, a conceptual entity represents many logical data model entities. Logical entities contain properties, often called 'attributes,' which we discuss in Chapter 16.

At a physical level, the entities correspond to technology-specific objects such as tables in a DBMS or collections in the NoSQL database MongoDB. The physical level is similar to the logical level but may include compromises that were needed to make up for deficiencies in technology, often related to performance or storage.

The physical entities also contain database-specific information such as the format and length of an attribute (**Author Last Name** is 50 characters), and whether the attribute is required to have a value (**Author Tax Identifier** is not null and therefore required to have a value, but **Author Birth Date** is null and therefore not required to have a value).

In a DBMS, these physical entities become tables or views. In NoSQL databases, these physical entities become transformed depending on the underlying technology. For example, in MongoDB, a document-based database, these entities become collections. The general term 'structure' is used to refer to the underlying database components independent of whether the database is a relational database or NoSQL solution.

An entity is shown as a rectangle with its name inside. Figure 168 contains several entities from the airline industry examples.

Figure 168. Sample Entities

Notice that there are two types of rectangles: those with square corners, such as **Passenger** and **Booking**, and those with rounded corners, such as **Ticket**. Without introducing archaic data modeling jargon, it is enough to know that in most tools, the rectangles with square corners are strong, and those with rounded corners are weak.

Strong entities stand on their own. They represent one occurrence of a person, place, or thing independent of any other entities. To find the information about a particular **Passenger**, for example, its **Passenger Identifier** could be used to retrieve it from the database. 'This is Bob, **Passenger Identifier** 123.' An **Aircraft Type** of 'Boeing 747-400' is retrieved with '747-4.' A **Passenger Gender** of 'Male' is retrieved with the letter 'M.'

Weak entities need to rely on at least one other entity. This means you *cannot* retrieve an entity instance without referring to an entity instance from another entity. For example, **Ticket** might be retrieved by a **Passenger** or **Booking** in combination with something within **Booking,** such as a **Sequence Number**.

A data model is a communication tool. Distinguishing strong from weak entities on the data model helps us understand the relationships and dependencies between entities. For example, a developer reading a data model showing that **Ticket** is a weak entity that depends on **Booking** would develop the application to ensure that a **Booking** is present before a **Ticket** is created.

Tutorial: Creating Entities in erwin DM

1. Open erwin DM.

2. Using the Quick Access Toolbar, click on the *Open* button.

3. Select the **MyMovie_Ver1** data model, from the previous portion of the tutorial, in the Open dialog.

4. Click on the *Open* button.

5. The MyMovie model opens in erwin DM. Maximize the model in the diagram window if needed.

Before going any further, lets first create a new diagram for the logical data model.

6. Right-click on the *ER Diagram* node in the Model Explorer pane, and select the *New* option. See Figure 169.

Figure 169. Right-Click ER Diagrams and Select New

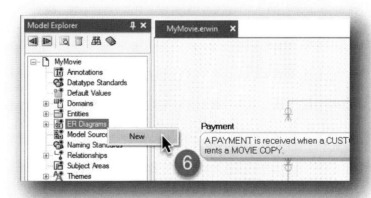

7. While the name of the newly created diagram is still highlighted, rename it to **Logical Model**.

8. Observe that the diagram pane changes to the newly created **Logical Model** diagram. Also, observe that there are no entities (or business objects) represented in the diagram.

9. Remember how we got to the Diagram Editor dialog in Chapter 10's tutorial—we are going to use another option this time to get to the same dialog. Right-click in the diagram, then select the *Properties* option. See Figure 170.

Figure 170. Right-Click in Diagram and Select the Properties Option

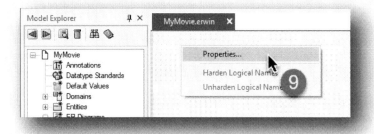

10. Because erwin DM remembers the last used tab for the dialogs, the Entity tab should be displayed. Click on the *Members* tab, as shown in Figure 171.

Figure 171. Click on the Members Tab

11. Observe on the Members tab there are two sides, the left being available objects and the right included objects. Also, notice that the entities that we created in the conceptual data model are all listed as available objects.

12. We are going to reuse the business objects from the conceptual data model in our logical data model as entities. Click on the *Move All Object to Included Objects* button (⬆) on the left-hand side, as shown in Figure 172.

13. Observe that all the objects moved from the left-hand side to the right-hand side, and also that all the objects appeared in the model in the background. Furthermore, observe that the entities are in the Attribute display level.

14. Press the *Close* button to dismiss the Diagram editor dialog.

Figure 172. Move All Objects from the Left-Hand Side to the Right-Hand Side

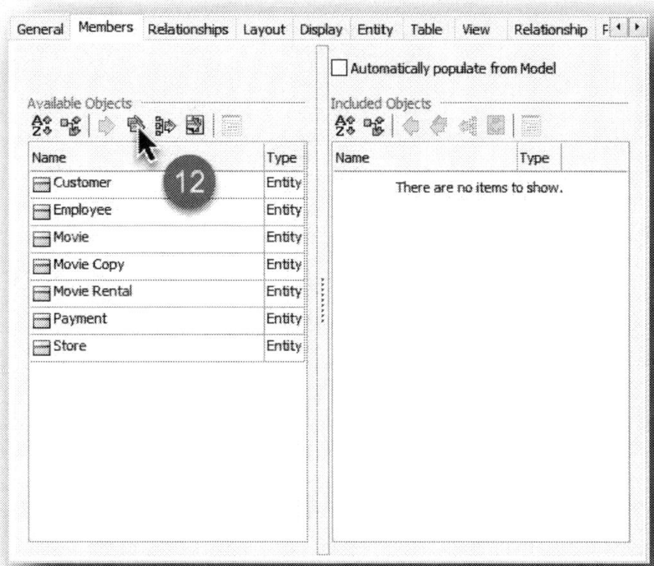

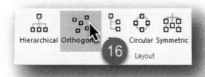

15. Click on the *Diagram* ribbon button.

16. Click on the *Orthogonal* layout option button. See Figure 173.

Figure 173. Click on the Orthogonal Layout Option Button

17. In the Model Explorer pane, click on the expand icon (⊞) next to the *Entities* node, to display all the entities in the data model.

18. Observe that all the entities in the data model display in the list under the *Entities* node. Right-click on the Customer entity and select the *Properties* option, observing the option to delete the entity and the Go To Diagram option. See Figure 174.

In erwin DM, when deleting an object from the Model Explorer pane, it deletes the object from the data model entirely. If deleting from the diagram pane, erwin DM gives the option of removing it from the diagram but still keeps it in the model, or deleting it entirely from the data model.

Figure 174. Right-Click on Customer Entity and Select the Properties Option

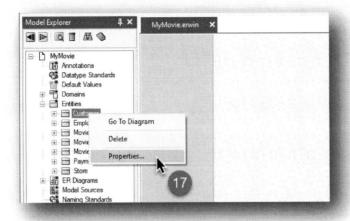

 The Go To Diagram option is a quick way to navigate to an object in the diagram pane.

19. Observe that the Entity Editor dialog displays. See Figure 175.

Figure 175. The Entity Editor Dialog

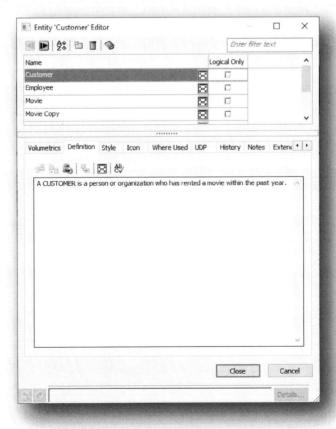

Before discussing the Entity Editor dialog, let us get an understanding of how the Object section of the dialog works.

Action Buttons

◄| **Previous**–Allows the user to position the editor on the previous entity in the Navigation Grid.

|► **Next**–Allows the user to position the editor on the next entity in the Navigation Grid.

A♦Z♦ **Sort**–Allows the user to sort the entities by alphabetic or reverse alphabetic order. Visual cues provide the current sort order:

  A♦Z♦ Specifies that the entity list sort order is in alphabetic order.

  Z♦A♦ Specifies that the entity list sort order is in reverse alphabetic order.

New–Allows the user to create a new entity that becomes the current object in the editor.

Delete–Allows the user to delete the selected entity.

Help–Allows the user to open online help for the editor.

| *Enter filter text* | The filter field allows for the filtering of extensive lists of entities in the Navigation Grid for the quick location of a particular entity. |

Grid Columns

Name Specifies the name of the entity. This field allows for the changing of the name of the entity.

Logical Only Specifies whether the entity is suppressed from a physical model as a table and appears in a logical model only.

20. When finished, click on the *Volumetrics* tab.

21. Observe the Volumetrics tab, as shown in Figure 176.

The Volumetrics tab is used to enter and maintain entity-level volumetric information from the logical side of a model. When specifying volumetric information, it is in place when you derive a physical model from the logical model. For logical/physical models, the information persists to the Table properties on the physical side.

Initial Row Count This field allows the user to enter an initial number of records.

Max Rows This field allows the user to enter the maximum allowable number of records that the entity is designed to hold. Leaving this field empty achieves open-ended growth. This option is used along with the Grow By option to determine when an entity reaches its designed record limit.

Grow By Month This field allows the user to enter the estimated number of records that the entity expects to grow per month. If a maximum record number in the Max Rows field is present, entity growth stops at that record number.

Figure 176. Volumetrics Tab

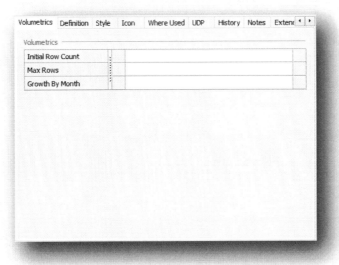

22. When finished, click on the *Definition* tab.

23. Observe the Definition tab, as shown in Figure 177.

Figure 177. Definition Tab

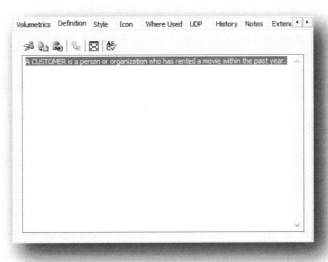

The Definition tab is used to enter a definition for the selected object. In a logical/physical model, or when deriving a physical model from a logical model, the definition migrates to the physical side as a comment.

Action Buttons

Cut–Allows the user to cut the selected text into the clipboard.

Copy–Allows the user to copy the selected text into the clipboard.

Paste–Allows the user to paste the text in the clipboard.

Reset Inheritance–Allows the user to reset the inheritance.

Edit–Allows the user to open the context-specific editor dialog.

Spell Check–Allows the user to invoke the spelling checker. For more details on the spelling checker, please refer to the tutorial in Chapter 7.

24. When finished, click on the *Style* tab.

25. Observe the Style tab, as shown in Figure 178.

Figure 178. Style Tab

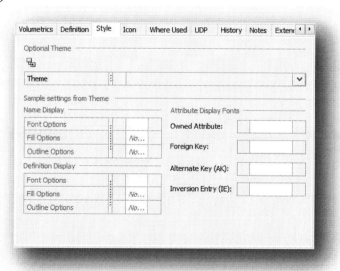

Use the Style tab to set the preferences for displaying the name and other definitions for a data modeling object, for example, tables, views, or columns. It either uses the default theme for the object that is defined in the Theme Editor dialog, or changes the style to apply only to the current object.

Action Buttons

	Allows the user to reset the inheritance of the theme.
Theme	Displays the currently used theme of the object. Use the drop-down list to select an existing theme to use. Click the *New* button (⬛) to create a theme or click the *Theme Editor* button (⬛) to open the Theme Editor dialog to modify the theme properties. Chapter 20 covers themes.

Name Display	Displays the Font, Fill, and Outline options used by the object's name in the diagram as defined by the current theme. Open the Theme Editor to change these settings.
Comment Display	Displays the Font, Fill, and Outline options used by the object's comments as defined by the current theme. Open the Theme Editor to change these settings.
Column Display Fonts	Displays the Font options used by the object's owned column and expression as defined by the current theme. Open the Theme Editor to change these settings.

26. When finished, click on the *Icon* tab.

27. Observe the Icon tab, as shown in Figure 179.

Figure 179. Icon Tab

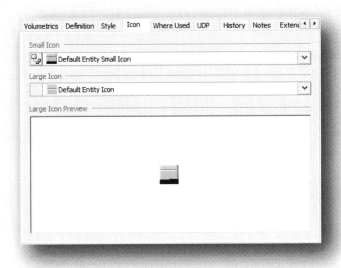

Use the Icon tab in the Entity Editor to attach small or large icons to an entity in the logical model. In Chapter 10, we demonstrated the usage of icons in the icon display level.

Small Icon	Specifies the small icon bitmap (*.bmp) that displays when selected to display the Entity Icon on the Display Style Sheet. Select an icon from the drop-down list or click *New* to open the Image Property Editor dialog where one can import, rename, or delete an image.
Large Icon	Specifies the large icon bitmap (*.bmp) that displays when selected to display the Entity Icon on the Display Style Sheet. Select an icon from the drop-down list or click *New* to open the Image Property Editor dialog where one can import, rename, or delete an image.

28. When finished, click on the *Where Used* tab.

29. Observe the Where Used tab, as shown in Figure 180.

Figure 180. Where Used Tab

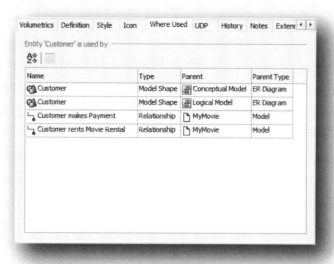

Use the Where Used tab to view where the usage of an object in the data model.

Action Buttons

Sort–Allows the user to sort the list by alphabetic, reverse alphabetic, alphabetic by object type, name, or reverse alphabetic by object type, name. Select the sort method by using the drop-down menu that opens after clicking the *Sort* button. The Sort button image indicates the currently selected sort order.

- Alphabetic
- Reverse Alphabetic
- Alphabetic by Object Type, Name
- Reverse Alphabetic by Object Type, Name

Edit–Allows the user to edit the properties of a selected object in the Where Used list. Select the object and click the button to open the selected object's property editor.

Grid Columns

Name	This column lists the name of the object used by the selected object in the editor.
Type	This column lists the object type.
Parent	This column lists the parent object of the selected object.
Parent Type	This column lists the parent object type.

30. When finished, click on the *UDP* tab.

31. Observe the UDP tab. For more information on the UDP tab, please refer back to the Chapter 7 tutorial that covered the UDP tab. We also explain more about UDPs in Chapter 25.

32. When finished, click on the *History* tab.

33. Observe the History tab. For more information on the History tab, please refer back to the Chapter 7 tutorial that covered the History tab.

34. When finished, click on the *Notes* tab.

35. Observe the Notes tab. For more information on the Notes tab, please refer back to the Chapter 7 tutorial that covered the Notes tab.

36. When finished, click on the *Extended Notes* tab.

37. Observe the Extended Notes tab. For more information on the Extended Notes tab, please refer back to the Chapter 7 tutorial that covered the Extended Notes tab.

38. Seeing that we have already captured all the known entities during the conceptual data model design phase, there is no more requirement to add entities. Therefore click on the *Close* button to close the Entity Editor dialog.

39. Save and close your MyMovie data model.

Key Learnings

- An entity represents a collection of information about something that the business deems important and worthy of capture. An entity fits into one of several categories - who, what, when, where, why, or how.

- A noun or noun phrase identifies a specific entity.

- Entity instances are the occurrences or values of a particular entity.

- An entity can exist at the enterprise, conceptual, logical, physical, operational level of detail, though not always called an entity.

- An entity can be strong or weak.

Domains are awesome
Reuse the metadata
Consistency rules

'A domain is a set of permissible values. A domain is defined in a schema and is identified by a <domain name>. The purpose of a domain is to constrain the set of valid values that can be stored in SQL-data by various operations. A domain definition **specifies a data type**. It may also specify a <**domain constraint**> that further restricts the valid values of the domain and a <**default clause**> that specifies the value to be used in the absence of an explicitly specified value or column default.'

Excerpt from *SQL-92 Standard*

Domains Explained

When it comes to domains, I always think back to my earlier data modeling days and a distinct situation I had to resolve. I had just started a data modeling competency for a retail company that had not seen data as an asset. Likewise, they also did not do any data modeling for their application development. As I started putting together a roadmap for the data modeling practice in the organization, I was pulled into a meeting in which the heads of the departments were discussing an issue regarding their store numbers. In the past, the company had adopted a three-character numeric value for their store numbers, and to complicate it, they had built-in intelligence into the numbering of the stores. They had broken down the store number into regions and zones.

As the company grew, they started running out of numbers in a zone and therefore had to duplicate zones to keep the system working. I was called in to define how complex of a task it would be to change the store numbering strategy to a four-character numeric value and to remove the intelligence behind the numbers. Sounds quite simple, go through all the databases and find wherever store number was found to get a list of all attributes that needed changing. But because there were no standard naming conventions in place, databases were built on the fly by developers, and there was no conformity to even data types. The task took over six months and had a success rating of about 75%.

Now, if we had implemented a data modeling practice earlier in the design of the databases, and had adopted a standard based on using domains, the task would have taken a couple of hours with a much higher success rating. All I would have done is to go through all the data models and looked at the store number domain to identify the usage of store numbers.

Domains are based on the SQL-92 Standards. Another way I look at domain are they are a named set of column properties or mini templates for attributes. The store number domain from the earlier discussion would have the following properties:

- Name   - <entity name> store number

- Data Type   - numeric characters

- Data Length   - 3 characters long

- Description   - A store number is a numeric value given to a store based on …

- Null Option   - May not be null

- Default Value   - 000 (head office, assigned if no store number is available)

- Validation Rule   - None

Typically domains are categorized into four core domain types:

- **Alphanumeric domains**. These domains are associated with attributes and columns that contain text string values. Values that do not perform any mathematical function or have any date constraints. For example, **Customer First Name**, **Address Line Text**, and **Postal Code**.

- **Numeric domains**. These domains are associated with attributes and columns that contain any mathematical numeric values. They may be whole numbers, fractions, decimal values, percentages—any value that could potentially have some form of math performed on them.

- **Temporal domains**. These domains are associated with attributes and columns that contain any date, datetime, or time values. It is vital to note that mathematical calculations may be performed on temporal domains, but the result of the calculation could be of a numeric domain. For example, the time difference in minutes from when a worker clocked in, to when they clocked out. The result would be in minutes, but would be a numeric value counted from 1 to 100s, not 1 to 60s.

- **Binary domains**. These domains are associated with attributes and columns that contain any binary data. Binary data is typically images, audio, or other multimedia objects, and sometimes even binary executable code is stored as binary data.

Domains provide lots of value, including efficiency in building new models and maintaining existing models. When a data modeler embarks on a project, they can use a standard set of domains, thereby saving time by not reinventing the wheel. Any new attribute can be assigned to an existing domain. With the assignment comes the pre-built properties of data type, data length, naming standard, definition, validation rules, default rules, and null options. This saves the time to define each of these individually and provides consistency across the design process.

Domains in erwin DM

erwin DM makes usage of the SQL-92 Standards domain concepts but expands on it to include other properties to assist in the automation of the data model design. erwin DM domains have two types of properties:

Non-inheritable properties	The non-inheritable properties do not migrate to child domains or attributes that are associated with the domain. This is because they are properties of the domain itself.
Inheritable properties	The inheritable properties migrate to child domains and to the attributes that are associated with the domain.

Inheritance in erwin DM is the ability to 'inherit' the property's value from the parent object. For example, if a data type property in the parent object is set to 'INTEGER,' and the child object's data type property has inheritance set to Inherit, then the child's data type will also be 'INTEGER.' In erwin DM, there are three states of inheritance:

Inherit. Specifies that inheritance is in place. Any changes to the parent property will cascade to the child's property.

Overridden. Specifies that the inherited property value has been overridden and that any changes to the parent property will not be carried forward.

Hardened. Specifies that the property value is hardened and cannot be changed without unhardening first. Hardening allows for the maintaining of the physical names that have been applied to a database, irrespective of any logical name changes. This option is only available on Name properties.

erwin DM structures the domains in a hierarchical structure, as shown in Figure 181, which contains the default built-in domains of a new logical data model.

Figure 181. erwin DM Hierarchical Structure of Domains

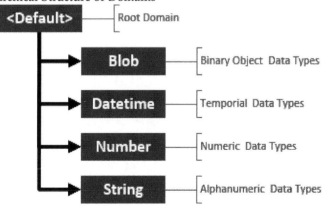

<Default> domain   This domain is the root of all domains; it does not hold any bias to data type families but is the parent of all subsequent domains. By default, all new attributes are created using this domain unless explicitly created otherwise.

Blob domains   These domains are associated with attributes and columns that contain binary data. Recall our earlier discussion on binary domains.

Datetime domains   These domains are associated with attributes and columns that contain any date, datetime, or time values. Recall our earlier discussion on temporal domains.

Number domains   These domains are associated with attributes and columns that contain any mathematical numeric values. Recall our earlier discussion on numeric domains.

String domains   These domains are associated with attributes and columns that contain any text string values. Recall our earlier discussion on alphanumeric domains.

The erwin DM domain properties are:

Domain Name   The name of the domain.

Child Domain = non-inheritable
Assigned Attribute = non-inheritable

Domain Image   In the Model Explorer and the Domain Editor, a unique image represents each domain. All new domains use a default image, but a different image can be used to represent the domain.

Child Domain = inheritable
Assigned Attribute = non-inheritable

Attribute Name   The name that an attribute inherits when assigned with the domain.

Child Domain = inheritable
Assigned Attribute = inheritable

Attribute Image   An image that represents the attribute assigned to the domain. By default, the attribute inherits the domain image but is overridable.

Child Domain = inheritable
Assigned Attribute = inheritable

Attribute Logical Only Option	Specifies the attribute assigned to the domain in the logical model only. Child Domain = inheritable Assigned Attribute = inheritable
Attribute Logical Data Type	The attribute assigned to the domain's data type and data length. It is essential to understand that the data type is limited to the data type family of the parent domain. Child Domain = inheritable Assigned Attribute = inheritable
Attribute Null Option	The attribute assigned to the domain's null option. Child Domain = inheritable Assigned Attribute = inheritable
Domain Definition	The definition of the domain. Child Domain = non-inheritable Assigned Attribute = non-inheritable
Attribute Definition	The definition of the attribute assigned to the domain. Child Domain = inheritable Assigned Attribute = inheritable
Attribute Validation Rule	The validation rule of the attribute assigned to the domain. Child Domain = inheritable Assigned Attribute = inheritable
Attribute Default Value	The default value rule of the attribute assigned to the domain. Child Domain = inheritable Assigned Attribute = inheritable
Domain UDPs	The UDP values of the domain. Child Domain = inheritable Assigned Attribute = inheritable
Attribute UDPs	The UDP values of the attribute assigned to the domain. Child Domain = inheritable Assigned Attribute = inheritable

Furthermore, erwin DM domains are extendable; in other words, one can add new domains at any level in the hierarchy. For example, we can create an employee **Gender** domain, with values

'M' for male or 'F' for female. This domain needs to be of string type. Therefore, we can use the parent domain of string as graphically represented in Figure 182.

Figure 182. Hierarchical Structure of Domains Including Gender

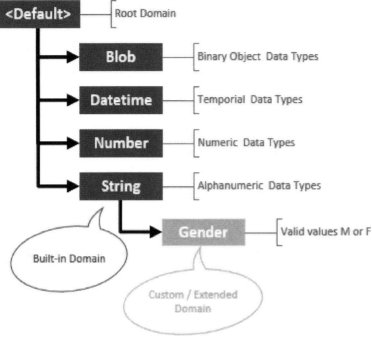

Now we want to use the domain to manage the gender for customers. Since we do not know the gender of all customers, we extend the **Gender** domain to include a valid value of 'U' for unknown. Since we do not want to allow unknown gender for employees, we need to use a new domain—an extended gender domain, as shown in Figure 183.

Figure 183. Hierarchical Structure of Domains Including Gender MFU

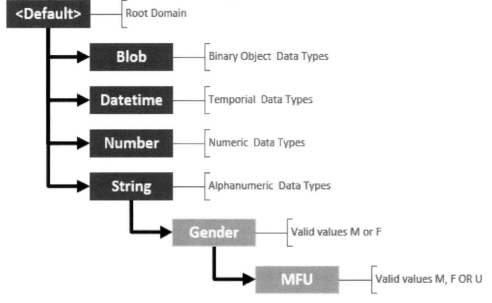

By extending a domain, the child domain inherits all the properties from the parent domain, and only the properties that need to change are changed.

Domains can also be used as placeholders for grouping of similar domains; for example, the **Address Line**, **City**, **State**, and **Zip Code** are all address-related domains. To group them, one can create an Address domain and have all the address-related domains as children to the **Address** domain, as demonstrated in Figure 184.

Figure 184. Hierarchical Structure of Domains Including Address Placeholder

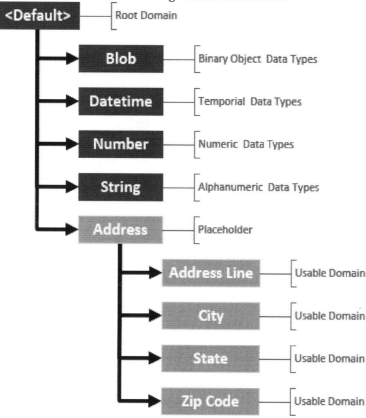

Although we use a hierarchical structure where the custom domains fall under the **<Default>** domain, there are alternatives to the hierarchical structure, such as where all the custom domains fall under a single placeholder for custom domains, as demonstrated in Figure 185.

The second being where all the custom domains fall under a family data type domains, as demonstrated in Figure 186.

Figure 185. Custom Domain Hierarchy Alternative 1

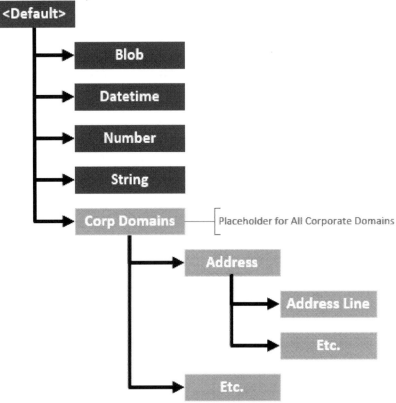

Figure 186. Custom Domain Hierarchy Alternative 2

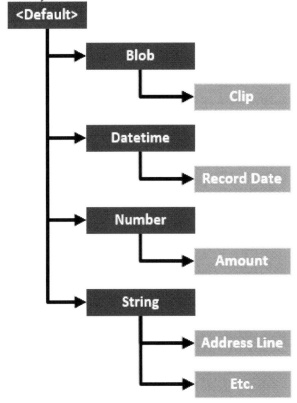

Tutorial: Further Requirements Gathering Session with 'MyMovie'

Now that we have sign-off on the conceptual data model for the MyMovie system, we meet again with John, the owner of MyMovie, to discover more details about the data that needs capturing. We identify several common attribute types and break them out, as shown in Table 30 through Table 37. We also find several generic attribute types, broken out in Table 38 through Table 41.

Table 30. MyMovie Name Attributes

Business Object	Property	Data Type	Nullable	Description
Customer	customer first name	String (20 Character)	No	The first name of the customer
Customer	customer last name	String (20 Character)	No	The last name of the customer
Employee	employee first name	String (20 Character)	No	The first name of the employee
Employee	employee last name	String (20 Character)	No	The last name of the employee
Movie	movie director	String (20 Character)	Yes	The last name of the movie director
Movie	movie star 1 name	String (20 Character)	Yes	The last name of the leading star of the movie
Movie	movie star 2 name	String (20 Character)	Yes	The last name of the second leading star of the movie
Store	store manager first name	String (20 Character)	Yes	The first name of the store manager
Store	store manager last name	String (20 Character)	Yes	The last name of the store manager

Table 31. MyMovie Address Line Attributes

Business Object	Property	Data Type	Nullable	Description
Customer	customer address line	String (30 Character)	Yes	The address line part of the address of the customer
Employee	employee address line	String (30 Character)	Yes	The address line part of the address of the employee
Store	store address line	String (30 Character)	No	The address line part of the address of the store

Table 32. MyMovie City Attributes

Business Object	Property	Data Type	Nullable	Description
Customer	customer city	String (20 Character)	Yes	The city part of the address of the customer
Employee	employee city	String (20 Character)	Yes	The city part of the address of the employee
Store	store city	String (20 Character)	Yes	The city part of the address of the store

Table 33. MyMovie State Attributes

Business Object	Property	Data Type	Nullable	Description
Customer	customer state	String (2 Character)	Yes	The state part of the address of the customer
Employee	employee state	String (2 Character)	Yes	The state part of the address of the employee
Store	store state	String (2 Character)	Yes	The state part of the address of the store

Table 34. MyMovie Zip Code Attributes

Business Object	Property	Data Type	Nullable	Description
Customer	customer zip code	String (5 Numeric Characters)	Yes	The zip code part of the address of the customer
Employee	employee zip code	String (5 Numeric Characters)	Yes	The zip code part of the address of the employee
Store	store zip code	String (5 Numeric Characters)	Yes	The zip code part of the address of the store

Table 35. MyMovie Phone Attributes

Business Object	Property	Data Type	Nullable	Description
Customer	customer phone	String (10 Numeric Characters)	Yes	The phone number of the customer
Employee	employee phone	String (10 Numeric Characters)	Yes	The phone number of the employee
Store	store phone	String (10 Numeric Characters)	Yes	The phone number of the store

Table 36. MyMovie Email Attributes

Business Object	Property	Data Type	Nullable	Description
Customer	customer email	String (50 Character)	No	The email of the customer
Employee	employee email	String (50 Character)	Yes	The email of the employee

Table 37. MyMovie Gender Attributes

Business Object	Property	Data Type	Nullable	Description
Customer	customer gender	String (1 Character)	Yes	The gender of the customer
Employee	employee gender	String (1 Character)	No	The gender of the employee

Table 38. MyMovie Generic Binary Attributes

Business Object	Property	Data Type	Nullable	Description
Movie	movie clip	Large Binary	Yes	The movie clip of the movie

Table 39. MyMovie Generic Datetime Attributes

Business Object	Property	Data Type	Nullable	Description
Employee	employee hire date	Date	No	The hire date of the employee
Movie Rental	movie rental date	Date	No	The date of the movie rental
Movie Rental	movie rental due date	Date	Yes	The due date of the movie rental
Movie Rental	movie rental record date	Date	No	The record date of the movie rental
Payment	payment date	Date	No	The date of the payment

Table 40. MyMovie Generic Number Attributes

Business Object	Property	Data Type	Nullable	Description
Employee	employee salary	Number 15 Characters, 2 decimal places)	No	The salary of the employee
Movie	movie rental rate	Number 15 Characters, 2 decimal places)	No	The rental rate of the movie
Movie Rental	movie rental overdue charge	Number 15 Characters, 2 decimal places)	Yes	The rental overdue charge of the movie rental
Movie Rental	movie rental rate	Number 15 Characters, 2 decimal places)	No	The rate of the movie rental
Payment	payment amount	Number 15 Characters, 2 decimal places)	No	The amount of the payment

Table 41. MyMovie Generic String Attributes

Business Object	Property	Data Type	Nullable	Description
Employee	employee soc sec number	String (9 Character)	No	The Social Security Number of the employee
Movie	movie description	String (255 Character)	Yes	The description of the movie
Movie	movie genre	String (10 Character)	Yes	The genre of the movie
Movie	movie rating	String (20 Character)	Yes	The rating of the movie
Movie	movie title	String (50 Character)	No	The title of the movie
Movie	movie url	String (50 Character)	Yes	The url of the movie
Movie Copy	movie copy format	String (15 Character)	No	The format of the movie copy, VHS or DVD.
Movie Copy	movie copy general condition	String (10 Character)	Yes	The general condition of the movie copy
Movie Rental	movie rental status	String (10 Character)	Yes	The rental status of the movie copy
Payment	payment check bank number	String (10 Character)	Yes	The check bank number of the payment
Payment	payment check number	String (20 Character)	Yes	The check number of the payment
Payment	payment credit card expiration date	String (4 Character)	Yes	The credit card expiration date of the payment
Payment	payment credit card number	String (16 Character)	Yes	The credit card number of the payment
Payment	payment credit card type	String (12 Character)	Yes	The credit card type of the payment, VISA, Master Card, or Amex
Payment	payment epay account number	String (20 Character)	Yes	The epay account number of the payment
Payment	payment epay vendor number	String (10 Character)	Yes	The epay vendor number of the payment
Payment	payment status	String (10 Character)	Yes	The status of the payment
Payment	payment type	String (20 Character)	No	The type of the payment, check, credit card, or e-payment

Tutorial: Creating Domains in erwin DM

With this information at hand, it is time to start setting up some of the domains in the MyMovie model.

1. Open erwin DM.

2. Using the Quick Access Toolbar, click on the **Open** button.

3. Select the **MyMovie_Ver1** data model, from the previous portion of the tutorial, in the Open dialog.

4. Click on the **Open** button.

5. The MyMovie model opens in erwin DM. Maximize the model in the diagram window if needed.

6. In the Model Explorer pane, click on the expand icon (⊞) next to the **Domains** node, to display all the built-in domains in the data model. See Figure 187.

Figure 187. Maximize the Domain Node

7. Observe all the built-in domains, as discussed earlier in this chapter.

8. Right-click on the **Domain** node and observe the pop-up menu. Notice the two sort orders, Sort Alphabetically, and Sort Hierarchical. Select the **Sort Hierarchical**. See Figure 188.

Figure 188. Select the Sort Hierarchical Sort Order

9. Expand all the nodes of the *Domain* node. Observe the built-in domains sorted hierarchically.

10. Right-click on the *<Default>* domain node, and notice the New, Delete, and Properties options added beyond the root node. Also, observe that the Delete option is greyed out because built-in domains cannot be deleted. Click the *New* option. See Figure 189.

Figure 189. Click the New Option

11. Observe the new domain with the name selected to rename. Furthermore, observe the location in the hierarchy for the new domain. Rename the domain to **Name**.

12. From the previous steps, by having the **<Default>** domain selected and then right-click to create a new domain, the selected domain becomes the parent domain for the new domain.

13. For our next domain, **First Name**, we are going to create it as a children domain under the **Name** domain. Right-click on the new *Name* domain node and click the *New* option. Rename the new domain to **First Name**. Observe the Delete option is now greyed out as this is a custom domain and can be deleted. See Figure 190.

Figure 190. Right-Click the Name Domain and Select the New Option

14. Observe the new domain created as a child to the **Name** domain.

15. As demonstrated in the above steps, a domain is creatable from the Model Explorer pane. But the properties of the domain have defaulted to the inheritance from the parent domain. Next, we are going to explore how to change the properties of a domain and create further domains from the Domain Editor dialog.

16. Right-click on the new **First Name** domain node and click the *Properties* option to open the Domain Editor dialog.

17. Observe the Domain Editor (Dictionary) dialog opens, with the **First Name** domain selected. See Figure 191.

Figure 191. Domain Editor (Dictionary) Dialog

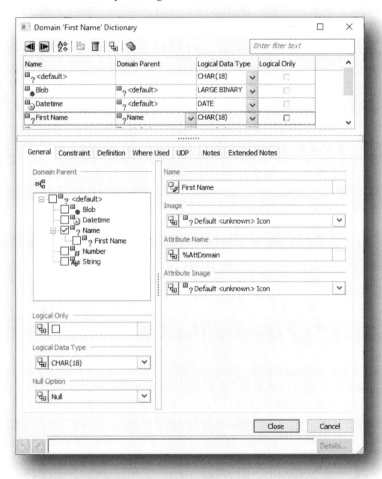

The Domain Editor lists all the domains for the data model, and they are arranged either hierarchically or alphabetically. The Model Explorer and the Domain Editor list the same domains and lets you sort the domains in hierarchical or alphabetic order. One can create and modify logical domains using the Domain Editor, whose components are described below.

Action Buttons

◀| **Previous**–Allows the user to position the editor on the previous entity in the Navigation Grid.

▶| **Next**–Allows the user to position the editor on the next entity in the Navigation Grid.

Sort–Allows the user to sort the domains by alphabetic or reverse alphabetic order. Visual cues provide the current sort order:

Alphabetic Order–Specifies that the domain list sort order is in alphabetic order.

Reverse Alphabetic Order–Specifies that the domain list sort order is in reverse alphabetic order.

New–Allows the user to create a new domain that becomes the current domain in the editor.

Delete–Allows the user to delete the selected domain.

Help–Allows the user to open online help for the editor.

Enter filter text — The filter field allows for the filtering of extensive lists of domains in the Navigation Grid for the quick location of a particular domain.

Grid Columns

Name — Specifies the name of the domain and allows for the changing of the name of the domain.

Domain Parent — The domain parent field specifies and allows for the changing of the parent domain.

Logical Data Type — Specifies the logical data type for the domain, and allows for the changing of the data type. Note that only data types of the parent domain's data type family are listed.

Logical Only — Specifies whether the domain is suppressed from a physical model as a physical domain and appears in a logical model only.

 The built-in (<default>, Blob, Datetime, Number, and String) domain's properties cannot be changed, and only custom domains are changeable.

---

18. When finished, click on the *General* tab to make sure that the General tab is visible. See Figure 192.

Figure 192. Click on the General Tab

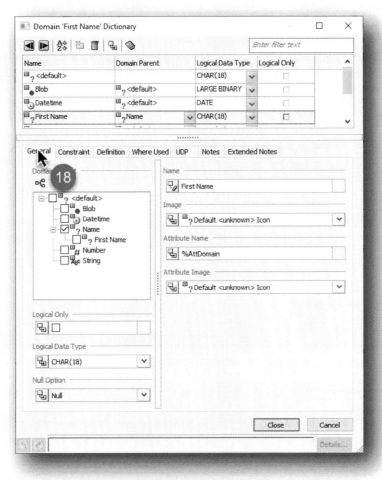

The General tab is used to enter and maintain core domain information and is broken down into key areas.

Domain Parent This section hierarchically displays and allows for the changing of the domain parent for the selected domain. Note that when changing the domain parent, all properties that have inheritance in place changes the property value of the new domain parent.

> **Alphabetic Order**–Specifies that the domain parents sort order is in alphabetic order.

> **Reverse Alphabetic Order**–Specifies that the domain parents sort order is in reverse alphabetic order.

> **Hierarchical Order**–Specifies that the domain parents sort order is in hierarchical order.

Logical Only Specifies whether the domain is suppressed from a physical model as a physical domain and appears in a logical model only.

    Inherit–Specifies that inheritance is in place. Any changes to the parent property will cascade to the child's property.

    Overridden–Specifies that the inherited property value has been overridden and that any changes to the parent property will not be carried forward.

Logical Data Type Specifies the logical data type for the domain and associated attributes, and allows for the changing of the data type. Note that only data types of the parent domain's data type family are listed.

    Inherit–Specifies that inheritance is in place. Any changes to the parent property will cascade to the child's property.

    Overridden–Specifies that the inherited property value has been overridden and that any changes to the parent property will not be carried forward.

Null Option Specifies the null option for the domain and associated attributes, and allows for the changing of the null option.

    Inherit–Specifies that inheritance is in place. Any changes to the parent property will cascade to the child's property.

    Overridden–Specifies that the inherited property value has been overridden and that any changes to the parent property will not be carried forward.

Name Specifies the name of the domain and allows for changing the domain name.

    Inherit–Specifies that inheritance is in place. Any changes to the parent property will cascade to the child's property.

    Overridden–Specifies that the inherited property value has been overridden and that any changes to the parent property will not be carried forward.

    Hardened–Specifies that the property value is hardened and cannot be changed without hardening first. This option is only available on Name properties.

Image Specifies the image for the domain and allows for the changing of the image. Although a new domain uses a default image, a different image can be used.

    Inherit–Specifies that inheritance is in place. Any changes to the parent property will cascade to the child's property.

    Overridden–Specifies that the inherited property value has been overridden and that any changes to the parent property will not be carried forward.

Attribute Name	Specifies the name that an attribute inherits when assigned with the domain. Allows for macros in the attribute name.

> **Inherit**–Specifies that inheritance is in place. Any changes to the parent property will cascade to the child's property.

> **Overridden**–Specifies that the inherited property value has been overridden and that any changes to the parent property will not be carried forward.

Attribute Image	Specifies the image that can be used to represent the attribute assigned to the domain. By default, the attribute inherits the domain image but is overridable.

> **Inherit**–Specifies that inheritance is in place. Any changes to the parent property will cascade to the child's property.

> **Overridden**–Specifies that the inherited property value has been overridden and that any changes to the parent property will not be carried forward.

19. For our **First Name** domain, we want to set it to the shared data type of 'String (20 Character).' Since the term 'string' is very generic, we would like to use the more specific data type of 'VARCHAR(20).'

20. Click on the dropdown of Data Type, and select the *VARCHAR()* option, and fill in the '20' between the brackets. See Figure 193.

21. Observe the inheritance button has changed to overridden; this is because we have broken the inheritance from the parent property by changing the data type.

22. Next, we want to change the null option to default to not null, as the specification that we received in the session emphasized that for the first name, nulls are not allowed.

23. Click on the dropdown of Null Option, and select the '*Not Null*' option.

24. We want to change the attribute name for the inherited attributes, and we have an attribute naming standard that we want to implement, '*<Entity Name> <Domain Name>*.' We could set the name for each domain and attribute individually, but the intention of using domains is to assist in automation and standardization. Therefore we want to change the root domain of all the domains to reflect our naming standard, which is the **<Default>** domain.

 When changing the focused object in an editor dialog, erwin DM keeps track of all the changes to the previous object. Then when clicking on the Close button, it applies all the changes permanently. Clicking on the Cancel button removes all the changes.

25. Click on the *<Default>* domain in the object section grid. See Figure 194.

Figure 193. Select the VARCHAR() Option

Figure 194. Click on the <Default> Domain

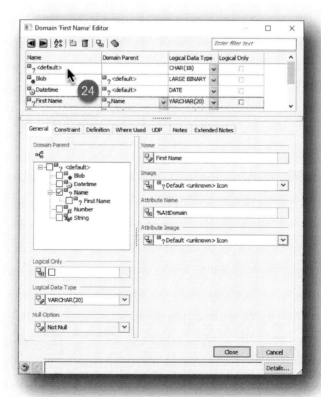

26. Notice that the attribute name field makes use of a naming standard rule macro to determine the name. We cover a more comprehensive understanding of naming standard rule macros in Chapter 26, but for the moment, the %AttDomain macro changes the attribute name to be the same as the domain name. From our session, we know that that is not what we want. Therefore, we need to change the macro to reflect the entity name first, then the domain name, as per our attribute naming standard.

27. Change the *Attribute Name* field to '%OwnerEntity %AttDomain.'

28. Next, we want to automate the definition of the attributes too. Click on the *Definition* tab.

29. The Definition tab is used to enter a definition for the selected domain.

   Action Buttons

	Allows the user to cut the selected text into the clipboard.
	Allows the user to copy the selected text into the clipboard.
	Allows the user to paste the text in the clipboard.
	Allows the user to reset the inheritance.
	Allows the user to open the context-specific editor dialog.
	Allows the user to invoke the spelling checker. See Chapter 7 for more on the spelling checker.

30. For the *Definition* of the **<Default>** domain, set it to 'Corporate domain for setting attribute standards.'

31. For the *Definition Inherited by Attributes* of the **<Default>** domain, set it to 'The %Lower(%AttDomain) of the %Lower(%OwnerEntity).' Notice that macros are used in erwin DM to aid in the automation of tasks, like rewriting of definitions.

32. Now, let us go back to the First Name domain. Click on the *First Name* domain in the object section grid.

33. Observe that the Definition Inherited by Attributes field has inheritance in place and has automatically updated to the new definition macro from the **<Default>** domain, being 'The %Lower(%AttDomain) of the %Lower(%OwnerEntity).'

34. Furthermore, observe the absence of the Definition field value. It is done intentionally because when creating an inheritance for the Definition of a domain, it could result in the same definitions for different domains. Imagine having two domains that have the same definition of 'Corporate domain of LAST NAME attribute.' A modeler would not know which one to use if different naming standards are used. Change the *Definition* of the First Name domain to 'Corporate domain of FIRST NAME attributes.'

35. Click on the *Name* domain in the object section grid.

36. Change the *Definition* of the **Name** domain, set it to 'Corporate domain of NAME attributes.'

37. Click on the *General* tab.

38. Change the *Data Type* for the generic Name domain to 'VARCHAR(50).' For a detailed process, go back to step 20 to repeat.

39. Observe that the Attribute Name field automatically changed to '%OwnerEntity %AttDomain,' and that the inheritance button indicates that inheritance is in place.

40. Click the *New* (🖳) button to create a new domain for the Last Name domain.

41. Observe that a new domain created, rename it to **Last Name** in the object section grid under the column of **Name**.

42. Observe that the parent domain of the **Last Name** domain is the **Name** domain. The same behavior experienced in the Domain Editor dialog as in the Model Explorer pane, of the select domain becoming the parent domain.

43. Observe the inherited Attribute Name of '%OwnerEntity %AttDomain' inherited from the parent domain.

44. Furthermore, observe the inherited Data Type of VARCHAR(50) from the parent domain. But we need to change this to VARCHAR(20). Change the *Data Type* for the **Last Name** domain to 'VARCHAR(20).'

45. And change the Null Option to 'Not Null.'

46. Click on the *Definition* tab.

47. Observe the inherited Definition Inherited by Attribute of Name of '%Lower(%OwnerEntity).' inherited from the parent domain.

48. Furthermore, observe the absence of the inherited Definition field value. Change the *Definition* for the **Last Name** domain to 'Corporate domain of LAST NAME attribute.'

49. Now create the rest of the domains that we need in the MyMovie data model, as per the instructions in Figure 195.

Figure 195. MyMovie Domains

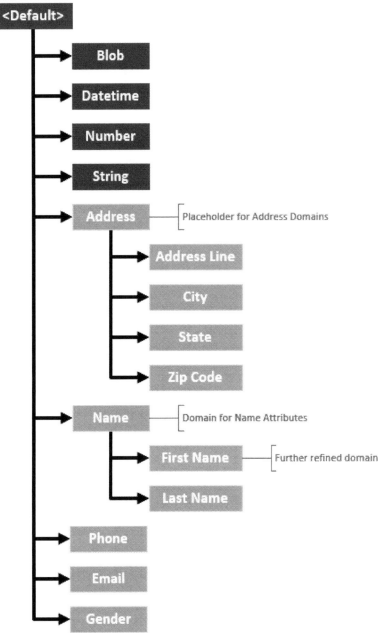

Address Domain

Parent Domain	<Default>
Name	Address
Attribute Name	–Leave Inherited–
Logical Data Type	–Leave Inherited–
Null Option	–Leave Inherited–
Definition	Corporate placeholder domain for all address domains.
Definition Inherited	–Leave Inherited–

Address Line Domain

Parent Domain	Address
Name	Address Line
Attribute Name	–Leave Inherited–
Logical Data Type	VARCHAR(30)
Null Option	–Leave Inherited–
Definition	Corporate domain of ADDRESS LINE attribute.
Definition Inherited	–Leave Inherited–

City Domain

Parent Domain	Address
Name	City
Attribute Name	–Leave Inherited–
Logical Data Type	VARCHAR(20)
Null Option	–Leave Inherited–
Definition	Corporate domain of CITY attribute.
Definition Inherited	–Leave Inherited–

State Domain

Parent Domain	Address
Name	State
Attribute Name	–Leave Inherited–
Logical Data Type	CHAR(2)
Null Option	–Leave Inherited–
Definition	Corporate domain of STATE attribute.
Definition Inherited	–Leave Inherited–

Zip Code Domain

Parent Domain	Address
Name	Zip Code
Attribute Name	–Leave Inherited–
Logical Data Type	NCHAR(5)
Null Option	–Leave Inherited–
Definition	Corporate domain of ZIP CODE attribute.
Definition Inherited	–Leave Inherited–

Phone Domain

Parent Domain	<Default>
Name	Phone
Attribute Name	–Leave Inherited–
Logical Data Type	NCHAR(10)
Null Option	–Leave Inherited–
Definition	Corporate domain of PHONE attribute.
Definition Inherited	–Leave Inherited–

Email Domain

Parent Domain	<Default>
Name	Email
Attribute Name	–Leave Inherited–
Logical Data Type	VARCHAR(50)
Null Option	–Leave Inherited–
Definition	Corporate domain of EMAIL attribute.
Definition Inherited	–Leave Inherited–

Gender Domain

Parent Domain	<Default>
Name	Gender
Attribute Name	–Leave Inherited–
Logical Data Type	CHAR(1)
Null Option	–Leave Inherited–
Definition	Corporate domain of GENDER attribute.
Definition Inherited	–Leave Inherited–

50. When finished, click the **Close** button to close the Domain Editor dialog and apply all the changes and additions. Did you notice how many times the fields were automatically populated from the inheritance? This is an excellent example of the power of using macros and inheritance in erwin DM. This is only the beginning of this power—wait until we get to creating the attributes themselves. The completed MyMovie domain hierarchy is shown in Figure 196.

51. Save and close your MyMovie data model. And this concludes the tutorial for this part.

Figure 196. Completed Domain Hierarchy

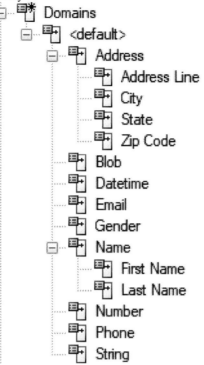

 If you accidentally created a domain under the wrong parent domain, open the Domain Editor dialog for that domain and change the Domain Parent in the general tab to the correct parent domain.

Key Learnings

- Domains originate from and conform to SQL-92 Standard.

- A domain is a named set of column properties or mini templates for attributes that apply to more than one attribute.

- There are different types of domains, including alphanumeric, numeric, temporal, and binary domains.

- erwin DM fully supports the domain standard from the SQL-92 Standard.

- erwin DM expands on the SQL-92 Standard to include other properties and a hierarchical structure of domains.

- erwin DM provides powerful functionality to automate a lot of tasks, such as inheritance and macros.

Spreadsheets have columns
Similar to attributes
Models all around

This chapter defines the concept of an attribute and the three different levels at which an attribute can exist: conceptual, logical, and physical.

Attributes Explained

An attribute is an individual piece of information whose values identify, describe, or measure instances of an entity. The attribute **Claim Number** identifies each claim. The attribute **Student Last Name** describes the student. The attribute **Gross Sales Amount** measures the monetary value of a transaction.

Returning to our spreadsheet analogy, the column headings on a spreadsheet are attributes. The cells beneath each column heading are the values for that column heading. Attributes can be thought of as the column headings in a spreadsheet, the fields on a form, or the labels on a report.

Attribute Types

As with entities, attributes can be described at an enterprise, conceptual, logical, physical, and operational level. An attribute at the enterprise or conceptual level must be an object, both *fundamental* and *critical* to the business. We do not usually think of attributes as business objects, but depending on the business need, they can be. When I worked for a telecommunications company, **Phone Number** was an attribute that was so important to the business that it needed representation on several conceptual data models.

An attribute on a logical data model represents a business property. Each attribute shown contributes to the business solution and is independent of any technology, including software and hardware. For example, **Passenger Last Name** is a logical attribute because it has business significance regardless of whether records are kept in a paper file or within the fastest database in the world. An attribute on a physical data model represents the physical 'container' where the data is stored. The attribute **Passenger Last Name** might be represented as the column **PSSNGR_LST_NAM** within the DBMS table **PSSNGR** or represented as the field name **PassengerLastName** within the MongoDB collection **Passenger**.

Tutorial: Creating Attributes in erwin DM

After creating the domains, it is now time to create the attributes in our model. Recall the attributes identified in the last chapter shown in Table 30 through Table 41.

1. Open erwin DM.

2. Using the Quick Access Toolbar, click on the *Open* button.

3. Select the **MyMovie_Ver1** data model, from the previous portion of the tutorial, in the Open dialog.

4. Click on the *Open* button.

5. The MyMovie model opens in erwin DM. Maximize the model in the diagram window if needed.

6. In the Model Explorer pane, click on the expand icon (⊞) next to the *Domains* node and all children domains, to display all the domains in the data model.

7. Observe all the built-in and custom domains created in Chapter 15.

8. There are several methods of adding an attribute to an entity. The first we are going to use is directly in the attribute itself. Select on the **Customer** entity. See Figure 197.

Figure 197. Select on the Customer Entity

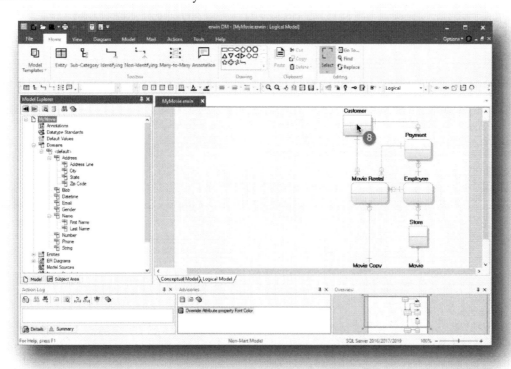

9. Press the *Tab* key. Observe that the focus jumps from the entity to the primary key group section of the entity, ready to create a new attribute in the primary key group section. See Figure 198.

Figure 198. Focus on Primary Key Group of Entity for Creating New Attribute

10. Press the *Tab* key a second time. Observe that the focus jumps from the primary key group section to the non-primary key group section of the entity, ready to create a new attribute in the non-primary key group section.

11. Press the *Tab* key a third time. Observe that the focus jumps from the non-primary key group section to the entity name section of the entity, ready to rename the entity. By using the Tab key, one can jump between the different sections of the entity for renaming or creating new objects within an entity.

12. Press the *Tab* key two more times to get back to the non-primary key group for adding our first attribute. Name it **customer first name**.

13. Press the *Enter* key. Observe that the focus jumps to the creation of another attribute in the non-primary key group section. Name it **customer last name**.

14. When finished, click outside of the entity on the background. Your entity should now have two attributes, as shown in Figure 199.

Figure 199. Customer Entity with Two Attributes

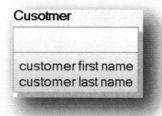

15. The second method of adding an attribute is by using the domains themselves, as set up in Chapter 15. Click and drag the **Gender** domain from the Model Explorer pane and drop it in the **Customer** entity, just below the **customer last name** attribute created in the previous step. See Figure 200.

Figure 200. Drag and Drop the Gender Domain

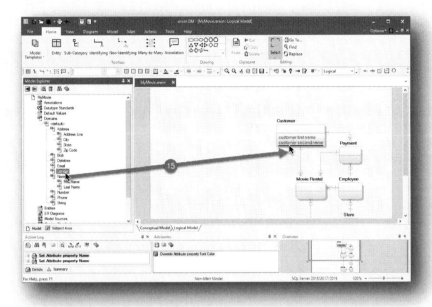

16. Observe that the attribute name was auto-populated with **Customer Gender**. This auto-populating was due to the macro that we put in the Attribute Name field in the domains. Also, take note of the intentional differences in case, which we will cover shortly.

17. If, in your model, the name of the attribute did not come out the same as the above step, go back to Chapter 15's tutorial and verify that all the steps were completed correctly.

18. Repeat the same steps for **Customer Address Line** from the **Address Line** domain, **Customer City** from the **City** domain, **Customer State** from the **State** domain, **Customer Zip Code** from the **Zip Code** domain, **Customer Email** from the **Email** domain and **Customer Phone** from the **Phone** domain, always adding them to the bottom of the **Customer** entity.

19. Make sure that the **Customer** entity is not selected, observed by the absence of the blue grip icons on the four corners of the entity. Right-click on the **Customer** entity and select the *Attribute Properties* option to open the Attribute Editor dialog. See Figure 201.

Figure 201. Right-Click Customer and Select Attribute Properties Option

20. The Attribute Editor dialog opens, as shown in Figure 202.

Figure 202. Attribute Editor Dialog

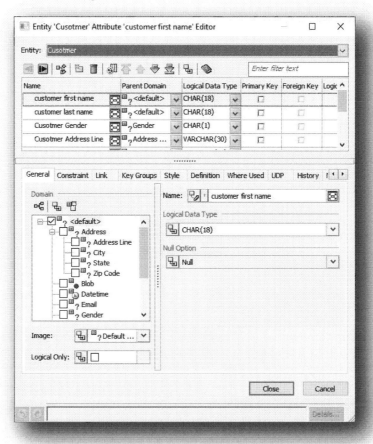

Let's discuss the sections of this dialog.

Parent Object Section

The parent object section is active in the Attribute Editor dialog. Note that it allows for the changing of the parent object, in this case, the entities, via the drop-down list. See Figure 203.

Figure 203. Parent Object Section

Object section

The object section allows for the changing of objects within the scope of the parent object—in this case, the attributes. It also allows for rudimentary changing of properties. Below are all the action buttons and grid columns of the Attribute Editor dialog's object section.

Action Buttons

◀ **Previous**–Allows the user to position the editor on the previous attribute in the Navigation Grid.

▶ **Next**–Allows the user to position the editor on the next attribute in the Navigation Grid.

Sort–Allows the user to sort the attributes by alphabetic, reverse alphabetic order, or attribute order. Visual cues provide the current sort order:

A
Z   Specifies that the attributes list sort order is in alphabetic order.

Z
A   Specifies that the attributes list sort order is in reverse alphabetic order.

        Specifies that the attributes list sort order is in attribute order.

New–Allows the user to create a new attribute that becomes the current object in the editor.

Delete–Allows the user to delete the selected attribute.

Reset Order–This button resets the order of the attributes in the logical model.

        Reset attribute to match column order (default order for physical model).

↶   Opens the reset order dialog, allowing for resetting the order of all entity attributes.

Move to Top–Moves the selected attribute to the top of the list. Only active when attributes list sort order is in attribute order.

Move Up–Moves the selected attribute up one level in the list. Only active when attributes list sort order is in attribute order.

Move Down–Moves the selected attribute down one level in the list. Only active when attributes list sort order is in attribute order.

Move to Bottom–Moves the selected attribute to the bottom of the list. Only active when attributes list sort order is in attribute order.

Help–Allows the user to open online help for the editor.

`Enter filter text`   The filter field allows for the filtering of extensive lists of attributes in the Navigation Grid for the quick location of a particular attribute.

Grid Columns

Name   Specifies the name of the attribute. This field allows for the changing of the name of the attribute.

Parent Domain   Specifies the current parent domain for the attribute. This field allows for the changing of the domain using the drop-down control.

Logical Data Type	Specifies the logical data type for the attribute. This field allows for the changing of the data type using the drop-down list. The drop-down list contains the data types related to the current domain's family data types.
Primary Key	Specifies whether the attribute is part of the primary key group. This field allows for the changing of the attribute from being a primary key attribute to a non-primary key attribute, and vice versa.
Foreign Key	Specifies whether the attribute is part of a foreign key group.
Logical Only	Specifies whether the attribute is suppressed from a physical model as a column and appears in a logical model only.
PII	Specifies that the selected attribute contains Personally Identifiable Information (PII). Select the checkbox to set this property. In the case of a child entity, for a PII enabled migrated parent attribute, the PII property is applicable in the child entity too.

21. When finished, click on the *General* tab.

22. Observe that when we created the attribute directly in the entity, the attribute was created with a parent domain of **<Default>** and inherited all the **<Default>** domain's properties, besides the name of the attribute.

23. For the **customer first name** attribute, we want the parent domain to be **First Name**, and for the **customer last name** attribute, we want the parent domain to be **Last Name**. We can change the attribute's parent domain via the Parent Domain column in the object section grid. Click the drop-down list button and select the **First Name** domain. See Figure 204.

 erwin DM drop-down lists often have the Invoke Editor button next to the list of objects. By using the Invoke Editor button, it opens the relevant editor for the list, with the object next to the button in focus. This functionality allows for the easy drilling through of editors for making quick changes to objects.

24. After changing the parent domain, observe the inherited properties changed, according to the domain of **First Name**.

25. Notice the overridden icon on the button next to the name of the attribute.

   Inherit–Specifies that inheritance is in place. Any changes to the parent property will cascade to the child's property.

   Overridden–Specifies that the inherited property value has been overridden and that any changes to the parent property will not be carried forward.

   Hardened–Specifies that the property value is hardened and cannot be changed without hardening first. This option is only available on Name properties.

Figure 204. Click the Parent Domain Drop-Down and Select the First Name Option

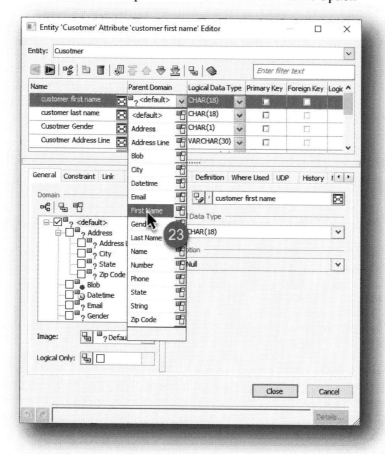

26. Click on the Overridden button next to the attribute name, and change the inherited state to Inherit (⬚).

27. Observe the name of the attribute changed to the macro from the domain, also observe the name changed in the object section of the grid to initial case.

28. Furthermore, observe that the toggle button (▶) next to the inheritance button is active. Click on the *Toggle* button to change the field view state.

29. Observe that the attribute name changes from the macro view state to the expanded view state. This functionality can be beneficial in seeing the changes to the macro and what they would do to the name.

30. Furthermore, observe the context-sensitive editor button (⬚) at the end of the attribute name field—we see these context editor buttons regularly in erwin DM. By clicking on these buttons, erwin DM opens the relevant editor for the object in focus. In this case, it opens an attribute name editor. Click on the *Context-Sensitive Editor* button. See Figure 205.

Figure 205. Attribute Name Context-Sensitive Editor Dialog

31. Observe that the attribute name context-sensitive editor dialog opens. Note the two fields, the macro filed and the expanded field. This dialog can be used to change the name of the attribute. Depending on the type of object in focus, the context-sensitive dialogs have a combination of the following action buttons:

    Save–Opens the Save As dialog so you can save the text.

    Print–Prints the text.

    Find–Opens the Find dialog to search the text.

    Find Again–Repeats the last search you entered in the Find dialog.

    Replace–Opens the Replace dialog, where you can enter text to find and replace.

    Cut–Cuts the selected text.

    Copy–Copies the selected text to the clipboard.

    Paste– Pastes the text from the clipboard.

    Macro Toolbox–Opens the macro toolbox.

    Spelling Checker–Checks the spelling of the text entered in the Text Editor.

    Help–Opens the help facility.

32. When finished, click the *OK* button to dismiss the attribute name context-sensitive editor dialog. Repeat the same steps for the **customer last name** attribute.

33. Observe the General tab.

    The General tab is used to enter and maintain core attribute information and is broken down into key areas.

    Domain   Displays and allows for the changing of the domain of the selected attribute. When changing the domain, all properties that have their inheritance in place changes to the property value of the new domain parent.

Image   Specifies the image for the domain and allows for the changing of the image. All new domains use a default image, or a different image can be used.

> **Inherit**–Specifies that inheritance is in place. Any changes to the parent property will cascade to the child's property.

> **Overridden**–Specifies that the inherited property value has been overridden and that any changes to the parent property will not be carried forward.

Logical Only   Specifies whether the attribute is suppressed from a physical model as a physical column and appears in a logical model only.

> **Inherit**–Specifies that inheritance is in place. Any changes to the parent property will cascade to the child's property.

> **Overridden**–Specifies that the inherited property value has been overridden and that any changes to the parent property will not be carried forward.

Name   Specifies the name of the attribute and allows for changing the attribute name.

> **Inherit**–Specifies that inheritance is in place. Any changes to the parent property will cascade to the child's property.

> **Overridden**–Specifies that the inherited property value has been overridden and that any changes to the parent property will not be carried forward.

> **Hardened**–Specifies that the property value is hardened and cannot be changed without hardening first. Only available on Name properties.

Logical Data Type   Specifies the logical data type for the attribute, and allows for the changing of the data type. Only data types of the parent domain's family are listed.

> **Inherit**–Specifies that inheritance is in place. Any changes to the parent property will cascade to the child's property.

> **Overridden**–Specifies that the inherited property value has been overridden and that any changes to the parent property will not be carried forward.

Null Option   Specifies the null option for the attribute, and allows for changing the null option.

> **Inherit**–Specifies that inheritance is in place. Any changes to the parent property will cascade to the child's property.

> **Overridden**–Specifies that the inherited property value has been overridden and that any changes to the parent property will not be carried forward.

34. When finished, click on the *Constraint* tab.

35. The Constraint tab specifies the validation and default value rules for attributes. One can select a validation and default value rule using the drop-down controls or select the checkbox to use an inherited constraint or default value. We cover the validation and default value rules more in-depth in Chapter 19.

36. When finished, click on the *Link* tab.

37. Observe the Link tab. The Link tab lets one work with the Link Wizard to link selected attributes and select the properties to synchronize between the linked objects. The Link feature provides support for column level denormalization by copying one attribute or column into one or more other entities or tables and allows for the applying of changes at any of the attributes/columns to update all the others automatically.

When a new link is defined, it maps an attribute or column to another existing attribute (or column) in another entity or allows for the creation of a new attribute in the target entity. The decision to map to an existing attribute or column or create a new one is a user choice made at the creation time of the link. The link can synchronize either or both ways for selected properties. Updates to a selected property of one linked attribute reflect the changes in its linked partner.

After creating a link, the link reflects in the link tab's grid for both of the attributes involved in the link. While an attribute may be involved in many links, each pair can only be involved in a single link. In other words, there cannot be multiple links connecting the same pair of attributes. Inheritance is not used to identify which properties are synchronized. The Link object holds an array of properties that are to be synchronized and the direction.

Action Buttons

> **Sort**–Allows the user to sort the links by alphabetic or reverse alphabetic order. Visual cues provide the current sort order.

> **New**–Allows the user to create a new link.

> **Delete**–Allows the user to delete the selected link.

⊞ **Choose Properties to Synchronize**–Allows the user to choose which properties to synchronize for the selected link.

⊞ **Column Editor**–Allows the user to change the selected attribute in the Attribute Editor dialog to the other side attribute for the selected link.

⊞ **Reset Property Inheritance**–Allows the user to open a dialog to allow for the resetting of the property inheritances for the selected link.

Grid Columns

Link Name	Specifies and allows for the changing of the name of the link.
Link To	Specifies the fully qualified attribute name on the other side of the link.
Synch direction	Specifies and allows for the changing of the direction of the synchronization, either *None, From This, To This* or *Two Way*.
Definition	Specifies and allows the changing of the definition of the link via the context-sensitive editor.

38. When finished, click on the *Key Groups* tab.

39. The Key Groups tab lets one manage the key group memberships for the selected attribute.

Action Buttons

⊞ **Sort**–Allows the user to sort the key groups by alphabetic, reverse alphabetic, or index order. Select the sort method using the drop-down menu that opens after you click the Sort button. Visual cues provide the current sort order:

    A⇕Z **Alphabetic Order**–Specifies that the key groups' list sort order is in alphabetic order.

    Z⇕A **Reverse Alphabetic Order**–Specifies that the key groups' list sort order is in reverse alphabetic order.

    ⊞ **Index Order**–Specifies that the key groups' list sort order is in index order.

⊞ **Key Group Editor**–Allows the user to open the Key Group Editor dialog with the current selected key group in focus.

Show FK Key Groups	**Show FK Key Groups**–This option box allows the user to switch on and off whether to show foreign key groups.

Grid Columns

☐	Specifies and allows for the changing of whether the currently selected attribute is part of the key group. We cover key groups in Chapter 17.
Key Group Name	Specifies the name of the key group.
Type	Specifies the type of the key group.

40. When finished, click on the *Style* tab.

41. The Style tab allows the user to set the preferences for displaying names and other definitions for an attribute. You can either use the default theme for the object that is defined in the Theme Editor dialog or change the style to apply only to the current attribute.

Option Theme

Reset–Allows the user to remove all style settings and to reset the inheritance of the theme to the parent diagram, subject area, or model.

Theme   **Theme**–Displays the currently used theme of the object. Use the drop-down list to select an existing theme to use. Click the *New* button (🔳) to create a theme or click the *Theme Editor* button (🔳) to open the Theme Editor dialog to modify the theme properties. We cover themes in more detail in Chapter 20.

Sample Settings from Theme

Name   Specifies and allows for the changing of the font name used for the attribute.

     Allows the user to reset the style setting for the selected setting for the attribute.

Size   Specifies and allows for the changing of the font size used for the attribute.

Color   Specifies and allows for the changing of the font color used for the attribute.

     Opens the color picker dialog.

Bold   Specifies and allows for the changing of the font boldness used for the attribute.

Italic   Specifies and allows for the changing of the font italics used for the attribute.

Strikethrough   Specifies and allows for the changing of the font strikethrough used for the attribute.

Underline   Specifies and allows for the changing of the font underline used for the attribute.

Sample   Provides a preview sample of the applied settings.

We cover themes in more detail in Chapter 20.

42. When finished, click on the *Definition* tab.

43. The Definition tab is used to enter a definition for the selected attribute. In a logical/physical model, or when you derive a physical model from a logical model, the definition migrates to the physical side as a column comment. Observe that the definition has been auto-populated from the First Name domain when we changed the attribute's domain in step 23.

Action Buttons

✂ Allows the user to cut the selected text into the clipboard.

📋 Allows the user to copy the selected text into the clipboard.

📋 Allows the user to paste the text in the clipboard.

🔲 Allows the user to reset the inheritance.

🔲 Allows the user to open the context-specific editor dialog.

🔤 Allows the user to invoke the spelling checker. For more details on the spelling checker, please refer to the tutorial in Chapter 7.

44. When finished, click on the *Where Used* tab.

45. Observe the Where Used tab. For more information on the Where Used tab, please refer back to Chapter 14 tutorial that already covered the Where Used tab.

46. When finished, click on the *UDP* tab.

47. Observe the UDP tab. For more information on the UDP tab, please refer back to Chapter 7 tutorial that already covered the UDP tab. We also explain more about UDPs in Chapter 25.

48. When finished, click on the *History* tab.

49. Observe the History Tab. For more information on the History tab, please refer back to Chapter 7 tutorial that already covered the History tab.

50. When finished, click the right arrow button (▶) on the tab scroll bar to display the remaining tabs. See Figure 206.

51. Click on the *Notes* tab.

52. Observe the Notes tab. For more information on the Notes tab, please refer back to Chapter 7 tutorial that already covered the Notes tab.

53. When finished, click on the *Extended Notes* tab.

54. Observe the Extended Notes tab. For more information on the Extended Notes tab, please refer back to Chapter 7 tutorial that already covered the Extended Notes tab.

55. When finished, click the left arrow button (◀) on the tab scroll bar to display the General tab.

56. Click on the *General* tab again.

57. Change the entity in the parent object section to **Employee** by clicking on the drop-down and selecting the *Employee* option.

58. Observe that the **Employee** entity has no attributes. We are going to use another alternative method of adding an attribute. Click the *New* button to add an attribute. See Figure 207.

Figure 206. Click the Right Arrow Button on the Tab Scroll Bar

Figure 207. Click the New Button

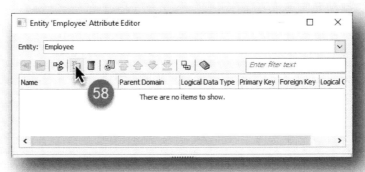

59. Observe the new attribute created, taking note of the parent domain, name, datatype, and null option of the new attribute. See Figure 208.

60. For **employee first name**, we could overwrite the name of the attribute, change the datatype, null option, and definition to reflect the correct information. But as seen before, using domains makes our task a lot easier, so let us continue using the domains. Change the domain using the Domain section on the General tab by clicking on the **First Name** domain. (You may have to scroll down to find the **First Name** domain)

Figure 208. Observe the New Attribute Created

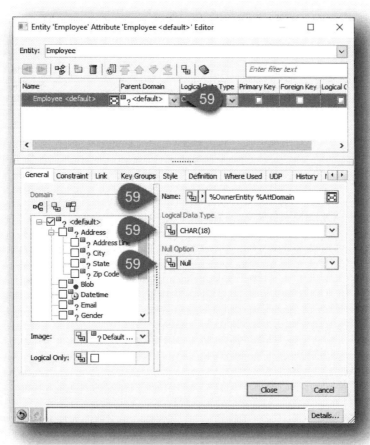

61. Now observe the attribute's name (both macro and expanded), datatype, and null option.

62. Next, it is your turn to create the **employee last name** and **gender** attributes on your own using the previous steps. Remember to change the null option for the **employee gender** attribute. See Table 42.

Table 42. Employee Entity Attributes (Part 1)

Entity	Attribute	Data Type	Nullable	Description
Employee	employee last name	String (20 Character)	No	The last name of the employee
Employee	employee gender	String (1 Character)	No	The gender of the employee

63. When finished, you should have three attributes.

64. For the next attribute (**employee hire date**), you will notice that we did not set up a domain for this. Seeing that this is a unique attribute, and is not used anywhere else, we chose not to create a domain for it. See Table 43.

Table 43. Employee Entity Attributes (Part 2)

Entity	Attribute	Data Type	Nullable	Description
Employee	employee hire date	Date	No	The hire date of the employee

65. For this attribute, you must use the built-in Datetime domain as the parent domain, so create a new attribute and assign it to the **Datetime** domain, as in the previous steps.

66. Observe the new attribute created, but noticing that the attribute name is not correct.

67. To resolve this, we need to rename the attribute. In the Name field, change the value to **employee hire date**.

68. Note that the inheritance for the attribute name is now overridden and that the macro name is no longer available.

69. Change the null option of the attribute to Not Null, as an employee must have a hire date.

70. Click on the *definition* tab.

71. Observe that the **Datetime** domain still defines **employee hire date** attribute as 'The datetime of the employee.'

72. Change the definition to the correct definition of 'The hire date of the employee.'

73. When finished, click the *General* tab again and create the remaining attributes for the **Employee** entity, as listed in Table 44.

Table 44. Employee Entity Attributes (Part 3)

Entity	Attribute	Data Type	Nullable	Description
Employee	employee salary	Number (15 Characters, 2 decimal places)	No	The salary of the employee
Employee	employee soc sec number	String (9 Character)	No	The Social Security Number of the employee
Employee	employee address line	String (30 Character)	Yes	The address line part of the address of the employee
Employee	employee city	String (20 Character)	Yes	The city part of the address of the employee
Employee	employee state	String (2 Character)	Yes	The state part of the address of the employee

Entity	Attribute	Data Type	Nullable	Description
Employee	employee zip code	String (5 Numeric Characters)	Yes	The zip code part of the address of the employee
Employee	employee email	String (50 Character)	Yes	The email of the employee
Employee	employee phone	String (10 Numeric Characters)	Yes	The phone number of the employee

Employee Salary

For **employee salary**, you should have done the following:

- Created a *New* attribute
- Selected the *Number domain*
- Changed the *Datatype* to DECIMAL(15,2)
- Renamed the attribute *Name* to **employee salary**
- Set the *Null Option* to Not Null
- Change the attribute *Definition* to 'The salary of the employee.'

We chose DECIMAL(15,2), as this is the logical representation for Number (15 Characters, 2 decimal places). Furthermore, we use Number as the root domain as this is a field that may have mathematical calculations performed on it.

Employee Soc Sec Number

For employee soc sec number, you should have done the following:

- Created a *New* attribute
- Selected the *String domain*
- Changed the *Datatype* to VARCHAR(9)
- Renamed the attribute *Name* to employee soc sec number
- Set the *Null Option* to Not Null
- Change the attribute *Definition* to 'The Social Security Number of the employee.'

Even though **Social Security Numbers** are generally numerical in nature, one never performs mathematical calculations on an SSN, and we need to allow for alternative identification numbers that may have an alphabetical character in it; therefore, we chose to use VARCHAR(9) as the data type.

Employee Address Line

For employee address line, you should have done the following:

- Created a *New* attribute
- Selected the Address Line domain
- Verified the attribute *Definition*

 When creating a new attribute in this manner, if you don't change the domain first after the creation of the attribute, the definition will not update to the new domain definition automatically. If this occurs, press the inherit button on the definition tab to reset the definition again.

Employee City

For employee city, you should have done the following:

- Created a *New* attribute
- Selected the *City domain*
- Verified the attribute *Definition*

Employee State

For employee state, you should have done the following:

- Created a *New* attribute
- Selected the *State domain*
- Verified the attribute *Definition*

Employee Zip Code

For employee zip code, you should have done the following:

- Created a *New* attribute
- Selected the Zip Code domain
- Verified the attribute *Definition*

We never perform mathematical calculations on zip codes. Therefore, we chose to use NCHAR(9) as the data type, which still enforces a numeric value, but manages it as a string.

Employee Email

For employee email, you should have done the following:

- Created a *New* attribute
- Selected the *Email domain*
- Verified the attribute *Definition*

Employee Phone

For employee phone, you should have done the following:

- Created a *New* attribute
- Selected the *Phone domain*
- Verified the attribute *Definition*

74. Now is time for you to fly solo, let us try adding all the other attributes to our logical data model, as reproduced below for ease of access in Table 45 through Table 49. We have included the domains that need to be assigned and the logical datatypes for those that are assigned to built-in domains.

Table 45. Movie Entity Attributes

Entity	Attribute	Data Type	Domain	Nullable	Description
Movie	movie title	VARCHAR(50)	String	No	The title of the movie
Movie	movie description	VARCHAR(255)	String	Yes	The description of the movie
Movie	movie genre	VARCHAR(10)	String	Yes	The genre of the movie
Movie	movie rating	VARCHAR(20)	String	Yes	The rating of the movie
Movie	movie rental rate	DECIMAL(15,2)	Number	No	The rental rate of the movie
Movie	movie director	VARCHAR(20)	Last Name	Yes	The last name of the movie director
Movie	movie star 1 name	VARCHAR(20)	Last Name	Yes	The last name of the leading star of the movie
Movie	movie star 2 name	VARCHAR(20)	Last Name	Yes	The last name of the second leading star of the movie
Movie	movie url	VARCHAR(50)	String	Yes	The url of the movie
Movie	movie clip	LARGE BINARY	Blob	Yes	The movie clip of the movie

Hint: When using a custom domain, you may need to overwrite the attribute name and description to change them accordingly when the standard macro does not reflect precisely what is required. For example, in **movie director**, **movie star 1 name**, and **movie star 2 name**.

Table 46. Movie Copy Entity Attributes

Entity	Attribute	Data Type	Domain	Nullable	Description
Movie Copy	movie copy format	VARCHAR(15)	String	No	The format of the movie copy (VHS, DVD)
Movie Copy	movie copy general condition	VARCHAR(10)	String	Yes	The general condition of the movie copy

Table 47. Movie Rental Entity Attributes

Entity	Attribute	Data Type	Domain	Nullable	Description
Movie Rental	movie rental date	DATE	Datetime	No	The date of the movie rental
Movie Rental	movie rental rate	DECIMAL(15,2)	Number	No	The rate of the movie rental
Movie Rental	movie rental status	VARCHAR(10)	String	Yes	The rental status of the movie copy
Movie Rental	movie rental due date	DATE	Datetime	Yes	The due date of the movie rental
Movie Rental	movie rental overdue charge	DECIMAL(15,2)	Number	Yes	The rental overdue charge of the movie rental
Movie Rental	movie rental record date	DATE	Datetime	No	The record date of the movie rental

Table 48. Payment Entity Attributes

Entity	Attribute	Data Type	Domain	Nullable	Description
Payment	payment type	VARCHAR(20)	String	No	The type of the payment (check, credit card, e-payment)
Payment	payment status	VARCHAR(10)	String	Yes	The status of the payment
Payment	payment amount	DECIMAL(15,2)	Number	No	The amount of the payment

Entity	Attribute	Data Type	Domain	Nullable	Description
Payment	payment date	DATE	Datetime	No	The date of the payment
Payment	payment check bank number	NCHAR(10)	String	Yes	The check bank number of the payment
Payment	payment check number	NCHAR(20)	String	Yes	The check number of the payment
Payment	payment credit card type	VARCHAR(12)	String	Yes	The credit card type of the payment (VISA, Master Card, Amex)
Payment	payment credit card number	NCHAR(16)	String	Yes	The credit card number of the payment
Payment	payment credit card expiration date	NCHAR(4)	String	Yes	The credit card expiration date of the payment
Payment	payment epay account number	NCHAR(20)	String	Yes	The epay account number of the payment
Payment	payment epay vendor number	NCHAR(10)	String	Yes	The epay vendor number of the payment

Table 49. Store Entity Attributes

Entity	Attribute	Data Type	Domain	Nullable	Description
Store	store address line	VARCHAR(30)	Address Line	No	The address line part of the address of the store
Store	store city	VARCHAR(20)	City	Yes	The city part of the address of the store
Store	store state	CHAR(2)	State	Yes	The state part of the address of the store

Entity	Attribute	Data Type	Domain	Nullable	Description
Store	store zip code	NCHAR(5)	Zip Code	Yes	The zip code part of the address of the store
Store	store phone	NCHAR(10)	Phone	Yes	The phone number of the store
Store	store manager first name	VARCHAR(20)	First Name	Yes	The first name of the store manager
Store	store manager last name	VARCHAR(20)	Last Name	Yes	The last name of the store manager

75. When finished, click the *Close* button on the Attribute Editor dialog.

76. Click on the *Diagram* ribbon button.

77. Click outside of the entities to release any selected objects. Then Click on the *Symmetric* layout option button.

78. By this stage, you might have noticed that we have different cases for the attributes that originated from our custom domains versus those from the built-in domains. Custom domains are initial case, and built-in domains (where we overwrote the names) are in lower case. There are two options to resolve this issue. The first is managing the types of objects in the data model through naming standards, which we deal with in Chapter 26. The other option is to modify the domain macros to force all custom domain macros to use lower case.

79. Right-click on the **Customer** entity, and click on the *Attribute Properties* again.

80. Observe that the Attribute Editor dialog opens. Click on the *Domain Editor* button.

81. Observe how erwin DM allows for the drilling through from one editor dialog to another. Also, notice that the focused domain is the domain of the attribute from the previous editor dialog. See Figure 209.

82. Scroll up in the object selection section and select the **<Default>** domain.

83. Change the *Attribute Name* field to '%Lower(%OwnerEntity %AttDomain).'

84. Click *Close* on the domain editor dialog.

85. Observe that the macro for the **customer first name** attribute automatically changed; this is due to inheritance being in place.

86. Click Close on the Attribute Editor dialog.

87. Observe the fully attributed logical data model.

88. Save and close your MyMovie data model.

Figure 209. Domain Editor Dialog Opens

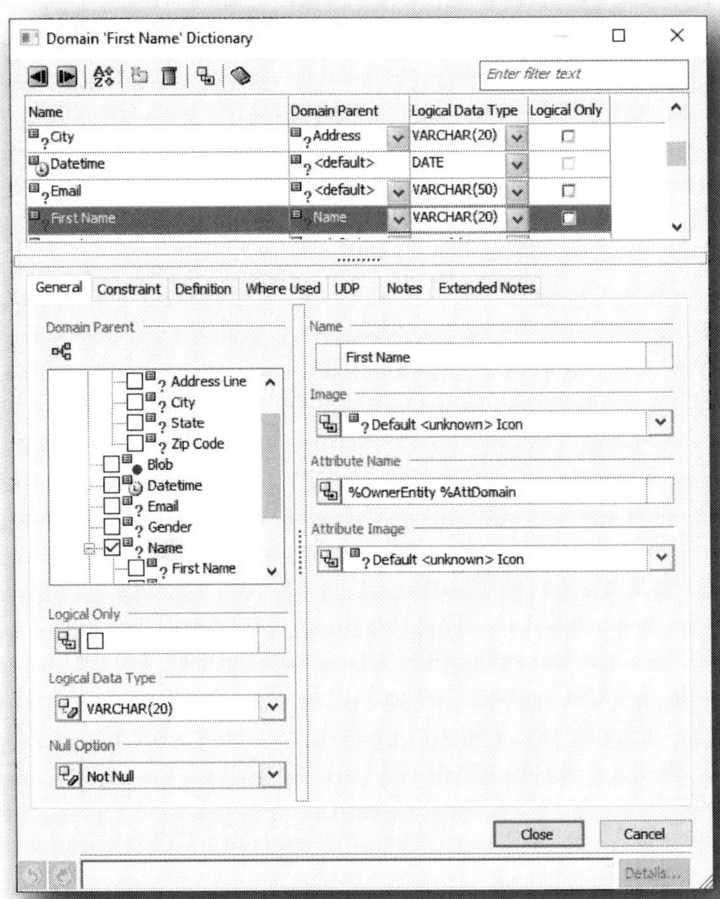

Key Learnings

- An attribute is a property of importance to the business whose values contribute to identifying, describing, or measuring instances of an entity.

- Attributes have different properties that form the basis of the logical data model design, such as name, datatype, definition, and null options, to only name a few.

- Domains make the process of adding attributes easier, more consistent in our logical data models.

- erwin DM provides a rich set of capabilities to create, manage, and update attributes.

More than one John Doe
Which is the right Customer?
Recall by the key

There is a lot of data out there, but how do you sift through it all to find what you're looking for? That's where keys come in. A key is one or more attributes whose purposes include enforcing rules, efficiently retrieving data, and allowing navigation from one entity to another. This chapter defines keys and distinguishes between the terms candidate, primary, and alternate keys. Also explained are surrogate keys and foreign keys.

Candidate Keys Explained

A candidate key is one or more attributes that uniquely identify an entity instance. Assigning an **ISBN** (International Standard Book Number) to every book title, uniquely identifies each book title and is, therefore, the title's candidate key. **Tax ID** can be a candidate key for an organization in some countries such as the United States. **Account Code** can be a candidate key for an account. A **VIN** (Vehicle Identification Number) identifies a vehicle.

Sometimes a single attribute identifies an entity instance such as **ISBN** for a book title. Sometimes it takes more than one attribute to identify an entity instance uniquely. For example, both a **Promotion Type Code** and **Promotion Start Date** may be necessary to identify a promotion. When more than one attribute makes up a key, we use the term *compound key*. Therefore, **Promotion Type Code** and **Promotion Start Date** together are a compound candidate key for a promotion.

For a school, each **Student** may attend one or many **Classes**, and each **Class** may contain one or many **Students**. Figure 210 contains a data model with primary and alternate keys.

Figure 210. Student/Class Data Model Updated with Primary and Alternate Keys

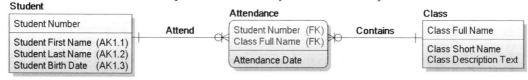

A candidate key consists of one or more attributes that uniquely identify an entity instance. The candidate key that is determined to be the best way to identify each record in the entity becomes the primary key. The other candidate keys become alternate keys. Keys containing more than one attribute are known as compound keys. Primary key attributes show above the line in the rectangles. Notice the two numbers following the key abbreviation 'AK.' The first number is the

277

grouping number for an alternate key, and the second number is the ordering of the attribute within the alternate key. So there are three attributes required for the **Student** alternate key: **Student First Name**, **Student Last Name**, and **Student Birth Date**. This is also the order in which the alternate key index will be created because **Student First Name** has a '1' after the colon, **Student Last Name** a '2,' and **Student Birth Date** a '3.'

Attendance now has as its primary key **Student Number** and **Class Full Name**, which appear to make a valid primary key. Note that the two primary key attributes of **Attendance** are followed by 'FK.' These are foreign keys, to be discussed shortly.

A unique index is the translation of a candidate key at the physical level.

Surrogate Keys Explained

A surrogate key is a unique identifier for a table, often a counter, usually fixed-size, and always system-generated without intelligence—that is, has no business meaning. (In other words, you can't look at a month identifier of '1' and assume that it represents the **Month** entity instance value of 'January.') Surrogate keys should not be visible to the business but should remain behind the scenes to allow for more efficient navigation across structures and to facilitate integration across applications.

Surrogate keys are also efficient. You've seen that a primary key may be composed of one or more attributes of the entity. A single surrogate key is more efficient to use than having to specify three or four (or five or six) attributes to locate a single record. Surrogate keys are useful for integration, which is an effort to create a single, consistent version of the data.

When using a surrogate key, always determine the natural key, which is what the business would consider being the way to uniquely identify the entity, and then define this natural key as an alternate key. For example, assuming a surrogate key is a more efficient primary key than **Class Full Name**, we can create the surrogate key **Class ID** for **Class** and define an alternate key on the natural key **Class Full Name**, as shown in Figure 211.

Figure 211. Student/Class Data Model Updated with Surrogate Key

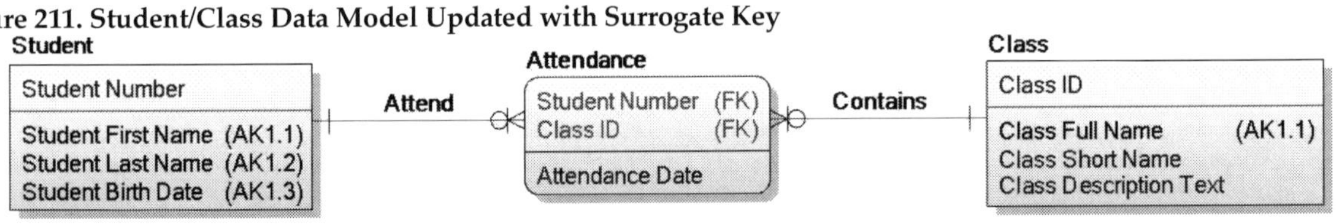

Foreign Keys Explained

The entity on the 'one' side of the relationship is called the parent entity, and the entity on the 'many' side of the relationship is called the child entity. When we create a relationship from a parent entity to a child entity, the primary key of the parent is copied as a foreign key to the child.

A foreign key is one or more attributes that provide a link to another entity (or in a case of a recursive relationship where two instances of the same entity may be related, a link to the same entity). At the physical level, a foreign key allows a relational database management system to navigate from one table to another. For example, if we need to know the customer who owns an account, we would want to include the **Customer ID** in the **Account** entity. The **Customer ID** in **Account** is the primary key for **Customer**.

Using this foreign key back to **Customer** enables the database management system to navigate from a particular account or accounts to the customer or customers that own each account. Likewise, the database can navigate from a particular customer or customers to find all of their accounts. Our data modeling tools automatically create a foreign key when a relationship is defined between two entities.

In our **Student/Class** model in Figure 211, there are two foreign keys in **Attendance**. The **Student Number** foreign key points back to a particular student in the **Student** entity, and the **Class ID** foreign key points back to a particular **Class** in the **Class** entity.

Secondary Keys Explained

Sometimes there is a need to retrieve data rapidly from a table to answer a business query or meet a specific response time. A secondary key is one or more attributes (if there is more than one attribute, it is called a compound secondary key) that is accessed frequently and needs to be retrieved quickly. A secondary key is also known as a non-unique index or inversion entry (IE for short). A secondary key does not have to be unique, stable, nor always contain a value. For example, we can add a secondary key to **Student Last Name** in **Student** to allow for quick retrieval whenever any queries require **Student Last Name**. See Figure 212.

Figure 212. Student/Class Data Model Updated with Secondary Key

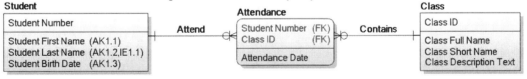

Student Last Name is not unique, as there can be two 'Murphy's, it is not stable and can change over time, and although it may be rare, there could be times when we may not know someone's last name, so that it can be empty.

Key Groups in erwin DM

There are two general categories of key groups in erwin DM, those that get automatically created, and those that get created manually. Primary key groups and foreign key groups get generated automatically, and alternate key groups and secondary key groups (erwin DM prefers the usage of the term 'inversion entry key groups') get generated manually by the modeler.

Every entity has a primary key group automatically created regardless of whether it has any members. Adding an attribute to or removing an attribute from the primary key section in an entity graphic changes the composition of the primary key group membership. Similarly, changes to the composition of the primary key group membership result in changes to the content of the primary key section of the entity graphic.

A foreign key group gets automatically created for every relationship, provided it has at least one member. The associated relationship manages the creation of the foreign key group. Furthermore, the associated primary key group of the parent entity manages the population of the foreign key group members for referential integrity purposes.

By default, relationships use the membership of the primary key group of the parent entity for referential integrity. Still, it is possible to select any alternate key group defined in the parent entity. There may be DBMS requirements concerning the definition and implementation of alternate key groups on the physical side as an index. (For example, in Oracle, a unique constraint has to be generated from the alternate key rather than a unique index.)

Key groups are one of only a few erwin DM objects where one can accept the default names generated. However, while it is not possible to auto-generate the logical key group names in a different format, it is possible to specify rules for the generation of the physical index names in a different form, which will be covered in Chapter 26.

erwin DM generates names for all key groups. These start with an 'X' followed by a key type indicator (PK = Primary Key, AK = Alternate Key, IF = Foreign key, and IE = Inversion Entry) and finish with the entity name. Apart from the primary key group, the type indicators also include a numerical suffix to ensure uniqueness.

Apart from the inversion entry key group, all the key groups can create both indexes and constraints at the DBMS level. If required, the primary key group generates both the primary key constraint and the primary key index in the physical database. (For some DBMS, generating both is not supported, or if both get generated, the index must appear before the constraint in the DDL.) Similarly, if an attribute or group of attributes requires a unique constraint, an alternate key needs to be defined in the model and is used to generate a unique constraint.

The foreign key group generates the foreign key constraint for the table, although the physical name of its associated relationship gets used as the foreign key constraint name.

We cover how to control what constraints and indexes get generated from key group objects in Chapter 27.

Tutorial: Creating Key Groups in erwin DM

In our MyMovie logical data model, we have already created the entities and their attributes, and we are now going to identify and promote the candidate keys to become our primary keys.

1. Open erwin DM.

2. Using the Quick Access Toolbar, click on the *Open* button.

3. Select the **MyMovie_Ver1** data model, from the previous portion of the tutorial, in the Open dialog.

4. Click on the *Open* button.

5. The MyMovie model opens in erwin DM. Maximize the model in the diagram window if needed.

6. Starting with the **Customer** entity, we identify that the **customer first name** and **customer last name** together have the potential of being a candidate key, but we know that there could be two (or more) people with the same first and last names. We can try to identify another attribute to add to the **customer first name** and **customer last name** that would make the entity instance unique. Seeing that all the other attributes are not required (nullable), we can deduce that there is no unique candidate key from the available attributes. We could make the **customer address line** or **customer phone** required attributes, and then add one of them to make a primary key. But this would break the business rule requirements of allowing the address line and phone to be nullable, and these attributes tend to change over time. Therefore, we are going to create a new surrogate attribute that can uniquely identify the entity instances.

7. Click on the name of the **Customer** entity and press the Tab key. Observe that a new attribute is created with the name of **<New>** in the primary key section of the **Customer** entity. See Figure 213.

    Figure 213. New Attribute Created in Customer Entity

8. While the new attribute is still highlighted, rename it to **customer number**. Then click outside of the entity to apply the new name.

9. Now open the Attribute Editor dialog with **customer number** attribute in focus. (If in doubt on how to open the Attribute Editor dialog, or to change the focus of the dialog to **customer number**, please refer back to the tutorial in Chapter 16.)

10. Change the Domain to **Number**, observe the data type changes to Integer.

11. Next, reset the inheritance of the Name of the attribute. See Figure 214.

Figure 214. Change Domain and Inheritance of Name of Attribute

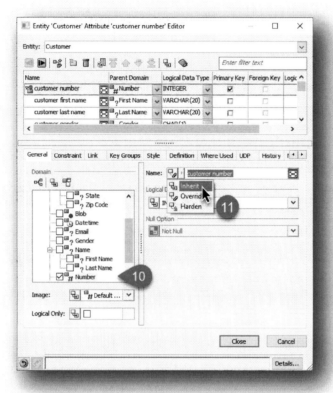

12. Observe that now the attribute name is inherited from the macro for the **Number** domain, and that the definition for the attribute inherits from the **Number** domain. When finished, close the Attribute Editor dialog.

13. Take note of how the **customer number** has migrated via the foreign key relationship into the **Payment** and **Movie Rental** entities.

14. Next, we are going to focus on the **Employee** entity. Following the same rationale, as followed for **Customer**, we can deduce that **employee first name** and **employee last name** is insufficient for a primary key. However, this time we have some other alternative attributes that could make a unique candidate key, such as **employee soc sec number**. However, Social Security Number as a primary key is not a good practice as this attribute contains sensitive data. For our MyMovie model, we also decide to make usage of a surrogate key for the **Employee** entity.

15. Repeat the same steps that we followed for the **Customer** entity, with the **Employee** entity, adding an **employee number** surrogate key attribute.

16. Repeat the same steps for the **Store** and **Movie** entities.

17. Observe how the primary keys have migrated as foreign keys to all the children entities wherever there is a relationship.

18. It is a good practice to deal with all the parent entities first and then drill down to the children entities. So let's now take a look at the children entities, starting with **Movie Copy**.

19. At first appearance, it appears that the **Movie Copy** entity is functional as it contains a primary key. However, looking closer, we realize that this primary key would not support the ability to identify each entity instance uniquely. Returning to the business rule, A **Movie Copy** is a single copy of a **Movie**, and we realize we could have more than one **Movie Copy** with the same movie number. To resolve this, we need to introduce another attribute to make each instance of the **Movie Copy** unique.

20. Instead of using the same method we used in the previous steps for adding a new attribute to an entity, we are going to drag the **Number** domain from the Model Explorer pane into the **Movie Copy** entity. Drop it below the **movie number** attribute in the primary key section of the entity. (For more details on this method, please refer to step 15 in Chapter 16.)

21. Observe the addition of the new attribute in the primary key section of the **Movie Copy** entity.

22. Furthermore, observe the impact it had on the child entity, **Movie Rental**.

23. Following the explanation earlier in this chapter, we need to identify the minimum set of attributes that would uniquely identify an instance of the **Movie Rental** entity. After careful consideration, we identified that only the **customer number**, **movie number**, **movie copy number**, and **movie rental record date** were required to identify an instance of a **Movie Rental** uniquely.

24. Click and hold the mouse button on the **employee number** attribute, then drag it down to the top of the non-key attribute section. See Figure 215.

25. Repeat the same steps for the **store number** attribute. Then drag the **movie rental record date** attribute from the non-key attribute section to the key attribute section.

26. Observe the change to the relationships between **Payment** and **Movie Rental**, and **Employee** and **Movie Rental**. The relationships changed from identifying to non-identifying. For more information about relationships, please see Chapter 18.

Figure 215. Dragging an attribute out of the primary key

27. Using the same methodology explained in the previous set of steps, **move store number** in **Employee** from the key attribute section to the non-key attribute section. Next, add the new attribute **payment number** and **move customer number** and **employee number** from the key attribute section to the non-key attribute section.

28. We know that erwin DM automatically creates the primary key groups, and we have now successfully identified their members. Furthermore, we also know that erwin DM automatically manages the foreign key groups, and we have seen the relationship between the primary key groups and foreign key group members and how they change according to the interaction of the relevant attributes.

29. We now need to incorporate the alternative and inversion entry key groups and their members. After reviewing the logical data model, we have identified the alternative and inversion entry key groups in Table 50.

Table 50. Key Groups

Entity	Key Group	Rationale	Members
Customer	Inversion Entry	Allow for the lookup of a customer based on their first and last names, taking into consideration that there might be multiple customers with the same first and last name.	customer first name
			customer last name
Employee	Alternate Key 1	Allow for the lookup of an employee based on their first and last names, taking into consideration that we were informed that there could only be one employee with the same first and last name.	employee first name
			employee last name
	Alternate Key 2	Allow for the lookup of an employee based on their SSN.	soc sec number

Entity	Key Group	Rationale	Members
Movie	Alternate Key	Allow for the lookup of a movie based on its title, assuming no two movies have the same title.	movie title
	Inversion Entry 1	Allow for the lookup of movie/s of a genre.	movie genre
	Inversion Entry 2	Allow for the lookup of movie/s directed by a specific person.	movie director
	Inversion Entry 3	Allow for the lookup of movie/s in which a specific person stared in.	movie star 1 name
			movie star 2 name

30. Right-click on the **Customer** entity, and select the Key Group Properties option.

31. Observe that the Entity Key Group Editor dialog opens, with the **Customer** entity in focus. See Figure 216.

Figure 216. Entity Key Group Editor dialog

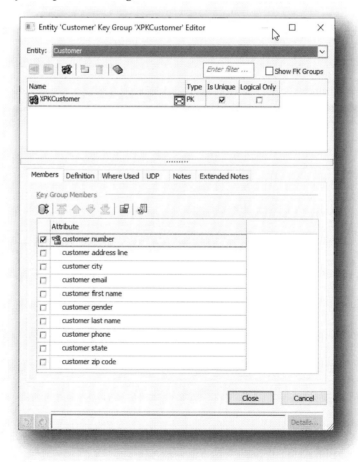

Before going further, let us get an understanding of how the Entity Key Group Editor dialog works.

Parent Object Section

The parent object section is active in the Entity Key Group Editor dialog. Note that it allows for the changing of the parent object, in this case, the entities, via the drop-down list.

Object section

The object section allows for the changing of objects within the scope of the parent object, in this case, the key groups. It also allows for rudimentary changing of properties. Below are all the action buttons and grid columns of the Entity Key Group Editor dialog's object section.

Action Buttons

Previous–Allows the user to position the editor on the previous key group in the Navigation Grid.

Next–Allows the user to position the editor on the next key group in the Navigation Grid.

Sort–Allows the user to sort the key group by alphabetic, reverse alphabetic order, or key group order. Visual cues provide the current sort order:

Specifies that the key group list sort order is in alphabetic order.

Specifies that the key group list sort order is in reverse alphabetic order.

Specifies that the key group list sort order is in key group order.

New–Allows the user to create a new key group that becomes the current object in the editor.

Delete–Allows the user to delete the selected key group.

Help–Allows the user to open online help for the editor.

Enter filter text — The filter field allows for the filtering of extensive lists of key groups in the Navigation Grid for the quick location of a particular key group.

☐**Show FK Groups** — Displays FK (foreign key) groups in the Navigation Grid.

Grid Columns

Name — Specifies the name of the attribute. This field allows for the changing of the name of the attribute.

Type — Specifies the type of key group. (PK = Primary Key, AK = Alternate Key, IF = Foreign key, and IE = Inversion Entry)

Is Unique — Specifies whether the key group is a unique key group. (Selected for PK and AK, unselected for IF and IE)

Logical Only — Specifies whether the key group is suppressed from a physical model as an index and appears in a logical model only.

32. When finished, click on the *Members* tab.

33. Observe the Members tab shown in Figure 217.

Figure 217. Members Tab

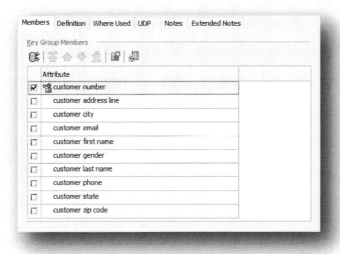

The Members tab is used to select and maintain the key group member attributes and is broken down into several areas.

Action Buttons

Sort–Allows the user to sort the key group members (attributes) by alphabetic, reverse alphabetic order, or key group order. Visual cues provide the current sort order:

Specifies that the key group member list sort order is in alphabetic order.

Specifies that the key group list member sort order is in reverse alphabetic order.

Specifies that the key group list member sort order is in attribute order.

Specifies that the key group list member sort order is in key group order.

Move to Top–Moves the selected attribute to the top of the list. Only active when attributes list sort order is in key group order.

Move Up–Moves the selected attribute up one level in the list. Only active when attributes list sort order is in key group order.

Move Down–Moves the selected attribute down one level in the list. Only active when attributes list sort order is in key group order.

Move to Bottom–Moves the selected attribute to the bottom of the list. Only active when attributes list sort order is in key group order.

Attribute Editor–Allows the user to drill through to the Attribute Editor dialog, with the currently selected attribute in focus.

Reset Order–Opens the Reset Order dialog, allowing the user to reset the key group member order for the selected key group or all key groups to match the physical index order. Or to reset the physical index order to match the key group order.

Grid Columns

☐ Specifies whether the attribute gets included in the key group's members or not.

Attribute The attribute field specifies the name of the attributes.

34. When finished, click on the *Definition* tab.

35. Observe the Definition tab. One uses the Definition tab to enter a definition for the selected key group. In a logical/physical model, or when you derive a physical model from a logical model, the definition migrates to the physical side as an index comment.

Action Buttons

⮚ Allows the user to cut the selected text into the clipboard.

⮚ Allows the user to copy the selected text into the clipboard.

⮚ Allows the user to paste the text in the clipboard.

⮚ Allows the user to reset the inheritance.

⮚ Allows the user to open the context-specific editor dialog.

⮚ Allows the user to invoke the spelling checker. For more details on the spelling checker, please refer to the tutorial in Chapter 7.

36. When finished, click on the *Where Used* tab.

37. Observe the Where Used tab. For more information on the Where Used tab, please refer back to Chapter 14 tutorial that already covered the Where Used tab.

38. When finished, click on the *UDP* tab.

39. Observe the UDP tab. For more information on the UDP tab, please refer back to the Chapter 7 tutorial that covered the UDP tab. We also explain more about UDPs in Chapter 25.

40. When finished, click on the *Notes* tab.

41. Observe the Notes tab. For more information on the Notes tab, please refer back to Chapter 7 tutorial that already covered the Notes tab.

42. When finished, click on the *Extended Notes* tab.

43. Observe the Extended Notes tab. For more information on the Extended Notes tab, please refer back to Chapter 7 tutorial that already covered the Extended Notes tab.

44. When finished, click the *Members* tab again to add our first inversion entry key group.

45. Click on the new button.

46. Select the New Inversion Entry (Non-Unique) option. See Figure 218.

Figure 218. Select the New Inversion Entry Option

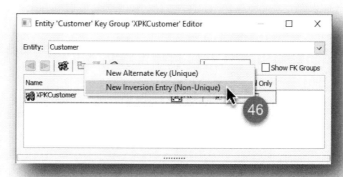

47. Observe a new inversion entry key group is created, but with no members. Also, notice the automatic assignment of the key group name. Select the checkbox next to the **customer first name** and **customer last name** attributes in the members' tab to assign the two attributes to the new inversion entry key group.

48. Next, change the object parent (entity) to **Employee** to add our next key group. See Figure 219.

Figure 219. Change the Object Parent to Employee

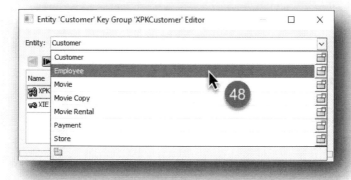

49. Observe that only the primary key group is shown. Select the checkbox to Show FK Groups to display the foreign key groups. erwin DM, by default, does not show the foreign key groups in the Key Group Editor dialog as the foreign key groups' definition is not manageable through this dialog, but instead through the primary key groups of the parent entity. See Figure 220.

Figure 220. Select the Show FK Groups Checkbox

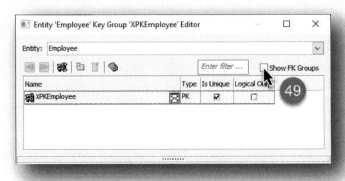

50. Observe the foreign key group is now displayed. The foreign key group is from the relationship where the **Employee** is the child entity in the relationship. (Store to Employee)

51. Click on the new button again to add our first alternative key group. See Figure 221.

Figure 221. Click the New Button

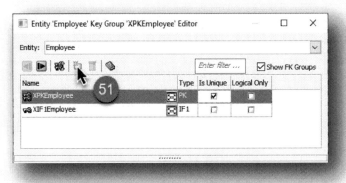

52. Select the New Alternate Key (Unique) option. See Figure 222.

Figure 222. Select the New Alternate Key Option

53. Observe the new alternative key group is created, but with no members. Also, notice the automatic assignment of the key group name. Select the checkbox next to **employee first**

name and **employee last name** attributes in the members' tab to assign the two attributes to the alternative key group.

54. Following the same above steps, create the remaining key groups for the model, as reproduced in Table 51.

Table 51. Remaining Key Groups

Entity	Key Group	Rationale	Members
Employee	Alternate Key 2	Allow for the lookup of an employee based on their SSN.	soc sec number
Movie	Alternate Key	Allow for the lookup of a movie based on its title, assuming no two movies have the same title.	movie title
	Inversion Entry 1	Allow for the lookup of movie/s of a genre.	movie genre
	Inversion Entry 2	Allow for the lookup of movie/s directed by a specific person.	movie director
	Inversion Entry 3	Allow for the lookup of movie/s in which a specific person stared in.	movie star 1 name
			movie star 2 name

55. Save and close your MyMovie data model.

Key Learnings

- A candidate key is one or more attributes that uniquely identify an entity instance.

- A candidate key has four primary characteristics: it is unique, mandatory, non-volatile, and minimal.

- A surrogate key is a unique identifier for a table, often a counter, usually fixed-size, and always system-generated without intelligence.

- A foreign key is one or more attributes that provide a link to another entity.

- A secondary key is one or more attributes that are accessed frequently and need to be retrieved quickly. A secondary key is also known as a non-unique index or inversion entry.

Rules all around us
Relationships tell the tale
Connecting the dots

This chapter defines rules and relationships and the different levels at which relationships can exist: enterprise, conceptual, logical, physical, and operational. Data rules are distinguished from validation rules. Cardinality and labels are explained so that you can read any data model as easily as reading a book. Other types of relationships, such as subtyping and many-to-many relationships, are also discussed.

Relationships Explained

Rules in our data models are visually captured through relationships. A line connecting two entities that captures the rule or navigation path between them is displayed as a relationship. If the two entities are **Employee** and **Department**, the relationship can capture the rules 'Each **Employee** must work for one **Department**' and 'Each **Department** may contain one or many **Employees.**'

Relationship Types

The levels of granularity (enterprise, conceptual, logical, physical, and operational) that apply to entities and attributes also apply to the relationships that connect entities. Enterprise and conceptual relationships are high-level rules or navigation paths that connect key business objects. Logical relationships are detailed business rules or navigation paths that enforce the rules between the logical entities. Physical relationships are detailed technology-dependent rules or navigation paths between the physical structures that the relationship connects. The operational relationships are the database constraints in a DBMS or references in a document-based database such as MongoDB.

Cardinality Explained

In a relationship between two entities, cardinality captures how many instances from one entity participate in the relationship with instances of the other entity. It is represented by the symbols that appear on each end of a relationship line. Without cardinality, the most we can say about a relationship is that two entities are connected in some way through a rule. For example, **Employee** and **Department** have some relationship, but we may not know more than this. Note that the same two entities may be related in more than one way; for example, each **Department** may contain one or many **Employees**, but there could be a separate relationship capturing the **Employee** who manages that **Department**.

For cardinality, we can choose any combination of zero, one, or many. *Many* (some people read it as *more*) means any number greater than one. Specifying zero or one allows us to capture whether or not an entity instance is *required* in a relationship. Specifying one or many allows us to capture *how many* of a particular instance participates in a given relationship.

The traditional data model diagramming approach has only three cardinality symbols—one can't specify an exact number (other than through documentation), as in 'A **Car** contains four **Tires**.' We can only say, 'A **Car** may contain many **Tires**.'

 Note that Class Diagram in the Unified Modeling Language (UML for short) allows for the specifying of the exact numbers in cardinality. erwin DM also provides an extension to the traditional data model diagramming approach, also allowing for the inclusion of the exact numbers in cardinality.

Illustrated in the following examples are each of the cardinality symbols. A booking is the origination for issuing a ticket. A booking may issue multiple tickets. Formalizing the rules between booking and ticket, we have:

- Each **Booking** issues zero, one, or many **Ticket**s.
- Each **Ticket** must be issued by one **Booking**.

Figure 223 captures these business rules. The small line means 'one.' The circle means 'zero.' The triangle with a line through the middle means 'many.' Some people call the 'many' symbol a *crow's foot*. Relationship lines are frequently labeled to clarify the relationship and express the rule that the relationship represents. Thus, the label 'issues' on the line in this example, helps in reading the relationship and understanding the rule. Having a zero in cardinality means we can use optional-sounding words such as 'may' or 'can' when reading the relationship. Without the zero, we use mandatory-sounding terms such as 'must' or 'have to.'

Figure 223. Cardinality Symbols. One-to-Many

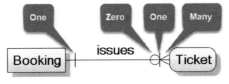

So instead of being redundant and saying:

- Each **Booking** issues zero, one, or many **Ticket**s.

We take out the word 'zero' because it can be expressed using the word 'may,' which implies the zero:

- Each **Booking** may issue one or many **Ticket**s.

A relationship has a parent and child. The parent entity appears on the 'one' side of the relationship, and the child appears on the 'many' side of the relationship. When I read a relationship, I always start with the entity on the one side of the relationship first. 'Each **Booking** may issue one or many **Ticket**s.' It's then followed by reading the relationship from the many side: 'Each **Ticket** must be issued by one **Booking**.' In truth, it doesn't matter which side you start from, as long as you are consistent.

I also always use the word 'each' in reading a relationship, starting with the parent side. The reason for the word 'each' is that you want to specify, on average, how many instances of one entity relate to a different entity instance. 'Each' is a more user-friendly term to me than 'A.'

Let's change the cardinality slightly and see how this impacts the resulting business rule. Assume that the airline industry changes the way airplane tickets are issued. A single ticket can be issued for multiple legs (flights) of a trip, listing all the flights on the same piece of paper. A passenger can make multiple bookings for a single trip, and they can make subsequent bookings to add to an existing trip. Figure 224 contains the updated cardinality.

Figure 224. Cardinality Symbols. Many-to-Many

Booking ▷————— issues —————◁ Ticket

This is known as a many-to-many relationship, in contrast to the previous example, which was a one-to-many relationship. The business rules here are read as follows:

- Each **Booking** may issue many **Ticket**s.
- Each **Ticket** may be issued by many **Booking**s.

Many modelers capture labels on both sides of the relationship line, instead of just one side, as shown in this chapter. In weighing simplicity versus verbosity, I chose simplicity. The other label can be inferred from the label that appears on the model.

 erwin DM allows for three options to display labels for relationships: the relationship name itself, the Parent to Child verb phrase, and the Child to Parent verb phrase. It is vital to choose a standard and always work according to that standard.

Role Naming Explained

We often require multiple foreign key groups to reference the same attribute in the parent entity, and therefore are required to rename the foreign key group attributes. In the IDEF methodology, the renaming of the foreign key group members (attributes) is referred to as Role Naming. For compound foreign key groups (more than one foreign key group member), it is only necessary to role name as many key group members as is required to support the business need. Data modeling tools, like erwin DM, traditionally unify the duplicate foreign key group members during the process of creating multiple relationships between two entities. See Figure 225 for a unified example, and Figure 226 for a role named example. In Figure 225, there is no distinguishing between the address of the employee's residence and the employee's workplace address. When creating the second relationship, the foreign key group attributes get unified into one foreign key group attribute. In Figure 226, we have role named the two unified foreign key attributes. Now there is a distinction between the address of the employee's residence and the employee's workplace address.

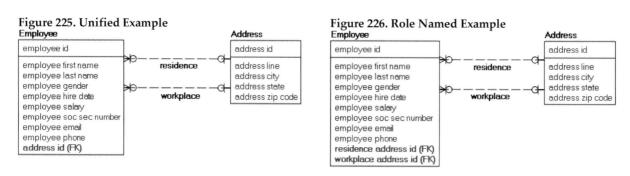

Figure 225. Unified Example   Figure 226. Role Named Example

Subtyping Explained

Subtyping allows grouping the common attributes and relationships of similar or related entities. Subtyping is an excellent way of communicating that certain concepts are very similar and for showing examples. In the airline industry example, we expand the business model to include not only flights tickets that a passenger can book but also bus and cruise tickets, as illustrated in Figure 227.

Figure 227. Airline Industry Example Before Subtyping

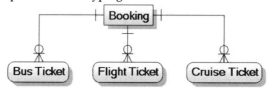

- Each **Booking** may issue one or many **Flight Tickets**.
- Each **Flight Ticket** must be issued by one **Booking**.
- Each **Booking** may issue one or many **Bus Tickets**.

- Each **Bus Ticket** must be issued by one **Booking**.
- Each **Booking** may issue one or many **Cruise Tickets**.
- Each **Cruise Ticket** must be issued by one **Booking**.

Rather than repeat the relationship to **Booking** three times, we can introduce subtyping, as shown in Figure 228.

Figure 228. Airline Industry Example After Subtyping

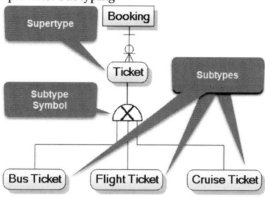

- Each **Booking** may issue one or many **Tickets**.
- Each **Ticket** must be issued by one **Booking**.
- Each **Ticket** may either be a **Bus Ticket**, **Flight Ticket**, or **Cruise Ticket**.
- Each **Bus Ticket** is a **Ticket**.
- Each **Flight Ticket** is a **Ticket**.
- Each **Cruise Ticket** is a **Ticket**.

The subtyping relationship implies that all the subtypes inherit all of the properties from the supertype. Therefore, there is an implied relationship from **Bus Ticket** to **Booking** as well as from **Flight Ticket** to **Booking** and well as from **Cruise Ticket** to **Booking**. Not only does subtyping reduce redundancy on a data model, but it also makes it easier to communicate similarities across what otherwise would appear to be distinct and separate concepts.

There are two types of subtype relationships, as illustrated in Figure 229.

Figure 229. Types of Subtype Symbols

- **Inclusive subtype relationship**–When an attribute in the subtype entity can derive its value from one or more subtype entities. For example, a **Ticket** may consist of a **Bus Ticket** <u>and</u> a **Flight Ticket** <u>and</u> a **Cruise Ticket**, or any combination thereof.

- **Exclusive subtype relationship**–When an attribute in the subtype entity can derive its value from only one subtype entity. For example, a **Ticket** may consist of a **Bus Ticket** <u>or</u> a **Flight Ticket** <u>or</u> a **Cruise Ticket**, but it may only be of one subtype.

In IDEF1X notation, the two types of subtypes are called 'Complete' and 'Incomplete.'

Tutorial: Creating Relationships in erwin DM

In our MyMovie conceptual data model, we started including some *fundamental* and *critical* relationships. After a better understanding of relationships and how they work, we are going to refine our relationships and revisit some of the attributes.

1. Open erwin DM.

2. Using the Quick Access Toolbar, click on the *Open* button.

3. Select the **MyMovie_Ver1** data model, from the previous portion of the tutorial, in the Open dialog.

4. Click on the *Open* button.

5. The MyMovie model opens in erwin DM. Maximize the model in the diagram window if needed.

6. Let us first start by understanding the Relationship Editor dialog. Right-click on the relationship line between the Payment and Employee entities, then select the *Properties* option. See Figure 230.

Figure 230. Right Click Relationship and Select Properties

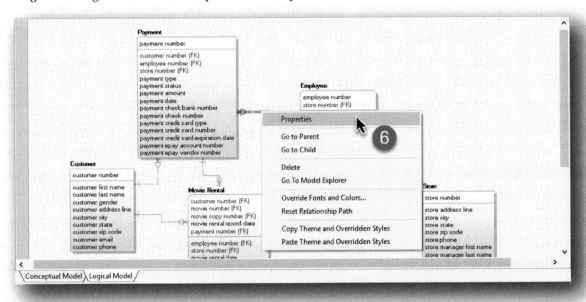

7. Observe the Relationship Editor dialog opens. See Figure 231.

Figure 231. The Relationship Editor Dialog

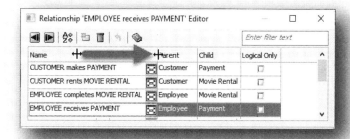

8. In the object section, drag the column divider between the Name and Parent column to the right to show the full names of the relationships. This functionality is present with all grids in erwin DM. See Figure 232.

Figure 232. Drag Column Divider to the Right

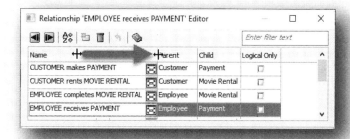

9. Make sure that you are on the General tab clicking on the General tab. See Figure 233.

The General tab is used to enter and maintain the core relationship information and is broken down into key areas.

Figure 233. Click on the General Tab

Type Properties

Type   The relationship Type defines the type of relationship. As explained earlier, there are two types of relationships possible, identifying and non-identifying.

Relationship Properties

Parent-to-Child   This is the verb phrase to describe the parent-to-child relationship.

Child-to-Parent   This is the verb phrase to describe the child-to-parent relationship.

Cardinality Properties

The relationship cardinality represents how a parent entity within a relationship connects to a particular number of instances of the child entity.

Cardinality   **Zero, One or More**–Specifies that each parent entity connects to zero, one, or more instances of the child entity.

One or More (P)–Specifies that each parent entity connects to one or more instances of the child entity.

Zero or One (Z)–Specifies that each parent entity connects to zero or one instance of the child entity.

Cardinality Value	Specifies that each parent entity connects to an exact number of instances of the child entity.

10. Notice that all the relationships and their properties created in the conceptual data model are carried forward in the logical data model.

11. Click on the *Definition* tab.

12. Observe the Definition tab, as shown in Figure 234.

Figure 234. Definition Tab

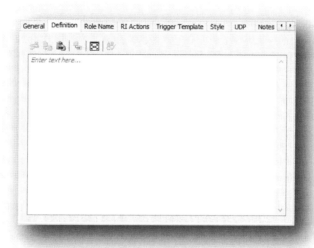

One uses the Definition tab to enter a definition for the selected relationship. Typically the name, parent-to-child, and child-to-parent adequately define the relationship. Still, erwin DM provides for a definition at all object levels, and therefore, the same applies to a relationship. The benefit of the definition is that it can add extra context to a relationship name, that might not be easily realized.

Action Buttons

- Allows the user to cut the selected text into the clipboard.
- Allows the user to copy the selected text into the clipboard.
- Allows the user to paste the text in the clipboard.
- Allows the user to reset the inheritance.
- Allows the user to open the context-specific editor dialog.
- Allows the user to invoke the spelling checker. For more details on the spelling checker, please refer to the tutorial in Chapter 7.

13. When finished, click on the *Role Name* tab.

14. Observe the Role Name tab, as shown in Figure 235. Using the Role Name tab, one can assign a Rolename to an attribute, delete a Role Naming, or migrate an alternate key as a foreign key.

Figure 235. Role Name Tab

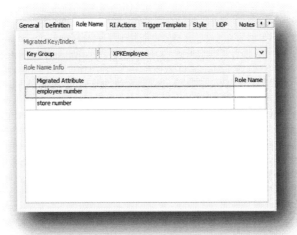

Migrated Key

Key Group   Let's one select the primary key group or the alternate key group that migrates from the parent entity to the child entity.

Relationship Properties

Migrated Attribute   Displays the primary key group attribute/s or the alternate key group attribute/s that migrate from the parent entity to the child entity and the role name associated with the attribute in the current relationship.

Role Name   Let's one enter a role name for the attribute selected from the Migrated Attribute list.

15. When finished, click on the *RI Actions* tab.

16. Observe the RI Actions tab, as shown in Figure 236.

Figure 236. RI Actions Tab

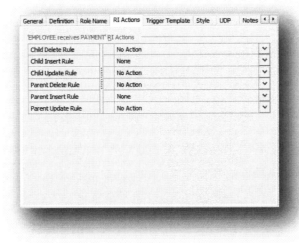

The RI (Referential Integrity) Actions tab lets the user override the default referential integrity rules for a specific relationship. The default referential integrity setting is set at mode level, as discussed in Chapter 7.

Grid Columns

Child Delete   Specifies the referential integrity trigger action that occurs when data in the child entity is deleted. Available actions include RESTRICT, CASCADE, SET NULL, SET DEFAULT, NO ACTION, or NONE. These actions are available for each of these settings.

Child Insert   Specifies the referential integrity trigger action that occurs when data in the child entity is inserted.

Child Update   Specifies the referential integrity trigger action that occurs when data in the child entity is updated.

Parent Delete   Specifies the referential integrity trigger action that occurs when data in the parent entity is deleted.

Parent Insert   Specifies the referential integrity trigger action that occurs when data in the parent entity is inserted.

Parent Update   Specifies the referential integrity trigger action that occurs when data in the parent entity is updated.

17. When finished, click on the *Trigger Template* tab.

18. Observe the Trigger Template tab, as shown in Figure 237.

Figure 237. Trigger Template Tab

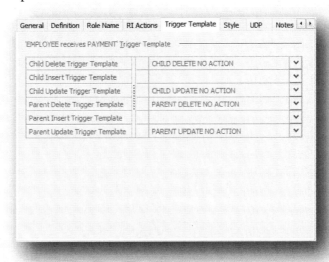

We cover triggers in more detail in Part IV, as triggers are the physical implementation of the referential integrity of the logical data model.

19. When finished, click on the *Style* tab.

20. Observe the Style tab, as shown in Figure 238.

Figure 238. Style Tab

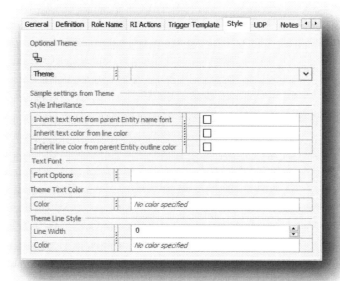

The Style tab allows the user to set the preferences for displaying names and other definitions for a relationship. One can either use the default theme for the object that is defined in the Theme Editor dialog or change the style to apply only to the current relationship.

Option Theme

Reset–Allows the user to remove all style settings and to reset the inheritance of the theme to the parent diagram, subject area, or model.

Theme   **Theme**–Displays the currently used theme of the object. Use the drop-down list to select an existing theme to use. Click the *New* button (🖳) to create a theme or click the *Theme Editor* button (🖳) to open the Theme Editor dialog to modify the theme properties. We cover themes in more detail in Chapter 20.

Sample Settings from Theme

Style Inheritance

Inherit text font from parent Entity name font   Specifies the inheritance state of the text font used for the relationship from the parent entity name font. It can only be changed via the theme.

Inherit text color from line color   Specifies the inheritance state of the text color used for the relationship from the line color. It can only be changed via the theme.

Inherit line color from parent Entity outline color	Specifies the inheritance state of the line color used for the relationship from the parent entity outline color. It can only be changed via the theme.

Text Font

Font Options	Specifies the font used for the relationship text. It can only be changed via the theme.

Theme Text Color

Color	Specifies the color used for the relationship text. It can only be changed via the theme.

Theme Line Style

Line Width	Specifies the style used for the relationship line. It can only be changed via the theme.
Color	Specifies the color used for the relationship line. It can only be changed via the theme.

We cover themes in more detail in Chapter 20.

21. When finished, click on the *UDP* tab.

22. Observe the UDP tab. For more information on the UDP tab, please refer back to the Chapter 7 tutorial that already covered the UDP tab. We also explain more about UDPs in Chapter 25.

23. When finished, click the right arrow button (▸) on the tab scroll bar to display the remaining tabs.

24. When finished, click on the *Notes* tab.

25. Observe the Notes tab. For more information on the Notes tab, please refer back to the Chapter 7 tutorial that already covered the Notes tab.

26. When finished, click on the *Extended Notes* tab.

27. Observe the Extended Notes tab. For more information on the Extended Notes tab, please refer back to the Chapter 7 tutorial that already covered the Extended Notes tab.

28. When finished, click the left arrow button (◂) on the tab scroll bar to display the General tab.

29. Click on the *General* tab again.

30. In Chapter 10, we learned to create relationships in the diagram pane. We are now going to use the relationship editor to create our next relationships. In our sessions with John, the owner of the MyMovie, we identify that there is a need to manage the manager of the store. This has two relationships that we need to capture. The first is the manager of the employees

relationship. A recursive relationship is a relationship that connects an entity to itself. Let's now create a recursive relationship to detail this information.

31. Click on the *New* button to create a relationship.

32. Observe the New Relationship dialog appears. Select the *Parent* of **Employee** and the *Child* of **Employee** and a *Type* of **Identifying**. When finished, click the *OK* button to create the new relationship.

33. Observe the pop-up windows, asking if you want to convert the relationship to a non-identifying relationship.

 Recursive relationships can only be non-identifying—if they were identifying, the parent and child attribute would both be the same attribute, thus causing the illegal cycle.

34. Click the *Yes* button to convert the relationship to a Non-Identifying relationship.

35. Observe the advisory note in the advisory section of the dialog. The advisory informs us that the relationship type got changed from a Non-Identifying to an Identifying relationship type.

36. In the object selection section, scroll down to the new relationship and select it. It should be the last relationship in the list. See Figure 239.

Figure 239. Select the New Relationship

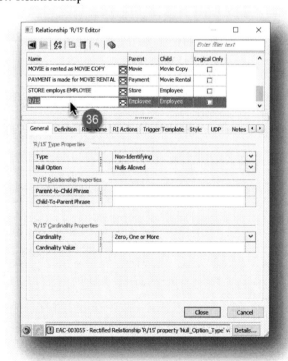

37. Rename the relationship to '**EMPLOYEE** manages **EMPLOYEE**.' Assign a Parent-to-Child Phrase of 'manages' and a Child-to-Parent Phrase of 'is managed by' to the relationship.

38. Click on the *Role Name* tab.

39. Observe the absence of the role name. By default, when we created the recursive relationship, erwin DM unifies the parent attribute with the child attribute and thus only reflects the single unified attribute. See Figure 240.

Figure 240. Observe the Absence of the Role Name

40. Change the role name for the **employee number** attribute to **manager employee number**. See Figure 241.

Figure 241. Change the Role Name for Employee Number

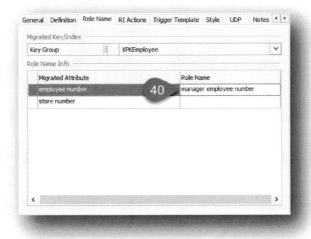

41. We only need to change the **employee number** to be role named as **manager employee number** because the **store number** for the manager and the employee will always be the same, as both will work at the same store. This is a business rule understanding that we gained from John, the owner of the MyMovie stores. Whenever using a role name, it is crucial to only role name the least number of attributes to satisfy the business case. In most instances, it usually is all the attributes, but sometimes it is only required to role name some of them.

42. Observe the creation of a new attribute, **manager employee number** in the **Employee** entity, and that the **store number** attribute stays unified. See Figure 242.

Figure 242. Employee Entity

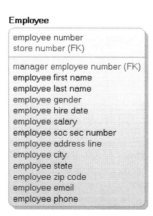

43. Next, we need to create a relationship from **Employee** to **Store** to maintain the relationship of **store manager first name** and **store manager last name** to satisfy the business requirement of tracking the store manager details at the store level. We could have these as standard text attributes, but the referential integrity would not be maintained. Secondly, we could also create a normal relationship and carry the **employee number** as a foreign key, but for simplicity of the front end, we decide to reflect the actual store manager's first and last names.

44. So to start, let's create the first relationship. Click the *New* button to create the new relationship.

45. Observe the New Relationship dialog appears. Select the *Parent* of **Employee** and the *Child* of **Store** and a *Type* of **Non-Identifying**. When finished, click the *OK* button to create the new relationship.

46. In the object selection section, scroll down to the new relationship and select it. It should be the last relationship in the list.

47. Rename the relationship to '**EMPLOYEE** manages **STORE**.'

48. Click on the *General* tab.

49. Assign a Parent-to-Child Phrase of 'manages' and a Child-to-Parent Phrase of 'is managed by' to the relationship.

50. Click on the **Role Name** tab.

51. Using the Migrated Key / Index section, change the Key Group to the **XAK1Employee**. This will change the migrated attributes in the relationship to the alternative key group attributes and not the primary key attributes. See Figure 243.

Figure 243. Change the Key Group to XAK1Employee

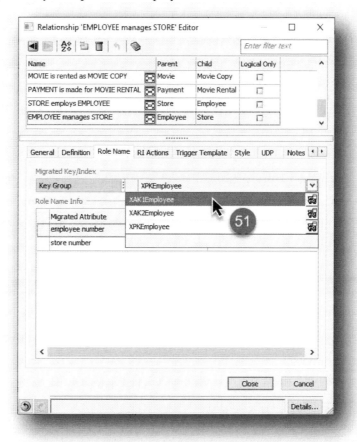

52. Observe that the migrated attributes change to the **employee first name** and **employee last name**.

53. Role name the **employee first name** to **store manager first name**.

54. Observe the pop-up Key Migration Conflict dialog. The dialog is informing us that the attribute **store manager first name** already exists, and provides us with the various options to resolve the duplicate attribute name conflict. The options are to either replace the existing attribute with the new foreign key attribute, rename the child attribute, or rename the rolenamed attribute.

55. For our requirements, we want to replace the child attribute with the foreign key attribute, as we previously created the attribute before creating the relationship. Click the *OK* button to accept the default option.

56. Repeat the same steps for the **employee last name** to **store manager last name** role naming.

57. When finished, click the *Close* button to close the Relationship Editor dialog.

58. You might notice that the two new relationships that we created are not displayed on the diagram. This is because we created the relationships in the editor and not directly in the diagram. Objects created in the dialogs and the model explorer do not automatically get included in the diagram, but they are in the data model. To make them visible and to fully understand the reasoning why you need to make them visible, see the chapters on Subject Areas and Diagrams in Chapter 20.

59. Save your MyMovie data model. Do not close it, as we will be continuing with it in the subtype relationship tutorial.

Tutorial: Creating Subtype Relationships in erwin DM

In reviewing our logical data model, that there are three different types of payments, each with their distinct information. We also learn that a payment may only be one of the three different types. Therefore, we decide to use a subtype relation to hold the specific payment type data.

1. Click on the new Entity button to create a subtype entity.

2. Place the new entity in your diagram and rename it to **Payment Check**.

3. Repeat the same steps, creating a **Payment Credit Card** and **Payment Epay** subtype entities.

4. Click on the new *Sub-Category* button to create the subtype relationships. See Figure 244.

Figure 244. Click the New Sub-Category Button

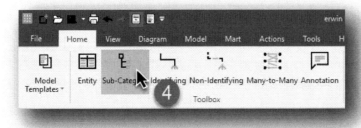

5. Click on the **Payment** entity.

6. And then the **Payment Check** entity. See Figure 245.

Figure 245. Create Subtype Relationship

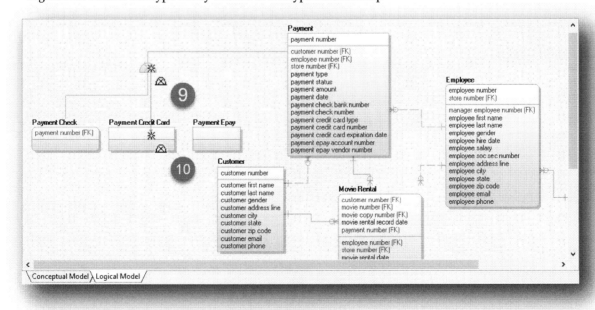

7. Observe the creation of the subtype relationship, and that the primary key from the **Payment** entity (Super-Type) has migrated to the **Payment Check** entity (Sub-Type).

8. Click on the Sub-Category button again.

9. This time, click on the sub-type symbol instead of the super-type entity. (If we click on the super-type entity, it creates a new sub-type relationship grouping.)

10. And then click on the **Payment Credit Card** entity. See Figure 246.

Figure 246. Second Subtype Entity Linked to Subtype Relationship

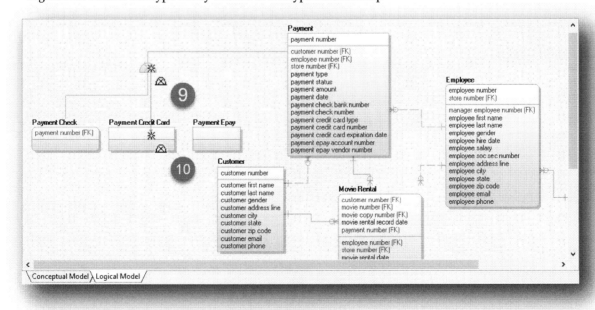

11. Repeat the same steps, linking the **Payment Epay** entity to the subtype relationship.

12. Next, we need to more the attributes into their respective entities. Click twice on the **payment check bank number** attribute, making sure that it is highlighted. (The first click selects the entity, the second click selects the attribute within the entity.)

13. Then drag the attribute, while holding the mouse button down, and drop it in the non-key section of the **Payment Check** entity. See Figure 247.

Figure 247. Drag and Drop the Attribute in the Payment Check Entity

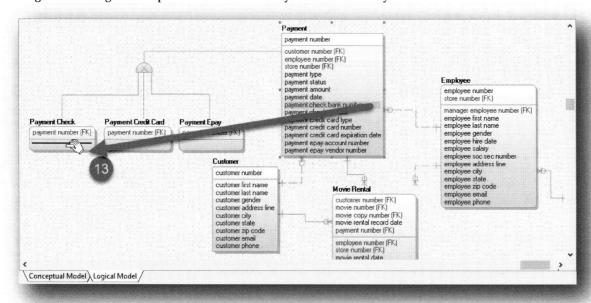

14. Repeat the same steps for the **payment check number** attribute.

15. Repeat the same steps for the **payment credit card type**, **payment credit card number**, and **payment credit card expiration date**. Dropping them in the **Payment Credit Card** entity.

16. Finally, repeat for the **payment epay account number** and **payment epay vendor number**, dropping in the **Payment Epay** entity.

17. From these steps, we learned that by dragging and dropping an attribute from one entity into another moves the attribute to the destination entity. This same functionality does not only operate for subtype entities but any two entities, even if they are not related to each other.

18. From our earlier section on subtyping, we learned that there are two types of subtype relationships, inclusive and exclusive. For our relationship, we need an exclusive relationship, but let us take a more in-depth look at the properties of the subtype relationship.

19. Right-click on the subtype symbol, and select the *Properties* option. See Figure 248.

20. Observe the Subtype Symbol Editor dialog displays. See Figure 249.

Figure 248. Right-Click the Subtype Symbol

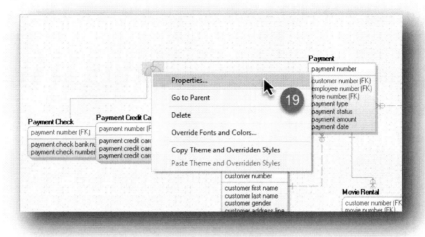

Figure 249. Subtype Symbol Editor Dialog

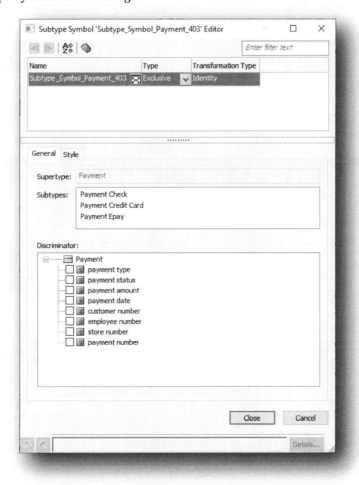

Before going further, let us get an understanding of how the Subtype Symbol Editor dialog works.

Object section

The object section allows for the changing of subtype symbols. Below are all the action buttons and grid columns of the Subtype Symbol Editor dialog's object section.

Action Buttons

Previous–Allows the user to position the editor on the previous subtype symbol in the Navigation Grid.

Next–Allows the user to position the editor on the next subtype symbol in the Navigation Grid.

Sort–Allows the user to sort the subtype symbol by alphabetic or reverse alphabetic order. Visual cues provide the current sort order:

> Specifies that the subtype symbol list sort order is in alphabetic order.

> Specifies that the subtype symbol list sort order is in reverse alphabetic order.

Help–Allows the user to open online help for the editor.

Enter filter text   The filter field allows for the filtering of extensive lists of subtype symbols in the Navigation Grid for the quick location of a particular subtype symbol.

Grid Columns

Name	Specifies the name of the subtype relationship. This field allows for the changing of the name of the subtype relationship.
Type	Specifies the type of subtype relationship.
	Complete subtype relationship (in IDEF1X, when all categories are known).
	Incomplete subtype relationship (in IDEF1X, when all categories may not be known).
	Inclusive subtype relationship (in IE, when an attribute in the subtype entity can derive its value from one or more subtype entities).
	Exclusive subtype relationship (in IE, when an attribute in the subtype entity can derive its value from only one subtype entity).
Transformation type	By default, all subtype relationships have a transformation type of Identity Transform. This identifies the movement of the primary key from the supertype to the subtypes.

21. Click on the subtype relationship name and rename to **Payment Type Subtype**.

22. When finished, click on the *General* tab.

23. Observe the General tab, as shown in Figure 250.

Figure 250. General Tab

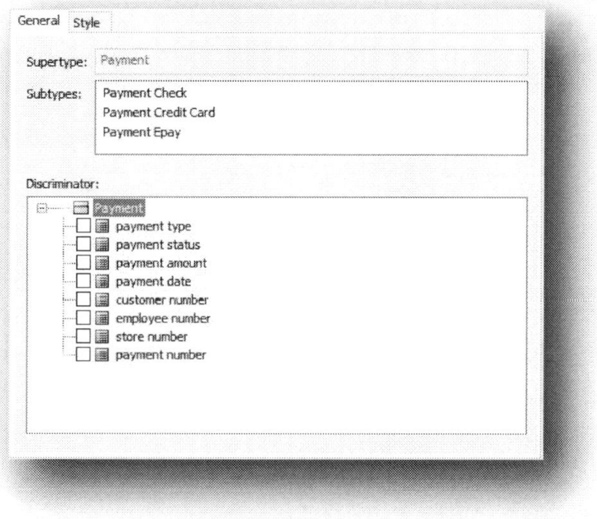

The General tab is used to select and maintain the subtype relationship details.

Supertype   Specifies the supertype entity of the subtype relationship.

Subtypes   Specifies the subtype entities of the subtype relationship.

Discriminator   It allows the user to select an attribute to assign as the discriminator, by selecting the checkbox next to the attribute name to assign as the discriminator. Clear the checkbox to remove the discriminator association.

24. Select the checkbox next to the **payment type** attribute to associate the **payment type** as the discriminator. See Figure 251.

25. When finished, click on the *Style* tab.

26. Observe the Style tab, as shown in Figure 252.

The Style tab allows the user to set the preferences for displaying names and other definitions for a subtype relationship. One can either use the default theme for the object that is defined in the Theme Editor dialog or change the style to apply only to the current relationship.

Option Theme

Reset–Allows the user to remove all style settings and to reset the inheritance of the theme to the parent diagram, subject area, or model.

Theme   **Theme**–Displays the currently used theme of the object. Use the drop-down list to select an existing theme to use. Click the *New* button (📋) to create a theme or click the *Theme Editor* button (🔠) to open the Theme Editor dialog to modify the theme properties. We cover themes in more detail in Chapter 20.

Figure 251. Select the Discriminator for the Subtype Relationship

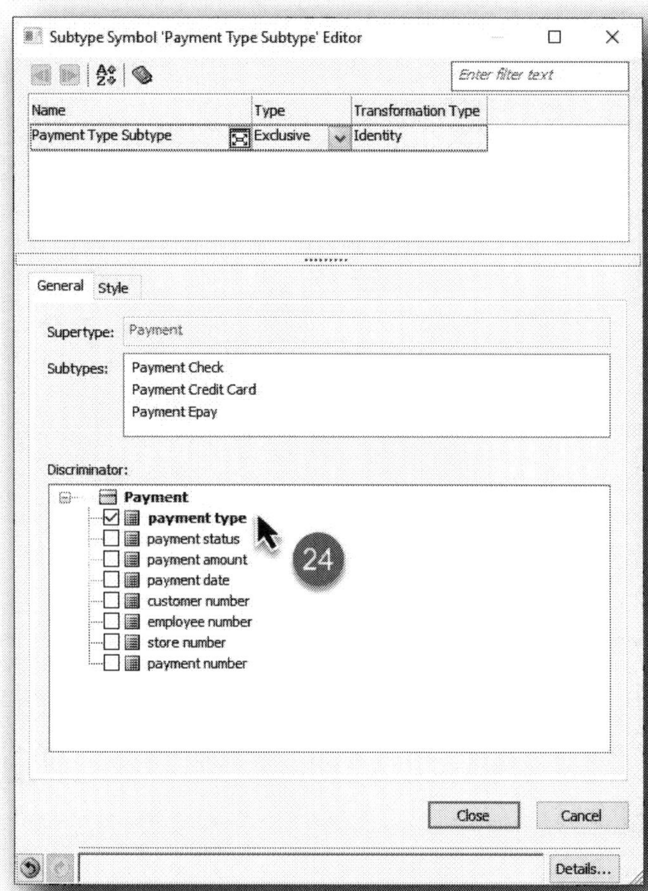

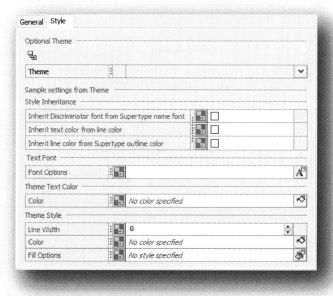

Figure 252. Style Tab

Sample Settings from Theme

Style Inheritance

Inherit Discriminator font from Supertype name font	Specifies the inheritance state of the text font used for the subtype relationship from the supertype entity name font. It can only be changed via the theme.
Inherit text color from line color	Specifies the inheritance state of the text color used for the subtype relationship from the line color. It can only be changed via the theme.
Inherit line color from Supertype outline color	Specifies the inheritance state of the line color used for the subtype relationship from the supertype entity outline color. It can only be changed via the theme.

Text Font

Font Options	Specifies the font used for the subtype relationship text. It can only be changed via the theme.

Theme Text Color

Color	Specifies the color used for the subtype relationship text. It can only be changed via the theme.

Theme Line Style

Line Width	Specifies the style used for the subtype relationship line. It can only be changed via the theme.
Color	Specifies the color used for the subtype relationship line. It can only be changed via the theme.
Fill Color	Specifies the fill color used for the subtype relationship symbol. It can only be changed via the theme.

We cover themes in more detail in Chapter 20.

27. When finished, click on the *Close* button to close the Subtype Symbol Editor dialog.

28. Observe the subtype discriminator is reflected next to the subtype symbol. See Figure 253.

29. In the past, we made usage of the auto-layout options, but there always comes a time when the auto-layout cannot always achieve the results that we desire. Unfortunately, erwin DM is an excellent data modeling tool, but it does not have a mind-reading function yet, and therefore cannot determine which entities we need close together and which ones don't matter. Therefore, erwin DM allows for the manual manipulation of the object in a diagram. We are now going to layout the new subtype entities and relationship lines manually.

Figure 253. Observe the Subtype Discriminator

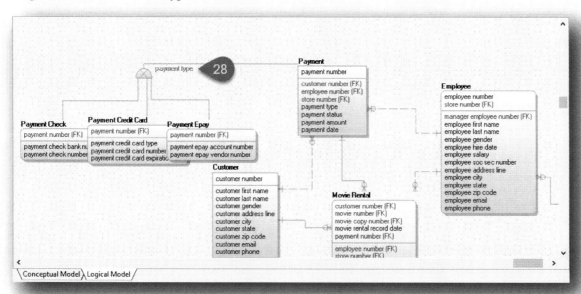

30. Click and hold the mouse button on the **Payment Epay** entity, and drag it to the bottom of the diagram, approximately where we have placed it on the diagram. See Figure 254.

Figure 254. Reposition the Payment Epay Entity

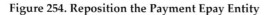

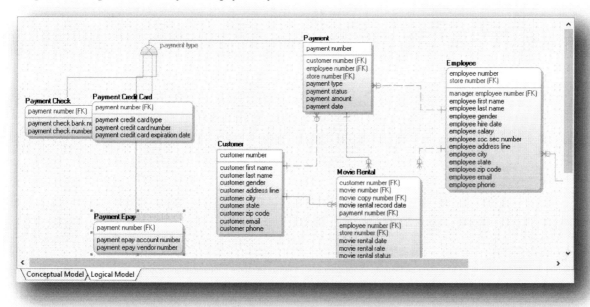

31. Reposition the **Payment Credit Card** entity roughly between the **Payment Check** entity and the **Payment Epay** entity, approximately where we have placed it on the diagram. See Figure 255.

32. Reposition the **Payment Check** entity approximately where we have placed it on the diagram. See Figure 256.

Figure 255. Reposition the Payment Credit Card Entity

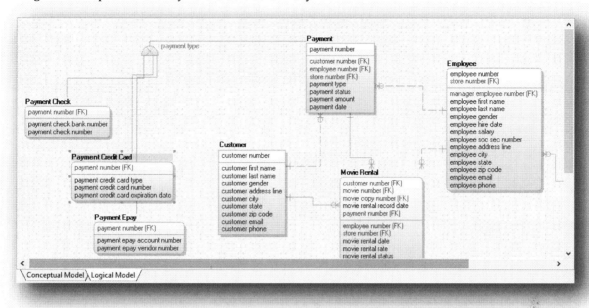

Figure 256. Reposition Payment Check Entity

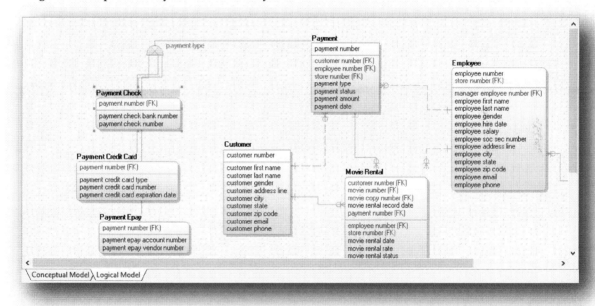

33. Then reposition the **Payment Type** Subtype to approximately where we have placed it on the diagram. See Figure 257.

34. Click on the *Diagram* ribbon tab to have the Diagram ribbon visible for the next steps.

35. Click once on the **Payment Check** entity, and then, while holding down the Ctrl key, select the **Payment Credit Card** and the **Payment Epay** entities too.

36. Click on the *Align Right* button on the Diagram ribbon. See Figure 258.

Figure 257. Reposition Payment Type Subtype

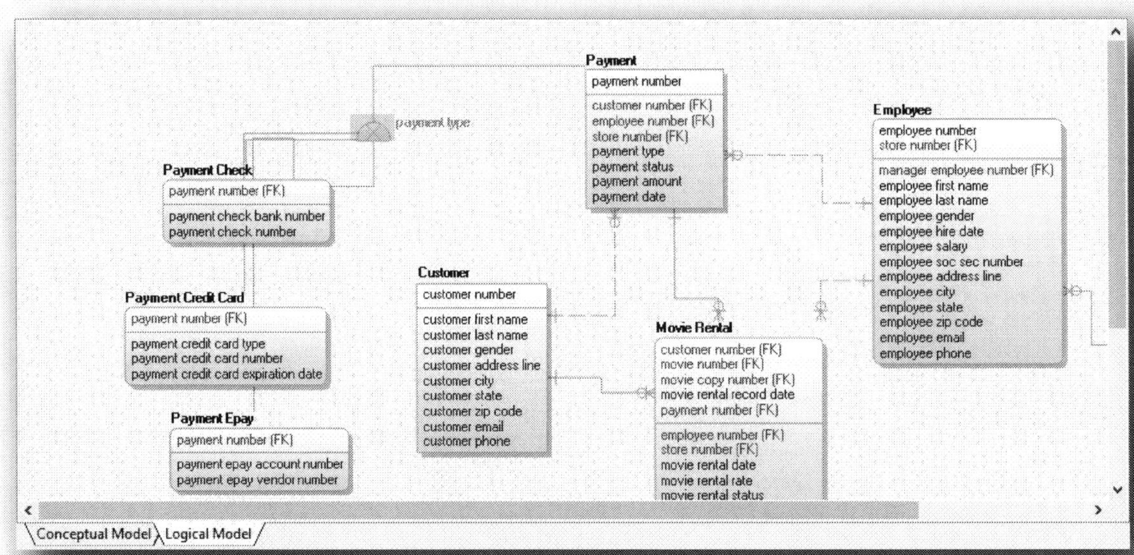

Figure 258. Click on the Align Right Button

37. Observe how the entities align all with their right-hand sides aligned, and how the right-hand sides are all according to the first entity that was selected, the **Payment Check** entity.

38. While keeping the three entities selected, click on the *Space Vertically* button on the Diagram ribbon.

39. Observe how the entities are spaced out vertically, with even gaps between the entities.

40. Right-click on the relationship between the **Payment Check** entity and the **Payment Type** subtype symbol and select the *Reset Relationship Path* option. See Figure 259.

41. Depending on the exact placement of your **Payment Check** entity and the **Payment Type** subtype symbol, your model should look something like what appears in Figure 260.

42. Repeat the same steps for the other two relationships out of the **Payment Type** subtype symbol. If they do not line up as in my diagram, select the relationship line and drag it to the desired location, taking not how easy it is to reposition the relationship lines.

Figure 259. Observe the Vertical Spacing of the Entities

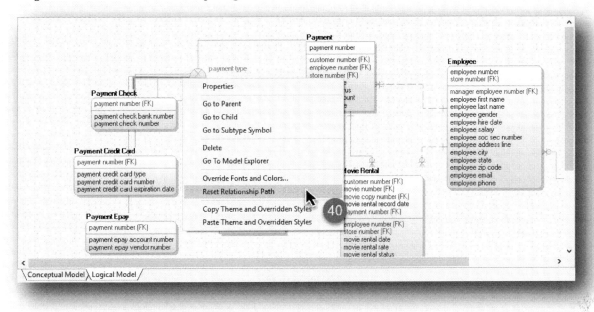

Figure 260. Observe the Reset of the Relationship Line

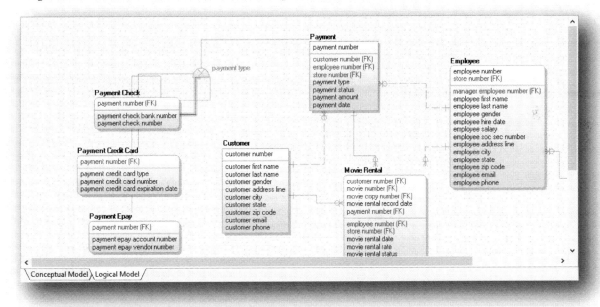

43. Perform the same action on the relationship line between the **Payment Type** subtype symbol and the **Payment** entity.

44. Play with the placement of the entities and relationship lines to layout your diagram as you would like to see it. Try and see how you can route relationship lines around objects, twisting and turning to suit the diagram. Figure 261 contains an example of how the relationship lines can twist and turn, not that you would want a diagram with this sort of relationship lines, but it demonstrates the functionality.

Figure 261. Sample of Relationship Line Re-layout Capability

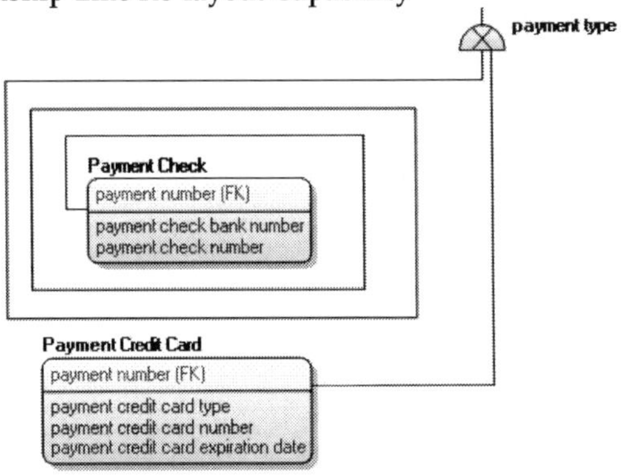

45. When finished, save and close your MyMovie data model.

Key Learnings

- A rule is visually captured in a data model by a line connecting two entities, called a relationship.

- Representing cardinality by symbols on both ends of a relationship defines the number of instances of each entity that can participate in the relationship. The three simple choices are zero, one, or many.

- Labels are the verbs that appear on the relationship lines. Labels should be as descriptive as possible to retain data model precision

- Subtyping allows grouping the common attributes and relationships of similar or related entities.

Specific values
What if there are no values
Validation rules

In Chapter 18, we discussed the data rule. In this chapter, we discuss the validation rule and its twin brother, the default value rule. Validation rules and default values are instructions on *what to do* when attributes contain specific values.

Validation Rules Explained

Validation rules are instructions on *what to do* when attributes contain specific values, for example:

- First-year students can register for at most 18 credits a semester.
- A policy must have at least three claims against it to be considered high-risk.
- Take 10% off of an order if the order contains more than five products.

In our data models, we can graphically represent the data and enforce data rules, but we cannot graphically represent validation rules, besides the format validation rule. A student data model can capture the level of the student, such as **First-year** or **Second-year** as an attribute, as well as the number of credits each student is taking each semester. However, we cannot graphically represent the enforcement that a first-year student registers for no more than 18 credits a semester. This is where the functionality of a data modeling tool overrides the concepts of data modeling. The data modeling tool may not be able to represent the validation rules graphically but is capable of capturing them for usage in the physical data model and subsequent DDL.

A validation rule is when an attribute must never contain a value outside of its assigned validation rule. The validation rule defines the actual list of values or a range of values or a specific set of SQL code that enforces the rule. For example, **Employee Gender Code** may limit the values of 'female' and 'male.' **Employee Hire Date** may be assigned a rule that it contains only valid dates, for example:

- February 15th, 2005
- 25 January 1910
- 20150410
- March 10th, 2050

Because **Employee Hire Date** is limited to valid dates, it cannot include 'February 30th.' An attribute may restrict an attribute with additional rules. For example, by restricting the **Employee**

Hire Date attribute to dates earlier than today's date, we would eliminate 'March 10th, 2100.' By restricting **Employee Hire Date** to YYYYMMDD (that is, year, month, and day concatenated), we would eliminate all the above examples given except for '20150410.' Another way of refining this set of values is to restrict the attribute of **Employee Hire Date** to dates that fall on a 'Monday,' 'Tuesday,' 'Wednesday,' 'Thursday,' or 'Friday' (that is, the typical workweek).

In an example of a Customer Relationship Management system, **Customer Name** may contain thousands or millions of values. This **Customer Name** attribute may need a bit of refining. It may be necessary to clarify whether a valid attribute value is composed of both a first and last name, such as 'Jeffrey Harris', or just a first name, such as 'Jeffrey.' Could this attribute contain company names such as 'Microsoft,' as well? Could it contain numbers instead of just letters, such as the name 'R2D2' from the movie Star Wars? Could it contain special characters, such as the name '⚥,' representing 'The Artist Formerly Known as Prince' (the musician Prince changed his name to this unpronounceable 'Love Symbol #2' in 1993 [⚥]).

There are four basic validation rule types:

- **Format Validation Rules**–These rules specify the standard types of data one can have in a database. For example, Integer, Character(30), and Date are all format validation rules. This rule is the most common validation rule, as almost all attributes have data type restrictions.

- **List Validation Rules**–These rules are similar to a drop-down list. They contain a finite set of values from which to choose. List validation rules are refinements of format validation rules. The format validation rule for **Order Status Code** might be Character(10). Further defined by a list validation rule through a list of possible values {Open, Shipped, Closed, Returned}.

- **Range Validation Rules**–These rules allow all values that are between a minimum and maximum value. For example, a **Student Score** might have a format validation rule of tiny integer (tinyint in SQL Server is 0 through 255), which ensures that the value is any whole number from 0 to 255. Applying a range validation rule of 0 through 100 ensures that a student may not receive a score above 100%.

- **User-Defined Validation Rules**–These rules allow the use of SQL code to validate a value for an attribute. For example, **Order Delivery Date** must be between today's date and three months in the future. By using SQL code, we can identify the current date and a date three months in the future and then verify that the value is within that period.

There are several reasons that validation rules are beneficial:

- **Improves data quality by checking against a validation rule before inserting data**. This is the primary reason for having a validation rule. Limiting the possible values of an attribute reduces the chances of bad data getting into the database. For example, if an attribute that represents a monetary value is assigned the data type (format validation rule) of decimal (15,2), then all decimal numbers up to 15 digits in length, including 2 digits after the decimal point would be included. **Gross Sales Amount,** which is assigned the data type of decimal (15,2), would not allow the insertion of the value 'R2D2'. An attribute that represents **Sales Month** may have the list validation rule ('January,' 'February,' 'March,' 'April,' 'May,' 'June,' 'July,' 'August,' 'September,' 'October,' 'November' and 'December').

- **The data model communicates even more**. When we are displaying data types (format validation rules) in a data model, the data model communicates that a particular attribute has the properties of a particular format, and therefore, the data model becomes a more comprehensive communication tool. For example, **Gross Sales Amount**, **Net Sales Amount**, and **List Price Amount** all share the decimal (15,2) data type and, therefore, share properties such that their valid values are limited to monetary values.

- **Greater efficiency in building new models and maintaining existing models.** When a data modeler embarks on a project, they can use a standard set of validation rules, thereby saving time by not reinventing the wheel. Any new attribute that stores a month value, can be assigned the list validation rule of month ('January,' 'February,' 'March,' 'April,' 'May,' 'June,' 'July,' 'August,' 'September,' 'October,' 'November' and 'December'). Or when a data modeler adds an attribute of **Social Security Number**, they can leverage the user-defined validation rule that ensures only valid **Social Security Numbers** get inserted.

Default Value Rules Explained

Where validation rules are instructions on *what to do* when attributes contain a specific value, default value rules are instructions on *what to do* when attributes contain no value (*NULL*).

It is crucial to understand that *NULL* does not mean *blank*; it means unknown. There may or may not be a value, and we just do not know what that value is. A great example that I read recently involved a hypothetical system at a blood bank. A patient comes into a hospital needing blood. And they enter the patient's details into the system, but the patient's blood type isn't known. If the system puts in a default value of a *blank* for the patient's blood type, then when they query the blood supply table, the returned values have all the unclassified pints of blood, as the same default of *blank* would apply for all the unclassified pints of blood. If they use one of the matched pints of blood, they could be giving the patient the wrong blood type. Now, if they were using *NULL* as the default value in the system, the result would return no matching pints of blood. *NULL* ≠ *NULL* (under the default settings of Microsoft SQL Server). And they would not be able to match a pint of blood for the patient until they knew the patient's blood type.

Some examples of default value rules are:

- All new bank accounts opened must start with a zero balance.

- Seeing that the majority of our chickens are hens, we want to default the gender to 'Female'.
- The default discount is 0% for all sales.

For us to accommodate a default value rule, we need to tell the database to set the value to a pre-defined value in the absence of the value when the attribute gets inserted into the database.

Tutorial: Creating Validation Rules in erwin DM

1. Open erwin DM.

2. Using the Quick Access Toolbar, click on the *Open* button.

3. Select the **MyMovie_Ver1** data model, from the previous portion of the tutorial, in the Open dialog.

4. Click on the *Open* button.

5. The MyMovie model opens in erwin DM. Maximize the model in the diagram window if needed.

6. To manage the validation rules, the user needs to interact via the Attribute Editor dialog. Right-click on the **Customer** entity, then select the *Attribute Properties* option.

7. In the Attribute Editor dialog, click on the *Constraint* tab. See Figure 262.

8. Remember that the Constraint tab allows for the specifying of the validation and default value rules for attributes. Observe the Constraint tab, as shown in Figure 263.

9. In our tutorial, we need to create a validation rule for all gender attributes, only allowing the capturing of 'M' for Male and 'F' for Female, with a default of 'M' for Male. Taking into consideration that all the gender attributes are attached to the gender domain, we could assign the gender validation rule at each of the gender attributes. The better practice is to assign the gender validation rule at the gender domain and allow for the natural inheritance to flow through to all attributes.

10. In the object section of the dialog, select the **customer gender** attribute. See Figure 264.

11. Observe that the Check Constraint (instance of a validation rule) and the Default (instance of a default value rule) are both set to inherit from the parent object, the domain associated with the attribute. Furthermore, notice that the Name of the Check Constraint and Default are blank, implying that there is no Check Constraint or Default rule in place.

12. In the Attribute Editor dialog, click on the *General* tab.

Figure 262. Click on the Constraint Tab

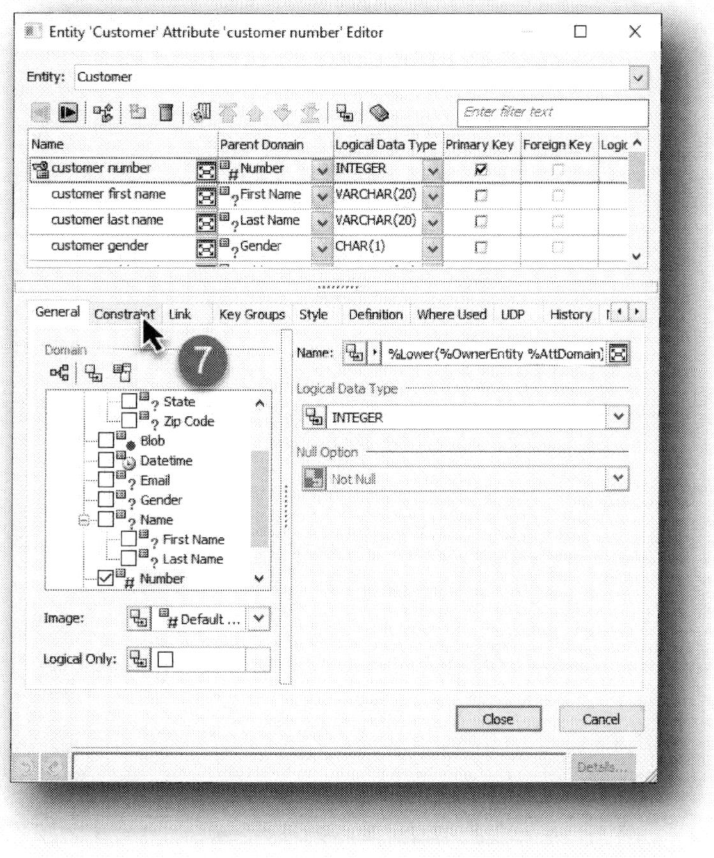

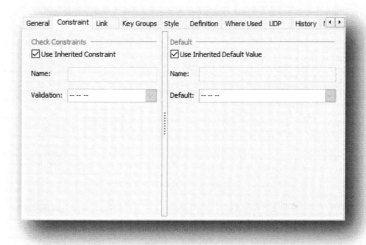

Figure 263. The Constraint Tab

13. Taking note that the **customer gender** attribute is associated with the **Gender** domain, click on the *Domain Editor* button. See Figure 265.

14. Observe the drill-through capability of the erwin DM dialogs, noting that the Domain Dictionary dialog opens, with the **Gender** domain in focus.

Figure 264. Select the Customer Gender Attribute

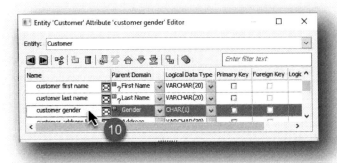

Figure 265. Click on the Domain Editor Button

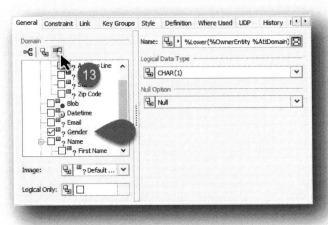

15. In the Domain Dictionary dialog, click on the *Constraint* tab.

16. Observe the Constraint tab, as shown in Figure 266.

Figure 266. The Constraints Tab

17. Unselect the **Use Inherited Constraint** checkbox to break the inheritance for the domain from its parent domain.

18. Click on the dropdown of the **Validation** option.

19. Observing the absence of validation rules, click on the *New* button (). See Figure 267.

Figure 267. Click the New Button

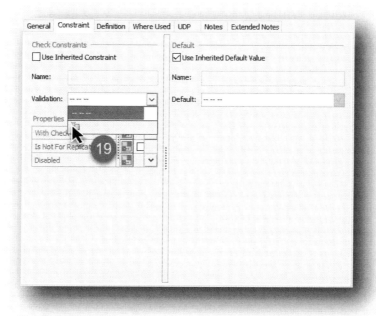

20. Observe that the Validation Rule Editor dialog opens.

21. Click on the validation rule *Name* and rename it to **Gender**. See Figure 268.

There are three types of validation rules:

User-Defined   Specifies an expression used to create the validation rule.

MinMax   Specifies a minimum and maximum values used to create the validation rule.

Valid Values Specifies a list of values used to create the validation rule.

22. Click on the **General** tab.

23. Observe the *Expression* text box for capturing a *User-Defined* expression.

24. Click on the dropdown of the **Type** option.

25. Observe the three types of validation rules.

26. Select the **MinMax** option, as shown in Figure 269.

27. Observe the change to the General tab. See Figure 270.

Figure 268. Rename the Validation Rule

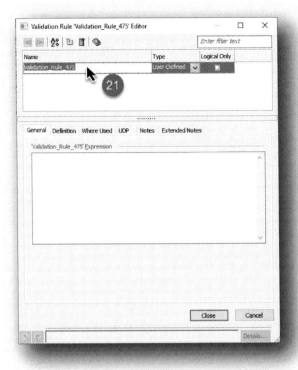

Figure 269. Select the MinMax Option

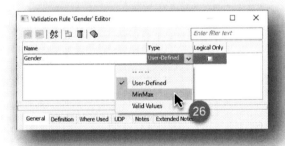

Figure 270. Observe the General Tab (MinMax)

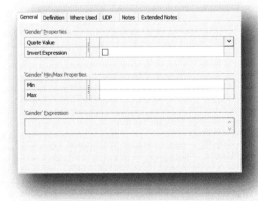

Quote Value   Specifies whether to quote (') the Min and Max value in the expression or not.

No = %AttFieldName BETWEEN 1 AND 10

Yes = %AttFieldName BETWEEN '1' AND '10'

Invert Expression   Specifies that the expression is inclusive or exclusive.

Unselected = %AttFieldName BETWEEN 1 AND 10

*Selected = %AttFieldName **NOT** BETWEEN 1 AND 10*

Min   Specifies the Min value of the equation, if required.

Max   Specifies the Max value of the equation, if required.

Expression   Represents a generic equivalent of the expression.

28. Select the *Valid Values* option. See Figure 271.

Figure 271. Select the Valid Values Option

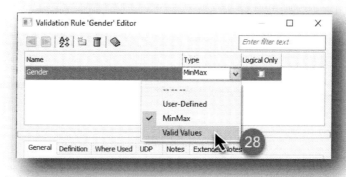

29. Observe the change to the General tab, as shown in Figure 272.

Figure 272. Observe the General Tab (Valid Values)

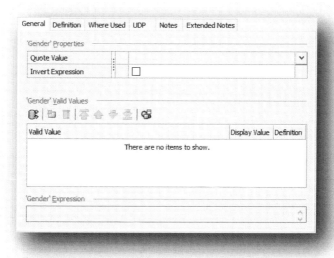

Quote Value	Specifies whether to quote (') the Min and Max value in the expression or not.
	No = %AttFieldName=M OR %AttFieldName=F
	Yes = %AttFieldName='M' OR %AttFieldName='F'
Invert Expression	Specifies that the expression is inclusive or exclusive.
	Unselected = %AttFieldName='M' OR %AttFieldName='F'
	Selected = NOT (%AttFieldName='M' OR %AttFieldName='F')
Valid Values	Specifies the Valid Values of the equation.

Allows the user to change the Valid Value record order.

Specifies that the Valid Value list sort order is alphabetical.

Specifies that the Valid Value list sort order is in reverse alphabetic order.

Specifies that the Valid Value list sort order is in creation order.

Allows the user to create a new Valid Value record.

Allows the user to delete the selected Valid Value record.

When using the Creation Order option, this button allows the user to move the selected Valid Value to the top of the list.

When using the Creation Order option, this button allows the user to move the selected Valid Value up one level of the list.

When using the Creation Order option, this button allows the user to move the selected Valid Value down one level of the list.

When using the Creation Order option, this button allows the user to move the selected Valid Value to the bottom of the list.

Allows the user to import a list of Valid Value records.

Expression	Represents a generic equivalent of the expression.

30. Change the *Quote Value* to **Yes**. See Figure 273.

31. Under the Valid Values section, click the *New* button to create a new Valid Value for **Male**.

32. Observe that a new valid value was created, rename it to **Male**. See Figure 274.

33. Repeat the above steps to create a **Female** valid value.

34. Observe the two newly created valid values, as shown in Figure 275. Also, note that erwin DM allows for the capturing of a display value and a definition.

Figure 273. Observe the General Tab (Valid Values)

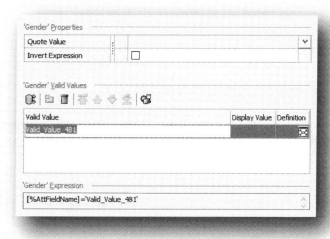

Figure 274. Rename the Valid Value to Male

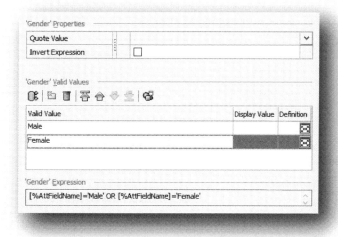

Figure 275. Observe the Two Created Valid Values

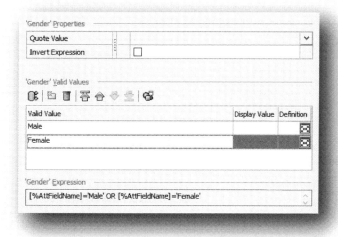

35. When finished, click the *Close* button on the Validation Rule Editor dialog.

36. Observe the automatic assignment of the newly created validation rule to the **Gender** domain. See Figure 276.

    Figure 276. Observe the Automatic Assignment

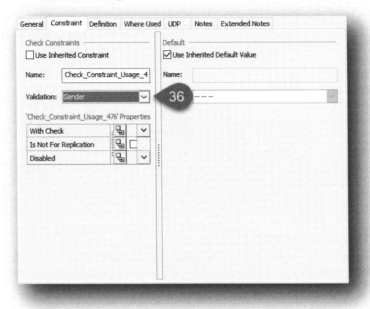

37. Click the *Close* button on the Domain Editor dialog.

38. On the Attribute Editor dialog, click the *Constraint* tab.

39. On the constraint tab, observe the following:

    The *Use Inherited Constraint* is selected; the attribute is inheriting the validation rule that we created and assigned to the **Gender** domain at the **Gender** domain.

    The *Name* of the check constraint has been pre-populated by erwin DM. Even though the name is changeable, erwin DM assigns a pre-populated name to ensure the uniqueness of the assignment of the validation rule.

The *Validation* rule is populated with the inherited validation rule from the domain.

40. In the parent object section of the dialog, change the parent object to the **Employee** entity. See Figure 277.

41. Scroll down in the object section, and select the **employee gender** attribute.

42. On the constraint tab, observe the following:

    The *Use Inherited Constraint* is selected; the attribute is inheriting the validation rule that we created earlier at the domain level. The *Name* of the check constraint has also been pre-populated by erwin DM. The *Validation* rule is populated with the inherited validation rule from the domain.

Figure 277. Change Parent Object to Employee

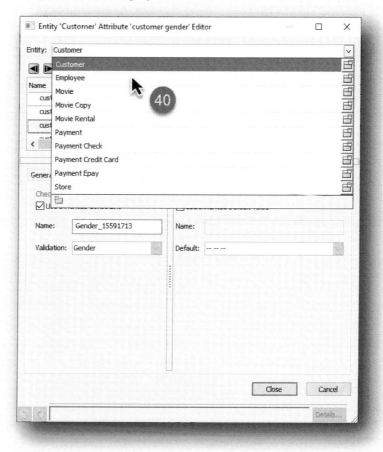

Tutorial: Creating Default Value Rules in erwin DM

1. While still on the Constraint tab of the **employee gender** attribute of the **Employee** entity, we are going to create a default value rule. Since we don't want to apply this default rule to all attributes that inherit from the **Gender** domain, we are going to create it at the attribute level.

2. Unselect the *Use Inherited Default Value* checkbox.

3. Click on the dropdown of the *Default* option.

4. Observing the absence of default value rules, click on the *New* button (▓).

5. Observe that the Default Value Rule Editor dialog opens.

6. Click on the default value rule *Name* and rename it to **M**. Good idea to use the default value as the name, as this makes it easier to find and interpret the default value rules. See Figure 278.

7. Click on the *Value* property on the General tab and give it a value of **M**. This is the value that gets applied to the attribute when there is an absence of a value provided when a record gets inserted into the database.

Figure 278. Rename the Default Rule

8.   Click the *Close* button on the Default Value Editor dialog.

9.   On the constraint tab of the Attribute Editor dialog, observe that the *Name* of the default value constraint has been pre-populated by erwin DM. The *Default* rule is populated with the default value rule that we just created. The default value gets represented below the name of the **Default** rule.

10.   When finished, click the *Close* button on the Attribute Editor dialog.

11.   Finally, save and close your MyMovie data model.

Key Learnings
• Validation rules are instructions on what to do when attributes contain specific values. Validation rules operate whenever a value is changed.
• Default Value rules are instructions on what to do when an attribute does not contain any values when the record gets created. Default Value rules only apply to the creation of the record.
• erwin DM provides advanced capabilities to manage and reuse both validation and default value rules.

Subject areas
Allow many diagrams
Tailor for user

Subject Areas Explained

A subject area is a subset of data model objects taken from the full pool of data model objects in a data model. One can create multiple subject areas in a data model. Subject areas are used to help you manage large data models to reduce the number of data model objects into functional groupings or to focus on particular business areas. Working with subject areas is especially useful when designing and maintaining a large or complex data model. By dividing a subject area into several smaller subject areas, you can allow different groups within an organization to concentrate on the processes and tasks pertinent to their business area.

You can create a subject area in the Subject Area Editor, which includes options for selecting the members of a subject area. In the Subject Area Editor, you name the subject area, set global options, and select members to include in the logical model, the physical model, or both. You can also exclude references, during schema generation, to tables that are not in the currently selected subject area. In addition, you can use the *Spanning Neighborhood* feature to specify how many generations of ancestors or descendants of the members you select to include in a subject area.

For each subject area that you create, its name is added to the Subject Area list in the Model Explorer. You can switch to a different subject area by selecting it from the list. If you have multiple subject areas in your model, you can create a set of diagrams for each subject area. When you switch to a different subject area, you only see the diagram tabs for that subject area.

When you create a subject area for the logical side of a logical/physical model, a similar subject area is automatically created for the physical side of the model. The reverse of this is also true. If you add or remove members from a subject area, the membership change is reflected in the corresponding physical or logical side of the model, but will not affect the membership of any other subject area. If you add or delete objects in one subject area, such as entities and attributes, it does not impact other subject areas.

When you create or edit a subject area, the edits are saved when you close the Subject Area Editor. When you save a model to a .erwin file, the subject areas are saved with the model, not as individual files. When you open a model, all previously created subject areas are available. In a logical/physical model, the logical and physical models share the same subject areas. Figure 279 illustrates how subject areas represent subsets of a data model.

Figure 279 Multiple subject areas in one data model

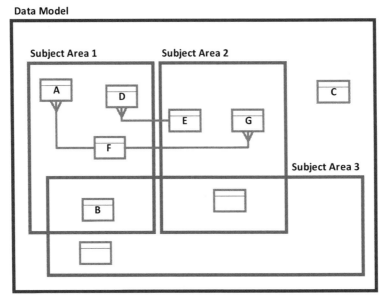

Objects A through G, are all owned by the data model.	=	Subject areas do not own objects; the data model owns them.
Object A is an object that is a member of a subject area.	=	Objects are members of subject areas.
Object B is an object that is a member of more than one subject area.	=	Objects can be members of more than one subject area.
Object C is an object of the Data Model but is not a member of any subject area.	=	Objects do not have to belong to a subject area.
Objects A and F are related to each other, and the relationship is a member of the subject area by default.	=	When two related objects are in a subject area, the relationship between them is included as a member of the subject area by default, but can be removed.
Objects D and E are related to each other, and the relationship between them is referred to as a dangling relationship and is a member of the subject area by default.	=	When two related objects are in a subject area, the relationship between them is included as a member of the subject area by default, but can be removed. When using forward engineering functionality, it generates the foreign key relationship as the parent entity is a member of the subject area.
Objects F & G are related to each other, and the relationship between them is referred to as a dangling relationship and is a member of the subject area by default.	=	When two related objects are in a subject area, the relationship between them is included as a member of the subject area by default but can be removed. When using forward engineering functionality, it <u>does not</u> generates the foreign key relationship as the parent entity is <u>not</u> a member of the subject area.

ER Diagrams Explained

ER Diagrams are a subset of a subject area and are owned by the subject area. The objects displayed in the ER Diagram are restricted to the membership of the owning subject area. If an entity is not in a subject area, then it cannot appear in that subject area's ER Diagrams. While the membership of an ER Diagram is restricted to the membership of its owning subject area, the membership of an ER Diagram can be a subset of the objects in the subject area.

At the model level, there are also ER Diagrams. These, by default, have the scope of the entire model, and all objects are available. Model-level ER Diagrams also can be subsets of the whole model.

As with Subject Areas, diagrams have an *Auto-populate* option, which, when set, ensures that all members of the owning subject area are also members of the diagram. When only a subset of objects is required, it is sometimes easier to turn the *Auto-populate* option on and off again and then remove unwanted objects.

When the auto-populate option is set, objects cannot be removed from a diagram. Each diagram in a subject area is individually definable. That is, each diagram can be separately configured in terms of:

- Content (within the scope of the subject area)
- Its type (logical, physical, or dimensional)
- The Display Level (Varies with type)
- Its theme (color, font, and so on)
- Data properties (domain, data type, and so on)
- Key group membership indicator
- Layout

While it is possible to work with a single diagram for each subject area and change its properties for the task in hand, the best practice is to create a diagram for each modeling need. The location of each object gets held at the diagram level, and changing properties, such as the type and display level, can result in the size of objects changing with a consequential impact on the diagram layout.

Tutorial: Creating Subject Areas in erwin DM

1. Open erwin DM.

2. Using the Quick Access Toolbar, click on the *Open* button.

3. Select the **MyMovie_Ver1** data model, from the previous portion of the tutorial, in the Open dialog.

4. Click on the *Open* button.

5. The MyMovie model opens in erwin DM. Maximize the model in the diagram window if needed.

6. In the Model Explorer pane, click on the expand icon (⊞) next to the *ER Diagrams* node, to display all the ER Diagrams in the data model at the root data model level.

7. Observe the two ER Diagrams that we have created, the **Conceptual Model**, and the **Logical Model**. See Figure 280.

Figure 280. Observe the Two ER Diagrams

8. Right-click on the *Subject Areas* node and select the *New* option.

9. Observe that a new subject area gets created, rename it to **Payment**. See Figure 281.

Figure 281. Rename the New Subject Area to Payment

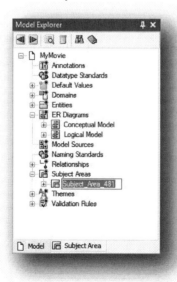

10. Right-click on the new *Payment* subject area, and select the *Properties* option.

11. Observe that the Subject Areas Editor dialog opens. See Figure 282.

Figure 282. Right-Click and Select Properties Option

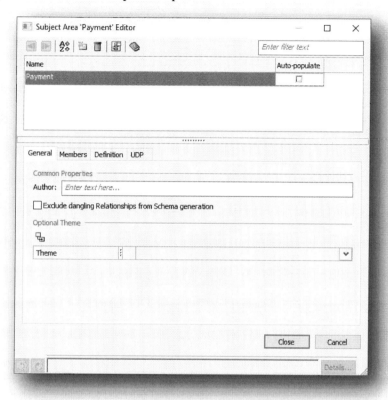

12. Click on the *General* tab.

13. In the Author property, fill in your name, as you are the author of the subject area.

14. As mentioned earlier about dangling relationships, the *Exclude Dangling Relationships from Schema Generation* checkbox excludes the dangling relationships from the forward engineering. For more information on forward engineering, please see Chapter 27.

15. Observe that there is no theme assigned to the subject area; the theme gets inherited from the model level.

16. Click on the drop-down for the *Theme* and select the *New* option. See Figure 283.

17. Observe the Theme Editor dialog opens, as shown in Figure 284.

18. In the *Name* column in the object section, rename the new theme to **Data Modeling Made Simple**.

19. Click on the *Fill Option Paint Can* button ( ). See Figure 285.

Figure 283. Right-Click on the Drop-Down and Select the New Option

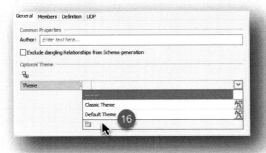

Figure 284. Right-Click on the Drop-Down and Select the New Option

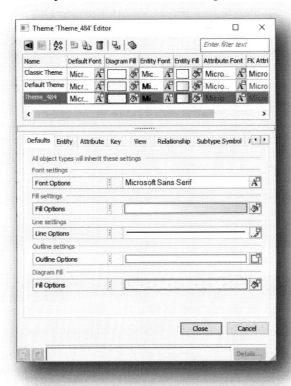

Figure 285. Click on the Fill Option Paint Can Button

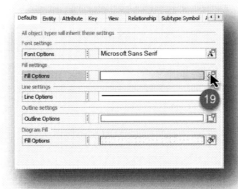

20. In the General Fill Editor dialog, change the ending color to *burnt orange*. See Figure 286.

Figure 286. Click on Ending Color to Burnt Orange

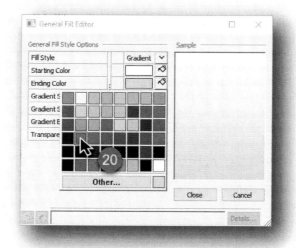

21. Observe all the other *Fill Options* available.

22. When finished, click the **Close** button on the General Fill Editor dialog.

23. Observe the change to the Fill Option for the subject area. All the other options available to change the colors and fonts are at the default level, or the individual object type levels.

 Explore all the other options available under themes and understand how each option can change the view of your data model.

24. When finished, click the **Close** button on the Theme Editor dialog.

25. Click on the **Members** tab.

26. Observe that the members tab is split into two sections. Those objects that are available to be included, and those objects that are already included in the subject area. See Figure 287.

Figure 287. Observe the Two Sides of the Members Tab

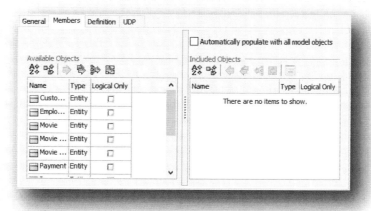

The user uses the Members tab in the Subject Area Editor to identify the entities, tables, and views that are members of a subject area. The *Available Objects* section displays the available entities, tables, views that can be members of the selected subject area. The *Included Objects* section displays the entities, tables, and views that are currently members of the selected subject area.

 When the user adds members to a subject area, the objects are not added to the corresponding diagram automatically. The user must add the objects manually.

Automatically populate from model Indicates whether to populate the Included Objects section automatically from all included objects of the model.

Action Buttons

Allows the user to change the entity, table, and view sort order.

    Specifies that the entity, table, and view list sort order is in alphabetic order.

    Specifies that the entity, table, and view list sort order is in reverse alphabetic order.

    Specifies that the entity, table, and view list sort order is in alphabetic order by the owner and then name.

    Specifies that the entity, table, and view list sort order is in reverse alphabetic order by the owner then name.

Allows the user to change the display names (logical versus physical).

    Specifies that the entity, table, and view list by logical names.

    Specifies that the entity, table, and view list by physical names.

    Specifies that the entity, table, and view list by physical names showing owner.

    Specifies that the entity, table, and view list by physical names showing owner for the non-current user.

Allows the user to move the selected objects to the Included Objects section.

Allows the user to move all the objects in the Available Objects section to the Included Objects section.

Allows the user to move the selected objects and neighboring objects to the Included Objects section. When clicking this button, the Spanning Neighborhood dialog opens, allowing the user to work with the options in the Spanning Neighborhood dialog.

Ancestors. Specifies the number of ancestors to include in the subject area. Ancestors are the parents of an entity. Select All or select Level and enter the number of ancestors to include.

Descendants. Specifies the number of descendants to include in the subject area. Descendants are the children of an entity. Select All or select Level and enter the number of descendants to include.

Allows the user to include all objects contained in another subject area in the model. When clicking this button, a dialog opens that contains a drop-down control for the user to select the other subject area from which to include objects.

Allows the user to remove the selected objects from the Included Objects section.

Allows the user to remove all the objects from the Included Objects section to the Available Objects section.

Allows the user to remove the selected objects and neighboring objects to the Available Objects section. When clicking this button, the Spanning Neighborhood dialog opens, allowing the user to work with the options in the Spanning Neighborhood dialog.

Allows the user to remove all objects contained in another subject area in the model. When clicking this button, a dialog opens that contains a drop-down control for the user to select the other subject area from which to include objects.

Allows the user to invoke the context-specific editor dialog.

27. Select the **Payment** entity.

28. Click the *Spanning Neighborhood* button in the *Available Objects* section. See Figure 288.

Figure 288. Click the Spanning Neighborhood Button

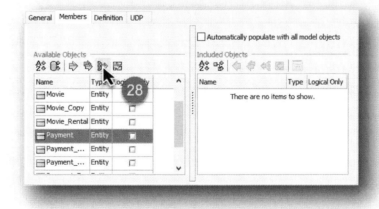

29. In the Spanning Neighborhood dialog, change the value for the *Descendants* to '*1.*' See Figure 289.

30. Click the *Add* button.

31. Observe the moving of all objects related by one level from the **Payment** entity gets moved to the Included Objects section.

Figure 289. Change the Value for Descendants to 1

32. Select the *Movie Rental* entity in the *Included Objects* section and click the *Move Selected Objects to Available Object Section* button. See Figure 290.

Figure 290. Move Movie Rental Entity to Available Objects Section

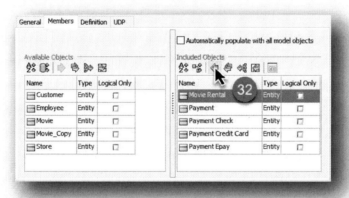

33. Take note of the *Auto-Populate* and *Automatically Populate With All Model Objects* checkboxes, as shown in Figure 291. By selecting these checkboxes, the subject area will be automatically populated with all objects in the model. After creating new objects, irrespective of where they are created, they will be included in the objects for the specific subject area.

34. When finished, click the *Close* button to dismiss the Subject Area Editor dialog.

Tutorial: Creating ER Diagrams in erwin DM

As was demonstrated in the tutorials in Chapter 10 and Chapter 14, we are now going to explore the settings and options of the ER Diagrams.

1. In the Subject Area Editor dialog, click the *ER Diagram Editor Drill-through* button, as shown in Figure 292.

Figure 291. Move Movie Rental Entity to Available Objects Section

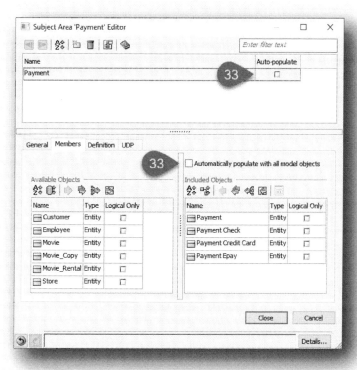

Figure 292. Click the ER Diagram Editor Button

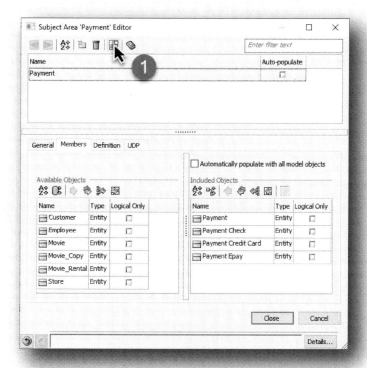

2. Observe the ER Diagram Editor dialog is displayed.

3. In the parent object section, change the focus of the parent object to the *MyMovie*, which is the model level. See Figure 293.

Figure 293. Change the Parent Object to the MyMovie

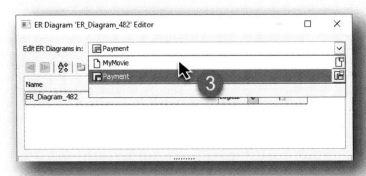

4. Observe the display of the two ER Diagrams that we created in the previous tutorials. Also, note that they were only visible once we change the parent object to the model level.

5. In the properties section, click on the *General* tab.

6. Observe the General tab, as shown in Figure 294.

Figure 294. The General Tab

    Author   Allows the user to specify the person responsible for the creation of the ER Diagram.

Optional Theme

Theme	Specifies the Theme (all the font, color, and display options) to use for the objects in the ER Diagram. The user can use the inherited theme or open the Theme Editor to create a new Theme.

Optional Override to Theme Background Fill

Fill Options	Specifies the fill option, such as style and color for the background fill. The choice overrides the style specified in the Theme.

7. When finished, click on the *Members* tab.

8. Observe the Members tab, as shown in Figure 295.

Figure 295. The Member Tab

Like the Subject Area Editor dialog's Members tab, the ER Diagram Editor dialog's Members tab allows for the including and excluding of objects in the ER Diagram. For more information on the relevant buttons, refer back to the previous tutorial on subject areas.

9. When finished, click on the *Relationships* tab.

10. Observe the Relationships tab, as shown in Figure 296.

When the user creates a new ER Diagram and adds members to it, erwin DM automatically includes the relationships associated with the members to the ER Diagram. They can manage these relationships using the Relationships tab in the Diagram Editor.

Figure 296. The Relationships Tab

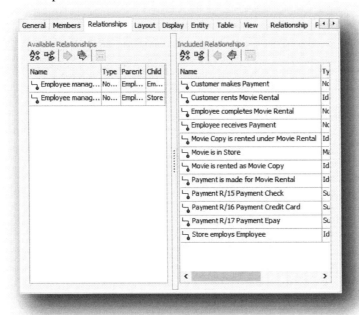

Action Buttons

 Allows the user to change the relationship sort order.

       Specifies that the relationship list sort order is in alphabetic order.

       Specifies that the relationship list sort order is in reverse alphabetic order.

   Allows the user to change the display names (logical versus physical).

       Specifies that the relationship list by logical names.

       Specifies that the relationship list by physical names.

   Allows the user to move the selected objects to the Included Objects section.

   Allows the user to move all the objects in the Available Objects section to the Included Objects section.

   Allows the user to remove the selected objects from the Included Objects section.

   Allows the user to remove all the objects from the Included Objects section to the Available Objects section.

   Allows the user to invoke the context-specific editor dialog.

11. When finished, click on the *Layout* tab.

12. Observe the Layout tab, as shown in Figure 297. The user uses the options in the Layout tab to set preferences for relationship line layout, entity and table sizing, object alignment, and diagram layout.

Figure 297. The Layout Tab

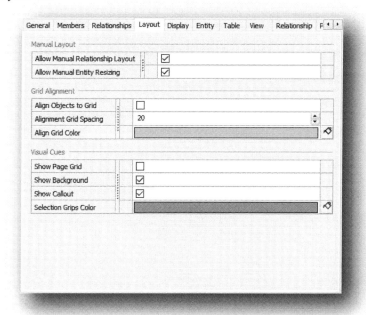

Manual Layout

Allow Manual Relationship Layout

Allows the manual reshaping of relationship lines. This checkbox is selected by default. Clear this checkbox to disallow the manual layout of relationship lines.

Allow Manual Entity Resize

Allows the manual resizing of selected entities, tables, or views. This checkbox is selected by default. Clear this checkbox to disallow manual resizing of entities, tables, and views throughout the ER Diagram.

Grid Alignment

Align Objects to Grid

Aligns entities, tables, or views to the nearest vertical and horizontal gridlines. New objects snap to the grid automatically. Existing objects are not automatically aligned with the grid unless they are copied, pasted, or moved. Clear this checkbox if the user does not want entities to align with the layout grid (default).

Alignment Grid spacing

Defines the distance in pixels between the gridlines. Enter a numeric value or click the arrows to increase or decrease the default value.

Align Grid Color

Defines the grid color. To change the default color, click the Align Grid Color Paint Can button ( ) and pick a color.

Visual Cues

Show Page Grid

Displays a grid for the ER Diagram.

Show Background	Displays a background for the ER Diagram. Clear the checkbox to have a white background.
Show Callout	Displays callouts for the relationship texts in the ER Diagram.
Selection Grip Color	Defines the color of the grip that surrounds a selected object. To change the default color, click the Selection Grip Color Paint Can button (⟁) and pick a color.

13. When finished, click on the *Display* tab.

14. Observe the Display tab, as shown in Figure 298.

Figure 298. The Display Tab

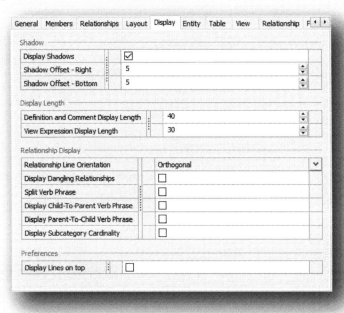

The user uses the options in the Display tab to set preferences for displaying shadows, comments, definitions, view expressions, and relationships.

Shadow

Display Shadow	Specifies whether or not to display the shadow effect for entities, tables, and views in the ER Diagram. Select the checkbox to display the shadow effect, or clear the checkbox to remove the shadow effect.
Shadow Offset - Right	Specifies the width of the shadow in pixels.
Shadow Offset - Bottom	Specifies the height of the shadow in pixels.

Display Length

Definition and Comment Display Length

Specifies the number of characters displayed on a single line for definitions and comments. Enter a numeric value or click the arrows to increase or decrease the default value. If the user exceeds this number, then they must resize the object to display the entire length of the text.

View Expression Display Length

Specifies the number of characters displayed on a single line for view expressions. Enter a numeric value or click the arrows to increase or decrease the default value. If the user exceeds this number, then they must resize the object to display the entire length of the text. Note that for the View Expression Display Length option to work, the user must select the Display View Column Expression option on the View tab.

Relationship Display

Relationship Line Orientation

Orthogonal

Specifies whether or not to display relationships with orthogonal lines which lay at right angles. Traditionally, orthogonal lines are used for relational models.

Diagonal

Specifies whether or not to display relationships with diagonal lines. Traditionally, diagonal lines are used for dimensional models.

Display Dangling Relationships

Specifies whether or not to show dangling relationship lines in the ER Diagram. Select the checkbox to display dangling relationship lines, or clear the checkbox to hide dangling relationship lines.

Split Verb Phrase

Splits the parent-to-child and child-to-parent verb phrases on each relationship line.

Display Child-to-Parent Verb Phrase

Select to display the child-to-parent verb phrase for relationships.

Display Parent-to-Child Verb Phrase

Select to display the parent-to-child verb phrase for relationships.

Display Subcategory Cardinality

Display the cardinality symbol for relationship lines in a supertype/subtype construct. Note that for the Display Subcategory Cardinality option to work, the user must select the Display Logical Relationship Name option on the Relationship tab.

Preferences

Display Lines On Top	When a relationship line passes through an object, it displays the relationship line on top of the object. Clearing the checkbox displays the relationship line behind the object which it is passing through.

15. When finished, click on the *Entity* tab.

16. Observe the Entity tab, as shown in Figure 299.

Figure 299. The Entity Tab

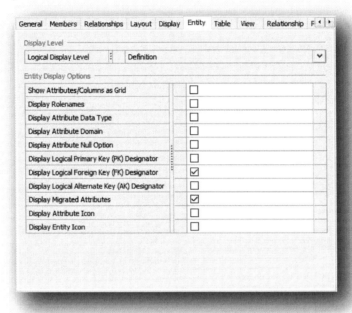

The user uses the Entity Tab on the Diagram Editor to set general display options for entities in the logical model.

Display Level

Logical Display Level	Specifies the display level for the ER Diagram. Select one of the following display levels from the drop-down list:

Entity. Specifies to use the Entity Display Level in the diagram, which displays the name of each entity in the entity box.

Attribute. Specifies to use the Attribute Display Level in the diagram, which displays the primary key and non-key attributes in the entity box.

Definition. Specifies to use the Definition Display Level in the diagram, which displays the entity definition in the entity box.

Primary Key. Specifies to use the Primary Key Display Level in the diagram, which displays the primary key attributes for each entity in the entity box.

Icon. Specifies to use the Icon Display Level (large entity icon) in the diagram, which displays a bitmap in the entity box.

Key. Specifies to use the Key display level in the diagram, which displays the key name in the entity box.

Entity Display Options

Show Attributes/Columns as Grid	Displays the attributes or columns as a grid.
Display Rolenames	Displays the rolename for the attributes in the diagram during migration. Clear to hide basenames of these attributes.
Display Attribute Data Types	Displays the logical data type for the attributes in the diagram. Clear to hide the datatype.
Display Attribute Domain	Displays the logical domain for the attributes in the diagram. Clear to hide the domain.
Display Attribute Null Option	Displays NULL or NOT NULL values for each attribute.
Display Logical Primary Key (PK) Designator	Displays the primary key designator (PK) for the attributes in the diagram. Clear to hide the primary key designator.
Display Logical Foreign Key (FK) Designator	Displays the foreign key designator (FK) for the attributes in the diagram. Clear to hide the foreign key designator.
Display Logical Alternate Key (AK) Designator	Displays the alternate key (AK) and inversion entry (IE) designator for the attributes in the diagram. Clear to hide the alternate key and inversion entry designator.
Display Migrated Attribute	Displays migrated (foreign key) attributes in the diagram. Cleared, hide all migrated attributes, including those that are assigned a rolename.
Display Attribute Icon	Displays attribute icons in the diagram. Cleared hides all attribute icons.
Display Entity Icon	Displays entity icons (small entity icon) in the diagram. Cleared hides all entity icons.

17. When finished, click on the *Table* tab.

18. Observe the Table tab, as shown in Figure 300.

Figure 300. The Table Tab

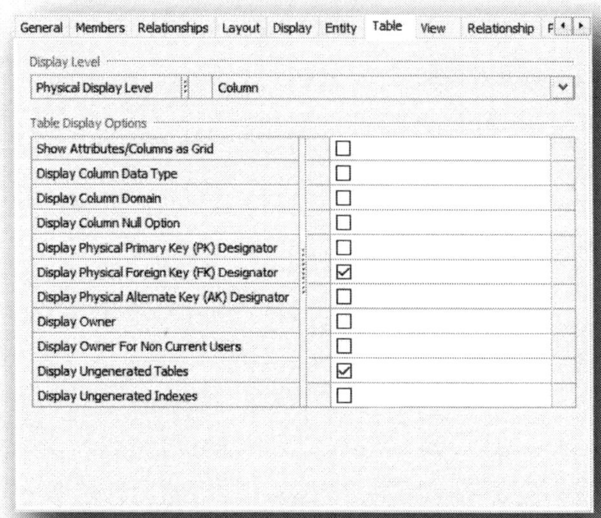

The user uses the Table Tab on the Diagram Editor to set general display options for tables in the physical model.

Display Level

Physical Display Level Specifies the default display level for the physical model. Select one of the following display levels from the drop-down list:

Table. Specifies to use the Table Display Level for the physical model, which displays only the table name in the diagram.

Column. Specifies to use the Column Display Level for the physical model, which displays the column names of the table.

Comment. Specifies to use the Comment Display Level for the physical model, which displays comments in the table.

Primary Key. Specifies to use the Primary Key Display Level for the diagram, which displays primary key columns in the table.

Physical Order. Displays the columns in the same order in which they appear in the physical database. This option lets you mirror the physical structure of your database in the erwin physical model. This display mode contrasts with the Column display level, which corresponds to the index order in the erwin logical model.

Icon. Specifies to use the Icon Display Level (large entity icon) in the diagram, which displays a bitmap in the diagram.

Key. Specifies to use the Key display level in the diagram, which displays the key name in the table box.

Collapse Fact. Specifies to hide fact table columns in a dimensional model. This option is only available if using the dimensional modeling notation for a physical model.

Collapse Dimension. Specifies to hide dimension table columns in a dimensional model. This option is only available if using the dimensional modeling notation for a physical model.

Table Display Options

Show Attributes/Columns as Grid	Displays the attributes or columns as a grid.
Display Column Data Types	Displays the physical datatype for columns in the physical model. Clear to hide column datatypes.
Display Column Domain	Displays the name of the domain attached to a column after the column name. Clear to hide the domain name.
Display Column Null Option	Displays NULL or NOT NULL values for columns in the diagram. Clear to hide NULL or NOT NULL values.
Display Physical Primary Key (PK) Designator	Displays the primary key designator (🗝) for columns in the physical model. Clear to hide the primary key designator.
Display Physical Foreign Key (FK) Designator	Displays the foreign key designator (FK) for columns in the physical model. Clear to hide the foreign key designator.
Display Physical Alternate Key (AK) Designator	Displays the alternate key (AK) and inversion entry (IE) designator for columns in the physical model. Clear this checkbox to hide the alternate key and inversion entry designators. The Alternate Key Designator (AK) display option displays extended notation to show the order of concatenation as defined in the Index editor.
Dimensional Icon	Displays dimensional table icons (Fact, Dimension, and Outrigger) in a dimensional model. Clear to hide dimensional icons. This option is only available if you use the dimensional modeling notation for your physical model.
Display Owner	Displays the name of the person who owns a table as a prefix to the table name. A TABLEOWNER.TABLENAME naming convention is used.

Display Owner for Non-Current Users	Displays the table owner information for tables owned by users other than yourself. A TABLEOWNER.TABLENAME naming convention is used.
Display Ungenerated Tables	Displays tables that will not be generated when you generate the schema. A table is generated only when you select the Generate checkbox in the Tables editor.
Display Ungenerated Indexes	Displays indexes that will not be generated when you generate the schema. An index is generated only when you select the Generate checkbox in the Index editor.

 The physical order may not be preserved when you forward engineer a physical model. When using the Forward Engineering functionality, the user can indicate physical order or column order for the generated schema. The column order is used to generate the database schema for Primary Keys and Alter statements.

19. When finished, click on the *View* tab.

20. Observe the View tab, as shown in Figure 301.

Figure 301. The View Tab

The user uses the View tab on the Diagram Editor to set display options for views in a physical model.

View Display Options

Display Views	Displays views in the physical model. Clear to hide your views.
Display View Relationships	Displays relationship lines for views in the physical model. Clear to hide view relationship lines.
Display View Column Expression	Displays the source table expression for view columns in the physical model. Clear to hide the source table expression.
Display View Column Data Type	Displays the physical datatype for view columns in the physical model. Clear to hide the datatypes.
Display View Column Null Option	Displays NULL or NOT NULL values for view columns in the physical model. Clear to hide NULL or NOT NULL values.
Display Ungenerated Views	Displays views that will not be generated when you generate the schema. Clear to hide views that will not be generated.

21. When finished, click on the *Relationship* tab.

22. Observe the Relationship tab, as shown in Figure 302.

Figure 302. The Relationship Tab

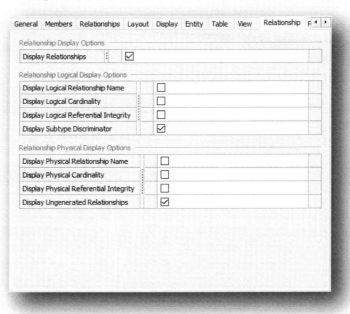

The user uses the Relationship tab on the Diagram Editor to set display options for relationships in either a logical or a physical model.

Relationship Display Options

Display Relationships	Displays relationships in the ER Diagram. Clear to hide the relationships.

Relationship Display Options

Display Logical Relationship Name	Displays relationship names in the logical model. Clear to hide the relationship name.
Display Logical Cardinality	Displays cardinality symbols (P, Z, or n) for the relationships in the logical model. Clear to hide relationship cardinality.
Display Logical Referential Integrity	Displays referential integrity symbols (for example, U:R, I:R, D:C) for the relationships in the logical model. Clear to hide referential integrity.
Display Subtype Discriminator	Displays the subtype discriminator assigned to the subtype relationship.

Relationship Display Options

Display Physical Relationship Name	Displays the physical relationship names in the model.
Display Physical Cardinality	Displays cardinality symbols (P, Z, or n) for the relationships in the physical model. Clear to hide relationship cardinality.
Display Physical Referential Integrity	Displays referential integrity symbols (for example, U:R, I:R, D:C) for the relationships in the physical model. Clear to hide referential integrity.
Display Ungenerated Relationships	Displays relationships that will not be generated when you generate the schema. Clear to hide relationships that will not be generated.

23. When finished, click the right scroll button to display the remaining tabs.

24. Click on the *Page Setup* tab.

25. Observe the Page Setup tab, as shown in Figure 303. The user uses the Page Setup tab on the Diagram Editor to set defaults that display on the General tab of the Page Setup Editor in the Print dialog.

Page Setup

Page Size	Specifies the page size for the print job. Select a page size from the drop-down list.
Orientation	Specifies the page orientation. Select portrait or landscape from the drop-down list.

Zoom Level   Specifies the zoom level used in the printout. Enter a number in the text box or click the arrow to increase or decrease the zoom level.

Figure 303. The Page Setup Tab

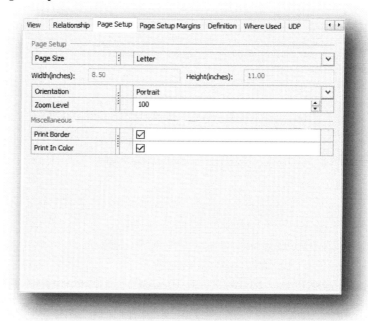

Miscellaneous

Print Border   Specifies to print the diagram with a border.

Print In Color   Specifies to print the diagram using color. Clear the checkbox to print in black and white, even if color choices were made in the diagram.

26. When finished, click on the *Page Setup Margins* tab.

27. Observe the Page Setup Margins tab, as shown in Figure 304. The user uses the Page Setup Margins tab on the Diagram Editor to set defaults that display on the Margins tab of the Page Setup Editor in the Print dialog.

Header/Footer

Current Page macro

Page Count macro

File Name macro

Subject Area Name macro

ER Diagram Name macro

Time macro

Date Macro

Figure 304. The Page Setup Margins Tab

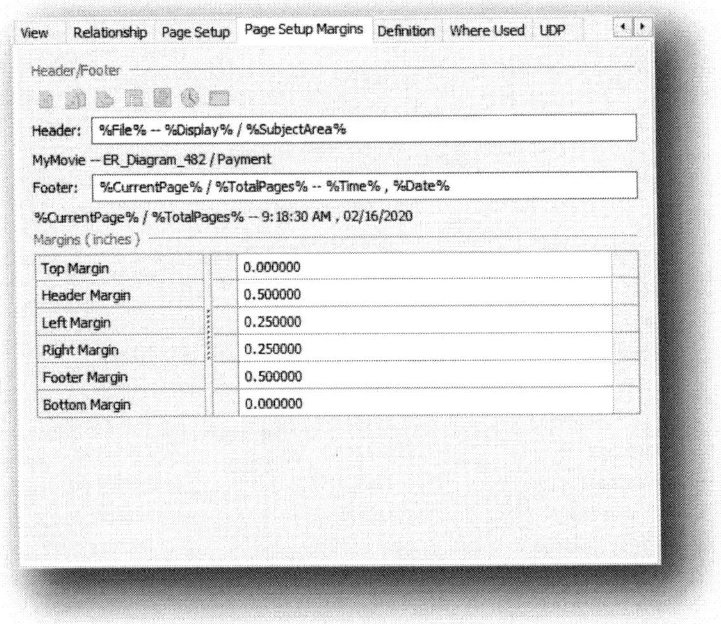

Header   Specifies elements that appear in the header of your printout. Click in the text box, then click an item on the Header/Footer toolbar to add a macro.

Footer   Specifies elements that appear in the footer of your printout. Click in the text box, then click an item on the Header/Footer toolbar to add a macro.

Margins

Top Margin	Specifies the margin (in inches) for the top.
Header Margin	Specifies the header margin (in inches) for the top.
Left Margin	Specifies the margin (in inches) for the left.
Right Margin	Specifies the margin (in inches) for the right.
Footer Margin	Specifies the footer margin (in inches) for the bottom.
Bottom Margin	Specifies the margin (in inches) for the bottom.

28. When finished, click the *Close* button on the ER Diagram Editor dialog.

29. Click the *Close* button on the Subject Editor dialog.

30. In the Model Explorer pane, click on the expand icon (⊞) next to the *Entity* node, and observe all the available entities at the model-level.

31. Click on the Subject Area tab in the Model Explorer.

32. Click on the expand icon (⊞) next to the *Entity* node, and observe all the subset of entities available at the subject area level. See Figure 305.

Figure 305. Expand the Entities Node

33. Drag and drop the four entities into the diagram pane.

34. Observe the following:

The color change of the entities, and the inclusion of the lines of the relationships, including the subtype symbol.

35. When finished, save and close your MyMovie data model.

Key Learnings

- A subject area is a subset of data model objects taken from the full pool of data model objects in a data model.

- When you create a subject area for the logical side of a logical/physical model, a similar subject area is automatically created for the physical side of the model.

- ER Diagrams are a subset of a Subject Area and are owned by the subject area. The objects displayed in the ER Diagram are restricted to the membership of the owning subject area.

Part V briefly explains the significant objects that form a physical data model. Although the physical data model is a very complicated and involved aspect of the data modeling practice, it also introduces aspects that are DBMS-specific. We will not go into great detail on all the nuances of each of the DBMSs but will skim over the generic aspects.

- **Chapter 21** explains tables, and their relationship to entities.
- **Chapter 22** drills into the concept of columns and how they interrelate with attributes.
- **Chapter 23** focuses on views, which are virtual tables.
- **Chapter 24** explains indexes and their logical counterpart, key groups.

Entities get real
Who, What, When, Where, Why, and How
Tables very real

Tables are the physical manifestation of the entities from the logical data model, which, when implemented in a database, compose records and fields that hold data. Each table in a database holds data about the object that the business deems important and worthy of capturing.

Tables Explained

In Chapter 14, we learned that an entity represents a collection of information about something that the business deems important and worthy of capture. And that a noun or noun phrase identifies each entity, and fits into one of six categories: who, what, when, where, why, or how.

In a DBMS, the entities become *tables* or *views*. In NoSQL databases, the entities become transformed depending on the underlying technology. For example, in MongoDB, a document-based database, the entities become *collections*. The general term *structure* is used to refer to the underlying database components independent of whether the database is a relational database or NoSQL solution.

Table Types

The beauty of data modeling is that you can take the same information and show it at different levels of detail, depending on the audience. The previous Part introduced design layer modeling and the various levels of detail at each: enterprise, conceptual, logical, physical, and operational. Entities are components of all these levels.

The enterprise means the high-level business, as a whole. In contrast, the conceptual means the high-level business solution to a business process or application effort, frequently defining scope, and essential terminology. The logical means the detailed business solution to a business process or application effort. And the physical means the specific technical solution to an application effort — finally, the operational reflects the business in motion.

At a physical level, the entities correspond to technology-specific objects such as tables in a DBMS or collections in the NoSQL database MongoDB. The physical level is similar to the logical level but may include compromises that were needed to make up for deficiencies in technology, often related to performance or storage.

The physical entities also contain database-specific information such as the format and length of an attribute (**Author Last Name** is 50 characters), and, whether the attribute is required to have a value (**Author Tax Identifier** is not null and therefore required to have a value, but **Author Birth Date** is null and therefore not required to have a value).

Tutorial: Managing Tables in erwin DM

1. Open erwin DM.

2. Using the Quick Access Toolbar, click on the *Open* button.

3. Select the **MyMovie_Ver1** data model, from the previous portion of the tutorial, in the Open dialog.

4. Click on the *Open* button.

5. The MyMovie model opens in erwin DM. Maximize the model in the diagram window if needed.

6. In the Model Explorer pane, right-click on the *ER Diagrams* node, and select the *New* option. See Figure 306.

Figure 306. Expand the ER Diagrams Node

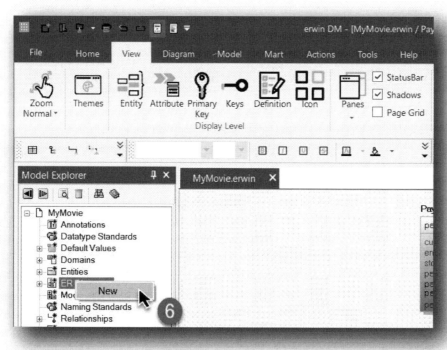

7. Rename the new ER Diagram to **Physical Model**.

8. Right-click on the background in the diagram pane and select *Properties* option. See Figure 307.

9. In the ER Diagram Editor dialog, change the View Mode to *Physical*. See Figure 308.

Figure 307. Right-Click and Select the Properties Option

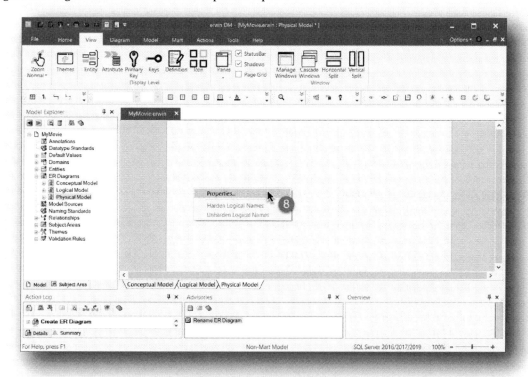

Figure 308. Change the View Mode to Physical

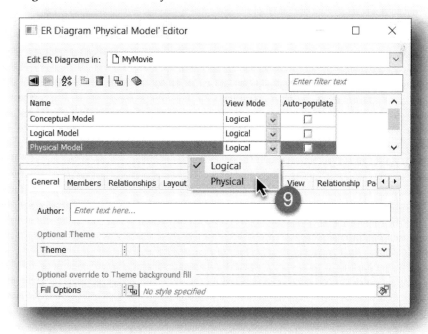

10. Select the *Auto-Populate* option to include all the objects.

11. Click the *Close* button on the ER Diagram Editor dialog and use the *Tree Auto-layout* option on the Diagram ribbon. For recapping on the layout options, please see Chapter 16.

12. Note that all the entities and attributes from the logical model get reflected as physical objects, taking note that the spaces get replaced with underscores (_).

13. Right-click on the **Employee** table name, and select the *Table Properties* option.

14. Observe the Table Editor dialog opens.

15. Although we are going to look at the physical model from a generic perspective, there are a few properties and tabs that are of importance.

16. In the properties section, click on the *General* tab.

17. Observe the General tab, as shown in Figure 309.

Figure 309. The General Tab

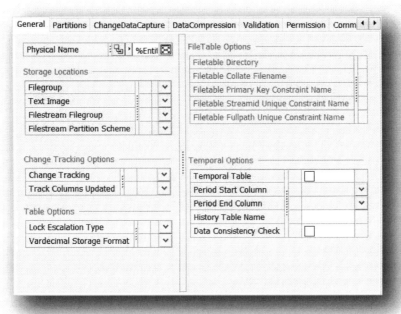

18. Take note of the *Physical Name* property; this is the name that is given to the table. erwin DM makes use of the macro and naming standards to translate the physical table name from the logical entity name. For more information regarding Naming Standards, see Chapter 26. The rest of the properties on the general tab are used for specifying the database-specific values.

19. Further, note that the Partitions, ChangeDataCapture, DataCompression, Validation, and Permissions tabs are all SQL Server database-specific, and hence we will not explore these tabs. Furthermore, note that these tabs change according to the chosen database for the physical data model, some DBMSs have fewer tabs, some have more—it depends on the functionality of the DBMS.

20. When finished, click on the *Comment* tab.

21. Observe the Comment tab, as shown in Figure 310.

Figure 310. The Comment Tab

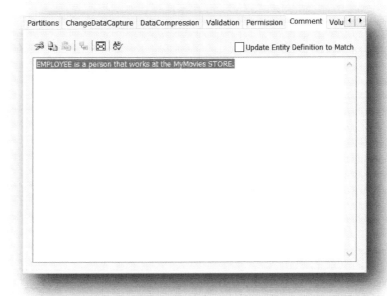

The comment property inherits its value from the logical entity's definition. As with most inherited properties, these are overwritable. Furthermore, take note of the option to Update Entity Definition to Match, which allows the user to update the logical entity's definition from the changes made to the comment in the physical table. For more information regarding the buttons, please refer to the Definition tab on the Entity Editor dialog in Chapter 14.

22. When finished, scroll to the right on the tabs to display the next set of tabs, then click on the *SQL* tab.

23. Observe the SQL tab, as shown in Figure 311.

Figure 311. The SQL Tab

The SQL tab provides a read-only version of the SQL command that gets generated during the forward engineering process. It is essential to note that the SQL displayed is based on the default option for forward engineering. During the forward engineering process, the user can change the format and structure of the SQL command to suit their specific requirements. For more information on the forward engineering process, please refer to Chapter 27.

24. Note that the Style and Icon tabs are the same as the Entity Editor dialog's tabs. Please refer back to Chapter 14 for more information on these tabs.

25. When finished, click on the *Object Creation Order* tab.

26. Observe the Object Creation Order tab, as shown in Figure 312.

Figure 312. The Object Creation Order Tab

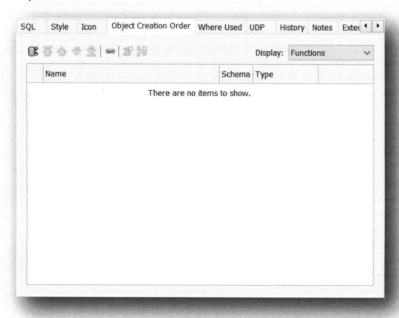

The Object Creation Order tab allows the user to set the order in which dependent objects get created during the forward engineering process. This allows for the changing of functions, scripts, and stored procedures' orders to ensure that the relevant objects get created first before the dependent objects get created.

For example, if the user needs to create a script to populate a table using a stored procedure. Therefore the table needs to be created before the stored procedure, and the stored procedure needs to be created before the script. The Object Creation Order tab assists in defining and managing this creation order.

For more information on the forward engineering process, please refer to Chapter 27.

27. When finished, click on the *Where Used* tab.

28. Observe the Where Used tab. For more information on the Where Used tab, please refer back to Chapter 14 tutorial that already covered the Where Used tab.

29. When finished, click on the **UDP** tab.

30. Observe the UDP tab. For more information on the UDP tab, please refer back to Chapter 7 tutorial that already covered the UDP tab. We also explain more about UDPs in Chapter 25.

31. When finished, click on the *Notes* tab.

32. Observe the Notes tab. For more information on the Notes tab, please refer back to Chapter 7 tutorial that already covered the Notes tab.

33. When finished, click on the *Extended Notes* tab.

34. Observe the Extended Notes tab. For more information on the Extended Notes tab, please refer back to Chapter 7 tutorial that already covered the Extended Notes tab.

35. When finished, click the *Close* button on the Table Editor dialog, then save and close your MyMovie data model.

Key Learnings

- Tables are the physical manifestation of the entities from the logical data model.

- Tables comprise of columns and records that hold the data about the objects that the business deems important.

- In a relational DBMS, the entities become tables or views.

- In NoSQL databases, the entities become transformed depending on the underlying technology.

- erwin DM provides a rich set of capabilities to create, manage, and update tables.

Make attributes real
Columns define a table
Columns have data

Columns are the physical manifestation of attributes from the logical data model, which, when implemented in a database, become fields that hold data. Each column in a database table holds data about the property of an object that the business deems important and worthy of capturing.

Columns Explained

In Chapter 16, we learned that an attribute is an individual piece of information whose values identify, describe, or measure instances of an entity. The same applies to columns—a column contains the value, or property, that identifies, describes, or measures an instance of a table. The column **student_last_name** describes the student. The column **gross_sales_amount** measures the monetary value of a transaction.

Tutorial: Managing Columns in erwin DM

1. Open erwin DM.

2. Using the Quick Access Toolbar, click on the **Open** button.

3. Select the **MyMovie_Ver1** data model, from the previous portion of the tutorial, in the Open dialog.

4. Click on the **Open** button.

5. The MyMovie model opens in erwin DM. Maximize the model in the diagram window if needed.

6. Make sure that the **Employee** table is not selected, and see that there are no blue grip icons on the four corners of the table. Right-click on the **Employee** table and select the *Column Properties* option to open the Column Editor dialog.

7. Observe the Column Editor dialog opens, as shown in Figure 313.

8. In the properties section, click on the *General* tab.

9. Observe the General tab, as shown in Figure 314.

10. Note that the General tab on the Table Editor dialog has the same look and feel like the logical counterpart, the Attribute Editor dialog.

Figure 313. Attribute Editor Dialog

Figure 314. The General Tab

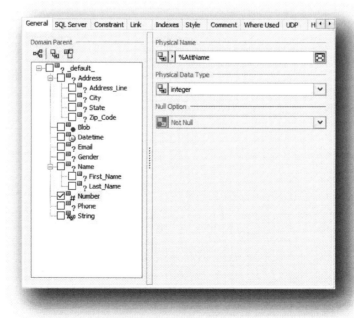

11. When finished, click on the *SQL Server* tab.

12. Observe the SQL Server tab, as shown in Figure 315.

Figure 315. The SQL Server Tab

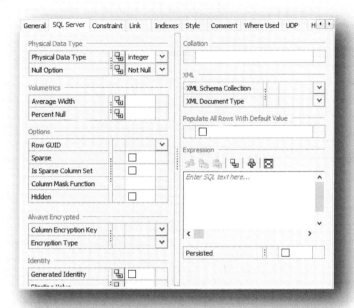

13. The SQL Server tab houses all the SQL Server database-specific properties that are associated with the selected column. Since our physical data model is based on SQL Server, this tab is labeled SQL Server. When a physical data model is based on a different DBMS, the tab will be labeled according to the database specified. That is, a physical data model based on an Oracle database is called Oracle, as shown in Figure 316.

Figure 316. The Oracle Tab

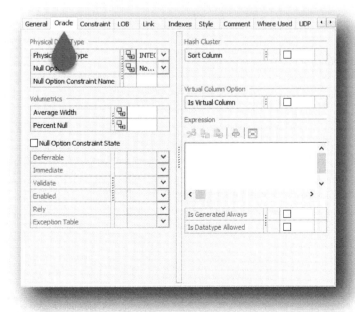

14. When finished, click on the *Constraint* tab.

15. Observe the Constraint tab, as shown in Figure 317.

Figure 317. The Constraint Tab

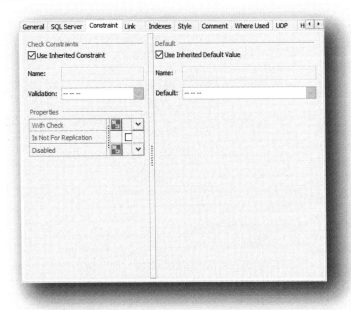

16. Once again, take note of the similarity between the Attribute Editor dialog's Constraint tab and the Column Editor's Constraint tab, with only the additional SQL Server database-specific properties. Please refer back to Chapter 16 for more information on this tab.

17. When finished, click on the *Indexes* tab.

18. Observe the Indexes tab, as shown in Figure 318.

Figure 318. The Indexes Tab

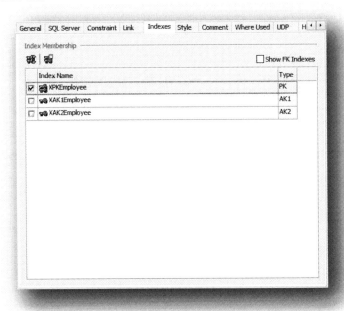

19. In the physical data model, the logical key groups are transformed into the physical indexes, as explained in Chapter 12. Also, observe the similarity of the tab from the Attribute Editor dialog's Key Groups tab, as explained in Chapter 17.

20. When finished, click on the *Style* tab.

21. Observe the Style tab. For more information on the Style tab, please refer back to Chapter 16 tutorial that already covered the Style tab.

22. When finished, click on the *Comment* tab.

23. Observe the Comment tab. The comment property inherits its value from the logical attribute's definition. As with most inherited properties, these are overwritable. Note the option to *Update the Attribute Definition to Match*, which allows the user to update the logical attribute's definition from the changes made to the comment in the physical column. For more on these buttons, refer to the Definition tab on the Attribute Editor dialog in Chapter 16.

24. When finished, click on the *Where Used* tab.

25. Observe the Where Used tab. For more information on the Where Used tab, please refer back to Chapter 14 tutorial that already covered the Where Used tab.

26. When finished, click on the *UDP* tab.

27. Observe the UDP tab. For more information on the UDP tab, please refer back to Chapter 7 tutorial that already covered the UDP tab. We also explain more about UDPs in Chapter 25.

28. When finished, click on the *Notes* tab.

29. Observe the Notes tab. For more information on the Notes tab, please refer back to Chapter 7 tutorial that already covered the Notes tab.

30. When finished, click on the *Extended Notes* tab.

31. Observe the Extended Notes tab. For more information on the Extended Notes tab, please refer back to Chapter 7 tutorial that already covered the Extended Notes tab.

32. When finished, click the *Close* button to close the Column Editor dialog, then save and close your MyMovie data model.

Key Learnings

- Columns are the physical manifestation of the attributes from the logical data model.

- Columns have different properties that form the basis of the physical data model design, such as name, datatype, comment, and null options, to only name a few.

- erwin DM provides a rich set of capabilities to create, manage, and update columns.

Don't reinvent wheel
Views can run the same query
Again and again

A view is a virtual table that is a dynamic 'view' or window into one or more tables where the actual data is stored.

Views Explained

A SQL query is a request that is made of the database, such as *'Bring me back all **Customer IDs** where the **Customer** is 90 days or more behind in their bill payments.'* The difference between a query and a view is that the instructions in a view are already prepared and stored in the database as the definition of the view, whereas a query is not stored in the database. Figure 319 contains a view of **Ticket** and **Booking**, which creates a simple way to display tickets along with the corresponding booking information. Behind this view is the following SQL query needed to retrieve the tickets and their bookings.

Figure 319. A View Creating a Listing of Offerings With Their Categories

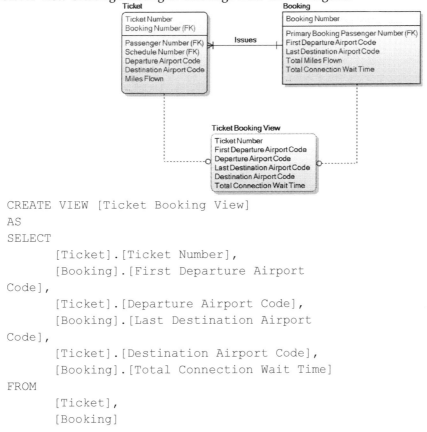

```
CREATE VIEW [Ticket Booking View]
AS
SELECT
      [Ticket].[Ticket Number],
      [Booking].[First Departure Airport
Code],
      [Ticket].[Departure Airport Code],
      [Booking].[Last Destination Airport
Code],
      [Ticket].[Destination Airport Code],
      [Booking].[Total Connection Wait Time]
FROM
      [Ticket],
      [Booking]
```

Table 52. Sample View Results

Ticket Number	First Departure Airport Code	Departure Airport Code	Last Destination Airport Code	Destination Airport Code	Total Connection Wait Time
0012348342101	CLT	CLT	YVR	PHX	4 hrs 35 min
0012348342102	CLT	PHX	YVR	PDX	4 hrs 35 min
0012348342103	CLT	PDX	YVR	YVR	4 hrs 35 min
0012347498912	DFW	ORD	DFW	ORD	0 hrs 0 min
…	…	…	…	…	…

Tutorial: Creating Views in erwin DM

1. Open erwin DM.

2. Using the Quick Access Toolbar, click on the **Open** button.

3. Select the **MyMovie_Ver1** data model from the previous portion of the tutorial.

4. Click on the **Open** button.

5. The MyMovie model opens in erwin DM. Maximize the model in the diagram window.

6. Make sure that you are on the Home ribbon, and click the **View** button. See Figure 320.

    Figure 320. Click the View Button

    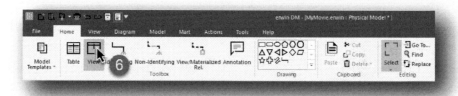

7. Click on the background of the diagram pane to place your new view. See Figure 321.

    Figure 321. Click Background of The Diagram Pane

    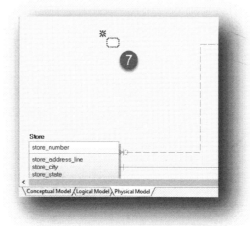

8. Rename the View to **Movie Movie Copy View**.

9. Right-click on the *Movie_Movie_Copy_View* view, and select the *View Properties* option.

10. Observe that the View Editor dialog appears, as shown in Figure 322.

Figure 322. The View Editor Dialog

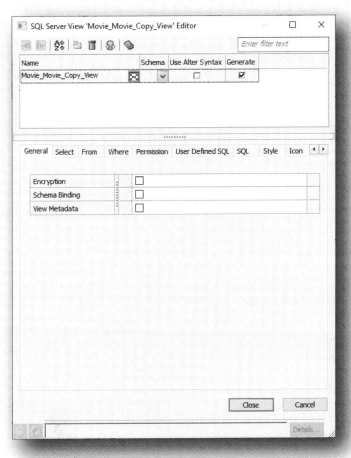

Object Selection Section Columns

Name	Specifies the name of the view and allows the user to change the name of the view.
Schema	Specifies the schema of the database to which the view belongs. The user can select the schema from a drop-down list.
Use Alternative Syntax	Generates a combined CREATE and ALTER statement during forward engineering. It creates a view if it does not exist or alters the view if it exists.
Generate	Generates the SQL during forward engineering. The user clears the checkbox not to generate the SQL.

11. In the properties section, click on the *General* tab.

12. Observe the General tab, as shown in Figure 323.

Figure 323. The General Tab

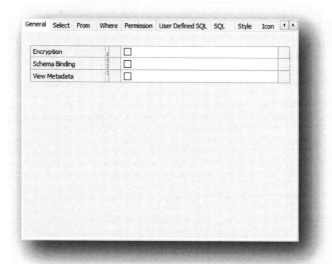

Encryption	Specifies to use encryption for the view so that the view is not published during SQL Server replication.
Schema Binding	Specifies to use schema binding on the view, which binds the view to the schema of tables upon which the view gets based.
View Metadata	Specifies that the instance of the database server returns the metadata information of the view and not the metadata of the tables upon which the view is based.

13. When finished, click on the *From* tab.

14. Observe the From tab, as shown in Figure 324.

Figure 324. The From Tab

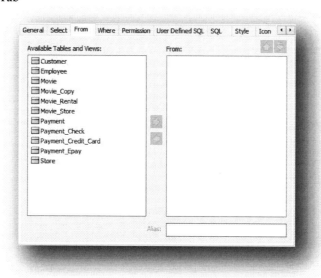

The From tab allows the user to specify which tables or views to base the view on. This would form the **FROM** portion of the SQL.

15. Select the **Movie** and **Movie_Copy** tables in the *Available Tables and Views* section and move them using the to the *Move Right* button to the **From** section. See Figure 325.

Figure 325. Move the Movie & Movie_Copy to The From Section

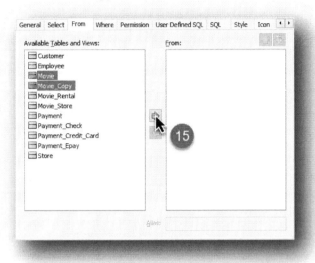

 Some versions of erwin DM require that the tables be moved one at a time.

16. When finished, click on the *Select* tab.

17. Observe the Select tab, as shown in Figure 326.

Figure 326. The Select Tab

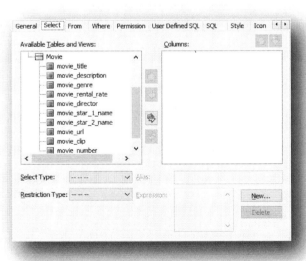

The Select tab allows the user to specify which columns to base the view on, noting that only the columns belonging to the tables selected on the From tab are listed. This would form the **SELECT** portion of the SQL.

Select Type	This allows the user to select a view type that automatically eliminates duplicate rows.
Restriction Type	This allows the user to specify the With Check Option for the view column. This option ensures that data remains visible through the view after any changes get committed.
Alias	Lets the user edit the alias of the selected view column.
Expression	Lets the user edit the selected view column expression. This option is available only if the selected view column is a user-defined expression.
New	Opens the New View Column dialog so the user can add a new view column expression to the view.
Delete	Deletes the selected view column expression.

18. Move the **movie_copy_format**, **movie_copy_general_condition**, **movie_copy_number**, **movie_title**, **movie_description**, **movie_genre**, **movie_rental_rate**, **movie_director**, **movie_star_1_name**, **movie_star_2_name**, **movie_url** and **movie_clip** from the *Available Tables and Views* section to the *Columns* section using the *Move Right* button.

19. When finished, click on the *Where* tab.

20. Observe the Where tab, as shown in Figure 327.

Figure 327. The Where Tab

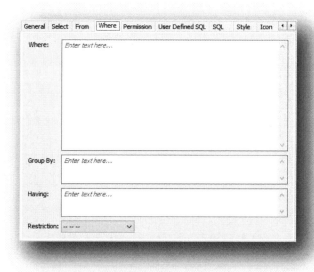

The Where tab allows the user to specify the search conditions for queries against a view. The information entered in the fields in this tab becomes the SQL script that gets generated.

Where Defines the search condition that must be satisfied by the results of the query. The text entered becomes the WHERE clause in the SQL script that gets generated. The WHERE clause excludes rows that do not meet the search condition.

Group By Defines the criteria to use to group rows returned by the query. The text entered becomes the GROUP BY clause in the SQL script that gets generated. The GROUP BY clause places the selected rows into one group for each unique value.

Having Defines the search condition that gets applied to each row group, and filter out rows that do not meet the specified search condition. The text you enter becomes the HAVING clause in the SQL script that gets generated.

Restriction Applies the With Check Option restriction to the WHERE clause.

21. Note that the Permissions tab is one of the database-specific tabs, and may not be present with all DBMSs.

22. When finished, click on the **User Defined SQL** tab. Observe the User Defined SQL tab, as shown in Figure 328. The User Defined SQL tab allows the user to define a custom SQL script for the bases of the SQL script. Selecting the User-Defined SQL checkbox allows for the input of the custom SQL script.

Figure 328. The User Defined SQL Tab

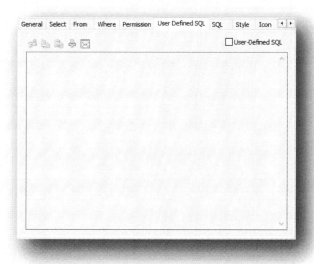

23. When finished, click on the **SQL** tab.

24. Observe the SQL tab, as shown in Figure 329. The SQL tab displays the SQL script that gets used in the forward engineering process.

When using the User Defined SQL script, all links to the FROM tables and all links to the SELECT columns are lost.

Figure 329. The SQL Tab

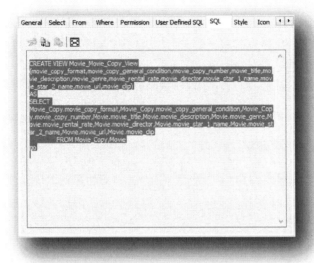

25. Note that the Style, Icon, Comment, Object Creation Order, UDP, History, Notes, and Extended Notes tabs are the same as the Table Editor dialog's tabs from Chapter 21.

26. When finished, click the *Close* button on the View Editor dialog.

27. Observe the newly created view, including the listing of the columns and the relationship lines to the from tables. See Figure 330.

Figure 330. The Newly Created View

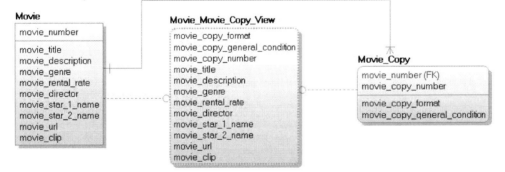

28. When finished, save and close your MyMovie data model.

Key Learnings
• Views are virtual tables that are pre-prepared, making it easier for the user not to have to re-type the query each time.
• A view is defined by a SQL query that can combine multiple tables into one result set.

Different indexes
Faster data retrieval
Key group to index

There is a lot of data out there, but how do you sift through it all to find what you're looking for? That's where indexes come in.

Indexes Explained

An index is a value and a pointer to instances of that value in a table. In Chapter 17, we covered primary keys, alternate keys, and inversion entries—these get converted into indexes on the physical data model. Primary and alternate keys get converted into unique indexes, and inversion entries get converted into non-unique indexes.

Tutorial: Managing Indexes in erwin DM

1. Open erwin DM.

2. Using the Quick Access Toolbar, click on the *Open* button.

3. Select the **MyMovie_Ver1** data model, from the previous portion of the tutorial, in the Open dialog.

4. Click on the *Open* button.

5. The MyMovie model opens in erwin DM. Maximize the model in the diagram window if needed.

6. Right-click on the **Employee** table, and select the *Index Properties* option.

7. Observe that the Index Editor dialog appears. See Figure 331.

8. In the properties section, click on the *Members* tab.

9. Observe the Members tab, as shown in Figure 332.

   The Members tab on the Index Editor dialog allows for the selection of the members of the index. Furthermore, there is the SQL Server specific functionality of being able to also include other columns in the index.

10. When finished, click on the *General* tab.

11. Observe the General tab, as shown in Figure 333.

Figure 331. The Index Editor Dialog

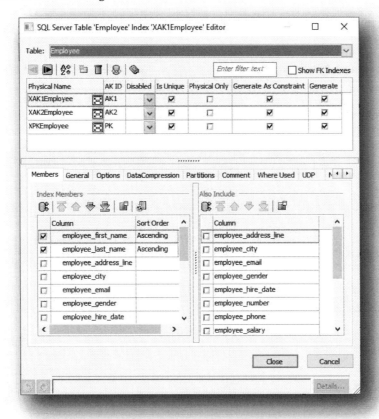

Object Selection Section Columns

Physical Name   Specifies the physical name of the index, and allows the users to change the physical name of the index.

AK ID   Displays key designation of the index.

Disabled   Specifies if the index is disabled or not.

Is Unique   Specifies if the index is unique or non-unique. Select the checkbox if it is a unique index.

Physical Only   Specifies whether the index should be suppressed from a logical model and appear in a physical model only.

Generate As Constraint   It generates the index as a constraint. When this option is enabled, the Constraint Name field on the General tab gets populated with the index name.

Generate   Generates SQL during forward engineering. Clear the checkbox if you do not want to generate SQL.

Figure 332. The Members Tab

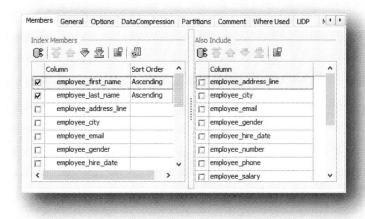

Figure 333. The General Tab

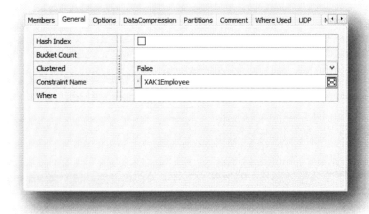

The General tab provides for some of the database-specific properties of the index.

12. When finished, click on the *Options* tab.

13. Observe the Options tab. The Options allows for the specifying of relevant SQL Server properties.

14. When finished, click on the *DataCompression* tab.

15. Observe the DataComression tab. The DataComression allows for the specifying of relevant SQL Server properties.

16. When finished, click on the *Partitions* tab.

17. Observe the Partitions tab. The Partitions allows for the specifying of relevant SQL Server properties.

18. When finished, click on the *Where Used* tab.

19. Observe the Where Used tab. For more information on the Where Used tab, refer back to the Chapter 14 tutorial.

20. When finished, click on the **UDP** tab.

21. Observe the UDP tab. For more information on the UDP tab, please refer back to the Chapter 7 tutorial that covered the UDP tab. We also explain more about UDPs in Chapter 25.

22. When finished, click on the **Notes** tab.

23. Observe the Notes tab. For more information on the Notes tab, please refer back to the Chapter 7 tutorial that covered the Notes tab.

24. When finished, click on the **Extended Notes** tab.

25. Observe the Extended Notes tab. For more information on the Extended Notes tab, refer back to the Chapter 7 tutorial that already the Extended Notes tab.

26. When finished, click the **Close** button on the Index Editor dialog, then save and close your MyMovie data model.

Key Learnings

- Logical Key Groups transform into the physical Indexes.

- Indexes add data integrity to a database.

- Indexes also provides for database performance benefits.

erwin DM provides several advanced functions to make the data modeler's life easier and more accurate. In **Part VI**, we are going to explore some of these functions in more detail. Although each of the functions are quite complex, this book provides the basics for the user to understand how they operate and the benefits that can be achieved using them.

- **Chapter 25** covers User Defined Properties in erwin DM.
- **Chapter 26** explores how to maintain a naming standard in a data model and how logical names translate into physical names.
- **Chapter 27** provides the knowledge to generate a database or DDL script with the forward engineering functionality.
- **Chapter 28** leverages the reverse engineering functionality in erwin DM to create a data model for an existing database or DDL script.
- **Chapter 29** explains the reporting functionality provided by erwin DM.
- **Chapter 30** explores the options to edit the data model in a bulk fashion.
- **Chapter 31** walks through the Complete Compare functionality.

Where can I store this?
Need some custom properties?
UDPs are here!

User Defined Properties, more commonly referred to as UDPs, are a custom property for an object instance. They are available for every instance of the object type. UDPs holds a value for each instance of the object, but can also hold a default value.

User Defined Properties Explained

We need to distinguish between the custom property (the UDP) and the value the custom property holds for each instance. A UDP gets defined for a specific object type, such as ENTITY or COLUMN, and every instance of the object type will then have that property. The property can have a different value for each instance of the object type. It is the same as a column or field in a database table. Every row in the table has the column, but each row can have a different value in it, including the option to have a NULL value.

There are six different types of UDPs:

- Int   Holds an integer value (whole numbers).
- Text   Holds a free text value.
- Date   Holds a date-time value.
- Command   Holds a path to a file or URL.
- Real   Holds a real numeric value (decimal value).
- List   Holds a value from a list of values.

In a physical data model and for some DBMSs, it is possible to use the UDP as an extended property that can be implemented in the database. Further to this, UDPs can also be used in macros. For example, I had a client that needed erwin DM to support a change control process implemented in their organization. The change control process needs to have a reference back to the originating request for the change, and it needed this to be implemented in the database as an extended property. To fulfill this requirement, I implemented a UDP in their data models, that when forward engineering, created an extended property holding the change control request number. Further to this, I implemented another UDP that held a URL link to the details of the change control request, thus allowing future viewers of the model to open the originating change control request.

Tutorial: Creating and Using UDPs in erwin DM

For our MyMovie model, we have identified three distinct UDPs that we need in our model: a UDP to keep track of the date that a table got created in the database, a UDP to keep track of the data steward for each of the entities, and a UDP which contains a link to the original design documents for the model. See Table 53 for the UDPs that suit our requirements.

Table 53. Table of UDPs

UDP	Class	Type	Default	Description
DB Creation Date	Table	Date	Today's date	This is the date that the table is created in the database.
Data Steward	Entity	List	Jeff Harris, Steve Hoberman, Andy Miles	This is the person who is the data steward for this table.
Design Document	Model	Command		This is the design document for this data model.

1. Open erwin DM.

2. Using the Quick Access Toolbar, click on the **Open** button.

3. Select the **MyMovie_Ver1** data model, from the previous portion of the tutorial.

4. Click on the **Open** button.

5. The MyMovie model opens in erwin DM. Maximize the model in the diagram window if needed.

6. Click on the *Model* ribbon tab.

7. Then click on the **User Defined Properties** button to open the User Defined Properties Editor dialog. See Figure 334.

Figure 334. Click on the User Defined Properties Button

8. Observe that the User Defined Properties Editor dialog appears, as shown in Figure 335.

9. Take special note in the label of the dialog; it refers to the *User Defined Properties: Physical*. It is important to note that when creating a UDP in a model, one needs to be on the same side of the model to be able to access the relevant objects. Remembering from our requirements, we need to create two UDPs on the logical model (Model and Entity level) and one on the physical model (Table level).

Figure 335. The User Defined Properties Editor Dialog

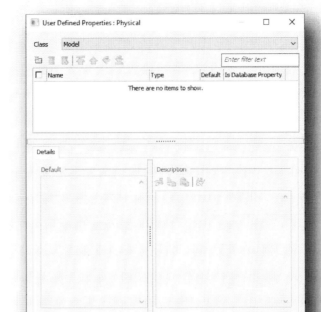

10. Expand the drop-down list of ***Class*** (object type), and select the ***Table*** option. See Figure 336.

Figure 336. Select the Table Option for Class

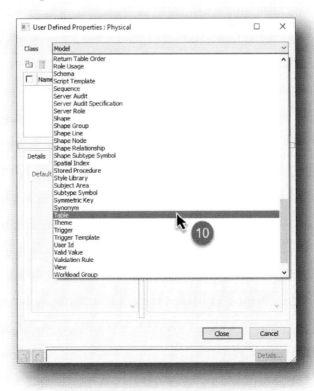

11. By selecting the *Table* option, we set the object class for the new UDP to be based on tables.

12. Click the *New* button (🔳) to create a new UDP.

13. Rename the new UDP to **DB Creation Date** and change the *Type* to *Date*, the default value to today's date, and the *Is Database Property* to **True**. Lastly, give a *Description* of the UDP as '**This is the date that the table is created in the database.**'

14. The *Is Database Property* is valid for the DBMSs that allow for the implementation of extended properties.

15. When finished, click the *Close* button.

16. Right-click on the **Employee** table, and select the *Table Properties* option.

17. In the Table Editor dialog, select the UDP tab.

18. Observe the new UDP that we created, and take note of the default value. See Figure 337.

Figure 337. Observe The New UDP

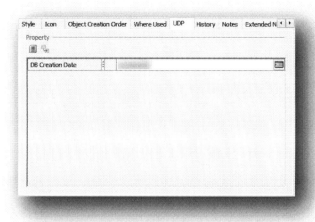

19. When finished, click the Close button to close the Table Editor dialog.

20. Click on the *Logical Model* tab in the Drawing pane to switch back to the logical model diagram.

21. Click on the *User Defined Properties* button to open the User Defined Properties Editor dialog again.

22. Observe that the User Defined Properties Editor dialog appears.

23. Once again, take special note in the label of the dialog; it refers to the *User Defined Properties: Logical*.

24. Now create the two logical UDPs, as per Table 53 above. Take special care to select the correct *Class* (object type) for each of the UDPs.

25. When finished, click the *Close* button.

26. Click the *Model Properties* button on the Model ribbon tab.

27. In the Model Editor dialog, select the *UDP* tab.

28. Click the *Open Folder* button. See Figure 338.

Figure 338. Click The Open Folder Button

29. Type in 'http://erwin.com' in the *File Name* field and press the *Open* button.

30. Observe the new **Design Document** UDP value and click on the *View* button. See Figure 339.

Figure 339. Click The View Button

31. Observe that the default browser opens on the erwin.com website. If a file were selected, the file would open using the default program associated with that file.

32. When finished, click the *Close* button.

33. Right-click on the **Payment** entity, and select the *Entity Properties* option.

34. In the Entity Editor dialog, select the *UDP* tab.

35. Observe, as shown in Figure 340, the newly created **Data Steward** UDP, with the default value of 'Jeff Harris.'

Figure 340. Observe The Data Steward UDP

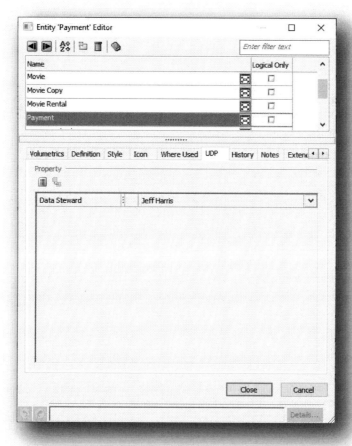

 When using the List option for a UDP, the list gets populated with the comma-separated values in the Default property. The default is always the first value in the comma-separated values. To prevent a default value, start the comma-separated list with a comma.

36. Change the *Data Steward* UDP for the **Payment** entity to 'Steve Hoberman,' and do the same for the **Payment Check, Payment Credit Card** and **Payment Epay** entities. Taking note that the different entities can all have different values.

37. When finished, click the *Close* button on the Entity Editor dialog.

38. Then click on the *Physical Model* tab in the Drawing pane to switch back to the physical model diagram.

39. Save and close your MyMovie data model.

Key Learnings

- UDPs allow a user to extend the properties stored in a data model.

- Macros can make usage of UDPs in the forward engineering process.

- To define a UDP, one needs to create the UDP at the object level, and then assign a value at the object instances.

- Most data modeling objects in erwin DM have a UDP capability.

Standardization?
Easier to understand
Naming standards rule

Many organizations wish to apply naming standards to their data models, and erwin DM has a range of features to support this requirement.

Naming Standards Explained

Recall from Chapter 15 that we can define attribute names using naming rules. Naming rules also define the generation of the physical names for the following dual state object types in a combined logical/physical model.

- Table names
- Index names
- Domain physical names
- Default rule physical names
- Column names
- Relationship physical names
- Validation rule physical names

All the physical objects listed above have an associated logical object, and the predefined naming rules merely returns the logical name of the object as the physical name with special characters replaced with underscores '_ '. However, this predefined naming rule can be changed to support different naming requirements. While the name of the logical object gets used as the basis for the physical name, there are other options to formatting the logical name before the final physical name gets derived.

In addition to the physical naming rules, a suffix and prefix can be defined for each of the object types listed above. These get added to the physical name of the appropriate objects. The naming rules are broken down into several key aspects:

- Case,
- Name length,
- Abbreviations, and
- Special characters and character substitution.

Case

For each of the dual object types, the case of the names is set separately. Therefore, the naming rule for tables can be different for those of columns. The case rule gets applied to both the logical and physical names individually. The case options are:

- **None**–Leaves the case the same as the user typed it in. (PaSSenGer nUmBER)
- **Upper**–Converts all characters into their upper case format. (PASSENGER NUMBER)
- **Lower**–Converts all characters into their lower case format. (passenger number)
- **Initial**–Capitalizes all the first characters in a word, and converts the remaining characters to lower case. (Passenger Number)

It is essential to note that the conversion is inline, and that the original format captured is still maintained. In other words, after applying a naming rule of upper case, the original mixed case text format is still maintained. Therefore, if the naming rule gets removed, the text reverts to the original mixed case format. It is also vital to note that wherever the object gets reflected, whether in a diagram, a report, or through any dialog, the case rule gets applied. Using a consistent style in erwin DM helps promote that material as a means of communication.

Name Length

For each of the dual object types, it is possible to set a maximum allowable length for the names. For physical objects, the default maximum length is the maximum allowed by the DBMS for the object type, and while this value can be reduced, it cannot be increased. For the logical objects, the default maximum length is 254 characters, which can be reduced or increased to suit the organizational requirements. If the name generated by a naming rule exceeds the max length setting for the object type, the name gets truncated. Where duplicate names arise, erwin DM renames the object by applying a numerical suffix to the name, which still complies with the maximum length setting for the object type.

Abbreviations

erwin DM allows for the usage of an abbreviation list, sometimes referred to as a glossary. The glossary converts words into their abbreviated form from the list of words and abbreviations in the glossary.

 erwin DM allows for multiple glossaries in a model, although only one standard can be active at a time. This can often lead to confusion or even incorrect information, and it is a good practice to ensure that only one glossary is present in a data model or to have a strict procedure for managing the multiple glossaries.

To fully appreciate how the glossary works, one needs to first understand the options for using the glossary. There are two switches (checkboxes) found on the Naming Standards Editor dialog that affect how the glossary function operates:

- Match whole words only
- Match whole name only

Table 54 contains a sample glossary entry.

Table 54. Glossary

Word	Abbreviation
First	Fst
Name	Nm

With neither of the checkboxes selected, the glossary gets applied to any substring within the logical name, irrespective if it is a whole word, whole name, or part of a word.

Table 55. Abbreviation Examples. None Selected

Attribute Name	Column Name
First	Fst
First Name	Fst_Nm
FirstName	FstNm

With the Match Whole Word Only selected, the glossary gets applied to any whole word in the logical name. It does not get applied when the glossary word is part of another word. Take a look at the **FirstName** example in Table 56. The glossary words **First** and **Name** appear in the **FirstName** attribute name, but because it is one word, neither of the glossary words gets applied.

Table 56. Abbreviation Examples. Match Whole Words Only Selected

Attribute Name	Column Name
First	Fst
First Name	Fst_Nm
FirstName	FirstName

With the Match Whole Name Only selected, the glossary gets applied to any whole logical name. It does not get applied when the glossary word is part of the whole logical name. Take a look at the **First Name** example in Table 57. The glossary words **First** and **Name** appear in the **First Name** attribute name, but because neither of the glossary words match the whole logical name, no abbreviation gets applied.

Table 57. Abbreviation Examples. Match Whole Name Only Selected

Attribute Name	Column Name
First	Fst
First Name	First_Name
FirstName	FirstName

Special Characters and Character Substitution

What constitutes a special character, and their significance varies from DBMS to DBMS. There are two properties (both found in the Model Naming Options dialog) that define how special characters in logical names get handled when generating physical names, and these properties need to be combined to get the desired result. The results of all combinations of these two properties are set out in Table 58. The second row represents the default settings in the table.

Table 58. Special Characters Behavior

Allow Special Characters	Special Characters	Result
✓	Leave	The special characters get included in the physical name.
	Leave	Special characters get replaced with an underscore '_'.
✓	Remove	Special characters, including spaces and underscores'_', get removed.
	Remove	Special characters, including spaces and underscores'_', get removed.
✓	Replace (with 'X')	Special characters get replaced by the replacement character, even when it is a special character.
	Replace (with 'X')	Special characters, including spaces and underscores, get removed. If the replacement character is a special character, the underscore '_' gets used in its place.

Some confusion can arise about the use of the underscore '_'. The underscore '_' is defined as a special character for some DBMSs but is acceptable by DBMSs in un-delimited identifiers. A common effect of including special characters in identifiers is the need to delimit them (for example, wrap them in double quotes or square brackets) in DDLs. Regardless of whether the DBMS defines the underscore '_' as a special character, it does not generally give rise to the need to delimit identifiers. Rows 2 and 6 do not allow special characters, but both can result in the underscore '_' getting included in the physical name.

Tutorial: Creating and Using Naming Standards in erwin DM

For our MyMovie database, we want to implement the following naming standards.

- Logical names to be in initial case,
- Physical names to be in upper case,
- Max length of physical names to be 60 characters long,
- Use pre-defined macros for physical relationships and indexes,
- Use the below-listed abbreviations for all physical names.

1. Open erwin DM.

2. Using the Quick Access Toolbar, click on the **Open** button.

Table 59. Abbreviation List

Word	Abbreviation
account	acc
address	addrs
amount	amnt
customer	cust
description	dec
employee	emp
gender	gendr
general	gen
number	nmbr
payment	pymnt
phone	phne

3. Select the **MyMovie_Ver1** data model, from the previous portion of the tutorial, in the Open dialog.

4. Click on the *Open* button.

5. The MyMovie model opens in erwin DM. Maximize the model in the diagram window if needed.

6. Click on the *Tools* ribbon tab.

7. Then click on the *Naming Standards* button to open the Naming Standards Editor dialog. See Figure 341.

Figure 341. Click on the Naming Standards Button

8. Observe that the Naming Standards Editor dialog appears, as shown in Figure 342.

9. Click on the *New* button to create our naming standard.

10. Rename the newly created Naming Standard to **MyMovie Naming Standard**, and select the *Is Active* option associated with the new Naming Standard. See Figure 343.

11. In the properties section, click on the *Glossary* tab.

12. Observe the Glossary tab, as shown in Figure 344.

Figure 342. The Naming Standards Editor Dialog

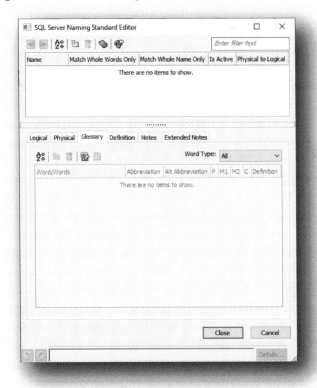

Action Buttons

Previous–Allows the user to position the editor on the previous Naming Standard in the Navigation Grid.

Next–Allows the user to position the editor on the next Naming Standard in the Navigation Grid.

Sort–Allows the user to sort the Naming Standard by alphabetic, or reverse alphabetic order. Visual cues provide the current sort order:

> Specifies that the Naming Standard list sort order is in alphabetic order.

> Specifies that the Naming Standard list sort order is in reverse alphabetic order.

New–Allows the user to create a new Naming Standard that becomes the current Naming Standard in the editor.

Delete–Allows the user to delete the selected Naming Standard.

Help–Allows the user to open online help for the editor.

Import–Allows the user to import an NSM file from an older version of erwin DM.

Enter filter text   The filter field allows for the filtering of extensive lists of Naming Standard in the Navigation Grid for the quick location of a particular Naming Standard.

Grid Columns

Name	Specifies the name of the Naming Standard. This field allows for the changing of the name of the Naming Standard.
Match Whole Words Only	Specifies whether to substitute glossary abbreviations on whole words only or to include parts of words or substrings. Select the checkbox to substitute glossary abbreviations on whole words only. Clear the checkbox to substitute glossary abbreviations for complete words, as well as on parts of words or substrings.
Match Whole Names Only	Specifies whether to substitute glossary abbreviations on the whole name only. Select the checkbox to substitute glossary abbreviations on the whole name only and to ignore parts of words and substrings.
Is Active	Specifies whether to apply the selected Naming Standard to the model.
Physical to Logical	Specifies whether the changes made to the Naming Standard in the Physical mode should be preserved and reflected in the Logical model.

Figure 343. Rename and Activate the Naming Standard

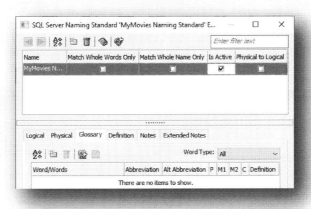

Figure 344. The Glossary Tab

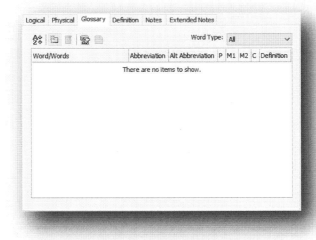

Action Buttons

Sort–Allows the user to sort the Words by alphabetic, or reverse alphabetic order. Visual cues provide the current sort order:

Specifies that the Word list sort order is in alphabetic order.

Specifies that the Word list sort order is in reverse alphabetic order.

New–Allows the user to create a new Word.

Delete–Allows the user to delete the selected Word.

Import–Allows the user to import a CSV file containing the words and abbreviations.

Export–Allows the user to export a CSV file containing the words and abbreviations.

Word Type   Allows the user to filter on the type of words.

Options are:

Prime = Prime words are the first word in the name.

Modifier 1 = Modifier 1 words are the first word that modifies the prime word. (Second word in name)

Modifier 2 = Modifier 2 words are the second word that modifies the prime word. (Third word in name)

Class = Class words are the words that define the type (data type) of the attribute. (Forth word in name)

Grid Columns

Column	Description
Word	Specifies the glossary word or words that you want to abbreviate.
Abbreviation	Specifies the standard abbreviation.
Alt Abbreviation	Specifies an alternate abbreviation.
P	Specifies whether you want to use the word as a prime word.
M1	Specifies whether you want to use the word as a modifier 1 word.
M2	Specifies whether you want to use the word as a modifier 2 word.
C	Specifies whether you want to use the word as a class word.
Definition	Specifies the definition for the glossary word and abbreviation.

13. Click on the *New* button to create the first word. See Figure 345.

14. Change the *Word* to 'account,' and the *Abbreviation* to 'acc' and enter a *Definition* of 'The standard corporate abbreviation for account.'

Figure 345. Click on The New Button

15. Note that by default, erwin DM sets the *Prime* option (P) on. Although the strict naming convention of PrimeWord_Modifier1_Modifier2_Class is generally not adhered to anymore, erwin DM still provides the functionality to manage this convention and to report on exceptions to this standard. Seeing that we are not worried about this naming convention, we are not going to worry about designating the Prime, Modifiers, and Class words, the default will work adequately well for our purposes.

16. Generally, in a real-world scenario, we would have a more extensive list of abbreviations, but then we would also make usage of the import from CSV function to import this list.

17. Follow the above steps to create the remaining words and their abbreviations:

Table 60. Abbreviation List

Word	Abbreviation	Alt Abbreviation	Definition
account	acc		The standard corporate abbreviation for account.
address	addrs		The standard corporate abbreviation for address.
amount	amnt		The standard corporate abbreviation for amount.
customer	cust		The standard corporate abbreviation for customer.
description	dec		The standard corporate abbreviation for description.
employee	emp		The standard corporate abbreviation for employee.
gender	gendr		The standard corporate abbreviation for gender.
general	gen		The standard corporate abbreviation for account.
number	nmbr		The standard corporate abbreviation for account.
payment	pymnt		The standard corporate abbreviation for account.
phone	phne		The standard corporate abbreviation for account.

18. When finished, click on the *Logical* tab.

19. Observe the Logical tab, as shown in Figure 346.

Figure 346. The Logical Tab

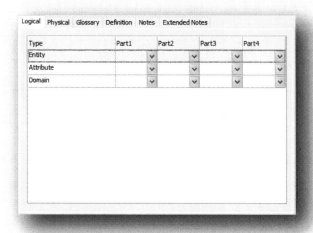

On the Logical tab, the user has the functionality to define the parts of the logical objects that need to comply with the PrimeWord_Modifier1_Modifier2_Class naming convention.

20. When finished, click on the *Physical* tab.

Observe the Physical tab, as shown in Figure 347. On the Physical tab, the user has the functionality to define the parts of the physical objects that need to comply with the PrimeWord_Modifier1_Modifier2_Class naming convention.

Figure 347. The Physical Tab

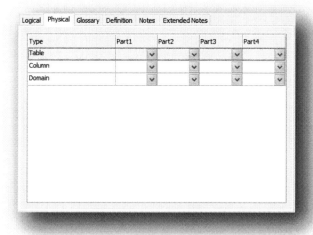

21. The Definition, Notes, and Extended Notes tabs all behave the same as the other dialogs.

22. When finished, click the *Close* button to close the Naming Standard Editor dialog.

You will most probably notice at this point that the naming standards have not been applied to the physical data model. Up to now, we have created the naming standard, but we need to still set the model naming options for this to take effect. Click on the ***Model Naming Options*** button to open the Model Naming Option dialog. Observe that the Model Naming Options dialog appears. Click on the ***Logical*** tab, if the Logical tab is not visible. See Figure 349. This tab allows the user to change the logical name options, case, and maximum length.

Figure 348. Click On The Model Naming Option Button

Figure 349. The Model Naming Options Dialog

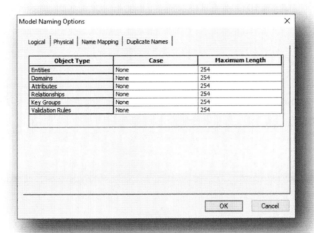

23. For our logical naming standards, we need to set the case to initial case. For each of the logical object types, click the Case property, and select the ***Initial*** option. See Figure 350.

Figure 350. Change The Case to Initial Case For All Logical Object Types

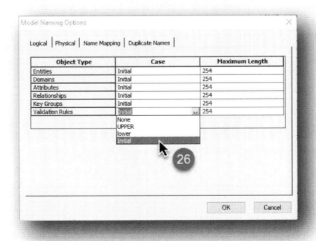

24. When finished, click on the *Physical* tab.

25. For our physical naming standards, we need to set the case to upper case. For each of the physical object types, click the *Case* property, and select the *UPPER* option. See Figure 351.

Figure 351. Change The Case to Upper Case For All Physical Object Types

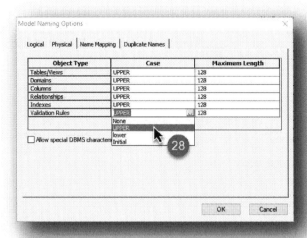

26. We need to set the maximum length for all physical object type to 60 characters. For each of the physical object types, click in the *Maximum Length* and change them to '*60*.' See Figure 352.

Figure 352. Change The Maximum Length to 60 For All Physical Object Types

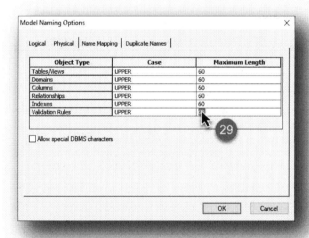

27. Take note of the *Allow Special DBMS Characters* checkbox, as was explained earlier in this chapter.

28. When finished, click on the *Name Mapping* tab.

29. Observe the Name Mapping tab, as shown in Figure 353.

Figure 353. The Name Mapping Tab

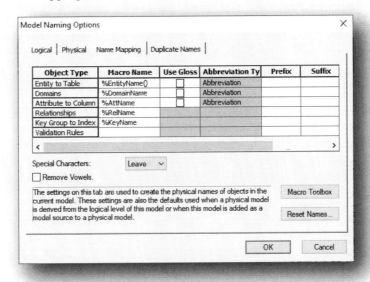

Grid Columns

Object Type   Specifies the object type that the macro and glossary gets applied.

Macro Name   Specifies the macro for converting the logical name to the physical name.

Object Type	Default Naming Rule	Comment
Entity to Table	%EntityName()	Returns the name of the entity as table name. Abbreviations may also be used to replace elements.
Domain (Physical)	%DomainName	Returns the logical domain name as the physical name. Abbreviations may also be used to replace elements. The physical name of validation rules can be used as the basis of the default constrain names.
Attribute to Column	%AttName	Returns the name of the attribute as column name. Abbreviations may also be used to replace elements.
Relationship (Physical)	%RelName	Returns the logical relationship name as the physical name. The logical relationship name is in the form R/n and is a different property to the business name of the relationship, which has no parallel on the physical side. A relationship's physical name can be used as an FK constraint name.
Key Group to Index	%KeyName	Returns the name of the Key Group as the index name.
Validation Rules	Although no rule set it behaves as if the rule is: %ValidationLogicalName	Returns the logical name of the rule. The physical name of validation rules can be used as the basis of a constrain names.

Use Glossary	Specifies whether the object type needs to use the glossary (abbreviations).
Abbreviation Type	If Use Glossary is set, specifies which glossary to use. Choose between the Abbreviation and the Alt Abbreviation.
Prefix	Specifies if the object type needs to prefix the object names with a prefix.
Suffix	Specifies if the object type needs to suffix the object names with a suffix.

Further to our physical naming standards, we need to set that all physical objects make use of the glossary. For the three object types that have an **Abbreviation** option, tick each of the checkboxes. See Figure 354. Observe that the *Abbreviation Type* becomes active after checking the *Use Abbreviation* checkbox.

Figure 354. Check The Abbreviation Checkboxes

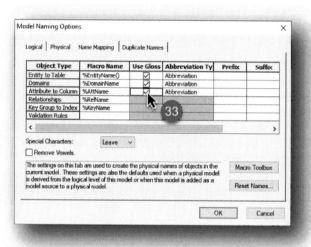

30. Next, change the Macro for the Relationships to the following:

```
FK_%Parent_%Child_%SubStr (%RelId,1,5)
```

Due to some complications in the naming of physical relationships, and the resultant foreign key constraints, this macro ensures it is unique even when multiple relationships exist between the same two tables. It is achieved by using the first five characters of the relationship's internal identifier, a GUID. The entire GUID would always be unique, but it is possible the first five characters are not. However, they only need to be unique between the same two tables. Lastly, change the *Macro* for the *Key Group to Index* to the following:

```
%Switch(%Substr(%KeyType,1,2))
{%Choose(PK) {PK_%Substr(%TableName,1,25)}
%Choose(IF) {FK_%Substr(%TableName,1,25)_%Substr(%KeyType,3)}
%Choose(AK) {UQ_%Substr(%TableName,1,25)_%Substr(%KeyType,3)}
%Choose(IE) {NU_%Substr(%TableName,1,25)_%Substr(%KeyType,3)}}
```

The macro above was generated to apply the index type to each type of index (PK, IF, AK, and IE).

Figure 355. Change The Macros

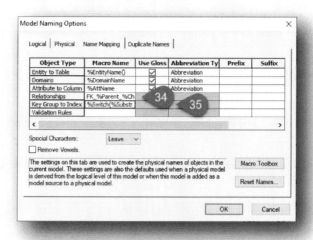

Observe the *Special Characters* options, as explained earlier in this chapter. Furthermore, take note of the *Remove Vowels* checkbox. This stems from an old practice in which the abbreviation was applied by removing all vowels. To support this old standard, erwin DM still provides this functionality. Lastly, take note of the *Macro Toolbox*, which opens a toolbox with all the possible macros that can be used in the naming macros, and the *Reset Names* button, which provides a tool to reset all inheritance of names on the model. Caution should be taken when using this feature, as it can result in unforeseen results, as inheritance is drawn from domains, and if no custom domains have been used, it will reset to the root domains.

31. When finished, click on the ***Duplicate Names*** tab.

    Observe the Duplicate Names tab, as shown in Figure 356.

    Figure 356. The Duplicate Names Tab

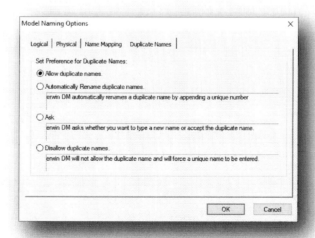

When attempting to create a duplicate name, and the user sets duplicate name preferences to *Ask*, they can accept the duplicate name, cancel the action that created the duplicate name, or have a new name generated for you.

32. When finished, click the *Close* button to close the Model Naming Options dialog.

33. Take a look at the physical model, now with the naming standards applied. See Figure 357.

34. Take special note of the case of the tables and columns, and the abbreviated names. Drill into the relationships and indexes to see how the naming standard has impacted these too.

35. When finished, save and close your MyMovie data model.

Figure 357. The Physical Data Model

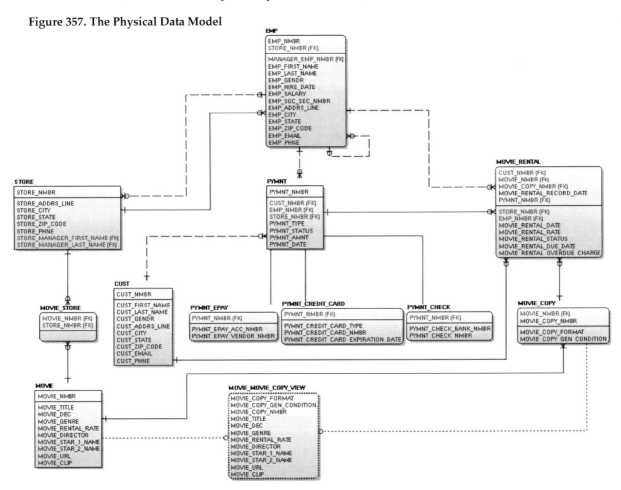

Key Learnings

- Naming standards are an easy way to apply uniform corporate naming standard rules, and in erwin DM include object names, abbreviations, lengths, and special characters.

- erwin DM has a macro language for defining the translation of logical names to physical names.

Requirements drive
DDL to PDM
Roll-out PDM

Forward Engineering is the process of generating the physical database or DDL script from a physical data model. The user can use the Schema Generation dialog to forward engineer a physical data model and generate the database or DDL script. The database or DDL script that gets generated includes all supported options for the target DBMS.

Forward Engineering Explained

Follow these steps to generate the schema:

Select the schema generation options–For each option you select, the appropriate SQL statement is included in the DDL script in the correct syntax for your target DBMS.

Review the schema generation options–The options appear in a hierarchical tree structure, and the user can review each group of options individually by expanding or collapsing the tree. They can change any of the selected options and generate the correct SQL statements.

Preview the DDL script–The DDL script is displayed based on the options selected. For example, if the target server is Oracle, and the user selected the CREATE TABLE option, a CREATE TABLE statement is displayed for each selected table in the physical data model.

Change the schema generation options–At any time, the user can change the schema generation options and generate the correct SQL statements.

Generate the database–When you generate the database, you can connect to the target server and generate the database, or you can generate an ASCII DDL script that can be run as a separate step on the server to generate the database. When generating a DDL script, one can save it as a text file that you can open in a word-processing package or load it into a utility that interprets SQL scripts.

When the DDL script gets executed, the user can preview the results of each generated statement. When the DDL gets successfully generated, they can change the statements and messages. The user can search for text strings, cut, copy, and paste text to a message log, and save the message log to an ASCII text file or print the script.

Tutorial: Using the Forward Engineering Engine in erwin DM

1. Open erwin DM.

2. Using the Quick Access Toolbar, click on the *Open* button.

3. Select the **MyMovie_Ver1** data model, from the previous portion of the tutorial, in the Open dialog.

4. Click on the *Open* button.

5. The MyMovie model opens in erwin DM. Maximize the model in the diagram window.

6. Click on the *Actions* ribbon tab.

7. Then click on the *Schema* button to open the Forward Engineering Schema Generation Wizard dialog. See Figure 358.

Figure 358. Click On The Schema Button

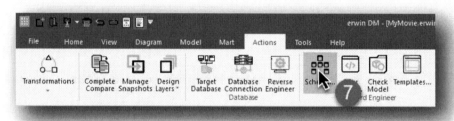

8. Observe that the Forward Engineering Schema Generation Wizard dialog appears. The Overview page of the Forward Engineering Schema Generation Wizard dialog provides the user with a brief overview of the wizard and the critical aspects of each of the pages.

9. Click on the *Option Selection* page tab, as shown in Figure 359.

Figure 359. Click The Option Selection Page Tab

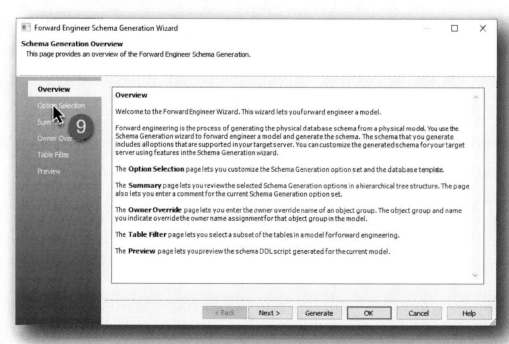

10. Observe the Option Selection page, as shown in Figure 360.

Figure 360. The Option Selection Page

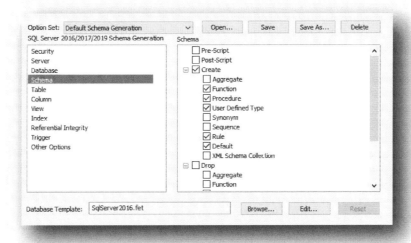

The Forward Engineering Wizard provides for the saving of custom *Option Sets*. By default, erwin DM opens with a **Default Schema Generation Option Set**. This *Option Set* has the most commonly used options for forward engineering. When selecting the objects and properties that need forward engineering, the user can filter specific objects by clearing the checkbox next to the objects. The user can furthermore save the selection as a new *Option Set* for reuse on other models.

Saving an *Option Set* to an XML file makes it available for performing the same Forward Engineering process on other models, thus standardizing the Forward Engineering process for an organization. The XML files are store independent of the data model and, therefore, are sharable amongst the users.

To save an *Option Set* as an XML file, the user needs to click the *Save As* button. A Save Current Option Set To A Destination dialog appears, allowing the user to select the type of *Option Set* to save. For Forward Engineering, the *Option Set* can be saved as an XML file, or embedded in the data model for future usage with the data model.

If the XML file option gets chosen, the dialog provides further options to choose the location for storing the XML file. Once saved, the user can update the XML file by using the *Save* button. To clear the *Option Set* selection, the user can use the *Delete* button. To open an existing *Option Set*, the user can use the *Open* button to load a customized option set into memory for the Forward Engineering process.

We also note that the Option Selection page has two major sides. The first is the object section, labeled based on the DBMS, in this case, SQL Server 2016/2017/2019 Schema Generation. The second is the properties section. Changing the focus on the object section results in the properties that are available for forward engineering appear for that specific DBMS in the properties section. Another powerful feature in erwin DM is the ability to redefine the forward engineering process. Forward engineering is built around a macro language that can be manipulated to generate different formats of the DDL code. This function is the Forward Engineering Templates, and we can find a reference to the specific Database Template that is in use at the bottom of the dialog.

11. For our tutorial, we are going to use the **Default Schema Generation Option Set** and therefore, do not need to make any changes to this page.

12. Click on the *Summary* page tab. Observer the Summary page, as shown in Figure 361. The Summary page presents the options from the Option page in a simplified format. It also allows for easy changing of options through a tree structure.

Figure 361. The Summary Page

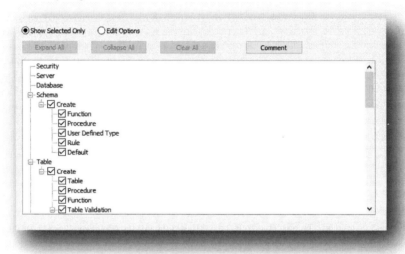

13. Click on the ***Owner Override*** page tab.

14. Observer the Owner Override page, as shown in Figure 362.

Figure 362. The Owner Override Page

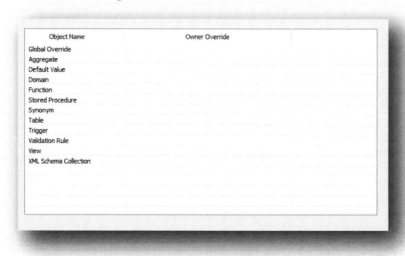

The Owner Override page allows the user to override the owner of the object types in the model with a different owner for the forward engineering process. This can be extremely useful for generating different schemas for development, test, and Q&A.

15. Click on the *Table Filter* page tab.

16. Observer the Table Filter page, as shown in Figure 363.

Figure 363. The Table Filter Page

The Table Filter page allows the user to select or unselect the instance of the tables and views for the forward engineering process.

17. Click on the *Preview* page tab.

18. Observer the Preview page, as shown in Figure 364.

Figure 364. The Preview Page

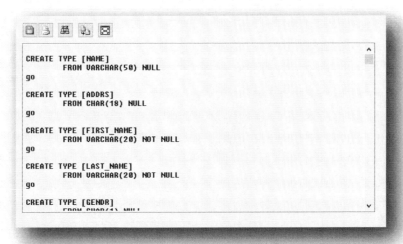

The Preview page allows the user to see a preview of the DDL code that gets generated from the forward engineering process.

Action Buttons

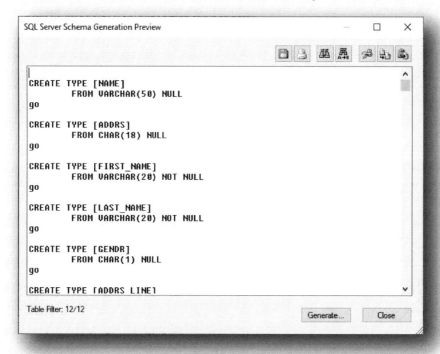

Save–Allows the user to save the DDL code to a file.

Print–Allows the user to print the DDL code.

Search–Allows the user to search through the DDL code for a specific word or phrase.

Copy–Allows the user to copy the DDL code to the clipboard.

Open Editor–Allows the user to open the DDL editor dialog.

19. Click on the *Open Editor* button (▦) to open the SQL Server Schema Generation Preview Editor dialog.

20. Observe that the SQL Server Schema Generation Preview Editor dialog appears, as shown in Figure 365.

Figure 365. The SQL Server Schema Generation Preview Editor dialog

The SQL Server Schema Generation Preview Editor dialog allows the user to preview and edit the DDL code. Note that the editing of the DDL code is not persisted back to the Forward Engineering Schema Generation Wizard dialog and does not have any validation of the changes applied to the DDL code. Although it is not a recommended process to edit the DDL code generated from erwin DM, this editor dialog provides the functionality for the rear case that requires the editing of the DDL code.

Action Buttons

Save–Allows the user to save the DDL code to a file.

Print–Allows the user to print the DDL code.

Search–Allows the user to search through the DDL code for a specific word or phrase.

Search & Replace–Allows the user to search and replace text within the DDL code.

Cut— Allows the user to cut the DDL code to the clipboard.

Copy–Allows the user to copy the DDL code to the clipboard.

Paste–Allows the user to paste from the clipboard.

Generate...   **Generate**–Opens the database connection dialog to apply the DDL code to the database. It is important to note that the DDL code that will be applied is the edited DDL code from the dialog and not the original DDL code from the Forward Engineering Schema Generation Wizard dialog.

21. When finished, click the *Close* button to return to the Forward Engineering Schema Generation Wizard dialog.

22. Observe the Generate button (Generate...) on the Forward Engineering Schema Generation Wizard dialog as well. This button also opens the database connection dialog but will apply the original, unedited version of the DDL code to the database.

23. Take some time and scroll through the DDL code, taking note of all the SQL commands for creating the objects from our physical data model, and the naming conventions used.

24. Click on the Save button (⊟) to save the DDL code to disk.

25. Navigate to the same folder that you have the MyMovie data model saved, and save the DDL code as **MyMovie_Ver1.DDL**.

26. Click the *OK* button to close the Forward Engineering Schema Generation Wizard dialog, then save and close your MyMovie data model.

Key Learnings

- The Forward Engineering engine generates a database from a physical data model.

- A DDL script can also be generated via the Forward Engineering Engine.

- erwin DM's Forward Engineering functionality allows for the customization of the DDL script.

Databases drive
DB to the PDM
Visualize it

Reverse engineering is the process of creating a data model from a database or a DDL script. erwin DM creates a graphical representation of the selected database objects and the relationships between the objects. This graphical representation can be a logical or a physical model.

Reverse Engineering Explained

A database can be reverse engineered for the following reasons:

- To understand how objects are related to each other and then to build upon the structure
- To demonstrate the database structure

After the reverse engineering process completes, one can perform the following tasks:

- Add new database objects
- Create the system documentation
- Redesign the database structure to suit your requirements

Most of the information that gets reverse engineered is explicitly defined in the physical database. However, reverse engineering also derives information from the schema and incorporates it into the data model. For example, if the target DBMS supports foreign key declarations, the reverse engineering process derives identifying and non-identifying relationships and default role names.

One can derive all the significant data model information, except subtype relationships, because currently, no SQL database management system supports explicit subtype relationships. Subtypes get supported as normal relationships. However, the target databases vary in the amount of logical data model information that gets included in the physical database. For this reason, the resulting data models can vary depending on the target database that is selected. It can also infer some logical information, including primary keys, foreign keys, and table relationships, by using the table index definitions or column names to infer these keys and relationships.

The reverse engineering process can include or exclude referential integrity. One can also choose to include or exclude these options during reverse engineering.

Reverse Engineer starts with a new blank data model. One cannot reverse engineer into an existing data model.

Tutorial: Using the Reverse Engineering Engine in erwin DM

1. Open erwin DM.

2. Click on the *Actions* ribbon tab with no model open.

3. Then click on the *Reverse Engineer* button to start the reverse engineering process.

4. Observe that the New Model dialog appears. Whenever reverse engineering a database, erwin DM always creates a new model. To apply changes from a database to an existing data model, the Complete Compare functionality, in combination with the Reverse Engineering functionality, would be used. For more information on Complete Compare, see Chapter 31.

5. In the New Model dialog, select the *Physical* option for the data model Type.

6. Select *SQL Server* for the database.

7. Select *2016/2017/2019* for the version of the database.

8. Leave all the rest of the settings as they are, then click the *Next* button. See Figure 366.

Figure 366. Populate the New Model Dialog

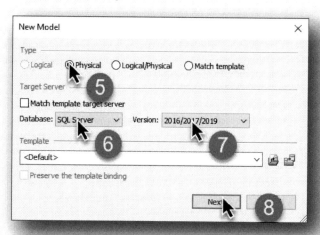

9. Observe that the Reverse Engineering dialog appears, furthermore, note that in the background erwin DM has created a new model. See Figure 367.

10. The Reverse Engineer dialog is broken into several sections, namely:

- **Reverse Engineer From section**–This section defines where the reverse engineering is coming from. The options are to either reverse engineer from a database itself, or a script file of a database. See Figure 368.

Figure 367. Populate the New Model Dialog

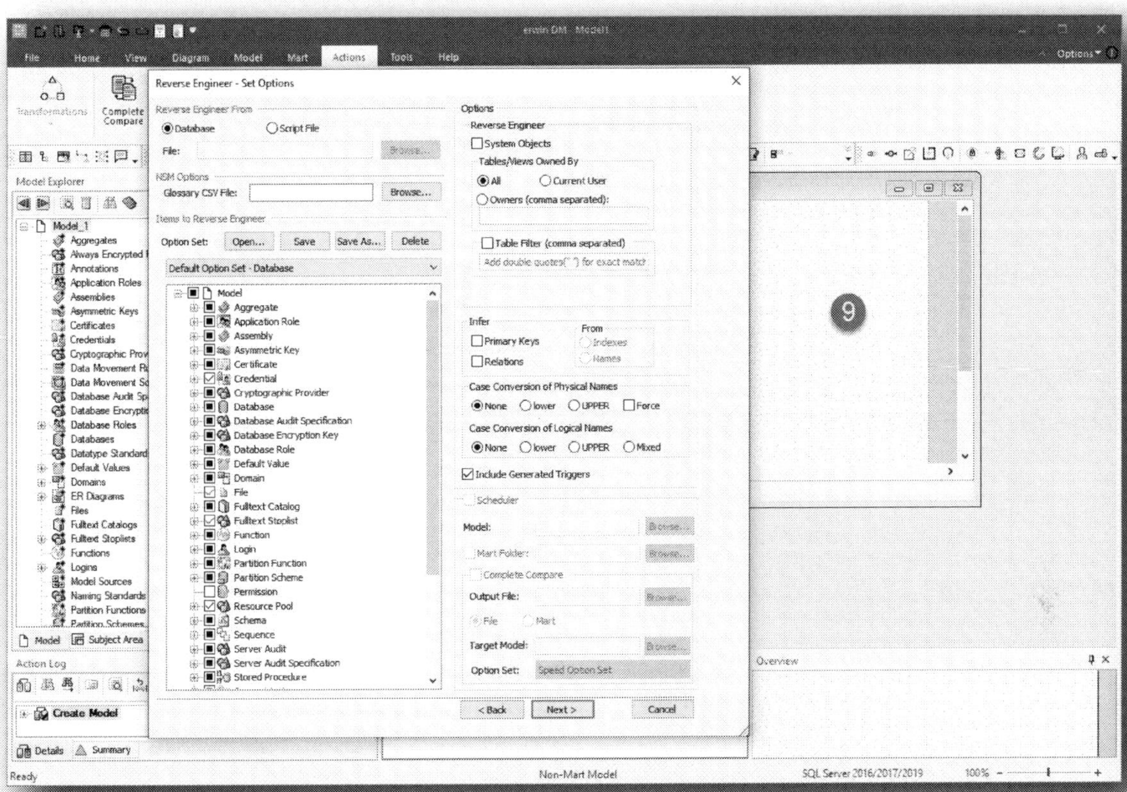

Figure 368. Reverse Engineering Dialog. Reverse Engineer From Section

- **NSM Options section**–This section is the Naming Standards options, like we used in the MyMovie physical data model. We applied a naming standard to convert (and abbreviate) the logical names to the physical names—the reverse works for reverse engineering. The NSM options allow the user to select a CSV file with the abbreviations to generate the words in the logical names from the abbreviated column names. See Figure 369.

Figure 369. Reverse Engineering Dialog. NSM Section

- **Items to Reverse Engineer section**–This section defines the items (object types) that the user wants to reverse engineer. Included in this section is the functionality to save and reuse predefined *Option Sets*. By default, erwin DM uses a **Default Option Set - Database**

Option Set. This *Option Set* has the most commonly used options for reverse engineering based on the previously chosen DBMS. For a better understanding of how the *Option Sets* behave, please refer to Chapter 29. See Figure 370.

Figure 370. Reverse Engineering Dialog. Item to Reverse Engineer Section

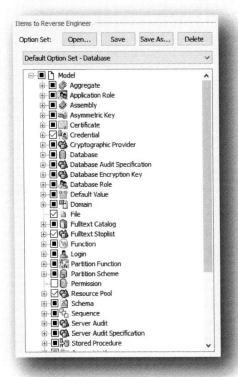

- **Options section**–The options section is further broken down into sub-sections.

  - **Options–Reverse Engineer section**–This section defines the object instances that the user wants to reverse engineer. It allows selecting if the System Objects (metadata tables) get reverse engineered. It also allows for the filtering of object instance based on the Owner, and lastly, based on a comma-separated list of Tables. See Figure 371.

    Figure 371. Reverse Engineering Dialog. Options. Reverse Engineer Section

  - **Options–Infer section**–This section defines the inference of objects during the reverse engineering process. When reverse engineering a database, one needs to take into consideration that relationships and primary keys are not really database objects; they are enforced via indexes and constraints. Hence during the reverse engineering process, the option to get them is inferred via the indexes and constraints. See Figure 372. Primary Keys allow for the inferring of primary key columns for the tables that get based on defined indexes. Relations allow for the inferring of relationships between tables that are based on either primary key column names or defined indexes. Selecting this option allows for specifying whether to use primary key column Names or defined Indexes:

Names–Infers the relationships from the primary key column names. Relationships are inferred from columns names only if all of the primary key columns of the parent are in the child table.

Indexes–Infers the relationships from the table indexes. Relationships are inferred from table indexes only if the primary key columns of the parent table are part of the index in the child table. If the target database or script supports primary and foreign key declarations, you do not need to use the Primary Keys, Relations, Indexes, or Names options.

Figure 372. Reverse Engineering Dialog. Options. Infer Section

- **Options–Case Conversion of Physical Names section**–This section defines how the case conversion of physical names gets handled during reverse engineering. See Figure 373. Work with the following options:

None–Preserves the case precisely as it appears in the script file or database.

Lower–Converts the names to lower case.

UPPER–Converts the names to upper case.

Force–Overrides the physical name property for all objects in logical/physical models automatically during reverse engineering. If this option is not enabled, all logical and physical names are set to the same value after the process completes. If this option is enabled, the logical/physical link gets broken between the logical and physical names.

Figure 373. Reverse Engineering Dialog. Options. Case Conversion Physical Names

- **Options–Case Conversion of Logical Names section**–This section defines how the case conversion of logical names gets handled during reverse engineering. See Figure 374. Work with the following options:

  None–Preserves the case precisely as it appears in the script file or database.

  Lower–Converts the names to lower case.

  UPPER–Converts the names to upper case.

  Mixed–Preserves mixed-case logical names.

  Figure 374. Reverse Engineering Dialog. Options. Case Conversion Logical Names

- **Options–Include Generated Triggers section**–This section specifies whether erwin-generated triggers get loaded during the reverse engineer process. This option is linked to the Automatically Create RI Triggers setting in the Model Editor dialog, RI Defaults tab. When choosing to create RI Triggers automatically, the triggers get treated as model objects. These objects can be forward-engineered into a model, database, or script file. See Figure 375.

  Figure 375. Reverse Engineering Dialog. Options. Include Generated Triggers Section

- **Options–Scheduler section**–This section is usually greyed out for the reverse engineering process, but gets used when initializing the reverse engineering from the erwin DM Scheduler. See Figure 376.

  Figure 376. Reverse Engineering Dialog. Scheduler Section

11. Under the Reverse Engineer From section, select the *Script File* option.

12. Click the *Browse* button to browse for the **MyMovie_Ver1.DDL** file that was created in Chapter 27; it should be in the same folder that you have the MyMovie data model. See Figure 377.

Figure 377. Select Script File and Then Browse for MyMovie_Ver1.DDL File

13. Accept all the other default options, and click the *Next* button.

14. Observe as shown in Figure 378 that the Reverse Engineering from Script dialog appears, and if no errors were encountered, it automatically disappears when finished reverse engineering.

Figure 378. The Reverse Engineering From Script Dialog

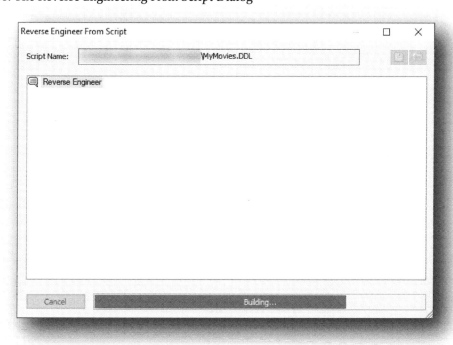

15. If errors in the DDL code are encountered, erwin DM Reverse Engineering engine provides a splash screen with the error details. See Figure 379.

Figure 379. The Reverse Engineering Error Screen

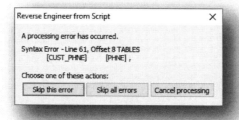

 When encountering errors during reverse engineering, Skip All Errors and then review the errors at the end by using the Advisory Details button (⬚), one by one.

16. If reverse engineering from a database, the Database Connection dialog gets presented first, as shown in Figure 380.

Figure 380. The Database Connection Dialog

17. When finished reverse engineering, the new model gets displayed in the Diagram pane.

18. Explore the reverse-engineered model and observe the similarities to the physical model of the MyMovie data model. Notice that the database objects have been reverse engineered, such as the table, columns, domains (database types), indexes, and the relationships got inferred. But the model level objects, like the ER diagrams, subject areas, and themes, did not get created. Only objects that exist in the database can be reverse engineered. Objects that are

at a model level do not get created in the DDL script, and therefore cannot be reverse-engineered.

19. When finished, save the model as **MyMovie_Ver1-OperationalDataModel.erwn**. Then close your data model, as this concludes the tutorial for this chapter.

Key Learnings

- Reverse Engineering creates a new data model from either a database or a DDL script.

- During the Reverse Engineering process, the user needs to specify the Model Type, Model Template, and the Target DBMS.

- The Reverse Engineering engine allows for the filtering of objects, object types, properties of selected object types, by owners and by DBMS specific tablespaces or databases.

- Reverse Engineering can infer the primary keys and foreign key constraints.

Distribute models
Reports on data models
Get the word out now

The Report Designer is an intuitive point-and-click interface for creating PDF, HTML, and text-based reports for both diagrams and metadata text.

Report Designer Explained

The Report Designer uses the concepts of report templates and solutions. Each report is defined and managed through its report template and can be used to generate output in any of the supported formats. A report template gets saved as a separate file with the extension '.erpt.' A solution is a package of one or more report templates, where many solutions may contain the same report template. This allows for the creation of different packages (solutions) containing shared report templates. Solutions get saved with the file extension '.erps.'

Defining a New Report Template in Five Steps

- **Step 1: Give the Report Template a Name**. Each report template should have a unique name that gets entered in the Report Editor. This name gets used to list the report templates in the Report Explorer and as the report template file name when saved.

- **Step 2: Specify the Model Type for the Report Template**. The Report Type defines whether the report gets based on the logical data model, the physical data model, a combined logical/physical data model, or on the mart (cross-model reporting and statistics).

- **Step 3: Specify a Report Subject Type**. The Report Subject Type specifies the root object type for the report template, and gets selected from the list displayed in the Select Report Subject pane. A report can have only one report subject type, but all children object types for the specified report subject type are available. For example, if the report subject type of entity is selected, all the attributes, check constraints, and key groups object types are available in the report template. If the selected model type is either physical or logical/physical, a DBMS specific node gets included, listing DBMS specific objects. After selecting a report subject type, a hierarchical tree of objects appears in the Select Report Fields pane. The object tree has the selected report subject type as its root, and this report subject type forms the root of the report. All children object types for the specified report subject type get listed below the root report subject type.

- **Step 4: Specify the Report Fields**. The fields required in the report gets selected from the properties listed in this hierarchy of objects in the Select Report Fields pane. The object tree not only reflects erwin DM's internal object hierarchy (Example: Model Object has children of type Entity which in turn have children of type Attribute), but also core references between objects which may sometimes be a link between objects of the same type. For example, the Attribute node holds a child node for Parent Domain, not because it is a child object of Attribute but because it is a core (and mandatory) reference held by the Attribute object. The domain object doesn't hold any reference to the attributes to which it is assigned, so it is necessary to have a clear idea of the report's requirements. Note that the Report Designer does not have access to all the model metadata. Only the API and the ODBC interface have access to all model metadata. Every object node has a child Properties node, which, when expanded, allows for the selection of the properties for the report. Properties get listed in alphabetical order. If an object has any child objects (Indexes have Members) or holds a core reference to an object, these object types also get included as child nodes. Some object nodes also include Filter By and Order By nodes. These can be useful when checking for specific features or issues in a data model, for example, trying to identify unified FK attributes which should be rolenamed. When selecting the required fields, it is critical to understand that the entire selection of properties gets displayed in a single row within the grid or when exported as text.

- **Step 5: Configure the Report Appearance**. Configuring a report includes changing the column heading, changing the column order, and overriding the HTML or PDF template properties for HTML or PDF output, respectively. When the report is defined and saved, it gets included in the Report Explorer, where its hierarchical structure is expandable. Once expanded, the properties for each node can be accessed by right-clicking on it and selecting Properties. The reports expanded view is a hierarchy of object and property types, where the property types get used as the default column name in the output. The object type nodes only appear in the HTML or PDF output, where they are section headings. For object types, the available settings relate to the HTML grid, while for the property types, the same options are available for both the column header and the column cell. The settings for the object type are inherited by its child property types unless overridden. If no customization gets performed, the default options in the standard template gets used, although it is possible to edit the template itself.

Report versus Solution

It is possible to generate either individual reports or a complete solution consisting of multiple reports. It is important to note that generating a complete solution is only available when exporting to TEXT (CSV), HTML, or PDF files, and is not available to export to the report grid (Run). When an entire solution gets exported to TEXT, a separate CSV file gets created for each report in the solution. When an entire solution gets exported to HTML, the generated index page includes separate references to each of the individual reports in the solution. When an entire solution gets exported to PDF, a separate PDF file gets created for each report in the solution. If the requirement is to display the data in the grid (Run), the reports need to be run individually to generate the individual outputs of each report.

Tutorial: Using the Report Designer in erwin DM

1. Open erwin DM.

2. Using the Quick Access Toolbar, click on the **Open** button.

3. Select the **MyMovie_Ver1** data model from the previous portion of the tutorial.

4. Click on the **Open** button.

5. The MyMovie model opens in erwin DM. Maximize the model in the diagram window.

6. Click on the **Tools** ribbon tab.

7. Then click on the **Report Designer** button to open the Report Designer. See Figure 381.

Figure 381. Click On The Report Designer Button

8. Observe that the Report Designer dialog appears, as shown in Figure 382.

Figure 382. The Report Designer Dialog

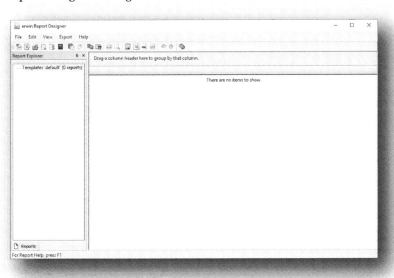

Action Buttons

Create a New Report–Allows the user to create a new report template in the solution.

Create New Solution–Allows the user to create a new solution for reports. If a solution is already open, the user gets prompted to save the open solution before creating a new solution.

Open a Report Solution–Allows the user to open an existing solution. If a solution is already open, the user gets prompted to save the open solution before open another solution.

Add an Exiting Report to the Solution–Allows the user to add an existing report from file to the solution. (Saved reports from another solution)

Open a Pinned Report from Disk–Allows the user to add a pinned report to the solution. Pinned reports is a legacy term in erwin DM for pre-built reports.

Count Objects–Allows the user to generate a report on the object counts in the data model.

Save Solution–Allows the user to save the solution to file as a '.erps' file. During the saving of the solution, the individual reports get saved too, as '.erpt' files.

Close Solution–Allows the user to close the current solution. The user gets prompted to save the current solution before closing.

Copy–Allows the user to copy the selected Report Designer Data Grid record.

Clear Data in Data Grid–Allows the user to clear the contents of the Report Designer Data Grid.

Print–Allows the user to print the contents of the Report Designer Data Grid, including headers.

Preview the Active Document–Allows the user to preview the print of the contents of the Report Designer Data Grid.

Run Current Report–Allows the user to run the current report and return the results into the Report Designer Data Grid.

Export to Text Format–Allows the user to run the current report or solution, whichever is selected, and returns the results into CSV text file/s. Options are allowed to define text qualifiers and delimiters.

Export to HTML–Allows the user to run the current report or solution, whichever is selected, and return the results into a collection of HTML files.

Export to PDF–Allows the user to run the current report or solution, whichever is selected, and return the results into a PDF file.

Prior Page to Browse–When a model has a large number of results, the Report Designer breaks the results into pages when displaying in the Report Designer Data Grid. This button then allows the user to browse the previous Report Designer Data Grid page of results.

Run Current Report for Next Page–When a model has a large number of results, the Report Designer, breaks the results into pages in the Report Designer Data Grid. This button then allows the user to browse the next Report Designer Data Grid page of results.

Help–Allows the user to open online help for the Report Designer.

9. Click on the *Create a New Report* button. See Figure 383.

Figure 383. Click the Create a New Report Button

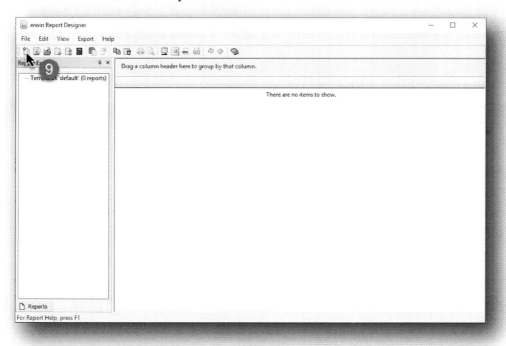

10. Observe that the Report Editor dialog appears.

11. In the Report Editor, change the *Name* of the report to **Entity and Attribute Names**.

12. Select the *Report Type* of *Logical*.

13. On the Report Designer tab, *Select the Report Subject* of *Entity*. See Figure 384.

The *Name* gets used to list the report templates in the Report Explorer and as the report template file name when saved. The *Report Type* defines whether the report gets based on the logical data model, the physical data model, a combined logical/physical data model, or a report based on the mart (cross-model reporting and statistics). The *Report Subject* defines the subject of the report and forms the root object in selecting the report fields.

Figure 384. The Report Editor Dialog

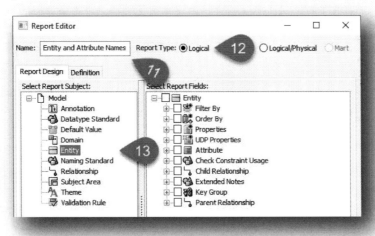

14. Observe that the *Select Report Fields* section gets populated with the report subject as it's root node and any sub-objects below it.

15. In the *Select Report Fields*, expand the **Order By** node, and select the '*Alphabet Order*' option.

16. Expand the **Properties** node and select the **Name** and **Definition** options. See Figure 385.

Figure 385. The Report Editor Dialog

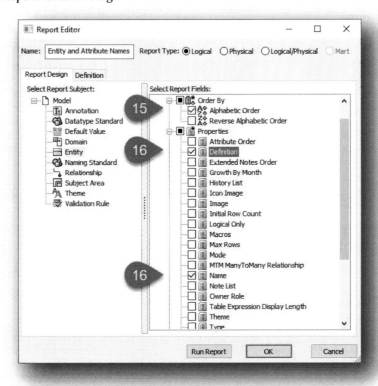

Most object types can have the results sorted in a particular order under an *Order By* node. For our report, we want them sorted alphabetically. Most object types also have a *Properties* node, and this node has all the properties that the object type holds. Take caution as to which is the parent of a particular node, as it gets confusing when multiple nodes are open.

17. Collapse the **Order By** and **Properties** nodes.

18. Expand the **Attribute** node, then the **Order By** and **Properties** under the Attribute node.

Figure 386. The Select Report Fields. Attribute Node

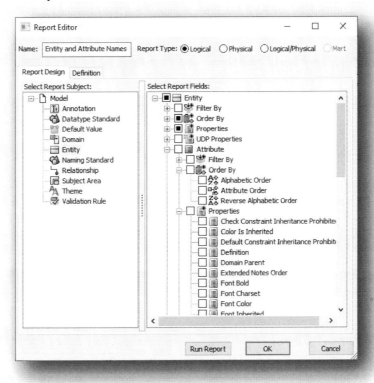

19. Observe the options under the *Order By* now includes an *Attribute Order*; this is the order as it gets displayed in the ER Diagram. Select the **Attribute Order** option.

20. Then, under the **Properties** node, select the **Name** and **Definition** nodes. See Figure 387.

21. When finished, click on the **Definition** tab.

22. The definition tab allows the user to capture the reason for the report; it is always a good practice to give definitions for the reports so that users in the future know why the report got created. Give the report a **Definition** of 'Corporate standard report of logical definitions.' Take note of the buttons to *Run Report* and *OK* to update the report. When using the *Run Report*, the report automatically gets updated and then runs the report.

23. When finished, click the **OK** button.

24. Expand all the nodes in the Report Explorer pane in the Report Designer dialog.

Figure 387. The Select Attribute Order, Name and Definition

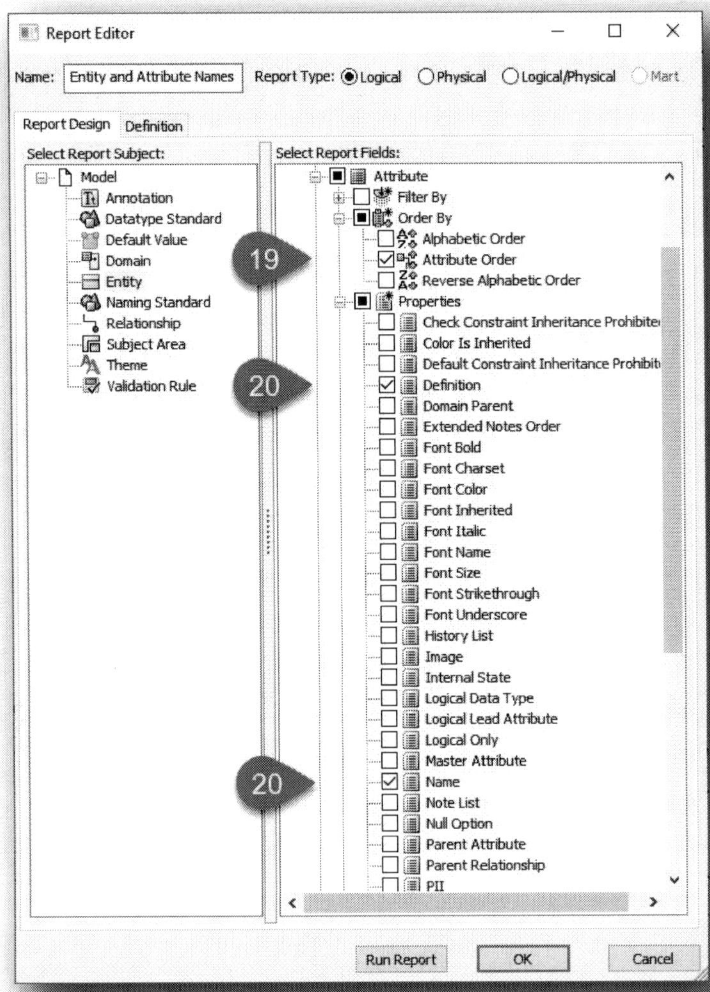

When updating a report, it does not mean that the report gets save to file; it just updates the definition of the report in the Report Designer. One needs to still save the Solution in the Report Designer to save the Report Definition.

25. Then Right-Click on the *Entity and Attribute Names* node in the Report Explorer, and click the *Run* option. See Figure 388.

26. Observe the Report Designer Data Grid gets populated with all the contents from the data model, as shown in Figure 389.

27. Observe the column headings, taking note of the duplication of the *Definition* column heading, one for the entity definition and the one for the attribute definition. Note that the *Name* column headings do not have the same issue.

Figure 388. Click the Run Option

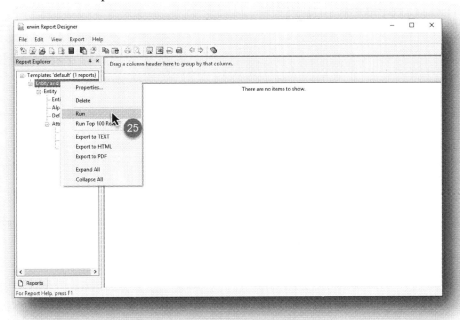

Figure 389. Click the Run Option

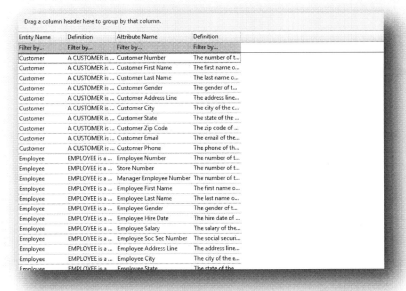

28. From the *Edit* drop-down menu in the Report Designer dialog, click the *Preferences* option. Note that the preferences does not have a button, and it is only accessible via the drop-down menus.

29. Observe the Report Designer Preferences dialog, as shown in Figure 390.

30. Take note of the *Add Object Type as Prefix for Properties 'Name' and 'Physical Name'* checkbox, and the fact that it is checked. This option defines that the *Entity* and *Attribute* part of the *Name* column headings will be added to differentiate the two names.

Figure 390. The Report Designer Preferences Dialog

31. Furthermore, take note of the *Add Object Type as Prefix for All Other Properties* checkbox, and the fact that it is unchecked. This option defines that all the other property column heading's get the object type added to differentiate what the column was referring to, such as *Definition* column headings in our Report Designer Data Grid.

 The prefixing of the object type is only applicable during the creation of the report, and cannot be retrofitted to an existing report.

32. Observe the options for optimizing the performance of the population of the Report Designer Data Grid.

33. When finished, click the **OK** button to dismiss the Report Designer Preferences dialog.

34. Right-click on the **Definition** under the *Entities* node in the Report Explorer and select the **Properties** option.

35. Observe the Properties dialog for the field in the report, as shown in Figure 391.

36. Change the **Name** to 'Entity Definition' and take note of the options to customize the report style for HTML and PDF output. See Figure 392.

37. When finished, click the **OK** button to close the Properties dialog.

38. Observe that the name of the *Definition* field in the Report Explorer has changed to **Entity Definition**, but the column heading has not. This is because the report has already been run, and any changes to the report template only take effect the next time it gets run. The same applies to the content of the data grid, and the data only gets updated after re-running the report.

Figure 391. The Properties Dialog

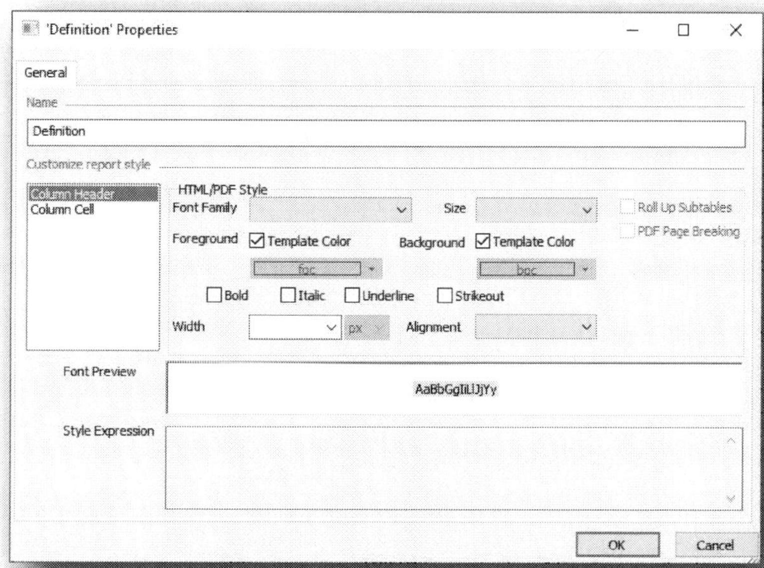

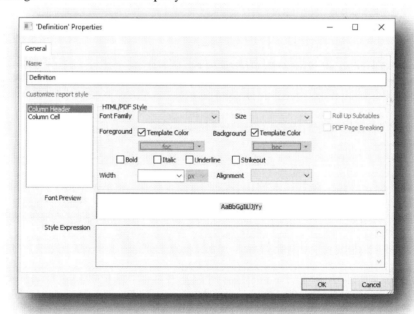

Figure 392. Change The Name of The Property

39. Click twice (not double-click) on the attribute's *Definition* field, change the name of the attribute's *Definition* to '*Attribute Definition.*' See Figure 393.

40. Re-run the report, and observe the updated column headings.

41. Click and hold the *Entity Name* header, and drag it above and release in the '*Drag a column here to group by that column.*' See Figure 394.

42. Observe the updated group by of **Entity Name** column.

Figure 393. The Changed Report Field Name

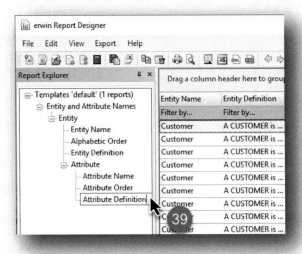

Figure 394. Drag Entity Name to Top

43. Click and hold the *Entity Definition* header and drag it above and release it to the right of the *Entity Name* column header. See Figure 395.

44. Observe the updated group by of **Entity Name** and then **Entity Definition** columns. See Figure 396.

45. Observe the group by of the **Entity Name** column.

46. And the group by of the **Entity Definition** column.

47. Re-run the report and observe that the group by columns is not maintained; this is because the report template maintains the definition of the report, but the group by is part of the output of the report.

Figure 395. Drag Entity Definition to Top

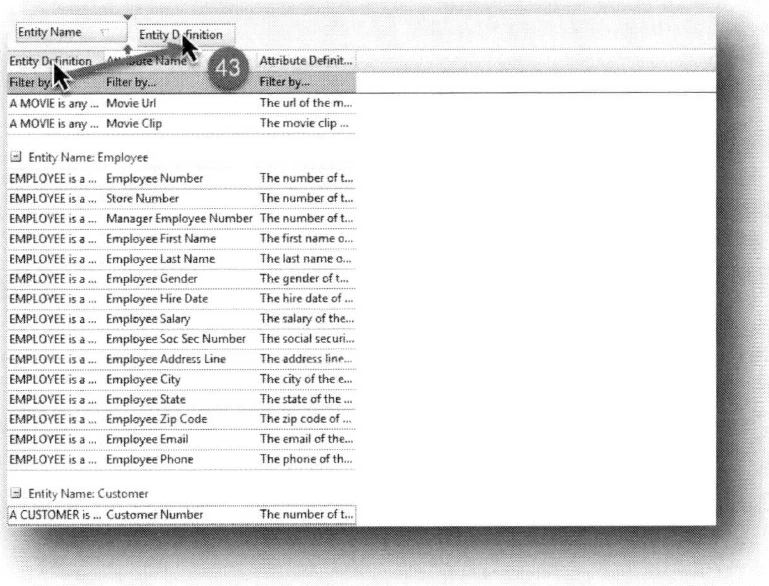

Figure 396. Observe the Group By of Two Columns

48. A quick way to interpret this is anything done in the Report Explorer side gets maintained in the report template, and anything done on the grid side is only for the instance of the data in the grid.

49. In the ***Filter By*** section for the *Attribute Name* column, type in '*Name*' and press the return key. See Figure 397.

50. Observe the filtered result set. It is important to note that the grid still maintains the full result set, as from the report template, it just hides the rows that do not meet the filtering requirements.

Figure 397. Filter Attribute Name Column by Name

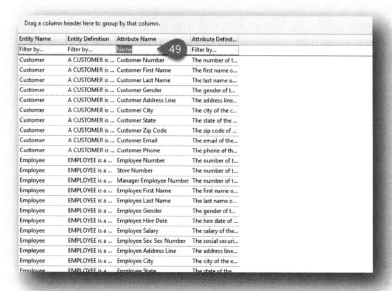

51. In the *Filter By* section for the *Attribute Name* column, remove the contents and press the return key. Observe that the results in the data grid return to the original contents.

52. In the Report Designer dialog, right-click on the solution and select the *Properties* option. See Figure 398.

Figure 398. Open the Properties for the Solution

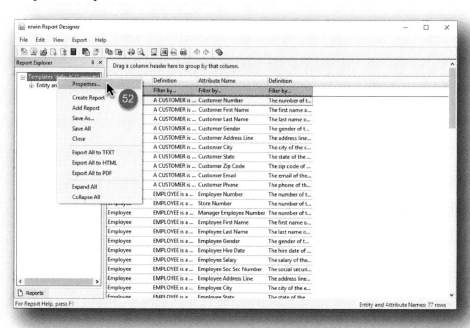

53. In the *Solution Properties* dialog, rename the solution to '**Standard Reports**.'

54. And then, click the *OK* button.

55. Right-click the solution again, this time, select the *Create Report* option. See Figure 399.

Figure 399. Create Report Option

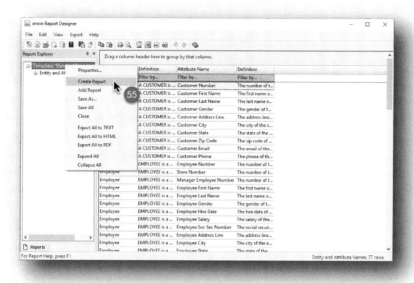

56. Define the new report with the following criteria:

Name	Diagrams Report
Report Type	Logical/Physical
Report Subject	Subject Area
Report Fields	Subject Area

        ↳ER Diagram

             ↳Filter By

                  ↳Specify Diagrams at Run Time

             ↳Order By

                  ↳Alphabetic Order

             ↳Properties

                  ↳Name

                  ↳Definition

             ↳Graphical Members

                  ↳Entity/Table

                       ↳Order By

                           ↳Alphabetic Order

                       ↳Properties

                           ↳Name

                           ↳Physical Name

                           ↳Definition

                    ↳Attribute/Column

                       ↳Order By

                           ↳Attribute Order

                       ↳Properties

                           ↳Name

                           ↳Physical Name

                           ↳Physical Data Type

                           ↳Null Option

                           ↳Definition

Definition	Corporate standard report of diagrams.

57. When finished, click the **OK** button to close the Report Editor dialog.

58. Expand all the nodes of the Diagram Report template in the Report Explorer and move the column headers to match the order, as mentioned above. See Figure 400.

Figure 400. Expand Nodes and Reorder Column Headers

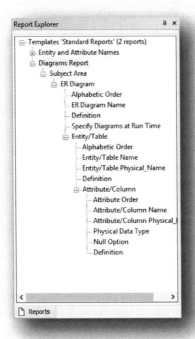

59. Right-click on the **Diagram Report** and **Run**. Observe that the Select Subject Area and Diagram dialog is displayed. This is due to the option of filtering the diagrams at run time.

60. Select the three diagrams that got created in earlier tutorials, namely the **Conceptual Model**, **Logical Model**, and **Physical Model**. See Figure 401.

Figure 401. Select the Three Diagrams Previously Created

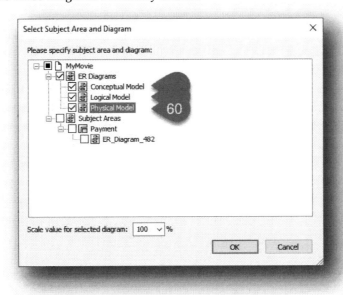

61. When finished, press the *OK* button to run the report into the grid.

62. Observe the list of all the objects in the grid, as per the previous steps in the tutorial. Also note that while in the grid, it is not possible to generate the diagrams.

63. Right-click on the Solution *Template 'Standard Reports' (2 reports)*, and select the *Export All to PDF* option. See Figure 402.

Figure 402. Select the Export All to PDF Option

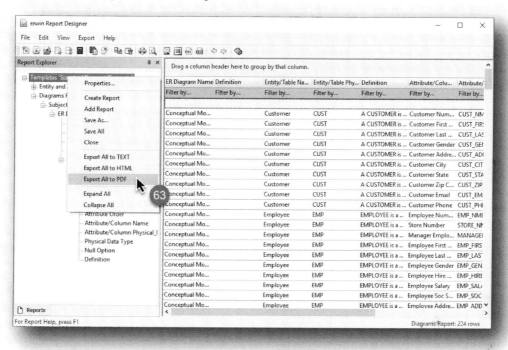

64. Observe the Export Report dialog opens.

65. Change the *Folder* for the exported report to the same folder in which you have stored the MyMovie data model.

66. Observe that the *Open After Exporting* checkbox is grayed out. This typically forces erwin DM into opening the PDF file, using the default program for PDFs, after exporting. Seeing that we are exporting a solution, with two reports in it, each of the reports gets exported as a separate PDF document, and therefore cannot open automatically.

67. When finished, click on the *PDF* tab. Observe the PDF tab. See Figure 403. The PDF tab allows the user to define the fonts, colors, and other variables used in the PDF document.

68. When finished, click the *Advanced* tab.

The Advanced tab allows the user to define further advanced variables used in the PDF document, such as selecting a logo and specifying the logo position and URL.

69. When finished, click the *OK* button.

Figure 403. The PDF Tab

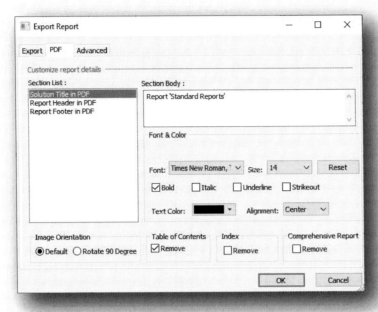

70. In the Select Subject Area and Diagram dialog, once again, select the three diagrams that were created in earlier tutorials, namely the **Conceptual Model**, **Logical Model**, and **Physical Model**. Take note of the *Scale Value for Selected Diagrams*. erwin DM attempts to scale each of the diagrams to fit the page, but this can be adjusted according to the user's specific needs.

71. When finished, click the *OK* button. Observe that erwin DM creates two PDF documents in the folder selected in the steps earlier.

72. Open the **Diagrams Report.PDF** file and observe the report output, including the diagrams and an index.

73. When finished, *close* the PDF viewer, and return to the erwin DM's Report Designer dialog.

74. In the Report Designer dialog, click the *Save Solution* button. See Figure 404.

75. Observe that the Report Designer opens the Save As dialog to allow for the navigation to the desired folder, and the renaming of the solution file. Navigate to the same folder in which you have stored the MyMovie data model, and accept the file name of **Standard Reports.erps**. Note that it only provides you the option to rename the solution, but the Report Designer also saves the separate reports, using their names in the same folder as *.ERPT files.

76. Open a Windows file explorer session, navigate to the folder, and observe the three new files created.

77. In the Report Designer dialog, click the *New Solution* button. See Figure 405.

Make sure of the difference between the *New Report* and *New Solution* buttons.

78. Observe the new solution has been created.

Figure 404. Click the Save Solution Button

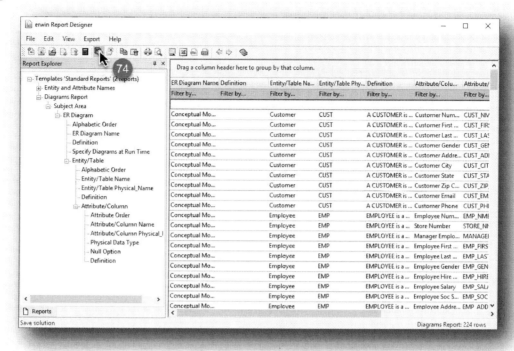

Figure 405. Click the New Solution Button

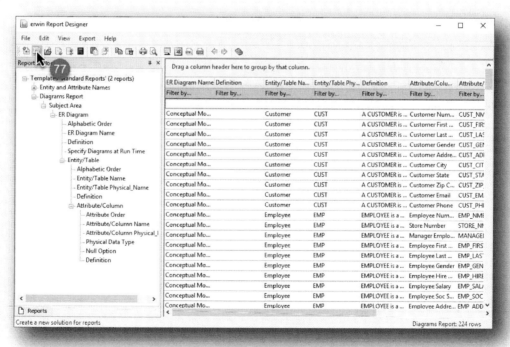

79. Click on the *Add Existing Report* button to add the **Entity and Attributes Names** report to our new solution. See Figure 406.

Figure 406. Click the Add Existing Report Button

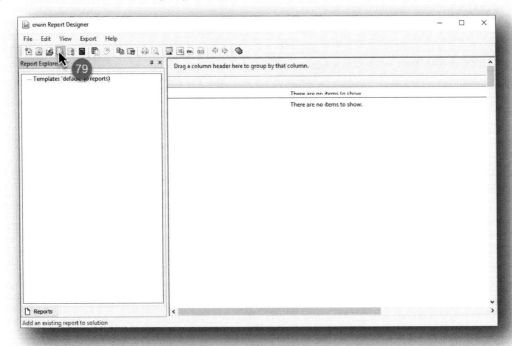

80. Select the *Entity and Attributes Names.ERPT* report and press the *Open* button.

81. Observe the added existing report in the Report Explorer pane.

82. Click on the *Open Pinned Report* button to add a pinned (predesigned) report to our solution. See Figure 407.

Figure 407. Click the Open Pinned Report Button

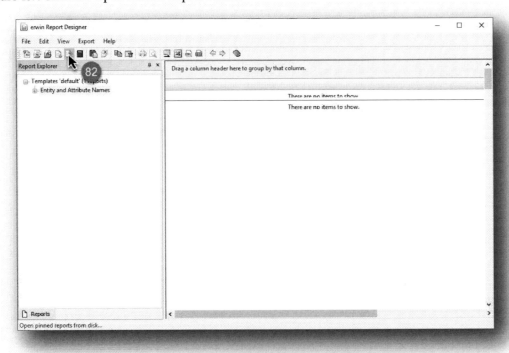

83. Observe the Pinned Reports dialog opens, allowing for the selection of a pinned report. The Report Repository is the location where all the pinned reports get stored on your hard disk. The Report Category is the general grouping of the pinned reports. The options are:

- **Mart Administrative Reports**–These pinned reports provide administrative reports of the Mart Server. These are only valid when using the erwin DM Workgroup Edition and connected to the Mart Server.

- **Mart Model Reports**–These pinned reports provide reports of models residing in the Mart Server. These are only valid when using the erwin DM Workgroup Edition and connected to the Mart Server.

- **Mart Model Validation Reports**–These pinned reports provide validation reports of models residing in the Mart Server. These are only valid when using the erwin DM Workgroup Edition and connected to the Mart Server.

- **Model Reports**–These pinned reports provide reports of models that are open in erwin DM.

- **Model Validation Reports**–These pinned reports provide validation reports of models that are open in erwin DM.

84. Change *the Report Category* to *Model Validation Reports*.

85. Select the **Attributes with no definitions.ERPT** report and click the *OK* button. See Figure 408.

Figure 408. Select the Attributes With No Definition Report

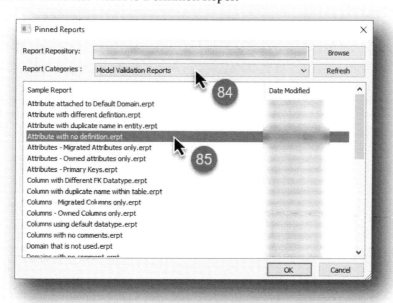

86. Observe the added pinned report in the Report Explorer pane.

87. Right-click on the *Attributes with no Definitions* report, and select the *Run* option.

88. Take note of the output of the report. Model validation reports help the user identify when there are issues in the data model. The **Attributes With No Definitions** report lists all the entities, and if there are any attributes within the entities, it lists the attributes that do not have *Definitions*. This pinned report is very handy to keep close to the **Definitions** report, as the user can run this report first to see if there are any attributes without definition, correct them and then run the full definitions report for sending to consumers of the model.

89. Another useful report in the Report Designer is the **Count Objects** report, which provides statistics on the data model in focus. Although this is not a pinned report, erwin DM provides a separate button to access this report.

90. Click on the *Count Objects* button. See Figure 409.

Figure 409. Click On The Count Objects Button

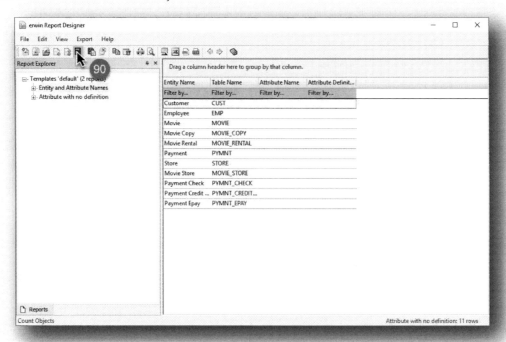

91. Observe the output of the **Count Objects** report.

92. Taking note that the report generates the statistics at the subject area level, but also the model level. In our tutorial, we named our model as MyMovie, note the line representing the MyMovie subject area, and this is the statistics for the entire model. We have created 11 entities, 79 attributes, 33 key groups, and 17 relationships.

93. When finished, *close* the Report Designer by using the default windows *Close* button on the top right of the screen. See Figure 410.

94. Observe that erwin DM always prompts the user when closing a model or a report designer session, as to whether they would like to save the changes before closing.

Figure 410. Close the Report Designer

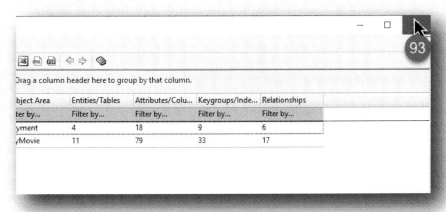

95. Select the *Yes* button and accept the default name and location. The Report Designer remembers the previous location used from the prior solution, and use the same location.

96. When finished, close your MyMovie data model.

Key Learnings

- erwin DM provides a reporting tool called the Report Designer for generating custom and predefined reports.

- The Report Designer is an easy and quick interface to generate meaningful reports for the consumers of the data model.

- Outputs from the Report Designer can be run into a grid utility for manipulating and viewing the metadata of the data model.

- The Report Designer also can export the metadata into CSV, HTML, and PDF files.

- Not only can the Report Designer generate spreadsheet type reports, but it can also generate graphical versions of the diagrams. In the HTML output, the graphical diagrams have hot-spots linking to the metadata of the object.

- There is also a tool in the Report Designer for generating model statistics.

Modify in bulk
Change metadata quickly
The Bulk Editor

Another very intuitive tool in erwin DM is the Bulk Editor. As the name implies, it allows the user to edit data objects in bulk capacity. The Bulk Editor is a grid-style tool that can list and edit objects and their properties in a grid. The real power comes from the ability to export a list of objects in the Bulk Editor grid to a CSV file, and then to use the power of a spreadsheet tool to manipulate the data and import it back into their data model. An everyday use case for the Bulk Editor is to export all the entities and their definitions into a spreadsheet. Then to send the spreadsheet to the business owners to edit and update the definitions of the entities, and finally to import all those updated definitions back into their data model.

Bulk Editor Explained

The Bulk Editor has several strengths, but its primary purpose is to allow users to update model metadata in a grid format without needing to navigate between objects and tabs in the traditional erwin DM dialogs. Although the Bulk Editor is not a reporting tool, it has some useful reporting capabilities.

The Bulk Editor can export to CSV files and to re-import those CSV files after editing, which makes it a potent tool for the data modelers. Users can define, name, and save templates for populating the grid from model data and thus allowing the user to use the same template on multiple data models. It presents model metadata in a grid and allows most of the metadata displayed to be updated. However, some metadata cannot be updated through the grid, typically where values are consequential on other actions or events. For example, it does not allow for the changing of the attribute order in an entity. Changing the order of one attribute would require subsequent changes to others. Read-only columns are shaded in the output to indicate they cannot be updated.

Tutorial: Update to MyMovie Data Model

After successfully forward engineering the first release of the MyMovie data model, the database administrators created the database from the DDL script that we provided, but the developers of the MyMovie system have asked for some changes to the database structure. As a good practice, we need to first model the changes and then provide an alter DDL script to the database administrators for them. The changes that the developers have requested are:

- Change all primary keys (and their relevant foreign keys) to SMALLINT.
- The customer phone number and email address need to be mandatory to be able to capture a customer.

Tutorial: Using the Bulk Editor Utility in erwin DM

1. Open erwin DM.

2. Using the Quick Access Toolbar, click on the *Open* button.

3. Select the **MyMovie_Ver1** data model from the previous portion of the tutorial.

4. Click on the *Open* button.

5. The MyMovie model opens in erwin DM. Maximize the model in the diagram window.

6. Click on the *File* ribbon tab.

7. Then click on the *Save As* button to save a copy of the MyMovie data model, as shown in Figure 411.

Figure 411. Click On The Save As Button

8. Change the data model name to **MyMovie_Ver2**.

9. And click the *Save* button.

 It is always a good practice to keep versions of release data models. The next time you are working on an existing data model that's released, increment the version number.

10. Click on the *View* ribbon tab.

11. Click on the *Panes* drop-down button to display the list of panes options. See Figure 412.

Figure 412. Click On The Panes Button

12. Click on the *Bulk Editor Pane* option to open the Bulk Editor pane. See Figure 413.

Figure 413. Click On The Bulk Editor Pane Option

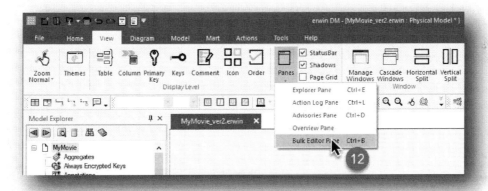

13. Observe the Bulk Editor pane is visible.

14. From Chapter 6, we learned that panes could be undocked, resized, and moved around the workspace. Depending on your requirements, the Bulk Editor pane can be undocked and resized to better interact with it. See Figure 414.

Figure 414. The Bulk Editor Pane Undocked and Resized

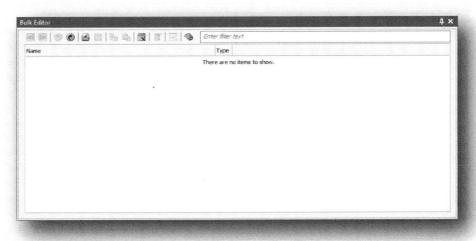

Action Buttons

◀️ **Previous**–Allows the user to position the cursor on the previous row in the Bulk Editor grid.

▶️ **Next**–Allows the user to position the cursor on the next row in the Bulk Editor grid.

↩️ **Undo** –Allows the user to undo the last action performed.

↪️ **Redo** –Allows the user to redo the last undo action performed.

📥 **Import Updates**–Allows the user to import a CSV file with updates.

💾 **Export Selected Rows**–Allows the user to export the selected rows to a CSV file for updating.

📋 **Copy** –Allows the user to copy the selected rows from the Bulk Editor grid into the clipboard.

📋 **Paste**–Allows the user to paste from the clipboard into the Bulk Editor grid.

🪄 **Bulk Editor Wizard**–Allows the user to open the Bulk Editor Wizard dialog. The Bulk Editor Wizard dialog allows the user to specify the contents of the Bulk Editor grid for the current editing session.

🗑️ **Delete** –Allows the user to delete the selected objects from the model.

📝 **Edit**–Allows the user to open the relevant editor dialog for the object selected, with the object in focus.

❓ **Help**–Allows the user to open online help for the Bulk Editor.

Enter Filter Text–This field allows the user to filter results on a specific text.

15. Click the *Bulk Editor Wizard* (🪄) button to invoke the Bulk Editor Wizard dialog. See Figure 415.

Figure 415. Click the Bulk Editor Wizard Button

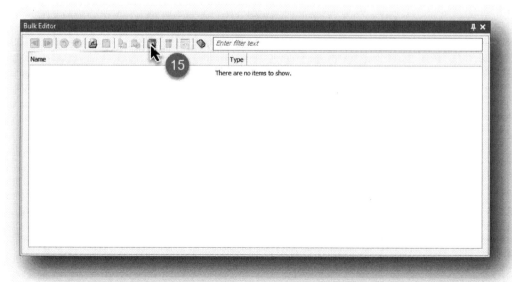

16. Observe the Bulk Editor Wizard dialog opens. The Overview page of the Bulk Editor Wizard dialog provides the user with a brief overview of the wizard and the critical aspects of each of the pages. During a modeling session, the wizard reopens to the same page and has the same settings as its last use in the same model.

 When on a wizard dialog, notice the flag next to a page tab. This is an indicator that there is a decision that needs to be made on that page before the wizard is runnable.

17. Click on the *Object Types* page tab.

18. Observe the Object Types page, as shown in Figure 416.

Figure 416. Observe the Object Types Page

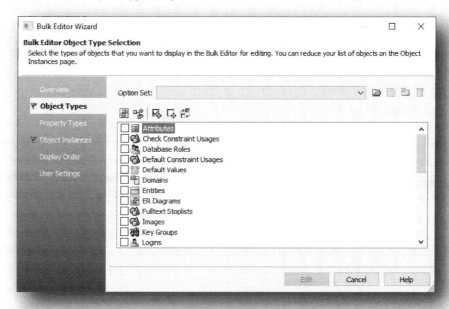

The Object Types page lets the user select the types of objects to use in the Bulk Editor. Selected objects get displayed as rows in the Bulk Editor. The names displayed here are consistent with the names displayed in the Model Explorer. Using this page, the user can save their selections as an *Option Set*, or they can select an existing *Option Set* to populate the selections, and then narrow the list using the options on the Object Instances page. This list of selected object types determines which types of objects are eligible for inclusion in this editing session.

The user can save the selection as a new *Option Set* for reuse on other models. Saving an *Option Set* to an XML file makes it available for performing the same Bulk Edit process on other models, thus standardizing the Bulk Edit process for an organization. The XML files are store independent of the data models and, therefore, are sharable amongst the users.

To save an *Option Set* as an XML file, the user needs to click the *New* button (🖼). A Save Current Option Set dialog appears, allowing the user to select the type of *Option Set* to save. The *Option Set* can be saved as an XML file, or embedded in the data model, for future usage with the data models.

If the XML file option gets chosen, the dialog provides further options to choose the location for storing the XML file. Once saved, the user can update the XML file by using the *Save* button (🖫). To clear the *Option Set* selection, the user can use the *Delete* button (🗑). To open an existing *Option Set*, the user can use the *Open* button (📂) to load a customized *Option Set* into memory for the Bulk Edit process.

Action Buttons

- 🔢 **Use Selected Objects**–Specifies to limit the list of object types to only those objects selected in the current diagram. Otherwise, all object types get shown.

- 🔧 **Display Names**–Allows the user to open a menu to select whether to display object names as either logical or physical. When the user selects one of the options, the toolbar button changes to provide a visual indication of choice:

  - 🔧 Logical Names
  - 🔧 Physical Names
  - 🔧 Physical Names, show owner
  - 🔧 Physical Names, show owner using User

  Note: The Logical Names option does not display when working in either a logical-only or a physical-only model.

- 🔲 **Select All**–Allows the user to selects the checkboxes for all the items in the list.

- 🔲 **Select None**–Allows the user to unselect all the checkboxes for all the items in the list.

- 🔲 **Toggle Selection**–Allows the user to select the checkboxes for any unselected items and unselect the checkboxes for all selected items.

19. Make sure that the *Display Names* is set to *Logical Names*, as shown in Figure 417.

20. Then click the *checkbox* of the *Attribute* object type.

21. Observe that the flag next to the Object Types page tab disappears.

22. When finished, click on the *Property Types* page tab.

23. Observe the Property Types page, as shown in Figure 418.

The Property Types page lets the user select the properties to edit for each of the objects. Selected properties get displayed as columns in the Bulk Editor. The property name is the column heading. Using this page, the user can save their selections as an option set, or they can select an existing option set to populate the selections.

Figure 417. Display Names Set to Logical Names

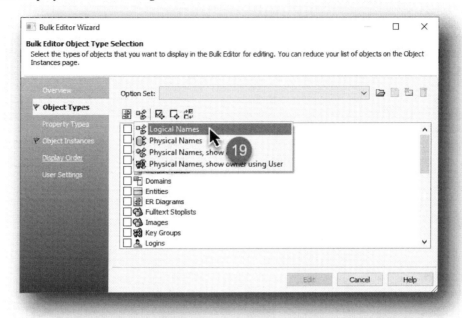

Figure 418. Observe the Property Types Page

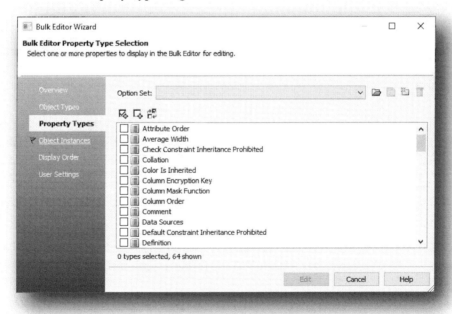

Action Buttons

Select All–Allows the user to selects the checkboxes for all the items in the list.

Select None–Allows the user to unselect all the checkboxes for all the items in the list.

Toggle Selection–Allows the user to select the checkboxes for any unselected items and unselect the checkboxes for all selected items.

24. Select the following Property Types:

- Attribute Order
- Definition
- Logical Data Type
- Name
- Null Option
- Physical Data Type
- Physical Name

25. When finished, click on the *Object Instances* page tab.

26. Observe the Object Instances page, as shown in Figure 419.

Figure 419. Observe the Object Instances Page

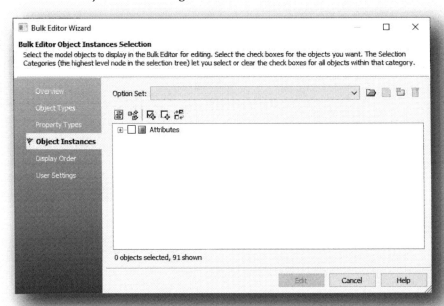

The Object Instances page lets the user select the specific objects from the data model to use in the Bulk Editor. This page lists all of the instances of the object types that were selected on the Object Types page as high-level nodes in the selection tree. The names displayed here are consistent with the names displayed in the Model Explorer.

Action Buttons

Use Selected Objects–Specifies to limit the list of object instances to only those objects selected in the current diagram. Otherwise, all object instances get shown.

Display Names–Allows the user to open a menu to select whether to display object names as either logical or physical. When the user selects one of the options, the toolbar button changes to provide a visual indication of choice:

Logical Names

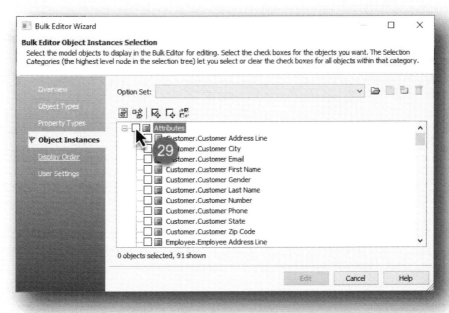

Physical Names

Physical Names, show owner

Physical Names, show owner using User

Note: The Logical Names option does not display when working in either a logical-only or a physical-only model.

Select All–Allows the user to selects the checkboxes for all the items in the list.

Select None–Allows the user to unselect all the checkboxes for all the items in the list.

Toggle Selection–Allows the user to select the checkboxes for any unselected items and unselect the checkboxes for all selected items.

27. Expand the *Attribute* node to display all the attributes in the data model.

28. Observe the list of all the attributes in the data model, as shown in Figure 420. Furthermore, take note of the naming conversion used ([Entity Name].[Attribute Name]) for ease of identifying the different instances correctly.

29. Click on the root node of *Attribute* to select all the attributes, as shown in Figure 420.

Figure 420. Click the Attribute Node

After selecting the root node of the Attributes, the flag next to the Object Instances disappeared and the *Edit* button now became active. This is because we have now satisfied the minimum requirements to populate the Bulk Editor grid. The minimum requirement is to have at least one Object Type and one Object Instance. Although, without selecting any Property Types, the population of the Bulk Editor grid is relatively meaningless, as there will be no properties that can be changed, but none the less, it is still a valid minimum requirement.

Furthermore, take note of the count of objects at the bottom of the page, '91 objects selected, 91 shown.' This is a visual cue to identify the number of objects, remembering that the Use Selected Objects button can filter the number of objects shown, and that the objects themselves can be individually selected, or at the root node, as we did in the tutorial.

30. When finished, click on the **Display Order** page tab.

31. Observe the Display Order page, as shown in Figure 421.

Figure 421. Observe the Display Order Page Tab

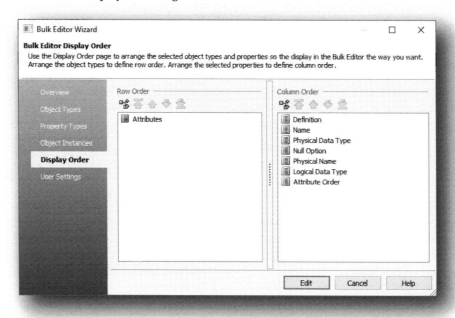

The Display Oder page lets the user specify how to arrange the rows for the object types and columns for the properties. The order specified is how the items get displayed in the Bulk Editor. As is observed, the Display Order page is divided into two sections, and the first (left) section defines the row order based on object types, as per the object types selected on the Object Types page. In our tutorial, we only selected one object type, being the Attributes, and therefore there is only one row order available. The second (right) section defines the column order based on property types, as per the property types selected on the Property Types page.

 Note that whenever storing the option set, that erwin DM does not store the display order with it. As the name 'Option Set' implies, it stores only the options selected.

 Note that once the wizard has been used to populate the Bulk Editor grid and dismissed, when re-invoking the wizard, it loads the options via a temporary option set and therefore, resets the display order.

Action Buttons

Display Names–Allows the user to open a menu to select whether to display object names as either logical or physical. When the user selects one of the options, the toolbar button changes to provide a visual indication of choice:

Logical Names

Physical Names

Physical Names, show owner

Physical Names, show owner using User

Note: The Logical Names option does not display when working in either a logical-only or a physical-only model.

Move to Top–Moves the selected object to the top of the list.

Move Up–Moves the selected object up one level in the list.

Move Down–Moves the selected object down one level in the list.

Move to Bottom–Moves the selected object to the bottom of the list.

32. Change the Column Order to the following by using the *Move Up* and *Move Down* buttons:

- Name
- Physical Name
- Attribute Order
- Logical Data Type
- Physical Data Type
- Null Option
- Definition

33. When finished, click on the *User Settings* page tab.

34. Observe the User Settings page, as shown in Figure 422. The User Settings page lets the user manage the optional behavior of the Bulk Editor.

- **Automatically update the current selection set**–Specifies whether changes made to the selection set are shown the next time entering the wizard.

- **Include Owner Path column for better model context**–Specifies that in addition to the standard Name and Type columns, an Owner Path column gets added to the Bulk Editor grid that shows the names of each object in the hierarchy of objects that own the current object. For example, having an Owner Path column present in the Bulk Editor can be useful when there is one column or index used in multiple tables, and you want to know the table to which that column or index belongs.

Figure 422. Observe the User Settings Page Tab

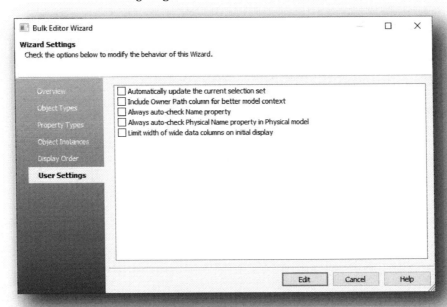

- **Always auto-check Name property**–Always automatically select the checkbox that is located next to the Name property on the Property Types page if working with a Logical or Logical/Physical model.

- **Always auto-check Physical Name property in Physical model**–Always automatically select the checkbox that is located next to the Physical Name property on the Property Types page if working with a Physical or Logical/Physical model.

- **Limit width of wide data columns on initial display**–Restricts the width of columns that contain lengthy text to 250 pixels upon the initial display in the Bulk Editor. All other columns get sized to match the best width so that a column's entire title and the widest data value is displayed.

 Once the data gets displayed in the Bulk Editor, the columns are resizable as needed by dragging the divider between column headings, or double-clicking on that divider to have the column automatically resized to match its contents.

35. When finished, click the *Edit* button to populate the Bulk Editor grid.

36. Observe the Bulk Editor grid in the Bulk Editor pane populated with the selections from the wizard. See Figure 423.

37. Click on the *Customer Number* cell in the Bulk Editor grid (first row, first column), and observe the following as shown in Figure 424.

Figure 423. Observe the Bulk Editor Grid

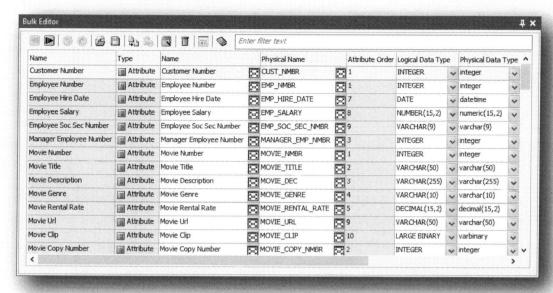

Figure 424. Observe the Following

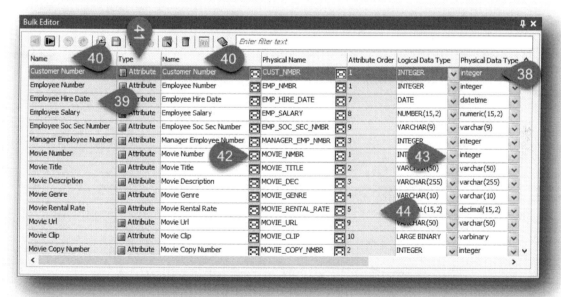

38. Blue highlighted row signifies the selected object. By holding down the Ctrl key, multiple selections can be made.

39. Greyed out cells are read-only cells, and no change can be made to the properties in these cells.

40. There are two Name columns, and the first is the internal column used by erwin DM to link back to the source object of the row. The second, the editable cell, the one that we selected earlier in the tutorial to display, is used to make changes to the name property.

41. There is always a Type column in the Bulk Editor grid, and this column identifies the type of object in the row. This is especially useful when having multiple object types selected on the Object Types page in the Bulk Editor Wizard dialog.

42. Most of the cells have an Edit button to open a context-sensitive editor screen for editing. This editor is at the property level and not at the object level.

43. Those cells that do not have an Edit button have a drop-down option list. These drop-down option lists get populated with the valid options for the object, based on whatever restrictions criteria that would be applied while using the respective editor dialog.

44. Some columns are greyed out and read-only due to them having a consequential impact on other objects. As in this example, by changing the value of the order results in potentially two attributes with the same order number and a missing number in the sequence.

45. In the *Enter Filter Text* field, type in 'Number' for us to filter all rows that have 'Number' in it. See Figure 425.

Figure 425. Type Number in Enter Filter Text

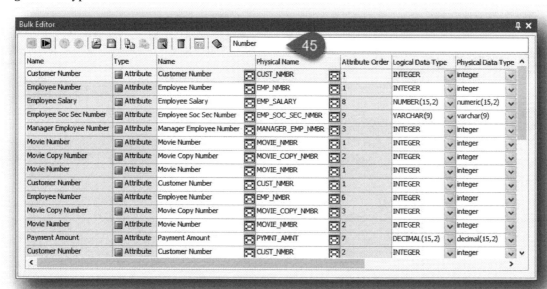

46. Observe the rows that are filtered, taking special note that not only the rows that had 'Number' in its name but also those that had 'Number' in its datatype, are included in the results.

47. If you examine the results, you will notice that it is difficult to identify which entities each of the attributes belong to. For example, look at the various versions of **Customer Number**. One of them is the primary key and the others are foreign keys, but it is difficult to identify in the Bulk Editor grid which is which.

48. Click on the Bulk Editor Wizard () button to invoke the wizard again. Refer back to step 15 for locating the Wizard button.

49. Observe that the Bulk Editor Wizard should open on the last page used, which should be the User Settings page. If not, click on the User Settings Page tab.

50. Select the *Include Owner Path column for better model context* checkbox. See Figure 426.

Figure 426. Select the Include Owner Path Option

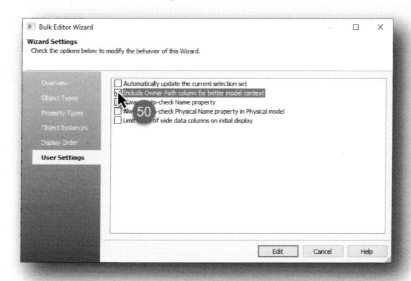

51. Return to the Display Order page and apply the order of the columns as below:

- Name
- Physical Name
- Attribute Order
- Logical Data Type
- Physical Data Type
- Null Option
- Definition

52. When finished, click the *Edit* button again.

53. Observe the inclusion of the Owner Path column.

54. Furthermore, observe how easy it is now to identify the entity that the attributes belong to.

> Note that the Owner Path provides the full path of the owner, and not just the owner. The MyMovie in the Owner Path of our tutorial is a reference to the name of the data model.

55. Identify the row of the **Customer Number** that belongs to the **Customer** entity (should be the first row). Then scroll to the right to find the *Logical Data Type* and click the drop-down button to display the options. See Figure 427.

Figure 427. Click the Logical Data Type Drop-Down Button

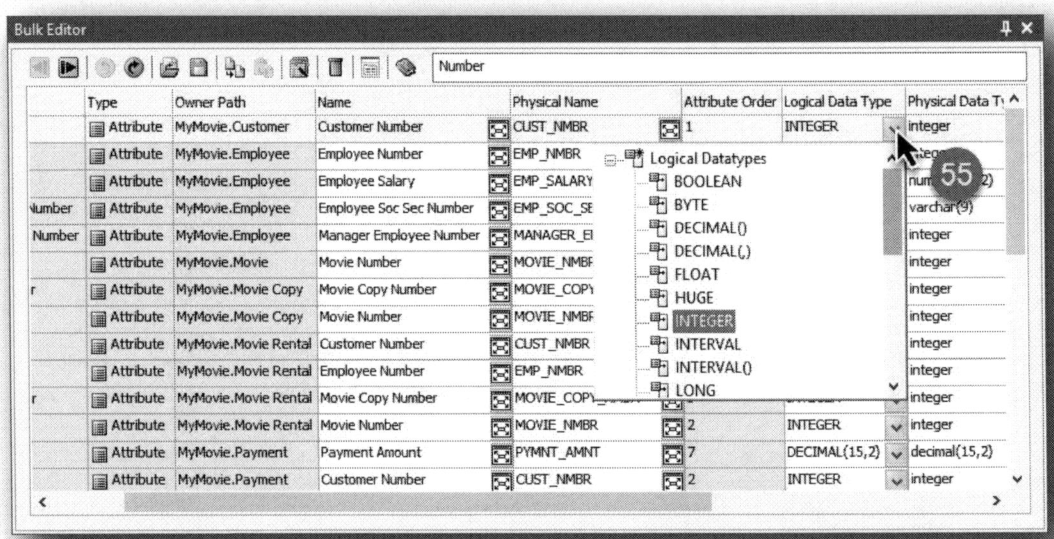

56. Scroll down the drop-down list. Observe that only numeric options are available. This is because the parent domain is **Number**. Remember from Chapter 15 that domains control the datatype, thus resulting in a list of only numeric datatypes. This is an example of how the Bulk Editor grid adheres to all the same restrictions and controls that get applied through the standard editor dialogs.

57. To satisfy our developer's first requirement, change the *Logical Data Type* for the **Customer Number** attribute to 'SMALLINT.'

58. Observe the ripple effect of the change through the data model, as shown in Figure 428. The *Physical Data Type* changed to 'smallint,' and all the foreign keys changed to 'SMALLINT.'

The *Physical Data Type* properties change due to the inheritance between the logical and physical side of the data model. Unless overridden on the physical side of the model, the physical properties inherit the DBMS specific equivalent of the logical property.

The foreign keys *Logical Data Types* change due to the inheritance via the relationship. It is a common practice that all foreign key datatypes are aligned to be the same as the primary key's datatype. erwin DM applies this practice via the inheritance established through the relationships.

59. To satisfy the rest of the primary key change request, perform the same change to the attributes (*Logical Data Type* = SMALLINT) in Table 61. Take caution that you are changing

the primary key attribute and not the foreign key attributes by inspecting the *Owner Path* column.

Figure 428. Observe the Ripple Effect of the Change

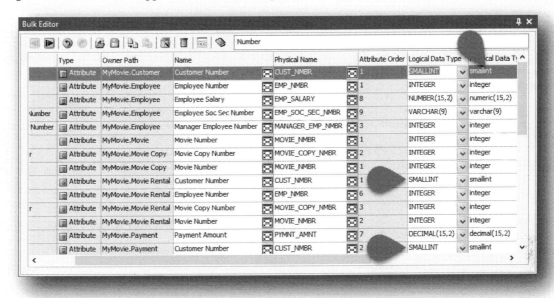

Table 61 –Primary Key Attributes to be Changed

Entity	Attribute
Employee	Employee Number
Movie	Movie Number
Movie Copy	Movie Copy Number
Movie Rental	Movie Rental Number
Payment	Payment Number
Store	Store Number

60. Clear the **Filter Text** field, and observe that all the rows are displayed again.

61. Scroll across to the right so that the *Null Option* column is visible, then scroll down until the **Customer Email** and **Customer Phone** is visible. Change the *Null Option* for the **Customer Email** attribute from 'Null' to 'Not Null,' as shown in Figure 429.

62. Repeat the same step for the **Customer Phone** attribute.

63. Scroll further across until the *Definition* column is visible.

64. Try and edit the *Definition* for the **Customer Email** attribute. Notice that the *Definition* property is not editable directly in the Bulk Editor grid. This is because multiline properties cannot be edited in a single line grid.

Figure 429. Change the Null Option for Customer Email and Customer Phone

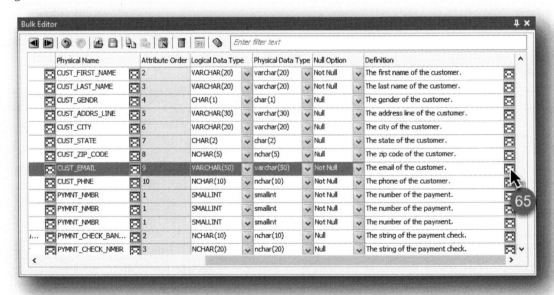

65. Click on the *Edit* button (⊡) in the *Definition* column of the **Customer Email** attribute. See Figure 430.

Figure 430. Click the Edit Button

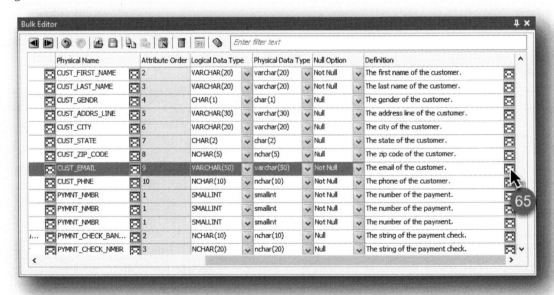

66. Observe the multiline editor dialog opens, and note that the multiline editor represents the macro version of the definition.

67. Change the text of the **Customer Email** attribute's *Definition* to 'The %Lower(%AttDomain) of the %Lower(%OwnerEntity) (manndatory).' Note that the incorrect spelling of the word 'manndatory' is intentional.

68. When finished, click the **OK** button and observe the updated *Definition* in the Bulk Editor grid.

69. Repeat the same steps for the **Customer Phone** attribute's *Definition* and observe the changed properties in the Bulk Editor grid.

70. In the next phase of the tutorial, we are going to look at the functionality of exporting and reimporting the contents of the Bulk Edit grid. As much as erwin DM has a spelling checker which is convenient for when capturing individual properties, it cannot perform a spelling check across an entire model. This is one of the use cases for the export and reimport functionality of the Bulk Editor.

71. Click on the Bulk Editor Wizard (🖼) button to invoke the Bulk Editor Wizard and click on the **Object Types** page tab. Refer back to step 15 for locating the Wizard button.

72. Then click the checkbox of the **Entity** object type, taking note that the Attribute object type is still checked. See Figure 431.

Figure 431. Click the Entity Object Type Checkbox

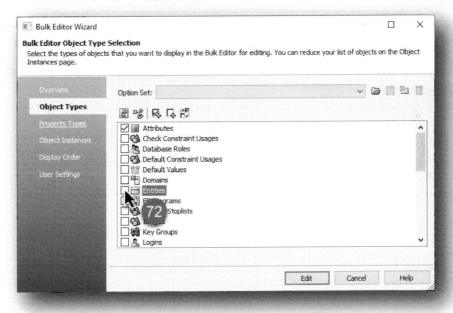

73. When finished, click the **Property Types** page tab.

74. Observe the Property Types page, taking note of the difference between the Property Types page when only the *Attribute* checkbox was checked. erwin DM's Bulk Editor can only work with properties that are common to the object types. For example, the properties *Name* and *Physical Name* are common to both attributes and entities. Therefore, they are valid common property types. But the *Logical Data Type* of an attribute does not have a corresponding property in entities. Therefore, it is not a valid common property type.

Figure 432. Entities Properties, Attribute Properties, and Common Properties

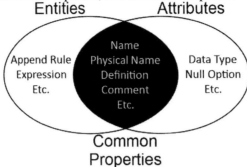

75. Unselect the checkbox for the *Physical Name*. We only want to check the spelling for the logical names and definitions. See Figure 433.

Figure 433. Unselect Physical Name Checkbox

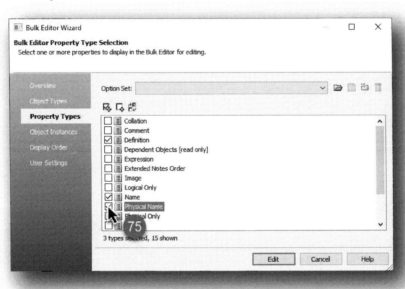

76. When finished, click on the **Object Instances** page tab.

77. Click on the root node of **Entities** to select all the entities, taking note that the root node of the *Attributes* should still be selected from before.

78. When finished, click the **Edit** button.

79. Observe the updated Bulk Editor grid with the new selection of objects and their properties. Furthermore, observe the row order, entities first, and then attributes. This is changeable via the Row Order section on the Display Order page.

80. Click on the Export Selected Rows button (▣) to export the contents of the Bulk Editor grid in CSV format. See Figure 434.

81. Save the CSV as **MyMovie-NameAndDefinitions.CSV** in the same folder that you have the MyMovie data model saved.

Figure 434. Export Metadata From Bulk Editor Grid

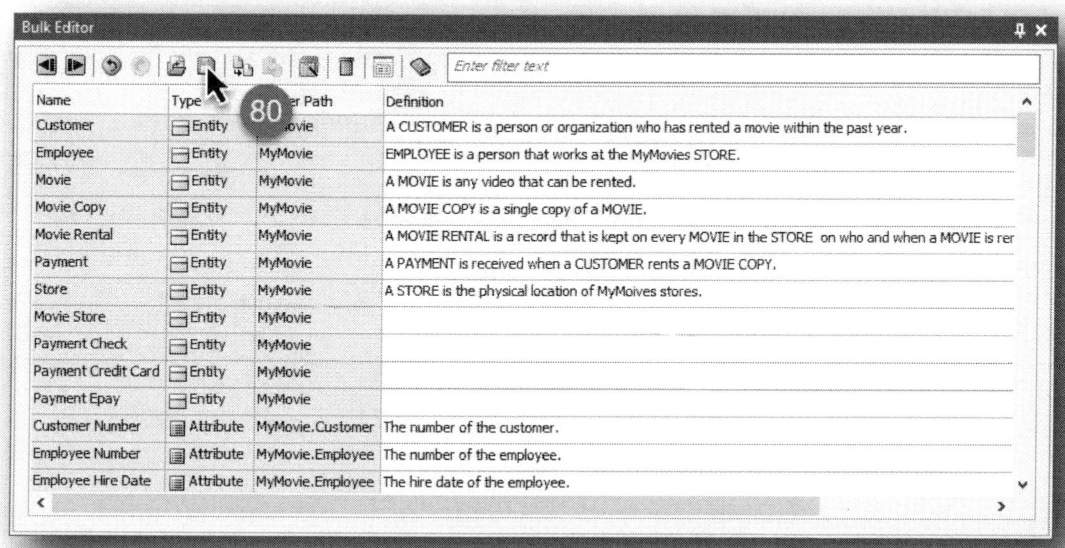

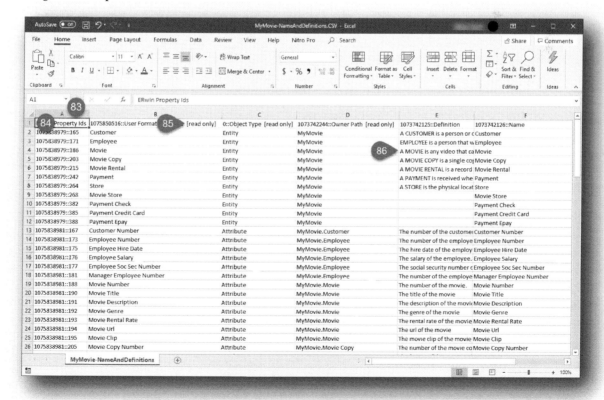

82. Depending on whether you had any rows selected, you might be presented with the prompt to save only the selected rows. Click the *No* button to export all rows.

83. Open Microsoft Excel (or an alternative spreadsheet editing tool) and navigate to and open the CSV file from the previous steps, and observe the following, as shown in Figure 435.

Figure 435. Exported Metadata in Excel

84. Column A contains erwin DM internal unique object identifiers to ensure updates are applied to the correct objects in the data model when reimported. Deleting or changing contents in this column breaks the ability to re-import the metadata via the Bulk Editor.

85. Row 1 contains erwin DM internal unique property identifiers to ensure updates are applied to the correct properties in the data model when reimported. Take note of the user-friendly name also provided in the headers. Deleting or changing contents in this row breaks the ability to re-import the metadata via the Bulk Editor.

86. Columns that are read-only in the Bulk Editor grid have the wording '[read only]' in the column header. Any changes made in these columns get ignored when re-importing. This is the reason for including the *Name* column in the Bulk Editor grid, as the *Name* column is the editable version.

87. The values of the macro-enabled properties, for example, the *Definition* column, reflects the result of the macro and not the macro itself.

88. Select the columns of **Definition** (1073742125::Definition) and **Name** (1073742126::Name) in Excel and use the spelling checker built into Excel to correct the spelling of all the definitions and names.

89. When finished, save and close the CSV file, making sure not to change the extension of the file.

 If the file is not closed before reimporting, erwin DM cannot open the file, as Excel locks the file while editing.

90. Back in erwin DM's Bulk Editor pane, click the **Import Updates** button (⬆) to re-import the CSV file. See Figure 436.

91. Navigate to and select the CSV file that got updated in Excel.

92. Observe the updated *Definition* for the **Customer Email** and **Customer Phone** attributes. See Figure 437.

93. Select the row on the **Customer Email**.

94. Then click the **Edit** button (▦) to open the relevant editor dialog, in this case, the Attribute Editor dialog.

95. Observer the Attribute Editor dialog opens.

96. Click on the **Definition** tab and observe the updated definition. See Figure 438.

97. When finished, close the Attribute Editor dialog by clicking the **Close** button.

Figure 436. Re-import Metadata Into Bulk Editor Grid

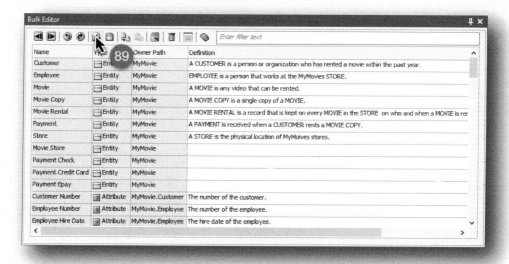

Figure 437. Observe the Updates in the Bulk Editor Grid

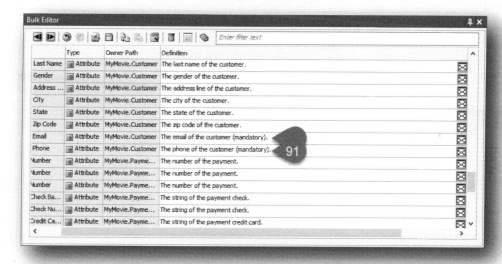

Figure 438. Observe the Updated Definition

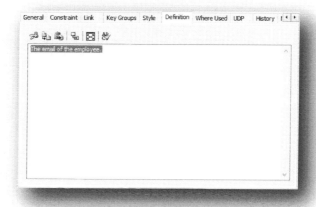

One of the limitations of using the Bulk Editor's reimport capability is that any macros used in updated properties get overwritten with the resultant values.

98. Then close the Bulk Editor pane by using the *Close* button (✕) on the top right of the pane.

99. Finally, save and close your MyMovie data model (remembering that is saving it as version 2 of the data model).

Key Learnings

- erwin DM's Bulk Editor functionality allows for the editing of the data model's metadata in a grid tool.

- All edits in the Bulk Editor grid comply with all limitations and controls that would get applied using the relevant editor dialog.

- The Bulk Editor provides functionality to export to CSV files, and reimport the modified CSV file to update metadata in the data model.

Differences exist?
Compare two databases
Use Complete Compare

The Complete Compare functionality automates bidirectional synchronization of data models, DDL scripts, and databases, compares one item with the other, displays any differences, allows the user to update either of the items selectively, and generates ALTER scripts when necessary.

Complete Compare Explained

Complete Compare is an advanced erwin DM function used to compare and synchronize two items, either data models, databases, or DDL scripts. Although the theory is that Complete Compare can perform comparisons on databases and DDL scripts, the reality is it leverages the reverse engineering functionality to reverse engineer the database or DDL script into a new data model. It then performs the Complete Compare function on the data model of the database or DDL script.

There are always two sides to the Complete Compare function, and they are commonly referred to as the left and right data models of the Complete Compare process. Within the Complete Compare process, the user gets presented with a Resolve Differences dialog, displaying all the differences identified and allowing updates to be made to either or both of the data models. The type of differences and updates are:

- Where an object is in one data model and not the other:
    - Import the object into the one data model from the other
    - Delete the object from the one data model

- Where an object is common to both data models
    - Update property values of one data model from the other

Any combination of updates is possible for either data model with a separate change record for each of the data models, allowing for bidirectional changes. The changes made to either or both data models during a Complete Compare session can optionally generate a DDL script. The usage of the DDL script can then be part of the change implementation. The Complete Compare function can also provide reports on differences between the two data models, databases, or DDL scripts.

There are Four Rules in Understanding the Complete Compare Process

- **Comparisons are always data model to data model**. Data model comparison in Complete Compare is always data model to data model, irrespective of whether one (or both), of the data models involved, is a database or a DDL script which has been reverse-engineered. Where a database is reverse-engineered during the Complete Compare process, the database connection remains open.

- **Changes to data models are in real-time**. Any changes applied to a data model through the Complete Compare Resolve Differences dialog are made in real-time to the data model. Where the data model is a reverse-engineer of a database or DDL script, the changes get applied via a DDL script, and not performed in real-time. The reason for this is due to the point above.

- **Changes to data models are consistent with manual changes**. Any changes applied to a data model through the Complete Compare Resolve Differences dialog are applied to the data model as though they were being made manually by the user. This requires users to be aware of the scope of individual changes and recognize where consequential changes made during the manual process need to be replicated in the Complete Compare process.

- **The Scope of DDL script generation is restricted to changes made in the Complete Compare session**. The record of changes made to each data model during the Resolve Differences session can be used to generate an ALTER script reflecting the changes to the data model. The ALTER scripts get generated by the Forward Engineering function, which can be called from within the Complete Compare process. The full scope of the Forward Engineering function is available, but the scope is restricted to the changes made during a single Complete Compare Resolve Differences session. The ALTER scripts for the two data models being compared get generated separately.

Complete Compare Use Cases

- **Identifying differences between two models**. This is one of the most common uses for Complete Compare. The two data models, in this case, can be different versions of the same data model, where there is a need to identify changes between versions, or they could represent different systems that share mutual objects, and there is a need for those mutual objects to be defined identically in both system.

- **Identifying differences between a model and a database**. This identifies changes made directly to a database, which haven't been updated into the data model and changes made to the data model as part of the development process. The database in question can be a development, test, or production database. The comparison can generate the DDL needed for the next incremental upgrade to the system.

- **Data model validation.** Where specific objects of a data model, such as domains or validation rules, must comply with a corporate standard, and a data model contains that standard, comparing data models with the standard data model can identify areas where some variance from the standard has occurred.

- **Comparing two databases.** The complete compare function can be used to compare two databases, for example, a signed-off test database and the current production database or two different databases with mutual objects.

- **Sharing objects between data models.** While erwin DM supports copying and pasting between data models, that approach gives little control over the sharing of complex data structures that exist inside data models. Complete Compare provides a more precise method of sharing objects between data models.

- **Populating new models.** While erwin DM's design layer approach provides the means of sharing and managing objects between data models, that approach creates a link between data models and has an overhead. Sometimes it is preferred to use the Complete Compare function between a new data model and an established data model to populate a new data model with previously defined objects.

- **Identifying version differences.** Where versions of data models are maintained, which reflect versions of a database, a comparison between two of the data model versions can indicate what differences existed between different versions of the database.

The Complete Compare Process is shown in Figure 439.

1. **Load left data model**–Load the data model from file, Mart Server, or reverse engineering.

2. **Load right data model**–Load the data model from file, Mart Server, or reverse engineering.

3. **Type selection**–Select object types for Complete Comparing.

4. **Left object selection**–Select object instance based on object types selected.

5. **Right object selection**–Select object instance based on object types selected.

6. **Complete Compare**–Perform the Complete Compare function.

7. **Resolve Differences**–Identify differences and apply them to left or right data models.

8. **Generate left ALTER script**–Generate the left ALTER DDL script, from changes applied to the left data model. (Optional)

9. **Generate right ALTER script**–Generate the right ALTER DDL script, from changes applied to the right data model. (Optional)

10. Apply change to left and right data models–Commit changes to the two data models.

The Complete Compare Process

Figure 439. The Complete Compare Process

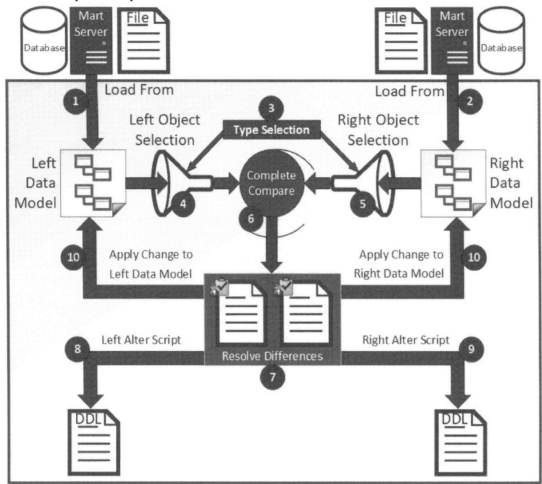

Tutorial: Using the Complete Compare Utility in erwin DM

1. Open erwin DM.

2. Using the Quick Access Toolbar, click on the *Open* button.

3. Select the **MyMovie_Ver1** data model, from the earlier portions of the tutorials, in the Open dialog.

4. Click on the *Open* button.

5. The MyMovie model opens in erwin DM. Maximize the model in the diagram window.

6. Once again, using the Quick Access Toolbar, click on the *Open* button.

7. Select the **MyMovie_Ver2** data model from the previous chapter.

8. Click on the *Open* button.

9. The MyMovie(2) model opens in erwin DM as the second model.

10. Click on the *Actions* ribbon tab.

11. Then click on the *Complete Compare* button to start the complete compare process. See Figure 440.

Figure 440. Click On The Complete Compare Button

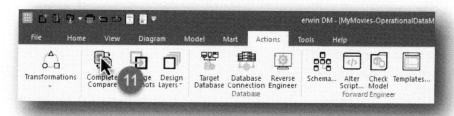

12. Observe that the Complete Compare Wizard dialog appears. By default, when opening the Complete Compare Wizard dialog with a data model in focus, the wizard opens on the Right Model page. The reason for this is that the open model in focus gets set as the left model with the assumption that the user wants to perform a Complete Compare from the current model in focus. But the choice of which model is on the left, and which model is on the right in the Complete Compare is changeable.

13. Click on the *Overview* page tab to open the Overview page.

14. Observe the Overview page, as shown in Figure 441.

Figure 441. The Overview Page

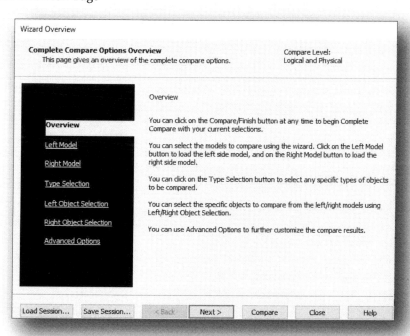

The Overview page gives a brief textual description of the Complete Compare function.

15. When finished, click on the *Left Model* page tab.

16. Observe the Left Model page. See Figure 442.

Figure 442. The Left Model Page

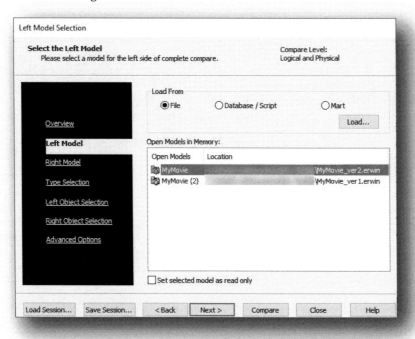

The Complete Compare Wizard dialog is already populated with all models currently open in erwin DM, and this page allows for additional data models to be opened and brought into the scope of the Complete Compare Wizard via the Load button. Models can be brought into the scope of the Complete Compare Wizard via a File version, the Mart Server (Mart), or reverse-engineered from a Database or DDL Script.

It is important to note that when opening a model via the Database or DDL Script option, a model gets created using the reverse engineering process, and the Complete Compare process does not directly compare against the database or the DDL script. For more information on the reverse engineering process, please see Chapter 28.

When the *Database/Script Load From* option is selected, an *Allow Demand Loading* option is visible. When this checkbox is selected, the initial reverse engineering, of either the database or the DDL script, gets restricted to high-level objects, such as tables, but excludes lower-level objects, such as columns and indexes. This feature allows for quicker execution of the reverse engineering process and allows for the lower-level details to be reverse engineered on-demand, once the object selection has been completed.

The *Set selected model as read only* option allows for ensuring that the model does not get changed through the Complete Compare process.

17. Select the ***MyMovie (MyMovie_Ver2.erwin)*** data model for the left side of the Complete Compare process. See Figure 443.

Figure 443. Select The MyMovie Data Model

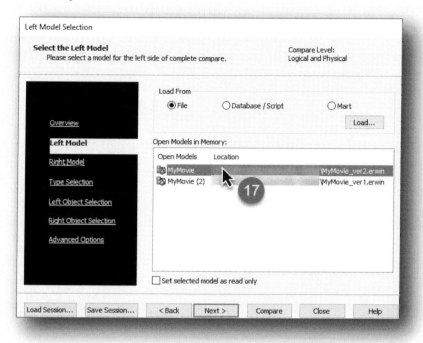

We have now completed step 1 of the Complete Compare process, as depicted in Figure 439.

18. When finished, click on the ***Right Model*** page tab.

19. Select the ***MyMovie (2) (MyMovie_Ver1.erwin)*** data model for the right side of the Complete Compare process. See Figure 444.

Figure 444. Select The MyMovie (2) Data Model

We have now completed step 2 of the Complete Compare process, as depicted in Figure 439.

20. When finished, click on the Type Selection page tab.

21. Observe the Type Selection page, as shown in Figure 445.

Figure 445. The Type Selection Page

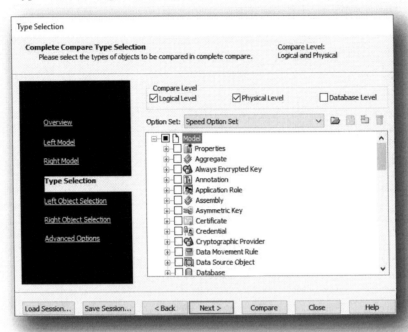

The Type Selection page is one of the most critical steps of the Complete Compare process. If the selection is too broad, the Complete Compare Resolve Difference dialog gets overrun with too much noise. But, on the other hand, if the selection is too narrow, vital differences get left off of the Complete Compare Resolve Difference dialog.

Compare Levels

The Type Selection page allows the user to set the compare level to either the logical level, physical level, or database level. The choice of *Compare Level* determines the default options set for the compare process. The default options are changeable via the option sets, or directly in the options section:

- **Logical Level**–All objects contained on the logical level of a data model.

- **Physical Level**–All objects contained on the physical level of a data model.

- **Database Level**–All objects on the database level of a data model.

The *Logical Level* and the *Physical Level* can be used in a combined mode for comparing both sides of the data models at the same time. But the *Database Level* cannot be combined with either of the other two.

Option Sets

When selecting the objects and properties that need comparing, the user can filter specific objects by clearing the checkbox next to the objects. The user can furthermore save the selection as a new option set for reuse on other models. There are three built-in *Option Sets* available:

- **Advanced Default Option Set**–This option set includes all objects in the selection tree, except those objects that are assigned generated values during forward or reverse engineering. Use this default option set for advanced compares, in which the user wants all objects to participate in the compare process.

- **Speed Option Set**–This option set includes the frequently used and required objects based on the best of practice. Use this option set to run a quick complete compare process.

- **Standard Default Option Set**–This option set filters many objects and properties from the selection tree. This option excludes physical-only object types, and includes a minimal set of property types. Use this default for standard compares where it is not necessary to include all objects and properties in the compare process.

Saving an *Option Set* to an XML file makes it available for performing the same Complete Compare process on other models, thus standardizing the Complete Compare process for an organization. The XML files are store independent of the data models and, therefore, are sharable amongst the users.

To save an *Option Set* as an XML file, the user needs to click the *New* button (🖷). A Save Current Option Set dialog appears, allowing the user to select the type of *Option Set* to save. For Complete Compare, the *Option Set* can be saved as an XML file, embedded in the left model, or embedded in the right model for future usage with the data models.

If the XML file option gets chosen, the dialog provides further options to choose the location for storing the XML file. Once saved, the user can update the XML file by using the *Save* button (🖫). To clear the *Option Set* selection, the user can use the *Delete* button (🗑). To open an existing option set, the user can use the *Open* button (📂) to load a customized option set into memory for the Complete Compare process.

22. Select the *Compare Level* for **Logical Level** and **Physical Level**. Seeing that we are comparing two data models that contain both logical and physical sides, this would be the most appropriate option. Further, make sure that the *Database Level* is not selected. See Figure 446.

23. Change the *Option Set* to the **Advanced Default Option Set**, as shown in Figure 447. For our tutorial, we will not be customizing the options, but will work with the built-in option sets, therefore accept the options as they are. We have now completed step 3 of the Complete Compare process, as depicted in Figure 439.

Figure 446. Select the Logical Level and Physical Level Options

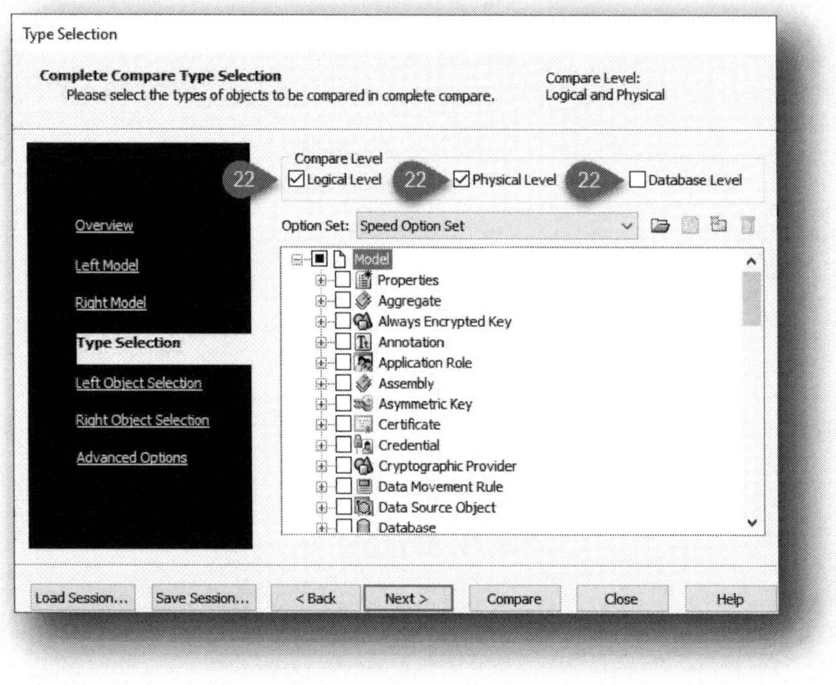

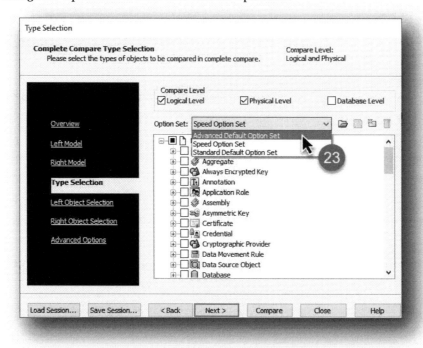

Figure 447. Change the Option Set to Advanced Default Option Set

24. When finished, click on the *Left Object Selection* page tab.

25. Observe the Left Object Selection page, as shown in Figure 448.

Figure 448. The Left Object Selection Page

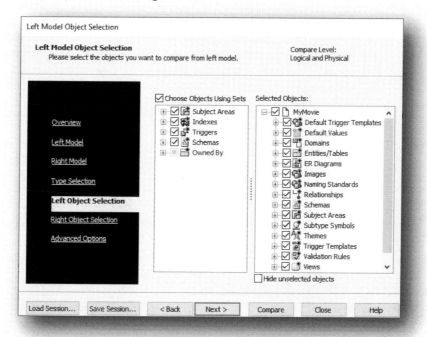

After selecting the object types for the comparison on the Type Selection page, the next step is to select the instances of those object types. This is where the object selection pages come in, and the first is the Left Object Selection page. This page selects the objects for the left side model that partakes in the Complete Compare session. It is essential to understand that if an object is excluded from the Complete Compare session, the Complete Compare engine assumes that the object does not exist. Therefore, it is critical on the object selection pages to ensure that all objects being compared have been included on both sides.

The object selection pages are broken into two sections to assist in the selection process. The left side, being the object selection using sets, for example, one could select all objects that are in a specific subject area only. The right side of the object selection page for selecting specific objects by their name.

26. In the left hand side of the object selection page, expand the *Subject Area* node.

27. Unselect the *<Model>* node, and observe the change on the right-hand side section of the object selection page, as shown in Figure 449.

28. Expand the *Entities/Tables* node in the right-hand side of the object selection page, and observe the absence of some of the Entities/Tables. Remember our selection of the members for the **Payment** subject area in Chapter 20.

29. Select the **Customer/CUST** entity and observe the left-hand side of the object selection page. The left-hand side of the object selection page is greyed out because the selection criteria are

no longer valid; it includes the **Customer** entity, which is not part of the **Payment** subject area.

Figure 449. Unselect the <Model> Node

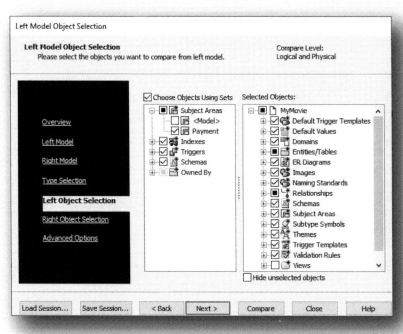

30. Click the *Choose Objects Using Sets checkbox*. See Figure 450.

Figure 450. Click the Choose Objects Using Sets Checkbox

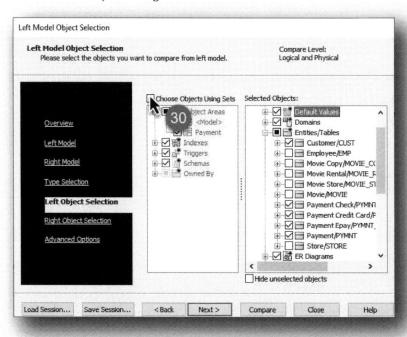

31. Click the *OK* button to accept the resetting of the selected objects.

32. Next, reselect the *<Model>* node. See Figure 451.

Figure 451. Reselect the <Model> Node

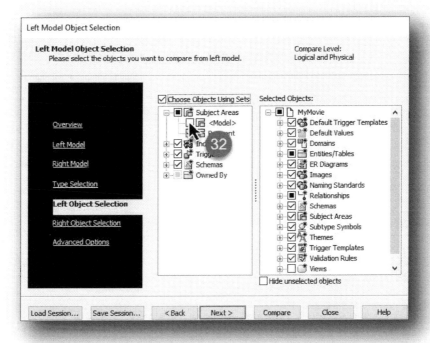

33. Observe that the selection on the right-hand side of the object selection page is all selected again. Expand the ***Entities/Tables*** node to verify. Take note of the *Hide Unselected Objects* option at the bottom of the page. This allows the user to remove from the display any objects that are not selected. This can aid the user in narrowing the selection criteria by not having to page through all the noise of unselected objects.

We have now completed step 4 of the Complete Compare process, as depicted in Figure 439.

34. When finished, click on the ***Right Object Selection*** page tab.

35. Observe the Right Object Selection page, as shown in Figure 452.

    Observe that the Right Object Selection page is the same as the Left Object Selection page, just operating on the right model in the Complete Compare process.

    We have now completed step 5 of the Complete Compare process, as depicted in Figure 439.

36. When finished, click on the ***Advanced Options*** page tab.

37. Observe the Advanced Options page, as shown in Figure 453.

    • **Auto dispose Database/Script Models**. Closes the model that is created from a database or script automatically when ending the Complete Compare session, if a model was reverse-engineered during the Complete Compare process. The option to save the model is not displayed.

Figure 452. The Right Object Selection Page

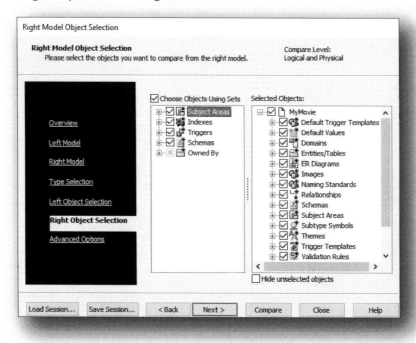

Figure 453. The Advanced Options Page

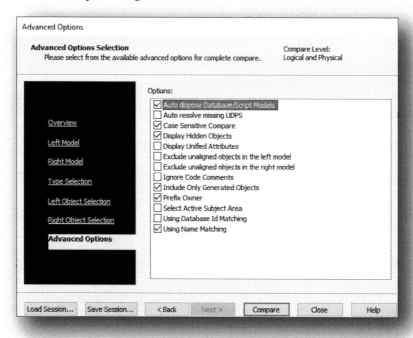

- **Auto resolve missing UDPs**. Copies the missing UDPs to the target model, when all the differences are due to missing UDPs. Complete Compare detects missing UDPs or property differences for common UDPs and displays the Type Resolution dialog before the Complete Compare session. Select this option to skip the Type Resolution dialog when all the differences are due to missing UDPs.

- **Case Sensitive Compare**. Instructs Complete Compare to perform a case-sensitive comparison. This option affects both the alignment of objects in the object tree and the equality of property values in the property pane. When the option gets cleared, the case gets ignored for alignment and equality testing of text property values.

- **Using Database Id Matching**. Matches by Database ID. This option is available for Informix, SAP ASE, and SQL Server database servers only. If the DB ID property is present, objects are aligned based on the property. Database IDs are present only in models that are reverse-engineered from a database. Select this property to compare a model with the same model that got reverse-engineered from a database.

- **Using Object Id Matching**. Aligns objects that are based on the Object ID property, where applicable. This option is available for the Db2 z/OS database server only.

- **Display Unified Attributes**. Simplifies the display of foreign-key attributes in the Resolve Differences dialog. When selected, a Unified Attributes group object gets used to display all unified attributes (role-named or not) of the same unified set of attributes. Any attributes that are aligned to the attributes under the Unified Group object appear as part of the Unified Group object, even if they are not unified attributes. The Unified Attributes group object carries the unified name if all the attributes under it are part of the same unified set. If not, the name consists of a comma-delimited list of names of all the attributes under it. For more information on unified attributes, please refer back to Chapter 18.

- **Exclude Unaligned Objects in the Left Model**. Instructs Complete Compare to exclude unaligned model-level objects from the left model in the Resolve Differences dialog. Use this option as a filter to distinguish between changes in a model subset and a larger model of which the subset is a part.

- **Exclude Unaligned Objects in the Right Model**. Instructs Complete Compare to exclude unaligned model-level objects from the right model in the Resolve Differences dialog. Use this option as a filter to distinguish between changes in a model subset and a larger model of which the subset is a part.

 The user can select to display only aligned model-level objects in the Resolve Differences dialog by selecting both the Exclude Unaligned Objects in the Left Model and Exclude Unaligned Objects in the Right Model options.

- **Ignore Code Comments**. Instructs Complete Compare to exclude blocks of comments from the body of a trigger, before including it in the compare process. If the only difference is in the comments, excluding comments enables Complete Compare to recognize that a trigger has not changed.

- **Prefix Owner**. Instructs Complete Compare to match objects by prefixing the table owner to the object. When the user selects this option, objects are aligned based on both the name and owner name property.

- **Select Active Subject Area**. Specifies that the user wants to select the active subject area by default in the Object Selection pane. Selecting a subject area by default simplifies the selection, especially in models that contain many subject areas.

- **Using Name Matching**. Instructs Complete Compare to match by object name. Relationship, index, and index members are aligned based on the name, in addition to the standard criteria used to align these objects. Use this property if the models that are getting compared have the same named objects with different owners. In this case, you can compare to see if the two models are similar other than the owner or schema name.

- **Tablespace in Database**. Instructs Complete Compare to align objects according to both, the IN_TABLESPACE and IN_DATABASE properties, where applicable. This option is available only for the Db2 z/OS database server.

- **Include Only Generated Objects**. Instructs Complete Compare to include objects for which the *Generate* option in the property editor is selected. The *Generate* option specifies whether you want to generate SQL for the object during forward engineering.

38. Make sure that your selection is the same as the selection in Figure 454.

Figure 454. The Advanced Options Page Selection

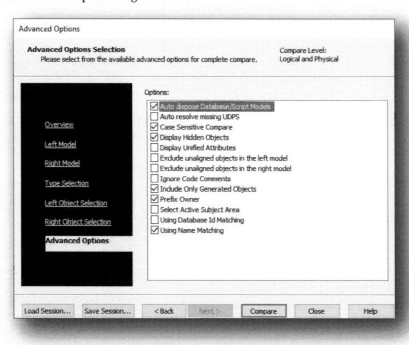

39. When finished, click the **Compare** button. This initializes the step 6 of the Complete Compare process, as depicted in Figure 439.

40. Observe the Resolve Differences dialog appears, as shown in Figure 455.

Figure 455. The Resolve Differences Dialog

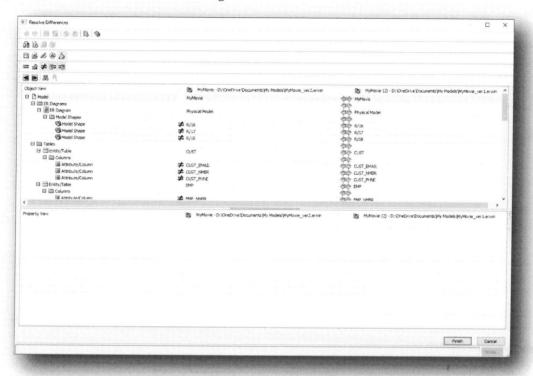

Note that the Resolve Differences dialog gets broken down into several sections.

- **Object View.** This section displays a list of differences between the models in an object tree. An icon illustrates the status of the comparison.

- **Property View.** This section displays the properties for the selected object in the Object View pane.

- **Status Bar.** This section displays the compare status of the current compare row. For example, 'The left and right items are not equal.'

41. Click on the line in the object section for the **Model Shape R/16**. See Figure 456.

Observe the properties section becomes populated with the properties for the object selected in the top section. Furthermore, take a look at the selected object and its properties. A *Model Shape* object is a reference to how an object gets shaped in a diagram. In the highlighted row, the shape is a reference to a relationship line, and the properties hold the bend points and connector points for the object.

Figure 456. The Resolve Differences Dialog

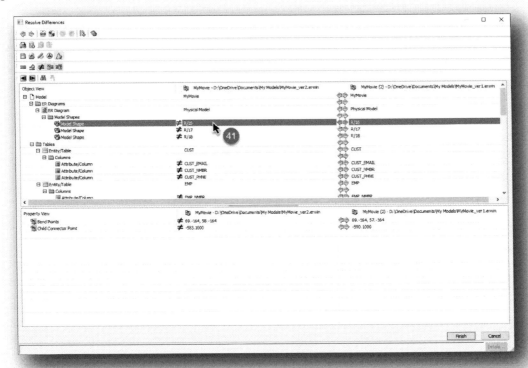

42. Click the **Show Equal Items** button to switch on the equal items; these are objects and properties that match and are equal. See Figure 457.

Figure 457. Click the Show Equal Items Button

Observe the result of the properties for the Model Shape. Scroll down, observing the full metadata of the object. As much as this information is interesting to see and understand, it is way too detailed for us to make usage of the Complete Compare process effectively. Remember, back in step 23, we selected the *Advanced Default Option Set*. This is what we refer to as noise, and the best approach is to use a narrow selection of details.

43. Click the **Cancel** button on the Resolve Differences dialog.

44. Back on the Complete Compare Wizard dialog, click on the Type Selection page tab. Then change the *Option Type* to **Speed Option Set**. See Figure 458.

Figure 458. Change Option Type to Speed Option Set

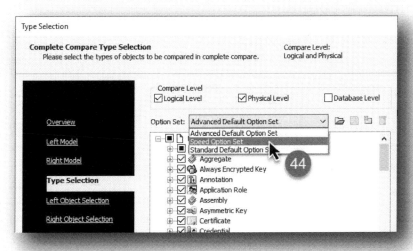

45. When finished, click the **Compare** button again. Note that when working with the Resolve Differences, it is easy to go back to the Complete Compare Wizard dialog to refine the selections.

46. Now observe the difference in the Resolve Differences dialog, the absence of the noise. See Figure 459.

Figure 459. Click the Cancel Button

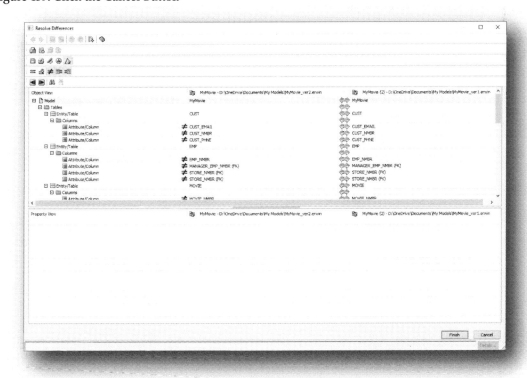

Before continuing, let us take a look at the Resolve differences Dialog.

Action Buttons

Standard Toolbar

Performs a specific action on a selected item in the list of differences.

Move Left–Allows the user to move any items that do not match, from the right model to the left model.

Move Right–Allows the user to move any items that do not match, from the left model to the right model.

Match–Allows the user to match two items. The user can use this feature to override the automatic matching. They need first to select an object, then click the match icon, finally click an object or property with which to match the first object. The items then appear on the same line in the Object View.

Unmatch–Allows the user to unmatch any items that have been matched.

Undo–Allows the user to undo the last operation.

Redo–Allows the user to redo a previous undo operation.

Report–Allows the user to open the Report Dialog to generate a report of the differences between the left and right models.

Help–Allows the user to open the online help for the Resolve Differences dialog.

Impact Analysis Toolbar

Invokes additional functionality as you resolve differences. The user can view the Impact Analysis dialog and the Message Log, and generate an alter script for either the left or the right model.

Action Log–Allows the user to display a read-only version of the Action Log. The two-pane window tracks the actions made in the Resolve Differences dialog. You can use the Find feature to search through long lists of transactions.

Advisory–Allows the user to display advisory messages in the Message Log dialog if they encounter these messages as they work in the Resolve Differences dialog.

Left Alter Script–Allows the user to generate an alter script for the data model in the left pane for a compare session that includes a database or script file. The Schema Generation Alter Script dialog opens, which guides them through the alter script generation.

Right Alter Script–Allows the user to generate an alter script for the data model in the right pane for a compare session that includes a database or script file. The Schema Generation Alter Script dialog opens, which guides them through the alter script generation.

Known Differences Toolbar

Marks known differences and work with snapshots. The user can select rows that they do not want to display in the Resolve Differences dialog, and save the list for retrieval in a future Complete Compare session.

Save Snapshot–Allows the user to save the known differences as a snapshot. The Save Snapshot dialog opens, where the user can set options for saving the snapshot.

Open Snapshot–Allows the user to load a saved snapshot to your current Resolve Differences session. The Load Snapshot dialog opens, where you can select the snapshot you want to load.

Mark–Allows the user to mark or unmarks a row as a known difference. When they select a row, and then click Mark Known Difference, it hides the selected rows in the Resolve Differences dialog.

Known Differences–Allows the user to display the known differences they hid using the Mark Known Differences option. This option is disabled when a snapshot is not active, or they have not marked rows as a known difference.

Changed–Allows the user to displays the rows (either the left or the right) for which the property value has changed since the snapshot was saved if they have loaded a snapshot.

Standard Filters Toolbar

Filters the display of differences to refine the compare process.

Equal–Allows the user to display objects and properties that are the same in both models.

Resolved–Allows the user to display the property and object rows that were resolved into equal rows during your Resolve Differences session. When they click this icon, the rows are marked with the change indicator color and the change indicator symbol in the status column.

Not Equal–Allows the user to display all of the differences between the objects and properties in both models. This filter is selected by default when the Resolve Differences dialog opens.

Unaligned Left–Allows the user to display objects that do not exist in the right model, but are present in the left model. This filter does not affect property rows. This filter is selected by default when the Resolve Differences dialog opens.

Unaligned Right–Allows the user to display objects that do not exist in the left model, but are present in the right model. This filter does not affect property rows. This filter is selected by default when the Resolve Differences dialog opens.

Navigation Toolbar

Lets the user navigate the list of known differences, search for an item, and expand or collapse the trees.

Previous–Allows the user to highlight the previous object or property difference.

Next–Allows the user to highlight the next object or property difference.

Search–Allows the user to search for an object or property.

Search Again–Allows the user to search again, using the search parameters already established.

47. Click on the line in the object section for the ***Attribute/Column CUST_NMBR***.

48. Observe the differences in the property section, specifically the *Physical Data Type*. See Figure 460.

Figure 460. Observe the Property Differences

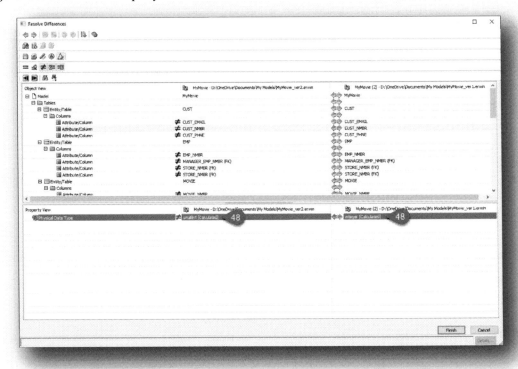

49. With the property row of *Physical Data Type* highlighted, click the **Move Right** button to apply the change that we performed in Chapter 30. See Figure 461.

Figure 461. Click the Move Right Button

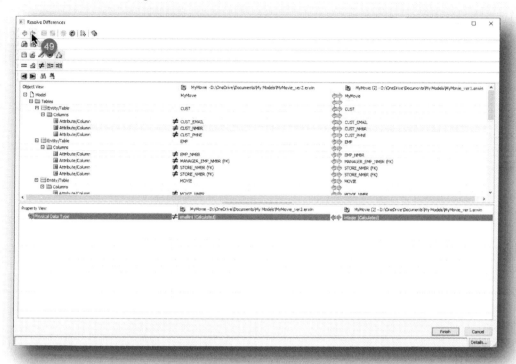

50. In the pop-up dialog, select the **Export Inherited State** option.

Export Inherited State versus Export Value

When a value gets exported using the Export Value option, the inheritance gets broken, and the property's value gets updated from the other model. When an update gets made by setting inheritance using the Export Inherited State, the value of the properties may not align if the property is inheriting from different sources in the two models.

51. Observe the disappearance of the difference, and this difference is marked as resolved.

52. Click on the line in the object section for the **Attribute/Column CUST_EMAIL**. Observe the differences in the property section, as shown in Figure 462.

For the **Customer Email**, we performed two changes, the first being the *Null Option,* and the second being the *Definition.* We can see the *Null Option* difference between the two models, but the *Definition* has resulted in two differences: the *Definition* and the *Comment* properties. The *Comment* property inherits its value from the *Definition* property, and therefore was also changed in the data model. Also, take note of the *[Calculated]* phrase behind the *Comment,* but not behind the *Definition.*

Figure 462. Click the CUST_EMAIL Line

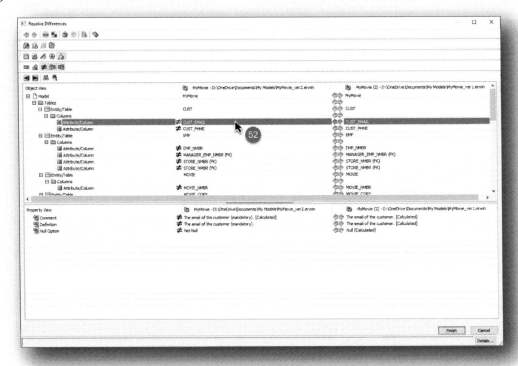

Remember that we edited the *Definition* in the Bulk Editor in Chapter 30, and by editing the definition, we broke the inheritance from the domain. This is the reason why the *Definition* property does not get marked as *[Calculated]*. The *Comment* property still has its inheritance from the *Definition* in place, and therefore maintains the *[Calculated]* phrase.

- **Calculated:** Indicates inheritance is in place, and the value is calculated (Derived), rather than holding it as a property value in its own right.

- **Filtered:** When a move is only partially successful, it means that a subset of what is being moved cannot be moved for some reason. It, therefore, remains behind but is tagged as 'Filtered.'

53. We could perform the same action we performed for the **Customer Number** attribute, but we would have to perform these for each of the three properties. Instead, we could perform the action at the object level, and then all three changes would be applied at once. Click the *Move Right* button in the line of the **CUST_EMAIL** object.

54. Observe the disappearance of all the **Customer Email** differences, and these differences are marked as resolved.

55. Perform the same steps to move all the differences for the **Customer Phone** attribute.

56. Observe the difference for the **Employee** entity. Taking special note of the differences for the **Employee Number (EMP_NMBR)** and **Manager Employee Number (MANAGER_EMP_NMBR)**.

57. Move the **Employee Number** differences to the right using the inline *Move Right* button).

Observe that the **Manager Employee Number (MANAGER_ EMP_NMBR)** also got resolved during the process. When applying changes to a model in Complete Compare, the changes behave the same as applying the changes manually in the data model. The **Manager Employee Number** is a foreign key to the **Employee Number**, and therefore was updated to match the datatype of the primary key, which was the change that we moved to the right model. Scrolling down, you would also notice that all the foreign keys to the **Customer Number** and the **Employee Number** have been resolved.

58. On your own, move the differences from the left model to the right model for the attributes shown in Table 62, making sure to move the primary key attributes, and not the foreign key attributes.

Table 62 –Attributes to be Changed

Entity	Attribute
Movie	Movie Number
Movie Copy	Movie Copy Number
Movie Rental	Movie Rental Number
Payment	Payment Number
Store	Store Number

59. When finished, you should have no more unresolved differences.

60. To check the resolved differences, click on the *Show Resolved Items* button. See Figure 463.

Figure 463. Click the Show Resolved Items Button

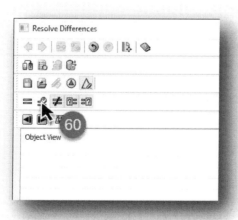

61. Now observe that all the differences have been resolved.

We have now completed step 7 of the Complete Compare process, as depicted in Figure 439. Seeing that we only need to generate a DDL script of the changes from the left model to the right model, we can bypass step 8.

62. To generate a DDL script of the changes from the left model that got applied to the right model, click the **Right Alter Script** button. See Figure 464.

Figure 464. Click the Right Alter Script Button

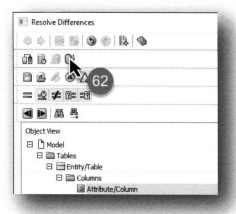

63. Observe the Forward Engineering Alter Script Schema Generation Wizard dialog appears. Click the **Preview** page tab.

64. Observe the preview of the DDL script to apply the changes, as shown in Figure 465.

Figure 465. Preview of DDL Script

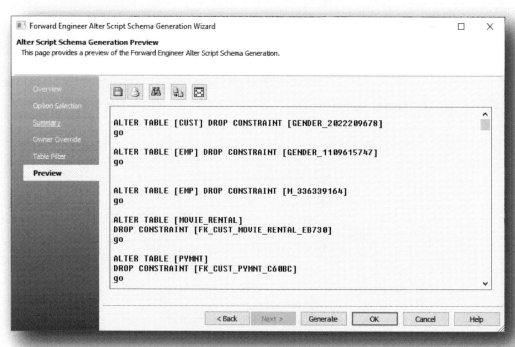

We have now completed step 9 of the Complete Compare process, as depicted in Figure 439.

65. When finished, click the **OK** button on the Forward Engineering Alter Script Schema Generation Wizard dialog.

66. Click the **Finish** button on the Resolve Differences dialog.

67. Click the *Close* button on the Complete Compare Wizard dialog.

At this point, we have now completed step 10 of the Complete Compare process, as depicted in Figure 439.

68. Finally, close the two data models without saving. And this concludes the last tutorial for this book. The choice of saving the models or not is dependent on the desired outcome. In our tutorial, the outcome was to generate a DDL of the differences from version 1 to version 2 of the MyMovies model, and it was not to apply the changes from one model to another.

Key Learnings

- Complete Compare is an advanced erwin DM function used to compare and synchronize two items

- Complete Compare can be performed on two data models, databases, DDL scripts, or any combination thereof.

- When performing a complete comparing with a database or DDL script, Complete Compare first performs a reverse engineering process and compares the resultant data model.

- There are always two sides to the Complete Compare, the left model, and the right model.

- Changes to data models are in real-time and consistent with doing them manually.

- The scope of DDL script generation from the Complete Compare are restricted to changes made in the Complete Compare session.

- Complete Compare can be used for:

    o Identifying differences between two models,
    o Identifying differences between a model and a database,
    o Data model validation,
    o Comparing two databases,
    o Sharing objects between data models,
    o Populating new models,
    o Identifying version differences.

erwin Inc. provides several data-related tools that enhance the capabilities of erwin DM, below is just a select few.

- **Chapter 32** covers erwin DM NoSQL, which enables a user to transform their logical data model designs into visual models that reflect native document database structures.
- **Chapter 33** explores the erwin Data Catalog tool, which automates enterprise metadata management, data mapping, code generation, and data lineage for faster time to value and greater accuracy for data movement and/or deployment projects.
- **Chapter 34** explains the erwin Data Literacy product, which enables organizations to curate and govern data assets so stakeholders can discover data relevant to their roles and understand it within a business context.

Extending the capabilities of erwin DM, erwin DM NoSQL enables a user to transform their logical data model designs into visual models that reflect native document database structures. erwin DM NoSQL also includes the code to create the data structures, plus it automates the capture and creation of visual models of document database instances that already exist. With erwin DM NoSQL, users can discover, visualize, document, analyze, design, and deploy, document database instances efficiently and cost-effectively while mitigating the risks inherent to managing this type of mission-critical data asset.

Solution Overview

erwin DM NoSQL gives technical and business users a complete and contextual view of their document database assets so that they can manage them with rigorous agility through the following features:

- **Software-as-a-Service** — SaaS-based tool for access anywhere, anytime with any device. No software to implement or install means access and use on day one, and support is included with automatic product updates.

- **Flexible SaaS options** — Hosting ensures high availability and robust, scalable infrastructure with no expensive overhead or resourcing requirements. Purchase the product as multi-tenant, with shared infrastructure in the United States or the United Kingdom, or a single-tenant, providing entirely dedicated infrastructure and resources.

- **Multi-target NoSQL document database support** — erwin DM NoSQL supports Couchbase and MongoDB.

- **Ease of use and guided task automation** — Web-based tool enables teams to work from anywhere. And the intuitive interface ensures all users are capable and effective in working with document databases out of the gate for faster time to value.

- **Import and visualization of erwin DM models** — Import erwin DM models for discovery, visualization, and analysis to drive document database data source definitions and design.

- **Transformation of entity relation designs to native document database structures** — Query-Optimized Modeling guided de-normalization options transform traditional data models and logical data designs into rich, visual NoSQL models that can be used to represent and engineer document databases.

- **Forward-engineering of document database schema generation scripts** — Pending physical design creation, automates the creation of JSON-like document definition scripts to instantiate your document database, enabling the efficient, accurate deployment of NoSQL designs into your hosted environment.

- **Reverse-engineering of hosted document databases** — Provides a connection manager to hosted document database instances for the automated creation of native NoSQL models from data source definitions previously deployed in document databases, based on statistical data analysis.

- **Relationship definition for documentation** — Specify relationships between data elements within a NoSQL model for documentation and analysis. These relationships guide developers and users in better understanding data value chains and analysis paths that naturally exist, but are not explicitly defined in an unstructured data management environment.

- **Model cloning** — Clone models for updating and editing while maintaining versions of the model for traceability, control, and lifecycle management.

- **Support for document database collections** — Create and maintain embedded collections, as well as reference collections, in support of scenario analysis to identify the proper structure.

- **Object properties editor** — Key model object properties can be edited and displayed in the erwin DM NoSQL properties pane that is context-aware and easily accessed through the right-hand menu.

- **Data model dashboard** — Stores all models centrally in the cloud and delivers a model access dashboard that hierarchically displays transformed, reversed, and cloned models, complete with source and other pertinent metadata. This makes it easy for teams to identify and access the appropriate model.

- **Diagram comments** — Create and store user comments for collaboration and extended documentation to promote business alignment and clarity of data sources deployed in document databases.

- **Internal and external notifications** — Provides end-user notifications both in-tool and via email, updating modelers about the status and results of essential tool operations and processes.

Key Benefits / Results

- Enable traditional DBMS teams and developers to work effectively with document databases.
- Break down the complexities of NoSQL through modeling and visualization.
- Document NoSQL data sources for easier discovery and understanding.
- Expose NoSQL data sources to the enterprise in a standardized and governed way.

Key Features

- Import and visualize erwin DM models.

- Transform entity relation diagrams to a visual document database representation using their patent-pending QueryOptimized Modeling.

- Forward-engineer document database schema generation scripts.

- Reverse-engineer hosted document databases.

- Define and visualize document database relationships for documentation.

Critical Differentiators

- **Support for any data from anywhere (Any^2)** — On-demand data modeling and visualization for document database data structures.

- **Native design and deployment for NoSQL data structures** — The first and only enterprise-class data modeling solution to provide native (non-relational) modeling support for document databases, automating the creation of platform-specific deployment scripts.

- **Discovery and visualization of NoSQL databases** — Reverse-engineering of existing document databases into graphical models, enables users to create documentation relationships to see how the data is logically related.

- **Simple transformation of relational schema to NoSQL constructs** — Guided de-normalization options through Query-Optimized Modeling takes the pain out of migrating traditional database models to the document database platform.

- **On-demand modeling for document database environments** — SaaS-based tool provides complete capabilities wherever and whenever using any device.

Adapted from *https://erwin.com/*

erwin Data Catalog automates enterprise metadata management, data mapping, code generation, and data lineage for faster time to value and greater accuracy for data movement and/or deployment projects. Harvest metadata from various data sources and map data elements from source to target, including 'data in motion,' and harmonize data integration across platforms. When combined with erwin Data Literacy, one can see an accurate picture of your business data assets for the data intelligence to govern and accelerate digital transformation projects, including Big Data deployments, Data Vaults, data warehouse modernization, and cloud migration, without heavy reliance on technical resources.

Solution Overview

erwin Data Catalog provides an automated metadata-driven approach to enterprise data management and data preparation through these features:

Easy data mapping — Use drag-and-drop and automapping features to accelerate the creation of metadata-driven mapping documents, eliminating manual work, and costly errors seen with the traditional Excel approach.

Impact analysis — Instantly identify the impact of change to an attribute or table across the warehouse in a matter of seconds, saving valuable time and resources.

Automated metadata harvesting, cataloging, and curation — Configure and schedule regular scans to harvest detailed technical metadata — from the mainframe to Big Data to business intelligence solutions — to establish a curated metadata backbone complete with the inference of expanded logical names on which to build data management and data governance practices.

- Datastores: relational, NoSQL, Big Data

- File connectors/cloud environments/packaged applications

- Data modeling tools

Key Benefits/Results

- Demonstrate faster time to value and greater accuracy for data movement and/or deployment.

- projects through automated metadata enrichment, data quality metrics, reuse, and guided workflows.

- Reduce the need for costly manual intervention by automating everything from the profiling of data, the generation of Big Data, ETL, and database procedural code to detailed data lineage and impact analysis views.

- Provide a central governance framework for data quality deployment and integration independent of siloed data management technologies.

- Support IT audits and regulatory compliance by governing enterprise data assets as well as data management processes and infrastructure for both IT and business stakeholders.

Key Features

- Accelerated pre-ETL mapping with the drag-and-drop approach, creating mapping specifications and eliminating human errors.

- Automated metadata harvesting and cataloging using erwin Data Catalog's wide range of data source and data movement connectors.

- Version mapping specifications for tracking changes instantly, as well as integrated requirements, testing, and deployment management for the development lifecycle.

- Easy import of legacy mappings, plus share and reuse mappings and transformations.

- Built-in reference data management, including code sets and 'crosswalks.'

- Plug-in code generation for Data Vault and leading ETL/ELT tools, Big Data systems, and scripts.

- Built-in data profiling and integrated data quality metrics.

- Integration with erwin Data Literacy for business glossary management and data discovery self-service.

Adapted from *https://erwin.com/*

erwin Data Literacy enables organizations to curate and govern data assets so stakeholders can discover data relevant to their roles and understand it within a business context. The creation of such data communities, especially for business users, promotes data literacy that leads to accurate, actionable insights and collaboration across the enterprise to produce the desired outcomes. Comprised of the erwin Business Glossary Manager and the erwin Business User Portal, the erwin Data Literacy software suite ensures your organization is fluent in the language of data. Used in combination with erwin Data Catalog, stakeholders have an integrated and contextual view of the semantic, business, and technical aspects of the entire data landscape.

Solution Overview

erwin Data Literacy lets stakeholders view data assets in context through the following key features:

- **Intuitive web interface for access from anywhere** — A web-based user interface provides broad access to approved organizational information. It enables distributed organizations to easily collaborate for improved information quality, compliance, and change management with lower risk and greater agility.

- **Business glossary** — Build glossaries of terms in taxonomies with synonyms, acronyms, and relationships to describe the organization's data assets. Publish approved standards for these terms to the broader organization to improve clarity/precision of language. Also prioritize terms, flagging information regarding regulatory requirements.

- **Data stewardship and data ownership** — Assign data stewards to manage the definition and approval process for terms and assign data owners and subject-matter experts to approve the definition of standards for terms.

- **Policy management** — Author, maintain, and publish information policies, combined with roles and responsibilities, to reuse across the enterprise data landscape to inform business and technical stakeholders, improving compliance.

- **Rule management** — Reduce risk and understand the impact of change by defining rules for the creation, use, and management of terms, in business language, to ensure regulatory compliance.

- **Sensitive data discovery** — Identify and document sensitive data elements to accelerate compliance efforts and reduce data-related risks.

- **Integration with erwin DC** — Automate the creation and maintenance of a detailed metadata landscape to underpin data governance with accurate, up-to-date business and technical metadata.

- **On-demand mind mapping** — Provide a one-click view of data elements and their relationships to physical, logical, and governance metadata.

Key Benefits/Results

- Provide visibility and governance for any data from anywhere.

- Enable enterprise data governance collaboration and organizational empowerment.

- Identify data connectivity, implications, and impacts across the enterprise to better manage change.

- Create an integrated ecosystem of people, processes, and technologies that manage and protect data.

- Easily create and configure a business-centric data asset framework for alignment and robust governance.

- Help mitigate a wide range of risks to provide regulatory peace of mind.

- Break down silos between disconnected systems, spreadsheets, reporting, and intelligence to enhance stakeholder understanding and trust in data to drive actionable insights.

Key Features

- Self-service visualization and navigation of crucial data governance constructs, including on-demand, configurable 'mind mapping' that shows metadata and governance relationships.

- Real-time data impact analysis to manage the risk and scope of changes to the data landscape.

- Data lineage analysis for business terms, data elements, and physical data sources.

- Flexible metamodel to create different business asset types, customize descriptive attributes, and support the full range of semantic associations between all business and technical asset types.

- Automated integration with the broader data governance ecosystem of people, processes, and technologies.

- Streamlined workflows, including notifications and compelling dashboards, and for on-demand visualizations.

- Integration with erwin Data Catalog for data governance in context.

Adapted from *https://erwin.com/*

Made in the USA
Middletown, DE
08 May 2021

38421743R00298